CW00819394

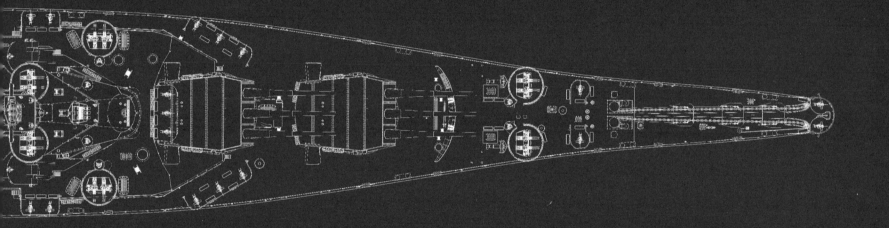

ANATOMY OF THE SHIP

# THE BATTLESHIP
# USS *IOWA*

OSPREY
PUBLISHING

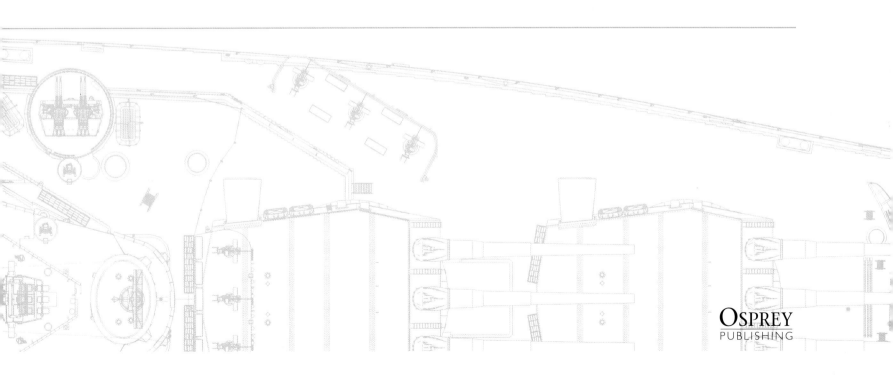

# ANATOMY OF THE SHIP

# THE BATTLESHIP USS *IOWA*

## Stefan Dramiński

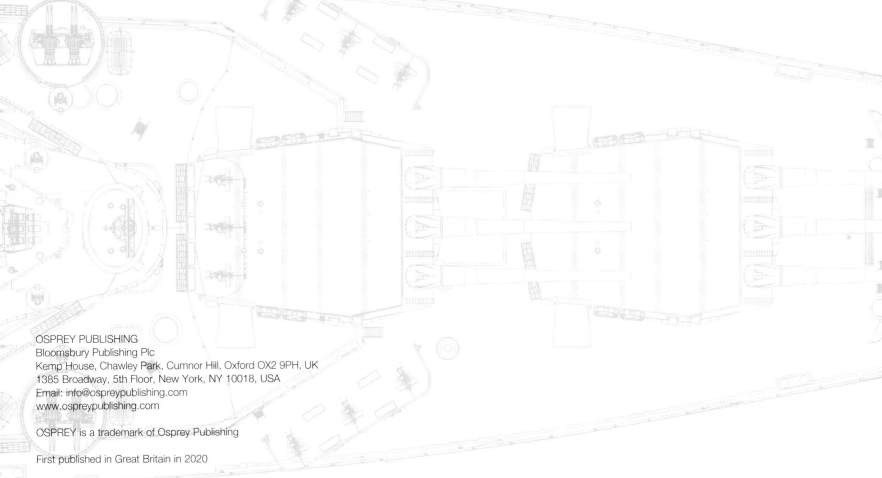

OSPREY PUBLISHING
Bloomsbury Publishing Plc
Kemp House, Chawley Park, Cumnor Hill, Oxford OX2 9PH, UK
1385 Broadway, 5th Floor, New York, NY 10018, USA
Email: info@ospreypublishing.com
www.ospreypublishing.com

OSPREY is a trademark of Osprey Publishing

First published in Great Britain in 2020

© Stefan Dramiński, 2020

Stefan Dramiński has asserted his right under the Copyright, Designs and Patents Act, 1988,
to be identified as Author of this work.

For legal purposes the Acknowledgements on page 8 constitute an extension of this copyright page.

All rights reserved. No part of this publication may be reproduced or transmitted in any form
or by any means, electronic or mechanical, including photocopying, recording, or any information
storage or retrieval system, without prior permission in writing from the publishers.

A catalogue record for this book is available from the British Library.

ISBN: HB 9781472827296; eBook 9781472827302; ePDF 9781472827289; XML 9781472827319

20 21 22 23 24    10 9 8 7 6 5 4 3 2

Originated by PDQ Digital Media Solutions, Bungay, UK
Printed and bound in India by Replika Press Private Ltd.

Front cover: Iwona Paszkowska-Dramińska
Back cover: Stefan Dramiński

Osprey Publishing supports the Woodland Trust, the UK's leading woodland conservation charity.

To find out more about our authors and books visit www.ospreypublishing.com. Here you will find
extracts, author interviews, details of forthcoming events and the option to sign up for our newsletter.

FSC
www.fsc.org
MIX
Paper from
responsible sources
FSC® C016779

# CONTENTS

## SECTION 1

## SECTION 2

## SECTION 3

# INTRODUCTION

The lead ship of the last US battleship class, the USS *Iowa*, entered service in 1943. She featured state-of-the-art armament, fire control, electronics, propulsion and protection. Since then, she has widely been considered as the best overall designed battleship in history.

Initially, six ships of the Iowa class were planned but only four were completed. *Iowa* (BB-61), *New Jersey* (BB-62), *Missouri* (BB-63) and *Wisconsin* (BB-64), all experienced extremely long and fruitful careers in the US Navy, after which they were converted to floating museums in various locations. *Iowa*, being commissioned and decommissioned several times over decades, saw service in World War II and the Korean War, ultimately earning 11 battle stars. It is an irony that the only occasion when her crew suffered a serious loss was during peacetime. Her 16in. gun turret suffered an explosion in the course of a routine artillery exercise in 1989, killing 47 men.

*Iowa* and her sisters served through several eras of naval warfare. During this time, the vessels were refitted many times, not only receiving the latest equipment but also being adapted to the changing role of a battleship in a naval conflict. Consequently, the Iowa class was among the most-modified capital ship classes in history. This created the main challenge when working on this book. As many as nine 3D models had to be created, each with different armament layout, superstructures, electronics and equipment. The reader will be able to follow the complex path of modifications that *Iowa* underwent from 1943 to 1990. When you compare the first and the last version, the dramatic change is most evident.

Due to the limited page count of the book, not all aspects of *Iowa*'s appearance have been covered in the planned extent. For example, it was not possible to fit all aircraft and helicopter types that were ever kept on board. In fact, this subject alone could make a separate book if processed in very high detail.

I would like to thank my wife Iwona for her constant support when working on this book. She created the artwork for the cover and prepared the whole material for print, thus greatly contributing to the quality of this publication.

Stefan Dramiński
Toruń, Poland, July 2019

# THE BATTLESHIP USS *IOWA* (BB-61)

The Washington Naval Treaty of 1922 put serious limitations on the construction of capital ships: not only did it set maximum allowed standard displacement to 35,000 tons and maximum gun calibre to 16in., but it also forbade the building of new battleships for the next ten years. Thus the so-called 'shipbuilding holiday' began. For the USA, this meant cancelling the six battleships of South Dakota class (BB-49 to BB-54). The First London Naval Treaty of 1930 extended the ban on shipbuilding until 1936, with only two exceptions: French Richelieu class and Italian Littorio class, which were supposed to replace older vessels. By the mid-1930s, however, the international situation was deteriorating. Another attempt was made to put a stop to the arms race, this time less successful; Japan and Italy withdrew from the Second London Naval Conference, which only left the USA, Great Britain and France as signatories in March 1936. The standard displacement limit was maintained at 35,000 tons, whereas maximum gun calibre was set to 14in. Two new vessels in accordance with these restrictions were authorized for the US Navy in June 1936. They were to become the North Carolina class (hull numbers BB-55, BB-56). Armed with twelve 14in. guns, they were designed to achieve a top speed of 27 knots. However, in early 1937 it became clear that the Japanese were secretly constructing a new, very powerful battleship type. This enabled the USA to implement the so-called 'escalator clause' of the Second London Naval Treaty, and change the North Carolina class vessels' armament to nine 16in. guns. The work was too advanced to modify the armour layout,

so the two battleships were constructed with inadequate protection in comparison with their main armament.

The Bureau of Construction and Repair began studies on the succeeding class of battleship for the US Navy in 1937. The main aim in designing the South Dakota class battleships (BB-57 to BB-60) was to improve the protection against enemy projectiles, at the same time retaining the same armament and speed as the North Carolina class. This was accomplished by shortening the hull and the armoured citadel, and also by moving the main armoured belt to the inside of the hull, together with inclining it by 19 degrees. The limit of 35,000 tons was exceeded only slightly. In the meantime, Japan's apparent unwillingness to comply with any naval treaties led the signatories of the Second London Naval Treaty to agree on a new displacement limit for capital ships. The figure was set to 45,000 tons in June 1938.

Work on a battleship with larger displacement had already been carried out in the USA since 1935. When designing the subsequent battleship class, the Americans had the additional 10,000 tons at their disposal. This could be used to either strengthen the armament and armour or to increase the speed of the new vessels. Eventually, it was decided to put a stress on the high speed; the new ships were designed to keep up with the fleet carriers. The armour scheme was similar to that of the South Dakota class. Main armament was the same (nine 16in. guns), but with the new gun type that had a longer barrel and better performance.

The bow of USS *Iowa* shortly before launch, New York Navy Yard, August 1942. The very slim clipper stem, a new feature of the *Iowa* class, is evident in this photograph. Chains are attached to the ship's sides in an effort to slow the hull down once it enters the water. A Navy Department safety poster is visible in the bottom right corner.
(National Archives, 80-G-K-13507)

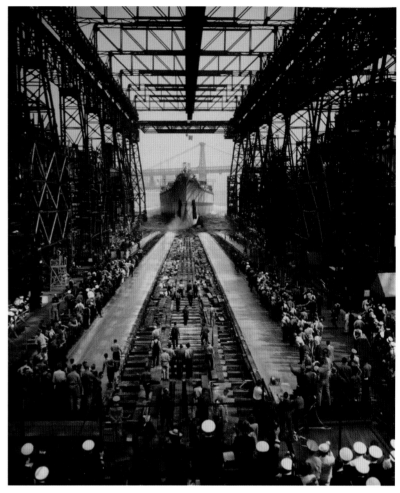

Launching of BB-61, New York Navy Yard, 27 August 1942. Yard workers and US Navy officers are gathered on the slipway and on the ship for the ceremony. A part of the Williamsburg Bridge is visible in the background.
(National Archives, 80-G-K-13514)

The first two vessels of what was to become the Iowa class were authorized on 17 May 1938. They were given hull numbers BB-61, BB-62, and the names *Iowa* and *New Jersey*, respectively. Another two battleships, *Missouri* (BB-63) and *Wisconsin* (BB-64), were authorized on 6 June 1939. As it turned out, all four ships were to have very long and successful service careers. Further vessels, *Illinois* (BB-65) and *Kentucky* (BB-66), were authorized on 19 July 1940 but their construction was halted due to the end of World War II.

## HULL STRUCTURE

As already mentioned, one of the main considerations in the Iowa class design was high speed. Another important factor was the limitation of the beam to 108ft 2in. (33m) to enable the ships to pass through Panama Canal locks. Taking these two points into account resulted in a very long and slim hull, which was able to incorporate very powerful propulsion and possessed good hydrodynamic performance.

| Principal characteristics of USS *Iowa* (BB-61) | |
|---|---|
| Displacement (standard) | 45,000 tons (1945)<br>48,425 tons (1984) |
| Displacement (full load) | 57,540 tons (1945)<br>57,500 tons (1984) |
| Length (overall) | 887ft 3in. (270.44m) |
| Length (waterline) | 860ft (262.1m) |
| Beam | 108ft 2in. (33m) |
| Draught | 37ft 9in. (11.5m) at 57,540 tons (1945) |
| Boilers | 4 x Babcock & Wilcox dual-furnace controlled superheat boilers, working at 850°F (454°C) and 656psi (38.5atm) |
| Turbines | 4 x General Electric geared turbine sets |
| Maximum machinery output | 212,000shp |
| Maximum speed | 33 knots |
| Fuel capacity | 8,811 tons |
| Electrical plant | 8 x turbogenerators, 1,250kW each (total 10,000kW)<br>2 x emergency diesel generators, 250kW each (total 500kW) |
| Range | Up to 20,150NM (37,318km) at 15 knots<br>Up to 4,830NM (8,945km) at 33 knots |
| Armour | Upper armour belt: 12.1in. + 1.5in. STS (307mm + 38mm STS)<br>Lower armour belt: 12.1in. tapering to 1.625in. below (307mm–41mm)<br>Decks: main deck 1.5in. STS (38mm STS); second deck 5.8in.–4.75in. + 1.25in. STS (147mm–121mm + 38mm STS); splinter deck 0.625in. STS (16mm STS); third deck outside the citadel 6.2in. + 1.5in. STS (158mm + 38mm STS), 5.6in. + 0.75in. STS (142mm + 19mm STS)<br>Fore and aft transverse bulkheads: 11.3in.–8.5in. + 0.625in. STS (287–216mm + 16mm STS)<br>Main artillery turrets: front 17in. + 2.5in. STS (432mm + 64mm STS); sides 9.5in. + 0.75in. STS (241mm + 19mm STS); rear 12in. (305mm); roof 7.25in. (184mm)<br>Main artillery barbettes: top to second deck 17.3in.–11.6in. (439–295mm); second deck to third deck 3in. STS (76mm STS); below third deck 1.5in. STS (38mm STS)<br>Dual-purpose artillery mounts: 2.5in. STS (64mm STS)<br>Conning tower: sides 17.3in. (439mm); roof 7.25in. (184mm); bottom 4in. (102mm) |
| Aircraft | 3 x Vought OS2U Kingfisher (1943–1945)<br>3 x Curtiss SC-1 Seahawk (1945–1947)<br>8 x AAI/IAI RQ-2A Pioneer (1986–1990) |
| Complement | 151 officers and 2,637 men (1945)<br>166 officers and 2,451 men (1949)<br>65 officers and 1,445 men (1984) |

The fore section of *Iowa*'s hull was clipper shaped and featured a prominent bulbous bow at the bottom. The aft part (from main artillery barbette no. 3) was supported by a pair of skegs. These improved the battleship's manoeuvrability, stiffened the hull and formed casings for the inner propeller shafts.

Inside, the hull was constructed of 215 frames, with a 4ft (1.22m) distance between each pair. The three top decks were continuous throughout the whole length of the hull. The main deck (also called weather deck or bomb deck) was almost entirely covered with wood planking. The battleship's superstructure was placed directly on it. The second deck, being the main armoured deck, housed compartments for the crew, galleys, messes and various workshops and offices. The central part of third deck, being inside the armoured citadel, contained ammunition magazines and vital compartments: plotting, damage control and communications rooms. A long corridor ran along the centre line of the ship at this level, commonly called 'Broadway' by the crew. It provided a main artillery ammunition transfer channel between the barbettes. Bow and stern sections were the area of crew quarters and storage rooms. Due to the height of the propulsion machinery, the next deck of most of the area between the barbettes was the hold. Forward and aft of the barbettes housed the following decks in between: first platform deck, second platform deck and third platform deck (the last one in the bow only). These contained mainly storage rooms of various materials, steering gear rooms being the only vital compartments.

Fitting-out of the ship at New York Navy Yard, autumn 1942. Main artillery turret no. 1 is in the foreground, trained to starboard and still lacking side sight hoods. Turret no. 2 has its guns slightly elevated and waiting to have its front armoured plate fitted. The fore superstructure tower has already been erected and is surrounded by scaffolding.
(National Archives, 80-G-K-518)

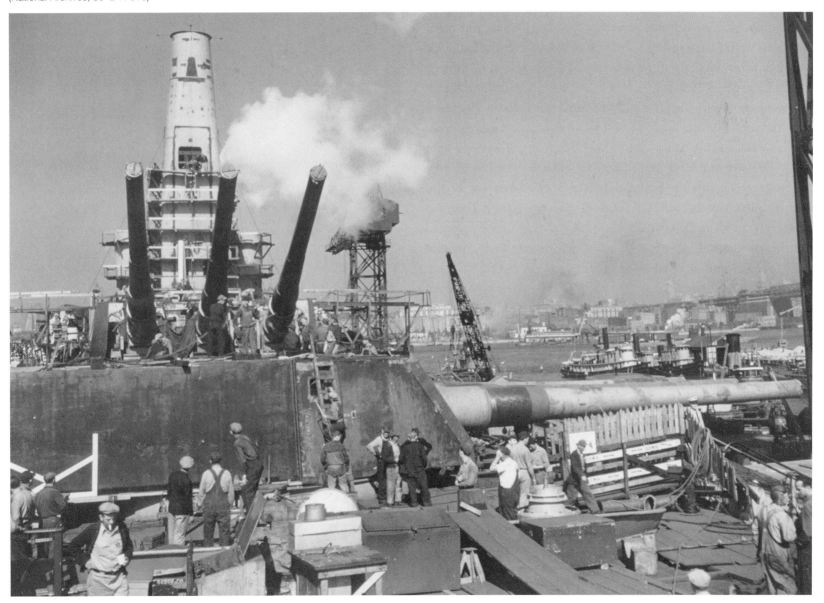

# ARMOUR

The battleship's armour scheme was essentially a repetition of successful solutions applied to the earlier South Dakota class vessels. The citadel was designed to withstand hits from 16"/45 projectiles at distances between 18,000 and 30,000 yards (16,460 and 27,432m). The types of armour included: A-type (face-hardened armour); B-type (homogeneous armour); and STS (Special Treatment Steel, homogeneous high-resistance construction steel).

The side armoured belt was placed well inside the hull. Moving it outboards would cause stability problems or would force the hull to be widened, which was out of the question (the ship had to fit through the Panama Canal locks). In order to improve performance against incoming amour-piercing projectiles, the belt was inclined by 19 degrees from the vertical plane. Being 38.5ft (11.74m) wide in total, its upper portion was 12.1in A-type armour plus 1.5in. STS (307mm + 38mm STS). The lower portion stretched down to the inner bottom in order to give protection against diving projectiles. Its thickness was 12.1in. B-type armour tapering to 1.625in. below (307mm–41mm). There was a narrower part of the belt that reached outside the citadel and protected the steering gear until frame 204. Its thickness was up to 13.5in. plus 1.5in. STS (343mm + 38mm STS).

The fore and aft transverse bulkheads of the citadel were positioned at frames 50 and 166 respectively. Made of A-type steel, the thickness of the fore bulkhead was 11.3in. tapering down to 8.5in. plus 0.625in. STS (287–216mm + 16mm STS). Similarly, the aft bulkhead as well as the steering gear bulkhead at frame 204 was 11.3in. plus 0.625in. STS (287 + 16mm STS).

*Iowa*'s horizontal armour was divided into several decks. The main deck was made of STS plates 1.5in.-thick (38mm). Its purpose was to detonate projectiles and bombs before they could reach the second deck, which formed the main armoured deck. Its B-type plate thickness was 5.8in. near the sides and 4.75in. inboards, plus 1.25in. STS (147mm–121mm + 38mm STS). The next barrier was the splinter deck placed immediately below. Designed to absorb any pieces of armour that would break off on projectile impact, it comprised STS plates 0.625in. (16mm) thick. Armour plating was also provided on the third deck, but only

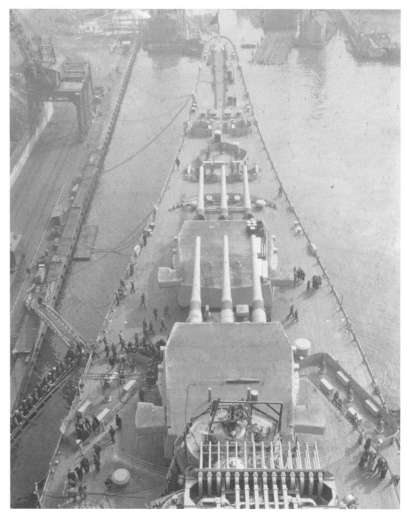

Commissioning day, New York Navy Yard, 27 February 1943. Photo taken from *Iowa*'s mast. Her fore triple 16in. turrets are in the centre, with the armoured roof of the conning tower and Mk8 radar antenna lower in the photograph. The pentagonal-shaped Oerlikon gun tub is visible just above the barrels of turret no. 1. Later in the year it was replaced with two Bofors gun tubs and the five 20mm mounts were removed. To the left, guests of the ceremony are visible boarding the ship.
(National Archives, 80-G-K-824)

outside the citadel, for protection of the steering gear. Its maximum thickness was 6.2in. plus 1.5in. STS (158mm + 38mm STS).

Main artillery turrets and barbettes, being outside the armoured citadel, also received strong protection. The turrets' plates had the following thicknesses: front 17in. B-type plus 2.5in. STS (432mm + 64mm STS); sides 9.5in. A-type plus 0.75in. STS (241mm + 19mm STS); rear 12in.

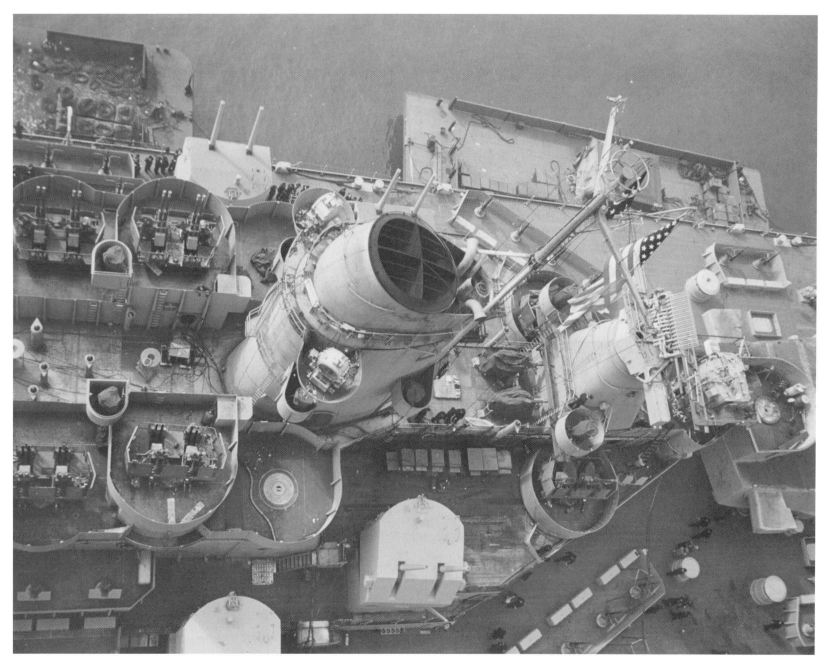

New York Navy Yard, 27 February 1943. An aerial view of funnel no. 2 and the aft superstructure. Although the battleship is being commissioned, fitting-out work in not finished yet; some of the equipment and armament is still missing, including several quadruple Bofors 40mm mounts.
(National Archives, 80-G-K-825)

A-type (305mm); roof 7.25in. B-type (184mm). The thickness of the barbettes' armour was the greatest at the sides and least at the front and back. Constructed of A-type armour, their thickness was

17.3–11.6in. (439–295mm) from top to second deck, 3in. STS (76mm STS) from second deck to third deck, and 1.5in. STS (38mm STS) below third deck. Dual-purpose artillery mounts and the ammunition magazines right below them were protected with 2.5in. (64mm) STS plates.

New York Navy Yard, 27 February 1943. The commissioning ceremony is being held on the *Iowa*'s aft deck. A shielded Bofors tub can be seen on the roof of turret no. 3, but its quadruple mount and gun director are not fitted yet. Note the Mk8 radar antenna on the top of main artillery director.
(National Archives, 80-G-K-825)

The conning tower received armour made of B-type steel: sides were 17.3in. (439mm) thick; roof was 7.25in. (184mm) thick; and the bottom was 4in. (102mm) thick.

Post-war studies showed that although *Iowa's* armour scheme did not incorporate the thickest plates, it was very well designed and balanced, thus giving solid protection to the vitals of the ship.

Bayonne, New Jersey, 29 March 1943. The anchor is being raised on USS *Iowa* in preparation to leave for Gravesend Bay near Brooklyn. The bow still lacks the distinctive double Oerlikon tube. This feature would be installed after the shakedown cruise. The ship is wearing Measure 22 camouflage scheme. The border between Navy Blue and Haze Gray is clearly visible on the hull. (Naval History & Heritage Command, NH 53264)

Underwater protection of *Iowa* against torpedoes, mines and bombs was provided by a multi-layered system. Four tanks were present on the outboard side of the hull, from the third deck downwards. The two outer tanks were filled with either fuel oil or ballast water, intended for absorbing the shock of the underwater explosion. The two inner tanks were void. The whole system was designed to withstand an explosion of a 700lb (320kg) torpedo warhead. However, at the outbreak of Pacific War, the Americans were unaware of the existence of Japanese advanced torpedoes; Japanese warheads actually contained as much as 1,080lb (490kg) of TNT.

None of the Iowa class battleships ever suffered from an underwater explosion so the actual effectiveness of the side protection system is hard to assess.

The *Iowa* had a double bottom running between the inner torpedo bulkheads along the entire length of the hull, and an additional third bottom under the citadel. The double bottom tanks were liquid-filled.

USS *Iowa* during her shakedown cruise, May 1943. Thick smoke is rising from funnel no. 2 during machinery trials. Photograph taken from the aft deck with turret no. 3 visible in the centre. The Oerlikon tub is in front of it, as well as vents and hatches. An aircraft cradle is present on the deck to the right, and a fragment of the port-side catapult can be seen to the left.
(National Archives, 80-G-K-6062)

## MACHINERY

In order to reach the designed maximum speed of 33 knots, exceptionally powerful machinery had to be fitted aboard the *Iowa*. Its total output equalled 212,000shp, driving four shafts and four propellers.

The propulsion machinery was placed in the middle part of the hull between barbettes nos. 2 and 3 (frames 87–151), and was distributed in the following way, starting from the bow:

- fire room no. 1, containing boilers nos. 1 and 2, producing steam for engine rooms nos. 1 and 2; uptakes headed for funnel no. 1;

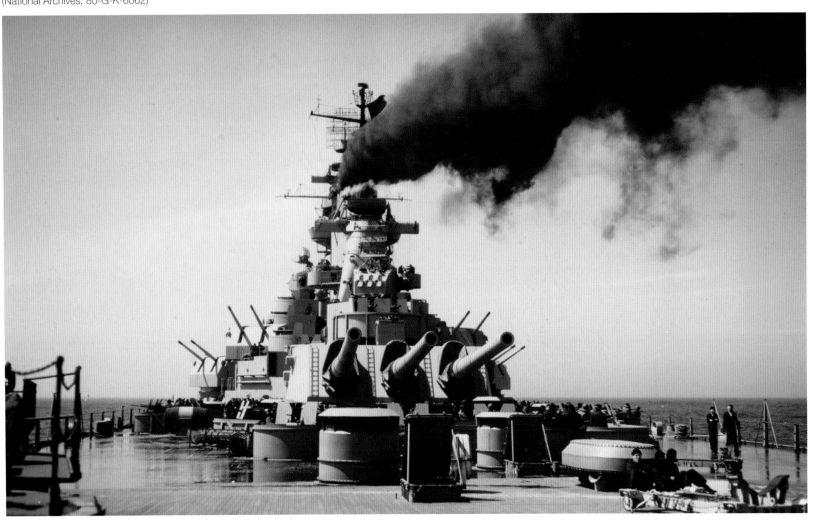

- engine room no. 1, containing geared turbine set no. 1, driving starboard outboard shaft; two turbogenerators on port side;
- fire room no. 2, containing boilers nos. 3 and 4, producing steam for engine rooms nos. 1 and 2; uptakes headed for funnel no. 1;
- engine room no. 2, containing geared turbine set no. 4, driving port outboard shaft; two turbogenerators on starboard side;
- fire room no. 3, containing boilers nos. 5 and 6, producing steam for engine rooms nos. 3 and 4; uptakes headed for funnel no. 2;
- engine room no. 3, containing geared turbine set no. 2, driving starboard inboard shaft; two turbogenerators on port side;
- fire room no. 4, containing boilers nos. 7 and 8, producing steam for engine rooms nos. 3 and 4; uptakes headed for funnel no. 2;
- engine room no. 4, containing geared turbine set no. 3, driving port inboard shaft; two turbogenerators on starboard side.

The turbines for *Iowa* were delivered by General Electric. Each of the four turbine sets consisted of a high-pressure turbine, a low-pressure turbine and a double reduction gear. The assumed power output of a single set was 53,000shp at 202rpm of the shaft for forward motion of the ship and 11,000shp at 123rpm for backward motion. Reverse shaft rotation was by provided by an astern element in the low-pressure turbine. All supplementary equipment necessary to operate the turbines was placed within the same compartment.

Steam was supplied by eight three-drum dual-furnace controlled superheat boilers delivered by Babcock & Wilcox. Fed with heavy fuel oil (mazut), the boilers worked at 850°F (454°C) and 656psi (38.5atm). During the 1980s' reactivation, boilers as well as their fuel storage and transport system were modified for compatibility with NATO F-75 light oil.

In order to provide power to lighting and more than 900 electrical motors on board (serving armament, fire control instruments, radars, electronics, etc.), eight turbogenerators, 1,250kW each, were fitted. There were two units in each of the engine rooms, on the opposite side to the turbine sets, giving the total output power of 10,000kW. The ship's electrical system worked on 450V, 60Hz alternating current. The design also allowed for two emergency diesel generators, 250kW each. They were placed in compartments immediately forward of fire room no. 1 and immediately aft of engine room no. 4.

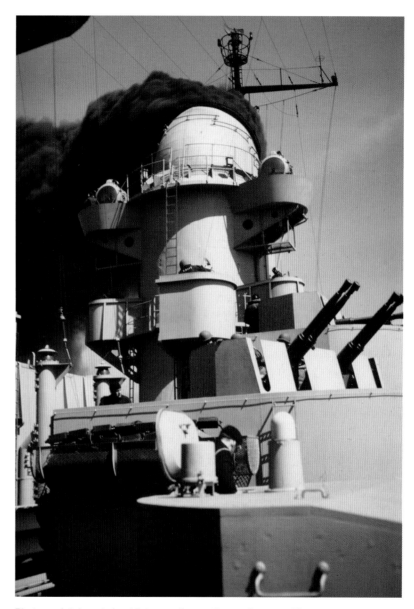

Photograph taken at about the same time as the previous one. The cameraman is standing in an Oerlikon tub on the flag bridge level of the fore superstructure. A fragment of 5in. mount is visible in the foreground, a floater net basket attached just behind. Note also the shielded positions of Bofors AA mounts and their Mk51 directors, wire antenna towers, searchlight platforms on funnel no. 2 and the SG radar antenna on the top of the mainmast.
(National Archives, 80-G-K-6063)

*Iowa* was fitted with a pair of rudders, each having a surface of 340ft² (31.59m²). They were positioned directly behind the inner propellers and could swing to a maximum 36.5 degrees to either side.

| Armament of USS *Iowa* (BB-61) | | | | | |
|---|---|---|---|---|---|
| Armament type\Year | 1943 | 1944 | 1947 | 1958 | 1984 |
| Main artillery | 9 x 16"/50 Mk7 (3 x III) | 9 x 16"/50 Mk7 (3 x III) | 9 x 16"/50 Mk7 (3 x III) | 9 x 16"/50 Mk7 (3 x III) | 9 x 16"/50 Mk7 (3 x III) |
| Dual-purpose artillery | 20 x 5"/38 Mk12 (10 x II) | 20 x 5"/38 Mk12 (10 x II) | 20 x 5"/38 Mk12 (10 x II) | 20 x 5"/38 Mk12 (10 x II) | 12 x 5"/38 Mk12 (6 x II) |
| Anti-aircraft artillery | 60 x 40mm/56 Mk1, Mk2 (15 x IV) 60 x 20mm/70 Mk4 (60 x I) | 76 x 40mm/56 Mk1, Mk2 (19 x IV) 52 x 20mm/70 Mk4 (52 x I) | 60 x 40mm/56 Mk1, Mk2 (15 x IV) 32 x 20mm/70 Mk4 (16 x II) | 52 x 40mm/56 Mk1, Mk2 (13 x IV) | – |
| Cruise missiles | – | – | – | – | 32 x BGM-109 (8 x IV) |
| Anti-ship missiles | – | – | – | – | 16 x RGM-84 (4 x IV) |
| Close-In Weapon System | – | – | – | – | 4 x 20mm/76 M61A1 (4 x I) |
| Chaff launchers | – | – | – | – | 48 x Mk36 SRBOC (8 x VI) |
| Saluting guns | – | – | 2 x 6-pdr (2 x I) | 2 x 6-pdr (2 x I) | 2 x 40mm (2 x I) |

# ARMAMENT

## MAIN ARTILLERY

*Iowa* carried nine 16"/50 (40.6cm) Mk7 guns, specially designed for the new battleship class. The guns were placed in three three-gun turrets: turret no. 1 in the bow section on frame 56; turret no. 2 just behind it in superposition on frame 74; and turret no. 3 in the stern section on frame 160.5.

The guns were installed in the uppermost level of the turret – the armoured gunhouse. They featured a Mk4 Welin-type breech block. Individual shell and powder hoists were provided for each gun. Shells were transported vertically to the breech, where they were rotated in a cradle and rammed. Powder bags were transported horizontally (hoists driven by respective 100KM electric motors), then rolled to the spanning tray from the side and rammed. Loading angle was +5 degrees. Electrohydraulic rammers were driven by 60KM electric motors.

The gunhouse was divided into several compartments with fireproof bulkheads. Each gun had a separate compartment, and there was also a commanding booth at the back of the turret. It featured a 46ft (14m) rangefinder, an analog computer, two periscopes and space for the turret's commanding officers. Train and point sights were positioned in compartments on both sides of each turret.

The next two levels under the gunhouse, pan floor and machinery floor, were protected by the armoured barbette. Most of the machinery necessary for driving the turret's mechanisms were placed here: elevating gear motors (60KM each), shell hoist motors (75KM each) and training gear electric motor (300KM). The whole turret revolved on a roller path, which rested on a fixed circular foundation between pan and machinery floors.

Further down the turret there were two (three in the case of superpositioned turret no. 2) projectile stowage and handling floors. Each floor consisted of three rings. The outer ring was fixed to a circular foundation around the turret and was used as a stowage place for projectiles standing vertically. The middle ring, revolving with the turret, was a working platform for the crew and featured six parbuckling capstans for moving the shells from their stowage places to the hoists. The inner ring was another stowage place for projectiles and could rotate inside the turret by means of a 40KM electric motor. The electric and communications cable column was in the centre.

At the very bottom of each turret there was a powder-handling floor. Propellant charges from the magazines around the turret were passed through special scuttles and then loaded to hoists.

Initially, it was planned to use the Mk5 armour-piercing projectile, weighing 2,240lb (1,016kg). However, in 1939 a much heavier Mk8 projectile was designed (2,700lb, 1,225kg). The new shell proved extremely successful, providing armour-penetration capability only a bit weaker than that of the much heavier Japanese battleship *Yamato*'s shell. In addition to the armour-piercing projectile, a high-capacity shell was provided – Mk13 (1,900lb, 862kg). Propellant charge could be either

| 16"/50 (40.6cm) Mk7 guns | |
|---|---|
| Gun weight | 267,904lb (121,519kg) |
| Gun length | 816in. (20.73m) |
| Number of grooves | 90 |
| Chamber volume | 27,000in.³ (442.5dm³) |
| Rate of fire per barrel | 2 rounds per minute |
| Barrel life | 290–350 rounds |
| Recoil | 47in. (119cm) |
| Weight of projectile | Armour-piercing projectile – AP Mk8: 2,700lb (1,225kg)<br>High-capacity projectile – HC Mk13: 1,900lb (862kg)<br>Nuclear projectile (after 1951) – Nuclear Mk23: 1,900lb (862kg)<br>Anti-Personnel Improved Conventional Munition (after 1984) – ICM Mk144: 1,900lb (862kg) |
| Bursting charge | AP Mk8: 40.9lb (18.55kg)<br>HC Mk13: 153.6lb (69.67kg)<br>Nuclear Mk23: about 15–20 kilotons |
| Length of projectile | AP Mk8: 72in. (182.9cm)<br>HC Mk13: 64in. (162.6cm)<br>Nuclear Mk23: 64in. (162.6cm)<br>ICM Mk144: 64in. (162.6cm) |
| Weight of propellant charge | Full charge until 1945: 660lb (299.4kg)<br>Reduced charge until 1945: 305lb (138.3kg)<br>Full charge after 1945: 655lb (297.1kg)<br>Reduced charge after 1945: 305lb (138.3kg) |
| Ammunition stowage per gun | About 130 rounds |
| Working pressure | 18.5 tons/in.² (3,200kg/cm²) |
| Muzzle velocity | AP Mk8: 2,500fps (762m/s)<br>AP Mk8 with reduced charge: 1,800fps (549m/s)<br>HC Mk13: 2,690fps (820m/s)<br>HC Mk13 with reduced charge: 2,075fps (632m/s) |
| Range with AP Mk8 | At 10° elevation: 17,650 yards (16,139m)<br>At 20° elevation: 29,000 yards (26,518m)<br>At 35° elevation: 39,500 yards (36,119m)<br>At 45° elevation: 42,345 yards (38,720m) |
| Striking velocity with AP Mk8 | At 10,000 yards: 2,074fps (632m/s)<br>At 20,000 yards: 1,740fps (530m/s)<br>At 30,000 yards: 1,567fps (478m/s)<br>At 40,000 yards: 1,607fps (490m/s) |

| Weight of turret | 1,701–1,708 tons |
|---|---|
| Loading angle | +5° |
| Elevation | Turrets nos. 1 and 3: -2/+45°<br>Turret no. 2: 0/+45° |
| Elevation rate | 12°/s |
| Train | -150/+150° |
| Train rate | 4°/s |
| Distance between gun axes | 122in. (310cm) |

full (660lb, 299.4kg) or reduced (305lb, 138.3kg) for higher striking angle at shorter distances. In both cases it consisted of six silk bags with powder.

Although the Iowa class battleships never had a chance to prove their main guns' effectiveness against an enemy capital ship, the Mk7 guns turned out to be very successful. They are widely considered as one of the best heavy-calibre artillery type ever mounted afloat.

## SECONDARY ARTILLERY

USS *Iowa*'s secondary battery consisted of twenty 5"/38 (12.7cm) Mk12 guns in ten twin mounts. The choice of this weapon was obvious, as it had been in service in the US Navy since 1934 and turned out to be among the most successful dual-purpose gun designs in history. It continued to be fitted to new ships after World War II and was used by several navies of the world for many years.

Four twin mounts were placed symmetrically on both sides of *Iowa*'s superstructure deck 1, and six on superstructure deck 2. Such a layout gave very good abeam arcs of fire, but the bow and stern sectors were not covered well because of the battleship's massive superstructures.

The twin mounts were armoured and featured a base ring underneath, from where ready-to-use ammunition was transported upwards by the means of integral hoists. Main magazines were placed inside the citadel, on the third deck.

There were a number of different projectiles intended for the Mk12 guns: anti-aircraft, high-capacity, armour-piercing and illuminating. The AA shells could use either Point Detonating (PT), Mechanical Time (MT) or Variable Time (VT) nose fuzes. The last ones, introduced in 1943 and commonly called proximity fuzes, greatly enhanced the guns' damaging capability against aircraft.

The guns' practical rate of fire depended heavily on their crews' level of training, which is why the battleship was fitted with a twin practice loading machine that was located between funnel no. 2 and aft of the rangefinder tower, flag bridge level.

Before her 1980s' reactivation, it was decided that some the *Iowa*'s 5in. mounts had to be taken away to make space for the new missile systems. Two aftermost mounts on each side of superstructure deck 2 were removed, and the battleship's total number of 5in. guns dropped to 12.

## ANTI-AIRCRAFT ARTILLERY

*Iowa* was equipped with 15 (increased to 19 soon after commissioning) quadruple 40mm/56 gun mounts. Developed by Swedish company Bofors, this automatic water-cooled weapon used four-round ammunition clips. Seeing its anti-aircraft potential, the Americans bought the licence from Sweden in June 1941. The Bofors gun had very good rate of fire, range and damaging capability, and soon became widely installed on virtually every ship in the US Navy.

| 5"/38 (12.7cm) Mk12 guns | |
| --- | --- |
| Gun weight | 3,990lb (1,810kg) |
| Gun length | 223.8in. (5.68m) |
| Number of grooves | 45 |
| Chamber volume | 654in.$^3$ (10.72dm$^3$) |
| Rate of fire per barrel | 15–22 rounds per minute |
| Barrel life | About 4,600 rounds |
| Recoil | 15in. (38.1cm) |
| Weight of projectile | 55.18lb (25kg) |
| Weight of bursting charge | 2.04–8.4lb (0.9–3.8kg) |
| Length of projectile | 20–20.75in. (50.8–52.7cm) |
| Weight of propellant charge | Full charge: 15.2–17.2lb (6.9–7.8kg) Reduced charge: 3.6lb (1.6kg) |
| Length of propellant cartridge | Full charge: 26.7in. (67.9cm) Reduced charge: 16.3in. (41.3cm) |
| Ammunition stowage per gun | About 450 rounds |
| Working pressure | 18 tons/in.$^2$ (2,835 kg/cm$^2$) |
| Muzzle velocity | Full charge: 2,600fps (792m/s) Reduced charge: 1,200fps (366m/s) |
| Range | At 10° elevation: 9,506 yards (8,692m) At 25° elevation: 14,804 yards (13,537m) At 45° elevation: 17,392 yards (15,903m) Ceiling: 37,200ft (11,887m) |
| Weight of mount | 170,635lb (77,399kg) |
| Loading angle | Any |
| Elevation | -15/+85° |
| Elevation rate | 15°/s |
| Train | -90/+90° |
| Train rate | 25°/s |
| Distance between gun axes | 84in. (213cm) |

| 40mm/56 Bofors Mk1, Mk2 guns | |
| --- | --- |
| Gun weight | 1,150lb (522kg) |
| Gun length | 148.8in. (3.780m) |
| Number of grooves | 16 |
| Chamber volume | 28.3in.$^3$ (0.464dm$^3$) |
| Rate of fire per barrel | 120 rounds per minute theoretical 80–90 rounds per minute practical |
| Barrel life | 9,500 rounds |
| Weight of projectile | 1.985lb (0.9kg) |
| Weight of bursting charge | 0.148–0.150lb (0.067–0.068kg) |
| Length of projectile | 7.25in. (18.4cm) |
| Weight of complete round | 4.75lb (2.15kg) |
| Weight of propellant charge | 0.694lb (0.314kg) |
| Length of complete round | 17.62in. (44.75cm) |
| Ammunition stowage per gun | About 2,000 rounds |
| Working pressure | 19.5 tons/in.$^2$ (3,070kg/cm$^2$) |
| Muzzle velocity | 2,890fps (881m/s) |
| Range | At 10° elevation: 6,844 yards (6,258m) At 25° elevation: 10,103 yards (9,238m) At 45° elevation: 11,133 yards (10,180m) Ceiling: 22,300ft (6,800m) |
| Weight of Mk2 quadruple mount without shield | 23,200–23,800lb (10,524–10,796kg) |
| Elevation | -15/+90° |
| Elevation rate | 24°/s |
| Train | 360° |
| Train rate | 26°/s |
| Train rate | 25°/s |
| Distance between gun axes | 84in. (213cm) |

| 20mm/70 Oerlikon Mk4 guns | |
|---|---|
| Gun weight | 150lb (68.04kg) |
| Gun length | 87in. (2.21m) |
| Number of grooves | 9 |
| Chamber volume | 2.127in.³ (34.855cm³) |
| Rate of fire per barrel | 450 rounds per minute theoretical<br>250–320 rounds per minute practical |
| Barrel life | About 9,000 rounds |
| Weight of projectile | 0.262–0.271lb (0.117–0.123kg) |
| Weight of bursting charge | 0.024–0.027lb (0.011–0.013kg) |
| Length of projectile | 3.025–3.275in. (7.68–8.31cm) |
| Weight of complete round | 0.53lb (0.241kg) |
| Weight of propellant charge | 0.061lb (0.028kg) |
| Length of complete round | 7.18in. (18.2cm) |
| Working pressure | 19.6 tons/in.² (3,090kg/cm²) |
| Muzzle velocity | 2,770fps (844m/s) |
| Range | At 10° elevation: 3,450 yards (3,154m)<br>At 25° elevation: 4,525 yards (4,138m)<br>At 45° elevation: 4,800 yards (4,389m)<br>Ceiling: 10,000ft (3,048m) |
| Weight of mount | Mk4 single mount: 1,695lb (769kg)<br>Mk24 twin mount: 1,400lb (635kg) |
| Elevation | -5/+87° |
| Train | 360° |

The quadruple mount was essentially a combination of two twin mounts fitted on a single carriage. Train and elevation was driven by electric motors, as well as cooling-liquid pumps. Each mount was fitted with a protective shield, and had an additional circular shield around it attached to the deck. Ready-to-use spare ammunition clips were stowed on racks on inner surfaces of these fixed shields.

In the 1950s it became clear that Bofors guns were becoming less effective against modern aircraft and their number was gradually reduced (down to 13 quadruple mounts in 1955). By the time of *Iowa*'s reactivation in 1984, all 40mm guns were gone.

In addition to the Bofors guns, much lighter 20mm/70 anti-aircraft guns were used on *Iowa*. Designed by the Swiss company Oerlikon and adapted by the US Navy in 1940, they provided anti-aircraft fire against closest targets. High rate of fire and simplicity of use were this weapon's biggest qualities. Ammunition was fed from spiral 60-round magazines.

USS *Iowa* carried 60 single manually operated Mk4 pedestal mounts when commissioned. They were equipped with modern Mk14 gun sights that enabled very effective aiming. However, after World War II it became clear that the Oerlikon gun was no longer a useful AA weapon. In 1946 all single mounts were removed and replaced with light Mk24 twin mounts, but these too were soon taken away.

## MISSILE BATTERY

When *Iowa* was being prepared for reactivation in the 1980s, it was decided that she should carry modern missile systems. Superstructures between funnel no. 1 and the aft main artillery director tower were rebuilt to accommodate the new launchers of Tomahawk and Harpoon missiles.

The BGM-109 Tomahawk is a long-range, subsonic, low-altitude missile that can hit targets both on land and at sea. It is propelled by a turbofan engine and features an advanced guidance system. It was first designed in late 1970s, and since then several improved versions had been released. Tomahawk can use a variety of warheads, including the following configurations: anti-ship, land-attack, cluster munition and nuclear.

| BGM-109 Tomahawk cruise missile | |
|---|---|
| Weight | 2,900lb (1,300kg) |
| Length | 18ft 3in. (5.56m) |
| Diameter | 20.4in. (51.8cm) |
| Wing span | 8ft 9in. (2.67m) |
| Range | Anti-ship: up to 470NM (870km)<br>Land attack: up to 675NM (1,250km)<br>Nuclear: up to 1,500NM (2,778km) |
| Speed | Up to about 550mph (885km/h) |
| Flight altitude | 50–325ft (15–100m) |

| RGM-84 Harpoon anti-ship missile | |
|---|---|
| Weight | 1,523lb (691kg) |
| Length | 15ft (4.6m) |
| Diameter | 13.5in. (34cm) |
| Wing span | 3ft (0.91m) |
| Range | Over 67NM (124km) |
| Speed | 537mph (864km/h) |
| Flight altitude | 7–325ft (2–100m) |

The *Iowa* was armed with 32 BGM-109 missiles in eight Mk143 ABLs (Armoured Box Launchers) on superstructure deck fore and aft of funnel no. 2. Each ABL contained four missiles stowed in a horizontal position and raised by a hydraulic drive for launch.

Another photograph from the same day aboard *Iowa*. Port-side 40mm and 5in. batteries are visible in this view from the fore superstructure tower bridge. All the Bofors tubs have ring racks for ammunition clip stowage on their inner sides. (National Archives, 80-G-K-6064)

The RGM-84 Harpoon is an anti-ship missile system that entered service in the US Navy in 1977. The missile is stored in Kevlar containers and fired at a fixed angle. The solid-fuel booster works only for a short time during the initial stage of flight (around 2.5 seconds), after which it is expended and then the turbojet engine takes over.

Iowa was armed with 16 Harpoons. The missiles were stored in four quadruple Mk141 launchers fitted on both sides of funnel no. 2 and aligned perpendicularly to the ship's centre axis.

As a supplementary defence weapon, five FIM-92 Stinger short-range missile launchers were provided. The launchers are portable and manually operated.

## CIWS (CLOSE-IN WEAPON SYSTEM)

During her 1982–84 refit, *Iowa* was equipped with four sets of Mk15 Phalanx CIWS. This weapon is intended for defence against airborne threats (mainly enemy anti-ship missiles) at short range. Fulfilling this task requires exceptional rate of fire and speed of operation of the mount.

The core of the Phalanx is the six-barrelled 20mm/76 M61A1 Vulcan gun, a weapon very successfully used by the US Air Force. It fires the Mk149 projectile, consisting of armour-piercing sub-calibre (12.75mm) penetrator, a 20mm sabot and a pusher, the two latter being

| Mk15 Phalanx CIWS Block 0 | |
|---|---|
| Gun type | 6 x 20mm/76 M61A1 Vulcan |
| Bore length | 59.8in. (1.52m) |
| Rate of fire per barrel | 3,000 rounds per minute |
| Weight of projectile | 0.22lb (0.1kg) |
| Length of projectile | 6.62in. (16.8cm) |
| Weight of complete round | 0.58lb (0.26kg) |
| Ammunition stowage | Integrated ammunition drum (989 rounds) |
| Muzzle velocity | 3,650fps (1,113m/s) |
| Range | Maximum: 6,000 yards (5,500m) Effective: 1,625 yards (1,490m) |
| Weight of mount | 12,500lb (5,625kg) |
| Elevation | -10/+80° |
| Elevation rate | 86°/s |
| Train | About -150/+150° |
| Train rate | 100°/s |

discarded immediately after the round exits the muzzle. Ammunition is automatically fed from a storage drum fixed underneath. The rotating six-barrelled gun has a capability of firing an impressive 3,000 rounds per minute, a figure necessary to take down a fast-approaching target. The Phalanx mount can operate in fully automatic mode, without any human operator input. The radome fitted above the gun cradle features both search and tracking radars. An advanced automated fire control system enables the mount to detect, identify and engage enemy missiles at close range.

Phalanx was introduced in 1980 and has received several revisions of its design since then. It is present aboard ships of numerous navies in the world, including almost every vessel of the US Navy. The mounts fitted on board *Iowa* were of the earliest version, Block 0. They were positioned symmetrically on both sides of fore superstructure's level 5 and on a special platform in front of funnel no. 2, thus providing coverage of all sectors around the battleship.

View from the forecastle during *Iowa*'s shakedown cruise, spring of 1943. AA crews are training. The Oerlikon tub in the foreground would later be replaced with Bofors tubs during the first refit of the battleship. (National Archives, 80-G-K-16469)

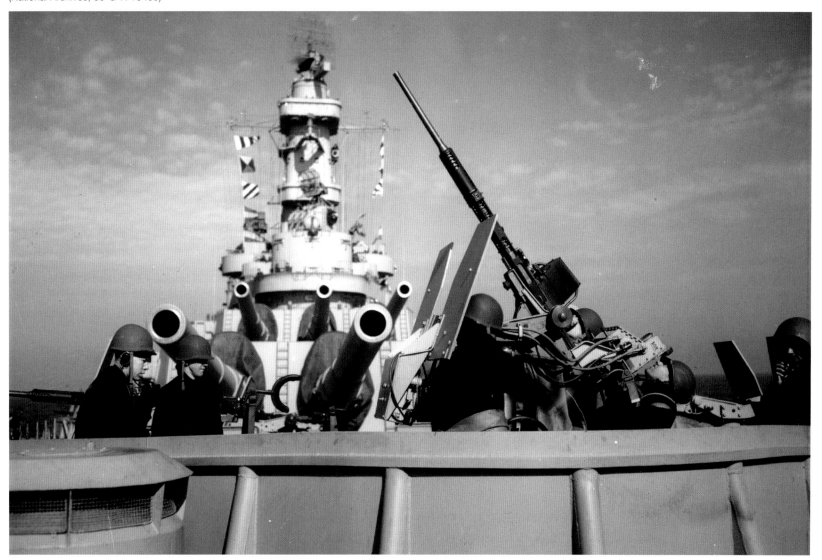

## FIRE CONTROL

When commissioned, *Iowa* was fitted with two separate fire control systems: Mk38 GFCS (Gun Fire Control System) for the main artillery and Mk37 GFCS for the secondary artillery.

Spring of 1943, sea trials of BB-61. Capt John L. McCrea, the commanding officer, tours the battleship with his staff. Visible in this photograph are the starboard-side catapult with liferafts stowed underneath, aircraft crane and OS2U Kingfisher floatplane sitting on a cradle.
(National Archives, 80-G-K-6118)

## MAIN ARTILLERY

The Mk38 system consisted of several elements. First, the data about the target was determined by rangefinders and directors. Each of the three main artillery turrets featured a 46ft (14m) rangefinder. The rangefinder in turret no. 1 was of a coincidence type and was removed in 1948, while the other two turrets had stereoscopic equipment. Two more rangefinders (26.5ft, 8.08m) were fitted in the Mk38 main artillery directors on top of the fore and aft fire control towers These directors also had Mk8 (FH) artillery radars mounted on their roofs that provided data about range

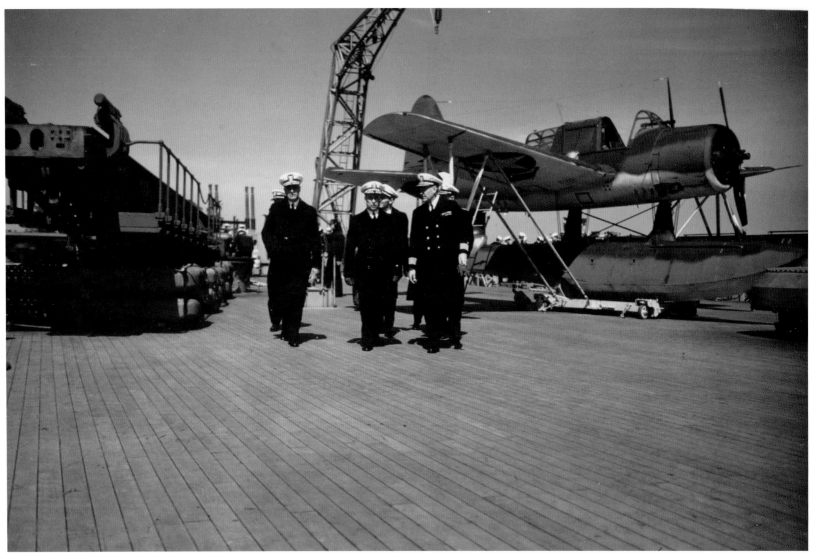

| Fire control radars | | | | | |
|---|---|---|---|---|---|
| Radar designation | Purpose | Period of service aboard *Iowa* | Wavelength | Peak output power | Antenna |
| Mk8 (FH) | Main artillery fire direction | 1943–1946 | 100cm | 15–30kW | Polyrod array antenna; 10.2 x 3.3ft (3.1 x 1m) |
| Mk13 | Main artillery fire direction | 1945–1990 | 3.3cm | 50kW | Parabola within a radome; 7.9 x 2ft (2.4 x 0.6m) |
| Mk3 (FC) | Main artillery fire direction | 1943–1945 | 40cm | 15–20kW | Half-cylinder; diameter 3 x 12.1ft (0.9 x 3.7m) |
| Mk27 | Surface target rangefinding | 1945–1955 | 10cm | 50kW | Parabolic section; 2.6 x 1.3ft (0.8 x 0.4m) |
| Mk4 | Dual-purpose artillery fire direction | 1943–1945 | 40cm | 40kW | 2 x half-cylinders; diameter 3 x 5.9ft (0.9 x 1.8m) |
| Mk12 | Dual-purpose artillery fire direction | 1945–1955 | 33cm | 110kW | 2 x half-cylinders; diameter 3 x 5.9ft (0.9 x 1.8m) |
| Mk22 | Air target height meter | 1945–1955 | 30cm | 25–35kW | 'Orange peel'; 1.6 x 6.2ft (0.5 x 1.9m) |
| Mk25 | Dual-purpose artillery fire direction | 1955–1990 | 10cm | 30kW | Dish antenna |
| Mk34 | AA artillery fire direction | 1945–1958 | 3cm | 30kW | Dish antenna |

| Air search radars | | | | | |
|---|---|---|---|---|---|
| Radar designation | Purpose | Period of service aboard *Iowa* | Wavelength | Peak output power | Antenna |
| SK/SK-2 | Air search | 1943–1946/1946–1951 | 100cm | 200kW | Flat square; 17.1 x 17.1ft (5.2 x 5.2m)/ parabolic antenna; diameter 17.1ft (5.2m) |
| SR | Air search | 1945–1948 | 150cm | 300kW | Flat rectangle; 13.5 x 5.5ft (4.1 x 1.7m) |
| SP | Air search | 1948–1955 | 10cm | 50kW | Parabolic antenna; diameter 7.9ft (2.4m) |
| SPS-6/SPS-12 | Air and sea surface search | 1951–1955/1955–1958 | 22.2–24cm | 500kW | Width 17.1ft (5.2m) |
| SPS-8 | Height meter | 1955–1958 | 8.4–8.7cm | 650kW | Height 14.1ft (4.3m) |
| SPS-49 | Air search | 1984–1990 | 31.8–35.3cm | 280–360kW | Width 24ft (7.3m) |

| Sea surface search radars | | | | | |
|---|---|---|---|---|---|
| Radar designation | Purpose | Period of service aboard *Iowa* | Wavelength | Peak output power | Antenna |
| SG | Sea surface search | 1943–1955 | 10cm | 50kW | 4.3 x 1.3ft (1.3 x 0.4m) |
| SU | Sea surface search | 1945–1948 | 3cm | 15kW | Protected by radome; diameter 2ft (0.6m) |
| SPS-10 | Sea surface search | 1984–1985 | 5.1–5.5cm | 500kW | Width 10.5ft (3.2m) |
| SPS-67 | Sea surface search | 1985–1990 | 5.1–5.5cm | 280kW | Width 10.5ft (3.2m) |
| SPS-64 | Sea surface search and navigation | 1984–1990 | 3.2cm | 20–50kW | Width 6ft (1.83m) |

and bearing to the target. The Mk8 sets were later replaced with newer Mk13 radars; on the fore director in 1945 and a year later on the aft director. Both antennas remained in place until Iowa's decommissioning in 1990.

As an addition to the Mk38 directors, a Mk40 director (consisting of two Mk30 and one Mk32 periscope) was present atop the conning tower. During the summer of 1943, a Mk3 (FC) radar antenna was added in this location to provide range information. This radar was later replaced by a Mk27 set (1945), which remained on board until 1955.

When *Iowa* was recommissioned in 1984, she received DR 810 muzzle velocity meter Doppler radars on the roofs of all main artillery turrets, just behind the middle barrels. These sets provided information about the last fired round, and thus greatly improved accuracy of fire.

A Mass is being held on the aft deck of *Iowa*, June 1944. Clearly visible in this colour photograph is the camouflage scheme that the battleship was wearing at the time – Measure 32/1B, consisting of spots in Light Grey 5-L and Navy Blue 5-N. (National Archives, 80-G-K-14182)

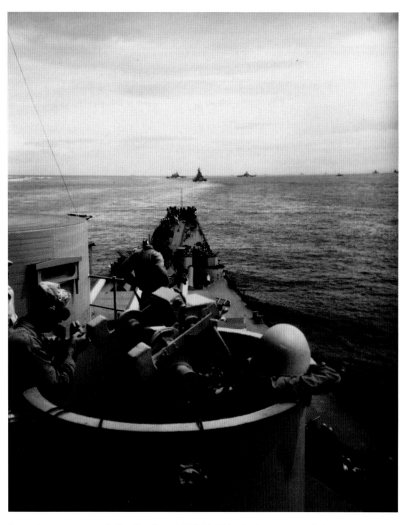

*Iowa* at an anchorage in the Pacific, mid-1944. This photograph was taken from the pilothouse top level, starboard side. A Mk51 Bofors gun director is in the foreground with the armoured conning tower slightly to the left. Judging by the camouflage schemes, the names of the battleships visible in distance can be determined: to the left is *North Carolina* (BB-55), and to the right is *Indiana* (BB-58). The identity of the third battleship in the middle, with her stern facing the observer, is hard to discern. (National Archives, 80-G-K-6120)

All the information gathered by the ship's optical and radar equipment was sent down to plotting rooms in the armoured citadel to evaluate appropriate train and elevation of the main artillery. For redundancy, *Iowa* had two plotting rooms: on the first platform (fore) and on the third deck (aft). Each of them contained several instruments. The Mk8 rangekeeper was a mechanical-analog computer that calculated orders for the turrets based on the information about the target, own motion, ballistics and stabilization. The Mk41 stable vertical was an instrument for measuring own roll and pitch, which consoles enabled the operators to read data from the radars, whereas the fire control switchboard was used to manage various work modes of the Mk38 GFCS.

The plotting rooms were changed very little during the battleship's career, the most important modification being the addition of the Mk48 electromechanical computers for shore bombardment fire control. They were installed in the fore and aft plotting rooms in 1950 and 1984 respectively.

## SECONDARY ARTILLERY

The Mk37 GFCS was a very reliable system and was widely used on US Navy ships during World War II. Iowa was fitted with four Mk37 directors, each with a cable connection with plotting rooms in the citadel. Two of the directors were on the ship's centre line

The battleship sitting in Dry Dock No. 4, Hunters Point Naval Shipyard, east terminus of Palou Avenue, San Francisco, January 1945. Having been damaged by a typhoon in December the previous year, *Iowa* had to be overhauled. The repairs and modernization lasted until mid-March. During this time the ship had her dazzle camouflage painted over with camouflage Measure 22.
(Library of Congress, Prints & Photographs Division, HAER, Reproduction number CAL,38-SANFRA,195A—13)

(on fore and aft superstructures), and two on both sides of funnel no. 1. The Mk37 director had an optical rangefinder (15ft, 4.57m), a sight and two telescopes. Radar equipment consisted of a Mk4 antenna mounted on the roof. In 1945 these sets were replaced on all directors with superior Mk12/22 radars (Mk22 being the height-finder antenna fitted on the right side). Another modification was made in 1955, when the new Mk25 radar dish antennas were fitted in place of the Mk12/22, and the directors received new square-shaped shields with new commanders' sights.

## ANTI-AIRCRAFT ARTILLERY

Each of the 40mm Bofors mount on board had its dedicated Mk51 director positioned nearby. This equipment was run by a single operator and its core was the Mk14 gun sight. A newer, superior director was developed by 1944: the Mk57, equipped with Mk34 radar. In her 1945

refit, *Iowa* received two of these sets. They were placed on both sides between the funnels, replacing a pair of Mk51s.

Further modernization came in 1951, when the two stern Bofors mounts were equipped with Mk63 directors. Their Mk34 radar dishes were too big and heavy to fit in the original position of the previous Mk51 director, so they had to be attached directly on the top of the Bofors guns. During the next refit in 1955 *Iowa* was equipped with six Mk56 directors. Originally intended for use with the 3in. guns, they gave blind fire capability to both the Bofors and 5in. mounts. Six units, each equipped with a Mk35 dish radar, were placed in pairs in front of the side Mk37 directors, in place of a pair of Bofors mounts amidships and on platforms at the base of aft fire direction tower. All remaining Mk51 directors, considered obsolete, were removed.

## SEARCH RADAR

During her long career, *Iowa* had a vast number of search radars fitted. These can be divided into two groups: air search radars and sea surface search radars.

When commissioned, the battleship only carried one air search radar: SK. Fitted on a platform on the foremast, it had a large square antenna. A smaller BL frame was present on its top – a part of the IFF (Identification Friend or Foe system). In 1945, a new SR air search radar with a rectangular antenna was fitted on the maintop. In the next year the SK antenna was replaced with an improved model: SK-2 (large dish antenna). During the 1948 refit the SR radar was replaced with a SP air search radar (dish antenna), and the SK-2 with a SR-3 air search radar. The latter one proved to be unsuccessful and was kept aboard briefly. When Iowa was being prepared for her Korean deployment in 1951, a newer SPS-6 was mounted in its place. This set was upgraded to a similar SPS-12 in 1955, together with replacing the SP radar with a SPS-8 unit. During her 1980s modernization, *Iowa* received a SPS-49 radar on her rebuilt foremast.

Two sets of SG sea surface search radar were present on the *Iowa* from 1943. This type had a relatively small antenna; one unit was mounted on a platform forward of the fire control tower and the other on the mainmast. During the 1945 refit the forward SG unit was replaced with a TDY jammer antenna, and a new SU surface search radar inside a small radome was mounted on the after end of the foretop. In 1948, the DBA antenna on *Iowa's* foretopmast was replaced with a SG-6 radar. The aft SG unit (upgraded to SG-1b) was not removed until 1955. For the battleship's reactivation in 1984, a new surface search set was installed (SPS-10), as well as a navigation radar (SPS-64). The SPS-10 unit was upgraded the next year to a similar SPS-67.

Two sisters out in the Pacific. This photograph was taken from the forecastle of *Iowa* with *Missouri* (BB-63) steaming alongside in the waters off Japan, 20 August 1945. The ships are clearly involved in a personnel transfer operation. Note that *Iowa's* original round open bridge had been replaced with square enclosed bridge during her January–March refit.
(Naval History & Heritage Command, NH 96781)

## OTHER ELECTRONIC EQUIPMENT

In addition to the radars, *Iowa* carried a large number of other electronic instruments, mainly for communication, IFF (Identify Friend or Foe) and ECM (Electronic Countermeasure). The most important World War II-era units included DBM radio direction finder, TDY radar jammer and AS-37, AS-56 noise amplifiers. During the 1980s' refit, Iowa received two SLQ-32 sets on her superstructure. This ECM gear worked together with the SRBOC chaff launchers. A SLQ-25 Nixie set was installed in the battleship's stern. This could launch a towed decoy in order to draw enemy torpedo off the ship. Other equipment included two OE-8 antennas for satellite communication (on the fore

| Specifications of the onboard aircraft of USS Iowa | | | |
|---|---|---|---|
| Aircraft type | Vought OS2U Kingfisher | Curtiss SC-1 Seahawk | AAI/IAI RQ-2A Pioneer |
| Wingspan | 35ft 11in. (10.95m) | 41ft (12.49m) | 16.9ft (5.2m) |
| Length | 33ft 10in. (10.31m) | 36ft 4in. (11.08m) | 14ft (4m) |
| Power plant | Pratt & Whitney R-985-AN-2 radial engine (450hp) | Wright R-1820-62 Cyclone supercharged radial engine (1,350hp) | Sachs two-cylinder engine (26hp) |
| Maximum speed | 164mph (264km/h) | 313mph (504km/h) | 125mph (200km/h) |
| Ceiling | 13,000ft (3,960m) | 37,300ft (11,370m) | 15,000ft (4,600m) |
| Range | 805 miles (1,296km) | 625 miles (1,006km) | 115 miles (185km) |
| Loaded weight | 6,000lb (2,721kg) | 9,000lb (4,082kg) | 452lb (205kg) |
| Armament | 2 x .30in. (7.62mm) Browning machine guns 650lb (295kg) of bombs | 2 x .50in. (12.7mm) Browning machine guns 2 x 325lb (150kg) bombs | – |

superstructure tower and funnel no. 2), as well as an NTDS antenna (Naval Tactical Data System) for exchanging combat information with other ships (on a large support frame on the bow).

## AIRCRAFT

Like earlier battleships of the US Navy, *Iowa* had aircraft facilities fitted on her stern. Board floatplanes could be employed in a variety of missions: spotting the main artillery's fall of shot, communication, reconnaissance and sea rescue. Two catapults were provided on either side for launch, and a crane for moving the aircraft on the very end of the stern. When commissioned, the battleship carried three Vought OS2U Kingfisher floatplanes. Two were usually sitting on the catapults and one on a cradle on the main deck nearby. By 1945 the US Navy adopted a superior aircraft: Curtiss SC-1 Seahawk. *Iowa's* aircraft were subsequently replaced with the new type.

After World War II the floatplanes lost their significance and were removed together with their catapults by 1948. In the following years *Iowa* landed several types of helicopters on her stern flight deck. These included Sikorsky HO3S-1 Dragonfly, Piasecki HUP-2 Retriever and Sikorsky SH-60B Seahawk (the last only in the 1980s). The stern crane used for operating the helicopters was removed by 1955.

After her reactivation, *Iowa* received eight AAI/IAI RQ-2A Pioneer aircraft. These light, unmanned aerial vehicles of RPV (Remotely Piloted Vehicle) system had a rocket-assisted take-off and were recovered with a special vertical net upon landing on the stern. The missions conducted by the Pioneers were primarily reconnaissance and weapons targeting.

## CAMOUFLAGE

The first camouflage worn by *Iowa* was Measure 22. The hull sides from the waterline to the level of the lowest hull edge were painted Navy Blue. All other vertical surfaces had the Haze Gray (5-H) colour. Horizontal surfaces were painted Deck Blue (20-B), but wooden decks were left in their natural colour (an unusual practice within the Measure 22).

Starting from January 1944, a dazzle camouflage Measure 32 Design 1B was applied. Iowa was the only ship to ever wear this pattern. It consisted of irregular geometric figures of Navy Blue (5-N) over a Light Gray (5-L) background. Some edges were feathered, a blurred colour border being very unusual in the US Navy. Around mid-1944 the camouflage was slightly modified: more Navy Blue was applied, some Light Gray areas painted over and blended edges were abandoned. All horizontal surfaces, including wooden decks, were painted Deck Blue while wearing Measure 32.

During her early 1945 overhaul, *Iowa* received again the Measure 22 camouflage and it was not changed until the end of the war. In the later years the battleship was painted Haze Gray with large shaded numbers '61' on her bow and stern.

# HISTORY OF THE BATTLESHIP USS *IOWA* (BB-61)

**17 May 1938:** The US Congress authorized the construction of two new battleships: *Iowa* (BB-61) and *New Jersey* (BB-62).

**1 July 1939:** The contract to build the BB-61 was awarded to New York Navy Yard in Brooklyn, New York.

**27 June 1940:** *Iowa* was laid down.

**27 August 1942:** Launch ceremony was held. The ship was sponsored by Ilo Browne Wallace, the wife of Vice President Henry A. Wallace, a resident of the Iowa state.

**22 February 1943:** *Iowa* entered service during an official commissioning ceremony. Secretary of the Navy Frank Knox described her as 'the greatest ship ever launched by the American Nation'. Capt John L. McCrea became the first commander of the battleship.

**Spring 1943:** *Iowa* conducted a series of training cruises along the US East Coast.

**16 July 1943:** While steaming through Hussey Sound in Casco Bay, Maine, the battleship hit the bottom. The damage to port side was serious enough to cause a month-long overhaul in Boston Navy Yard, Massachusetts.

**27 August 1943:** The battleship was sent on a patrol to the North Atlantic in order to protect Allied shipping against possible attack from German battleship *Tirpitz*, based in Norway. The threat was no longer real after 22 September, when British X-Craft midget submarines managed to severely damage *Tirpitz*.

**20 October 1943:** Return to Norfolk, Virginia.

**13 November 1943:** With President Franklin D. Roosevelt and almost 80 other guests on board, *Iowa* set course for Mers-el-Kébir in North Africa. The delegation was on its way to Tehran, where an Allied conference was to take place.

**14 November 1943:** In the course of a routine torpedo exercise during the Atlantic passage, an escorting destroyer, *William D. Porter* (DD-579), accidentally fired a torpedo at *Iowa*. The battleship was warned and was able to outmanoeuvre the torpedo just in time.

**9 December 1943:** After the Tehran Conference, Roosevelt and his staff came on board *Iowa* in Freetown, British West Africa.

**16 December 1943:** The delegation safely reached the USA and left the battleship.

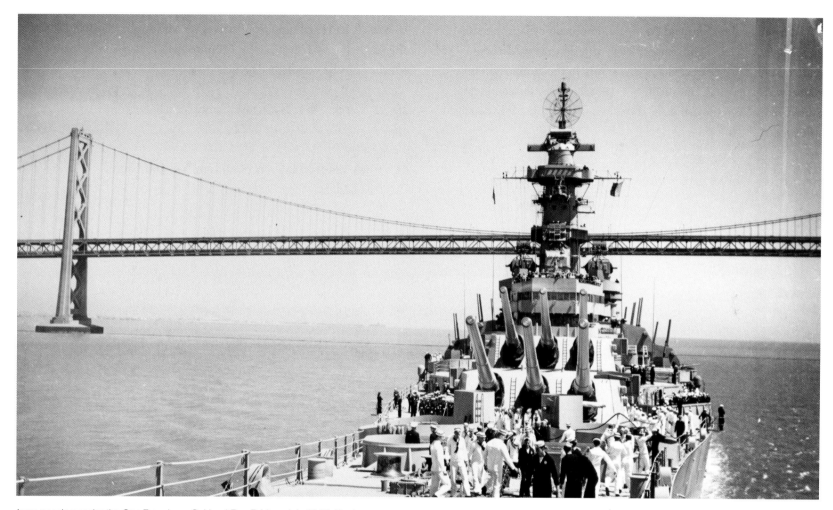

*Iowa* passing under the San Francisco–Oakland Bay Bridge, July 1947. Post-war modifications included replacing the SK search radar on the foremast with a newer SK-2 radar (large dish antenna at the top), as well as the removal of some of the AA guns. By this time the battleship carried no single Oerlikon mounts, and some of the Bofors mounts (including the ones from the tubs in the foreground) had also been taken away. (Naval History & Heritage Command, NH 70261)

**2 January 1944:** As the flagship of Battleship Division 7, *Iowa* left Norfolk, Virginia together with sister ship *New Jersey* (BB-62) and headed towards Panama Canal.

**22 January 1944:** Arrived at Funafuti, Ellice Islands.

**29 January 1944:** In support of carriers of Task Force 58, which began pre-invasion air raids on Kwajalein and Eniwetok atolls, Marshall Islands. The attacks lasted until 13 February.

**Early February 1944:** In support of carriers conducting air raids on a major Japanese base at Truk, Caroline Islands.

**16 February 1944:** Attacked by a single Mitsubishi A6M 'Zero' fighter. Its bomb was a near miss and the aircraft was soon shot down by carrier fighters.

**17 February 1944:** *Iowa* and *New Jersey* in pursuit of Japanese ships escaping from Truk: light cruiser *Katori* with destroyers *Maikaze* and *Nowaki*. BB-61 targeted the largest ship in the group and sank *Katori* with 16in. and 5in. shells. Shortly afterwards, she conducted evasive manoeuvres to avoid the torpedoes fired by the badly damaged *Maikaze*.

**18 March 1944:** In support of strikes on Mili Atoll, Marshall Islands. The battleship was hit twice by 120mm shells from a shore battery, but they caused very little damage.

**28–30 March 1944:** With Task Group 58 conducting attacks on Palau and Woleai, Caroline Islands.

**31 March 1944:** In support of raids on Yap and Ulithi, Caroline Islands.

In Korean waters, mid-1952. The photographer captured the moment of firing a projectile towards a North Korean target. The Bofors tubs in front of turret no. 1 have their quadruple gun mounts and directors fitted again during this deployment. (National Archives, 80-G-K-13195)

**21–22 April 1944:** As a part of TG 58, *Iowa* took part in bombardment of Hollandia and Aitape, New Guinea. These were followed by landings in Aitape and Humboldt Bay.

**29–30 April 1944:** In support of TG 58's carriers delivering final blows to the Japanese base at Truk.

**1 May 1944:** Together with other battleships, *Iowa* shelled Japanese shore installations at Ponape, Caroline Islands.

**6 June 1944:** After a stay at Majuro, Marshall Islands, *Iowa* left for the Mariana Islands to take part in Operation *Forager*.

**11–15 June 1944:** In preparation for the invasion on Saipan in the Mariana Islands, the battleship escorted attacking carriers and bombarded Saipan and Tinian.

**19–20 June 1944:** Battle of the Philippine Sea. The Japanese aircraft carrier fleet unsuccessfully attempted to destroy the American invasion force. Having suffered heavy losses, the Japanese were forced to retire. USS *Iowa*, while operating in escort of friendly carriers, was attacked by a Nakajima B5N 'Kate' torpedo bomber. The battleship managed to shoot the aircraft down. Later, three Mitsubishi A6M 'Zero' fighters also attacked but did not manage to score a hit.

**21–24 June 1944:** Shelled enemy positions on Guam, Rota and Pagan islands in the Mariana Islands.

**21–24 July 1944:** In support of landings on Guam and Tinian.

Pearl Harbor, 28 October 1952. *Iowa* anchored here briefly en route to the West Coast following her combat mission during the Korean War. Note the large hull number on her bow, which stands in contrast to the very small numbers painted during World War II. (Naval History & Heritage Command, NH 44538)

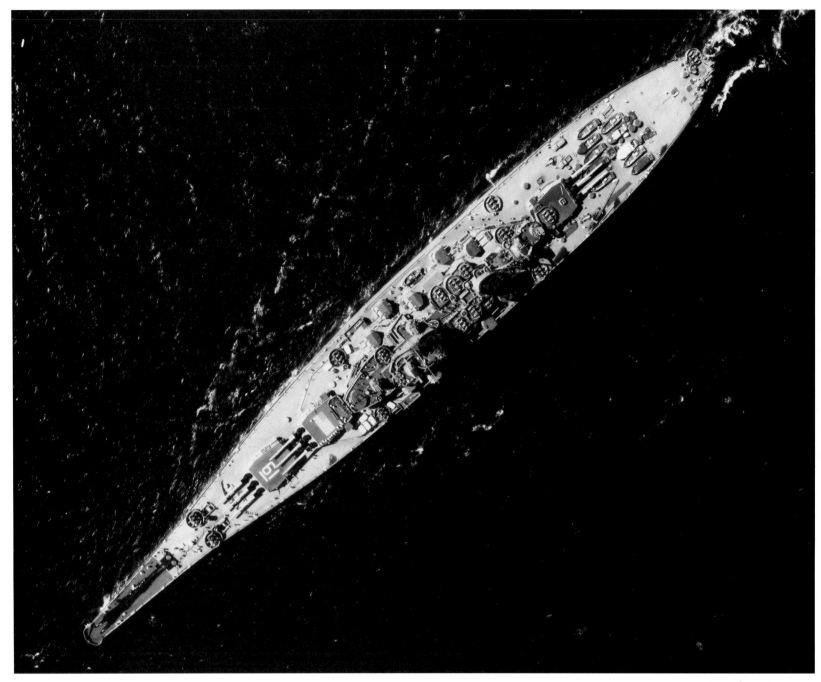

Off Pearl Harbor, 28 October 1952. In this aerial view the markings on the fore artillery turret tops are very visible: number 61 on turret no. 1 and the US flag on turret no. 2. The extremely slim hull, particularly in the bow section, is evident in this photograph. (Naval History & Heritage Command, NH 44536)

**25–27 July 1944:** The battleship took part in attacks on Palau, Yap and Ulithi.

**1–10 August 1944:** Supported further air strikes on Guam.

**6–8 September 1944:** With the carrier fleet attacking Palau.

**9–14 September 1944:** In support of strikes on Mindanao, Cebu, Negros, Legaspi and Panay islands in the Philippines.

**21–22 September 1944:** Attacked Japanese positions on Luzon, the Philippines.

**10–19 October 1944:** Took part in raids on Okinawa in Japan, Luzon and Formosa (now Taiwan). On the 14th, *Iowa* was attacked by a lone Yokosuka D4Y 'Judy'. The battleship's AA artillery shot down the bomber. Later, *Iowa* repelled an air raid by a group of Nakajima B6N 'Jill' torpedo bombers.

Anchorage off Hampton Roads, Virginia, 13 June 1957. The battleship is dressed overall and her crew is gathered on her decks in preparation for the International Naval Review. The helicopter flying above is a Piasecki HUP Retriever. (Naval History & Heritage Command, NH 97201)

**24 October 1944:** Battle of Leyte Gulf, a major effort of the Imperial Japanese Navy to destroy the American invasion fleet off Leyte island, the Philippines. Operating within Task Force 34 under V Adm Willis A. Lee, *Iowa* was sent to the north in pursuit of Adm Ozawa's task force. This group proved to be merely a decoy as the main part of Japanese surface fleet attempted to reach Leyte Gulf through San Bernardino Strait.

**25 October 1944:** Realizing their mistake, the Americans sent the fast battleships south to intercept Adm Kurita's force. However, it was too late and *Iowa* did not manage to fire a shell at an enemy ship from either task force.

**19–25 November 1944:** Supported further strikes on Luzon. On the last day of the operation, *Iowa*'s AA artillery shot down two Nakajima B6N 'Jills' and one Yokosuka D4Y 'Judy'.

**14–16 December 1944:** In support of task force delivering more attacks on Luzon.

*Iowa* as she appeared shortly before being decommissioned for the second time, 3 August 1957. Her sister ship USS *Wisconsin* (BB-64) can be seen in her wake, followed by USS *Boston* (CAG-1) and USS *Austin* (CA-123). (National Archives, L45-138.05.01)

**17–18 December 1944:** During her passage to Ulithi atoll, *Iowa* was hit by a strong typhoon, nicknamed Cobra. One of the battleship's floatplanes was washed off her deck, and vibrations of her propeller shaft, already noticeable earlier, became intolerably strong.

**28 December 1944:** Entered floating dry dock ABSD-2. Minor repair was conducted in preparation for the battleship's passage to the US West Coast.

**15 January–19 March 1945:** Repair and refit at Hunters Point Naval Shipyard, San Francisco, California. Among other modifications, *Iowa*'s radar suite was upgraded.

**15 April–12 May 1945:** *Iowa* operated in the waters off Okinawa, giving support to troops fighting on the island.

**2–10 June 1945:** After a short stay at Ulithi, *Iowa* escorted aircraft carriers in their strikes on Kyūshū and Okinawa in Japan.

**15–16 July 1945:** Together with other battleships and cruisers, *Iowa* shelled industrial targets on northern Honshū and Hokkaidō islands in Japan. These areas were out of the range of US strategic bombers.

**30–31 July 1945:** Having returned to Pearl Harbor, Hawaii, the battleship conducted artillery training.

**15 August 1945:** *Iowa* was operating in the waters south of Honshū when the news came of Japan's surrender.

**26 August 1945:** Entered Sagami Bay south-west of Tokyo. A detachment of *Iowa*'s crew members was formed to land on Japanese soil together with the Marines.

**29 August 1945:** Moved to Tokyo Bay to secure the occupying forces' landing that was planned for the next day.

**2 September 1945:** Official ending of World War II. Japanese representatives signed the surrender aboard *Iowa*'s sister ship, the *Missouri* (BB-63), in Tokyo Bay. BB-61 was also anchored nearby, serving as radio communication ship on that day.

**20 September 1945:** Left Japan heading for US West Coast. For the journey back from Japanese waters, *Iowa* carried around 1,500 passengers – prisoners of war and civil workers returning home.

**15 October 1945:** Entered the harbour in Seattle, Washington, ending her service in the Pacific War.

**Late 1945:** *Iowa* underwent an overhaul in Puget Sound Naval Shipyard, Bremerton, Washington, followed by several training cruises along the West Coast.

**27 January 1946:** Entered Tokyo Bay and took position of the flagship of the 5th Fleet.

**25 March 1946:** Having ended her service in Japanese waters, *Iowa* anchored in Long Beach, California.

**Spring 1946:** Conducted naval reserve and midshipmen training along the West Coast.

**4 June 1946:** Entered Puget Sound Naval Shipyard for an overhaul.

**1946–1948:** Conducted training cruises.

**September 1948:** Entered San Francisco harbour, where preparations where made for the battleship's deactivation.

**24 March 1949:** Decommissioned and put in the Pacific Reserve Fleet.

**Summer 1950:** As the Korean War began with an invasion of North Korea on South Korea, the US Navy was among the forces to intervene in the name of the United Nations. It was decided to engage the *Iowa* class battleships. *Missouri* was the first vessel of the four to sail to Korea.

**14 July 1951:** *Iowa* was towed to Hunters Point Naval Shipyard, San Francisco, where she was prepared for reactivation.

**25 August 1951:** Recommissioning ceremony of the battleship.

**March 1952:** Following several training cruises, *Iowa* sailed east.

**1 April 1952:** Arrived at Yokosuka, Japan, where she relieved he sister ship *Wisconsin* (BB-64) as the flagship of the 7th Fleet.

USS *Iowa* (right) lying decommissioned at Philadelphia Naval Yard, October 1978.
Beside her are USS *Wisconsin* (BB-64) and USS *Shangri La* (CVA-38).
Note that none of the ships have any light AA guns left on board; they have
also been stripped of the fragile electronic equipment.
(National Archives, K-121963)

**8 April 1952:** Shelled the supply route between Wonsan and
Kimchaek in North Korea.

**9 April 1952:** Bombarded the enemy position in the area
of Suwon-dan, North Korea.

**14 April 1952:** Fired at railroad facilities, ammunition magazines
and artillery posts in Wonsan.

**20 April 1952:** Destroyed four railroad tunnels in the area
of Tanch'on, North Korea.

**25–27 April 1952:** Shelled enemy positions near Chindong,
Kosong and Wonsan.

**25 May 1952:** Conducted bombardment of an industrial centre near Chongjin. This area was the furthest north that *Iowa* would sail during the war, only around 50 miles (80km) away from the territory of USSR. Soviet aircraft were being observed on the battleship's radar screens but they took no action.

**26 May 1952:** A helicopter based on *Iowa* rescued an American pilot.

**27 May 1952:** Shelled railroad facilities at Kimchaek, North Korea.

**1 June 1952:** Retired to Sasebo, Japan, for replenishment.

**June 1952:** Conducted artillery strikes in North Korea on Mayang-Do, Tanch'on, Chongjin, Ch'odo, Hongnam and Wonsan. Her helicopter recovered an American pilot that had been shot down.

**July–August 1952:** Shelled enemy positions around Hongnam, Wonsan and Kimchaek. Again, her helicopter helped a downed aircraft pilot.

**20 August 1952:** Operating in the area of Kimchaek, *Iowa* assisted destroyer *Thompson* (DD-627), which had been hit by coastal artillery. The battleship took aboard the wounded and screened the smaller ship's retirement.

**23 September 1952:** Hit and destroyed a large ammunition storage facility near Wonsan.

**25 September 1952:** Destroyed a train in the area of Wonsan.

**14–16 October 1952:** Took part in artillery bombardment in preparation for the UN's landing in the area of Kojo.

**17–19 October 1952:** In transit to Yokosuka, Japan. Shortly afterwards, *Iowa* headed for an overhaul in Norfolk, Virginia with a stop at Pearl Harbor. During her Korean War deployment, the battleship travelled around 35,000NM (64,820km) and fired twice as many salvos as she did during World War II.

**July 1953:** While serving as the flagship of the 2nd Fleet during operation *Mariner*, a major NATO exercise in Northern Europe, *Iowa* had occasion to operate together with HMS *Vanguard*, Britain's last battleship.

**7 July 1954:** For the only time in history, all four battleships of the Iowa class operated together; *Iowa*, *New Jersey*, *Missouri* and *Wisconsin* trained joint manoeuvres for several hours off the coast of Virginia.

**Late 1954–1955:** In the course of her several training cruises, *Iowa* visited multiple harbours in the Mediterranean Sea: Gibraltar; Mers-el-Kébir and Oran (North Africa); Genova and Naples (Italy); Istanbul (Turkey); Athens (Greece); Cannes (France); and Barcelona (Spain).

**August 1955:** Arrived at Portsmouth, Virginia for four-month-long overhaul.

**April 1956:** Visited Havana (Cuba) during her Caribbean training cruise.

**June 1956:** Another training cruise of the *Iowa,* involving anchoring in Bermuda, Portsmouth (England), Copenhagen (Denmark) and Guantanamo Bay (Cuba).

**January 1957:** On duty with the 6th Fleet in the Mediterranean Sea.

**13 June 1957:** Took part in the International Naval Review off Hampton Roads, Virginia.

**September 1957:** Participated in NATO's Operation *Strikeback*, an exercise in the North Atlantic. Shortly afterwards, arrived at Norfolk, Virginia.

**23 October 1957:** After the decision had been made to deactivate *Iowa* for the second time, the battleship was towed to Philadelphia Naval Shipyard, Pennsylvania.

**24 February 1958:** Decommissioned and put in the Atlantic Reserve Fleet.

**1981:** After Ronald Reagan was elected the President of the United States, his administration began to implement his '600-ship Navy' programme. This plan, the aim of which was to retain a strong navy to keep balance with the Soviet Union's forces, involved recommissioning all four Iowa class battleships.

**13 July 1982:** A contract was signed for conducting reactivation and modernization work on the *Iowa*.

**1 September 1982:** Left Philadelphia on tow.

**1 October 1982–30 January 1983:** In dry dock at Avondale Shipyard near New Orleans, Louisiana, where work on *Iowa*'s hull was carried out.

**Spring 1983–spring 1984:** In Ingalls Shipbuilding and Dry Dock Co, Pascagoula, Mississippi, where the rest of the modernization work was conducted. This involved removing two 5in. gun mounts on each side and placing modern missile systems in their place: Tomahawk cruise missile and Harpoon anti-ship missile launchers. In place of the old Oerlikon and Bofors mounts, four new Phalanx CIWS 20mm mounts formed the battleship's anti-aircraft and anti-missile armament. Search radar and fire control suite were upgraded, and modern ECM and communications systems were fitted. *Iowa*'s superstructures and masts were heavily modified. This was by far the biggest modernization that she received during her career, with a budget that reached around $500 million.

**28 April 1984:** After the reactivation work had been completed in a record time, *Iowa* was recommissioned.

**May 1984:** Conducted gunnery and machinery tests in Guantanamo Bay and off Vieques island (Puerto Rico).

Pascagoula, Mississippi, mid-1983. Covered with scaffolding, the *Iowa* is being refitted and heavily modernized for her last reactivation. She would enter service in April 1984. (National Archives, DN-SN-83-09081)

**June 1984:** During her training cruise, *Iowa* visited Venezuela, Colombia, Jamaica and the Virgin Islands.

**Early July 1984:** More artillery exercises off Vieques.

**Late July 1984:** Visited Martinique and Barbados.

**8 August 1984:** Crossed the Panama Canal and entered the Pacific. Later that month, *Iowa* operated off the Nicaraguan coast, conducting surveillance and providing medical support to Guatemala and El Salvador.

**26 August 1984:** Returned to the Atlantic via the Panama Canal.

**17 September 1984:** Entered harbour in Norfolk, Virginia.

**October 1984:** Made a week-long visit to New York, where the battleship received strong interest from the press and the public.

**November 1984:** *Iowa* took part in the *COMPUTEX 1-85* exercise off the Puerto Rican coast. She was back in Norfolk by the end of the month.

**January 1985:** Conducted sea trials.

**February 1985:** During her stay in the waters off Costa Rica and Honduras, *Iowa* completed several humanitarian operations. Later in the month she conducted training cruises developing tactics for the Battleship Surface Action Group (BBSAG).

**26 April–31 July 1985:** Underwent an overhaul in a dry dock at Norfolk Navy Yard, Portsmouth, Virginia. The workers mainly dealt with machinery-related problems.

**Early August 1985:** Loaded ammunition at Hamton Roads following her overhaul, and conducted ten-day-long sea trials.

**22 August 1985:** *Iowa* was awarded the Battenberg Cup for the best all-around ship in the Atlantic Fleet in 1984.

**27 August–20 September 1985:** As a member of BBSAG, *Iowa* took part in Operation *Ocean Safari* (escorting supply ships from Boston across the Atlantic). After its successful completion, the battleship visited Le Havre (France), Copenhagen and Aarhus (Denmark), and Oslo (Norway).

**12–18 October 1985:** The battleship was involved in the NATO exercise *BALTOPS 85*, together with many other surface ships, submarines and aircraft belonging to a number of other nations. In the course of the exercise, *Iowa* conducted main artillery firing off the Danish island of Bornholm in the Baltic Sea. After the operation was over, BB-61 visited the German base at Kiel.

**26 October–5 November 1985:** Underway from Europe back to the Norfolk base. *Iowa* conducted a number of drills during the cruise.

**January–early March 1986:** Visited several harbours in Central America.

**17 March 1986:** Beginning of the InSurv (Board of Inspection and Survey) examination aboard *Iowa*. Deficiencies in several areas were found, including propulsion machinery, main artillery turrets' equipment, and electrical installation. These problems were addressed in the following weeks.

**4 July 1986:** In New York at the ceremony marking the centennial of the Statue of Liberty, *Iowa* hosted President Reagan and his wife as they watched a number of American and foreign ships taking part in the International Naval Review on the Hudson River.

**Early August 1986:** Conducted Tomahawk cruise missile test launches as well as main and secondary artillery test firing in the Gulf of Mexico.

**5–6 September 1986:** Took part in Operation *Northern Wedding* near Cape Wrath in Scotland. During this exercise, *Iowa* supported the simulated marine landing with her artillery. After completing the training, the battleship visited Portsmouth (England) and Bremerhaven (Germany), where many visitors came on board.

**October 1986:** Return to Norfolk.

**9 December 1986:** First tests of the AAI/IAI RQ-2A Pioneer drones were conducted.

**10 January 1987:** Beginning of the *BLASTEX 1-87* exercise in the Caribbean. Further tests of the Pioneer drones were executed. Afterwards, the battleship visited Honduras, Columbia, American Virgin Islands, Guantanamo Bay and Vieques.

**February 1987:** Return to Norfolk.

**May 1987:** Conducted training within exercise *SACEX* near Puerto Rico.

**July 1987:** *FLEETEX 3-87* exercise in the West Atlantic. More test launches, landings and fire targeting procedures by the Pioneers were executed.

Waters off Vieques island near Puerto Rico, 1 July 1984. Following her recommissioning, *Iowa* fires a full broadside (nine 16in. and six 5in. guns) during target exercise. Note the spherical indentions in the water surface caused by the blast. (National Archives, DN-ST-85-05379)

**16 September–20 October 1987:** As a part of the 6th Fleet, *Iowa* took part in the exercise *Display Determination*. During this time the procedures regarding the use of the Pioneer drones were finalized.

**25 November 1987:** Passed the Suez Canal to support Operation *Earnest Will* in the Persian Gulf. Over the next few weeks, *Iowa* operated in escort of Kuwaiti tankers against attacks from Iranian forces.

**20 February 1988:** Transited the Suez Canal and headed west, reaching Norfolk on 10 March.

**Late March–early April 1988:** Underwent an overhaul at Norfolk.

**21–25 April 1988:** Took part in a Fleet Week in New York.

**June–August 1988:** Stayed in Portsmouth, Virginia for a propulsion machinery check-up.

**25 August 1988:** As a result of *Iowa*'s poor manoeuvrability in shallow water, she almost collided with frigate *Moinester* (FF-1097), guided-missile destroyer *Farragut* (DDG-37) and guided-missile cruiser *South Carolina* (CGN-37) while steaming through Chesapeake Bay. The battleship eventually moved off the ship channel and ran aground. It took one hour for *Iowa* to get safely off the shoal and return to harbour.

**September–October 1988:** *Iowa* continued her training in the waters off Florida and Puerto Rico.

**January 1989:** Experiments with super-heavy propellant charges for the 16in. guns were conducted off Vieques. On the 20th, *Iowa* set a record for the longest-ranged 16in. projectile ever fired, achieving 26.9 miles (43.3km). The accuracy rate at this range was exceptionally good. Towards the end of the month, an accident took place in turret no. 2 when a powder bag was unintentionally ignited while the breech of the left gun was open. Luckily, the gun's captain managed to close the breech before the explosion occurred.

**13 April 1989:** Left Norfolk to take part in the exercise *FLEETEX 3-89*.

**19 April 1989:** In the morning, *Iowa* was steaming north-east of Puerto Rico and starting to execute main artillery firing procedure. After a salvo from turret no. 1, guns of turret no. 2 were ordered to load. Left and right gun reported readiness shortly afterwards but there seemed to be a problem with the centre gun. About a minute and a half after the order to load, at 09.53, an explosion of the propellant charge occurred in the centre gun. All 47 crew members inside the turret were killed and the turret was wrecked. The blast doors worked properly and prevented flash from entering the powder magazines, which would likely result in sinking of the battleship. The magazines of turret no. 2 were ordered to be flooded. Firefighting crews immediately began spraying water on the turret and the fire was extinguished within an hour and a half.

**20 April 1989:** After water had been pumped out of turret no. 2, the bodies of the dead crew members were recovered and sent on board a helicopter to Puerto Rico, from where they were flown to the USA. Identification of the bodies was completed by mid-May.

**23 April 1989:** *Iowa* anchored at Norfolk. A memorial service was conducted the next day, with President George Bush attending.

**7 September 1989:** Conclusions of the US Navy investigation into the cause of the accident were presented to the public. The report stated that the explosion was most probably deliberately caused by Gunner's Mate 2nd Class Clayton Hartwig. He was allegedly involved in a homosexual relationship with another crew member and became suicidal as a result of disappointment in love. However, the Congress, the families of the killed and the public soon expressed serious doubts about the US Navy's conclusions as the evidence was very weak.

**25 May 1990:** During a hearing before the Senate, the results of a second investigation, conducted by the General Accounting Office and Sandia National Laboratories, were revealed. In their opinion, the explosion aboard *Iowa* was most likely caused by an unintentional

North-east of Puerto Rico, 19 April 1989. This was the most tragic day in *Iowa*'s service history, when an explosion in the centre gun of turret no. 2 killed 47 of the turret's crew members. This photograph shows the view from the battleship's superstructure just moments after the accident.
(National Archives, DN-SC-90-05388)

overram of the propellant powder bags inside the breech. A deliberate act was deemed highly unlikely. Under pressure from the public, the US Navy reopened its investigation.

**26 October 1990:** Due to the fact that after the collapse of the USSR the Soviet Navy no longer posed a great threat, it was considered to deactivate the Iowa class battleships. BB-61, her turret no. 2 having been completely wrecked by the 19 April explosion, was the first of the four vessels to be decommissioned. Her turret was never repaired.

**17 October 1991:** At a press conference in the Pentagon, the conclusions of the US Navy's second investigation were presented. It was admitted that no evidence of an intentional act had been found, but it was also stated that in the opinion of the Navy, the exact cause of the explosion could not be determined.

**12 January 1995:** *Iowa* was stricken from the Navy Vessel Register. The battleship's berthing place became Philadelphia Naval Shipyard, Pennsylvania.

**24 September 1998:** Moved under tow to Naval Station Newport, Rhode Island.

**4 January 1999:** *Iowa* was again added to the Navy Vessel Register as a reserve ship.

**8 March 2001:** As the decision had been made to move *Iowa* to the West Coast, she left Newport on tow and headed for the Panama Canal. The only other battleship in reserve, USS *Wisconsin*, was to be based on the East Coast.

**21 April 2001:** Reached the Pacific Reserve Fleet anchorage in Suisun Bay near San Francisco, California.

**17 March 2006:** Stricken from the Navy Vessel Register for the last time. This act officially opened the possibility for the aging *Iowa* to become a museum ship. Several cities were considered for her berthing place, including Vallejo, Stockton, San Francisco and San Pedro (Los Angeles). Ultimately, the last location was chosen.

**27 October 2011:** Towed from Suisun Bay to nearby Richmond.

**30 April 2012:** The battleship was officially donated by the US Navy to the Pacific Battleship Center, Los Angeles.

**26 May 2012:** Towed by tugboats, *Iowa* left Richmond.

**9 June 2012:** The battleship arrived at Berth 87 in San Pedro, Los Angeles, California. This would become her permanent place of anchoring.

**7 July 2012:** The museum ship USS *Iowa* was opened to the public.

# BATTLESHIP USS *IOWA*

**HULL NUMBER:** BB-61

**NICKNAMES:** 'The Big Stick', 'The Grey Ghost'

**BATTLE STARS:**

★ MARSHALL ISLANDS OPERATION ★

★ ASIATIC–PACIFIC RAIDS ★

★ HOLLANDIA OPERATION ★

★ MARIANAS OPERATION ★

★ TINIAN CAPTURE AND OCCUPATION ★

★ WESTERN CAROLINE ISLANDS OPERATION ★

★ LEYTE OPERATION ★

★ OKINAWA GUNTO OPERATION ★

★ THIRD FLEET OPERATIONS AGAINST JAPAN ★

★ SECOND KOREAN WINTER ★

★ THIRD KOREAN WINTER ★

SPRING 1943, SHAKEDOWN CRUISE, OFF US EAST COAST. The battleship
is wearing Measure 22 camouflage.

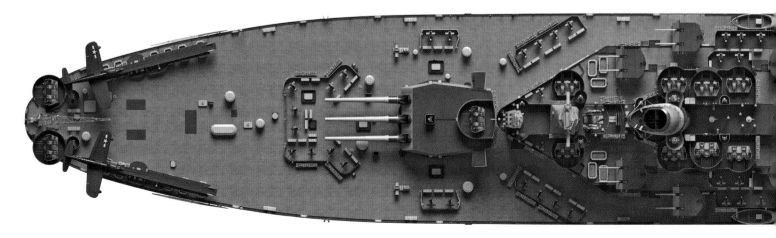

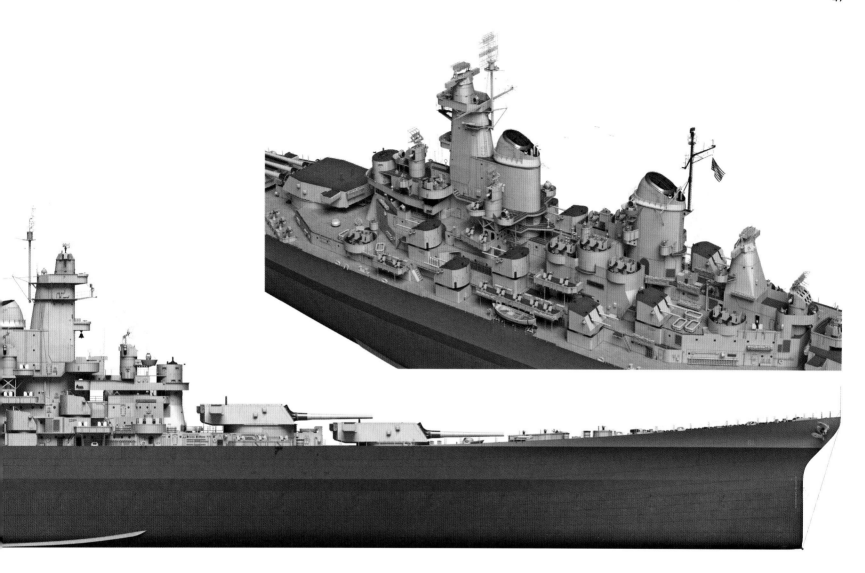

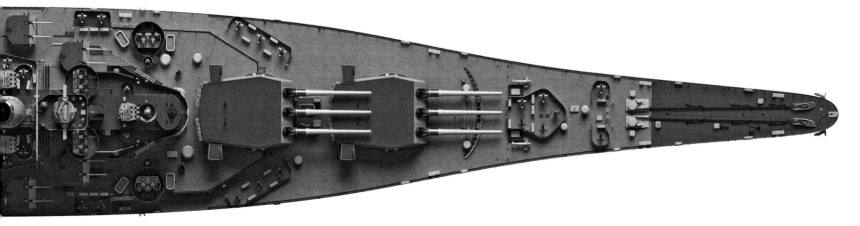

EARLY 1944, OFF KWAJALEIN ATOLL, PACIFIC OCEAN. A unique Measure 32 Design 1B camouflage has been applied to the battleship, with some edges feathered.

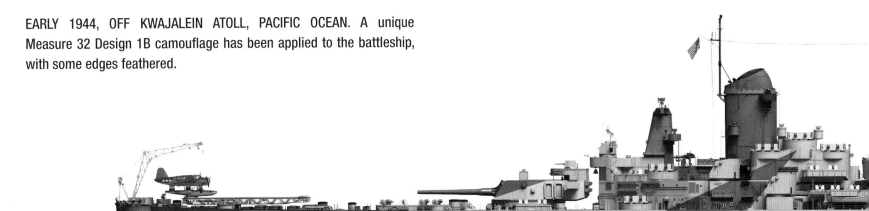

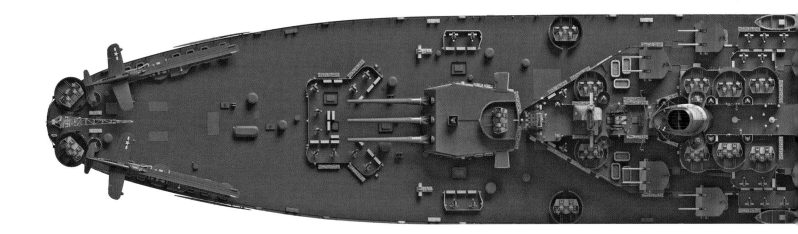

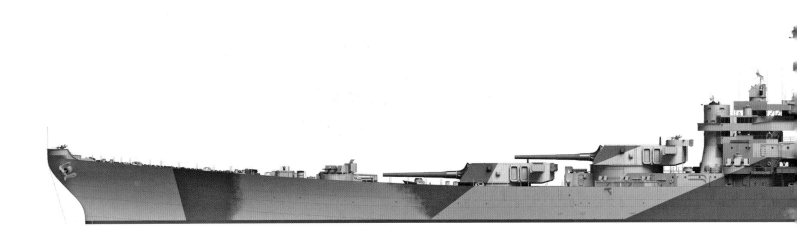

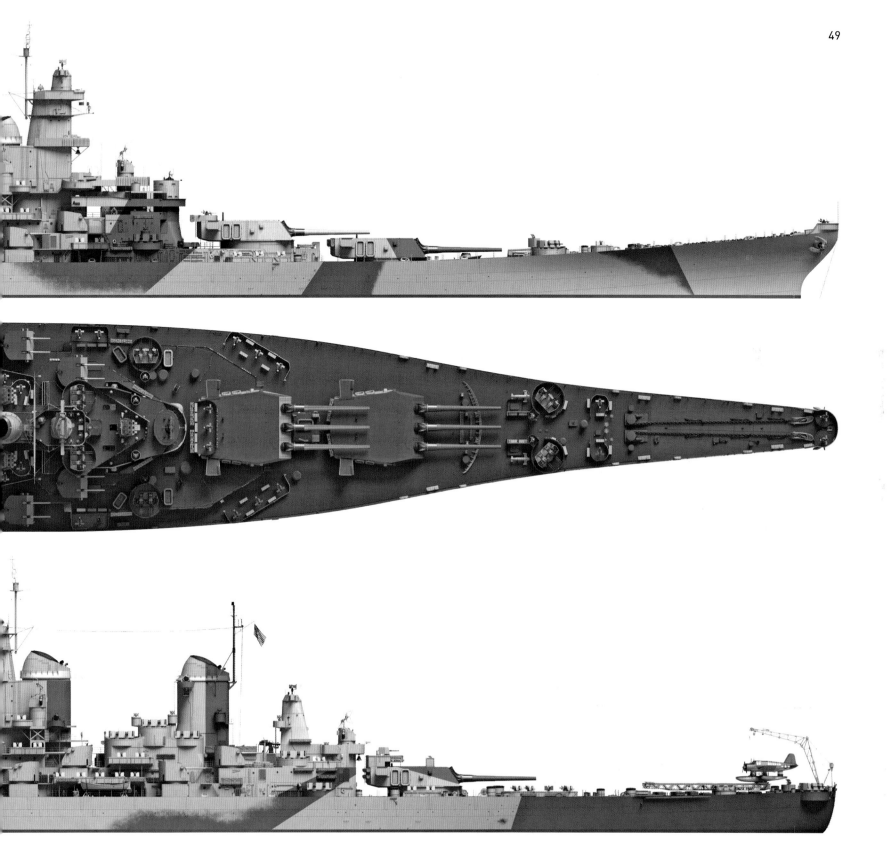

LATE 1944, ULITHI ATOLL, PACIFIC OCEAN. Following a modification to the camouflage scheme, some colour borders changed and no blurred edges were left.

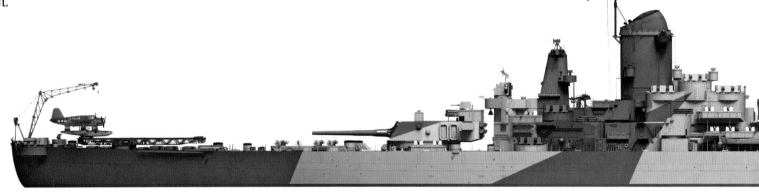

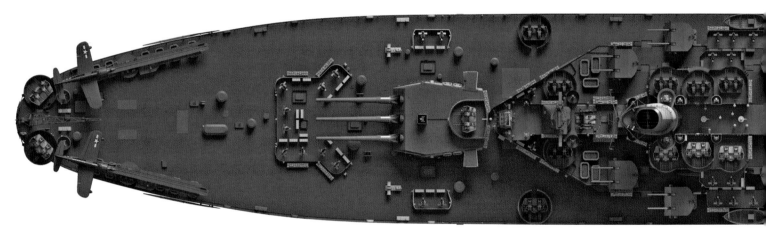

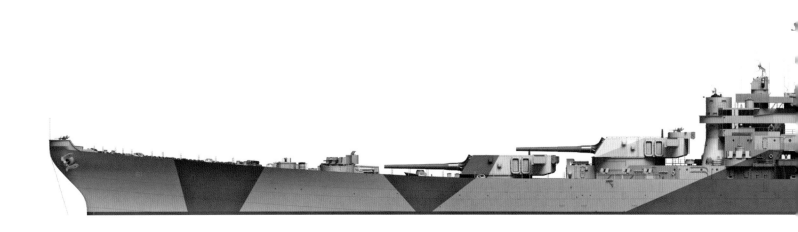

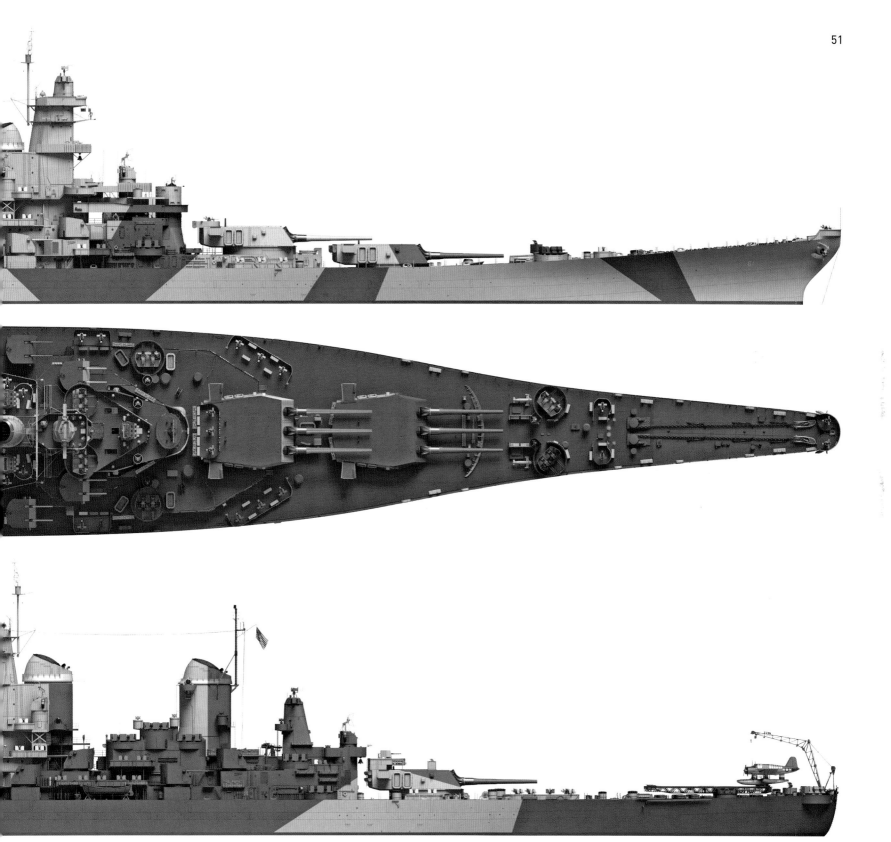

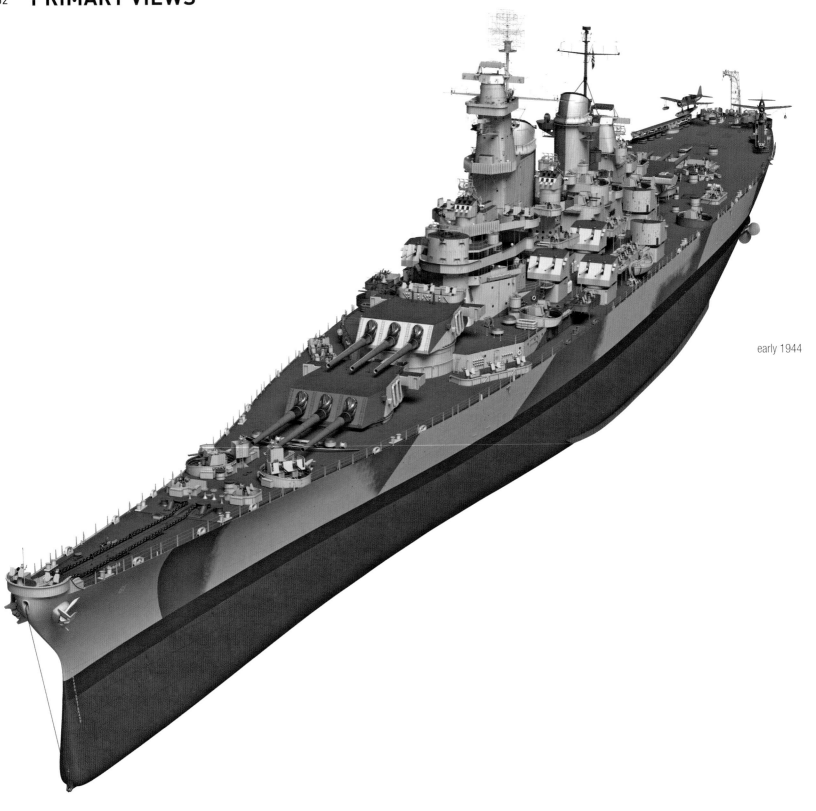

early 1944

early 1944

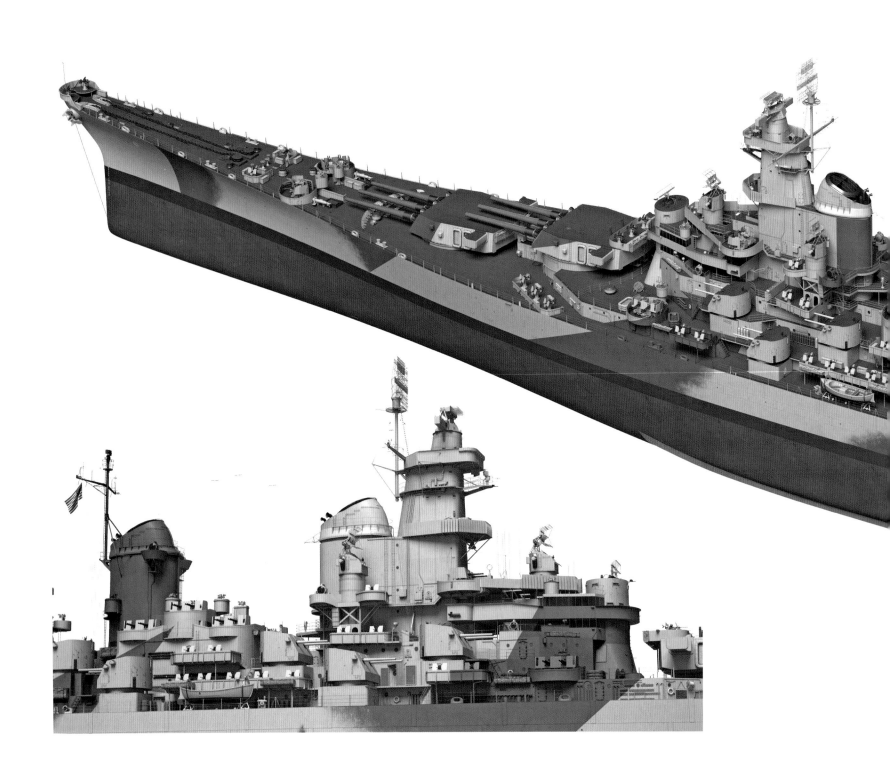

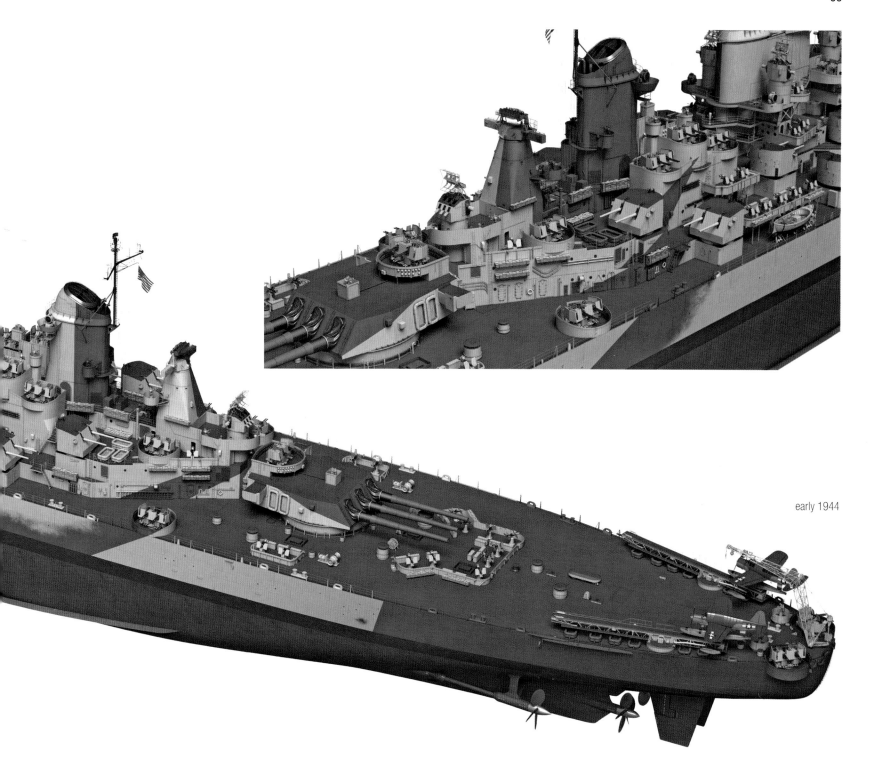

early 1944

late 1944

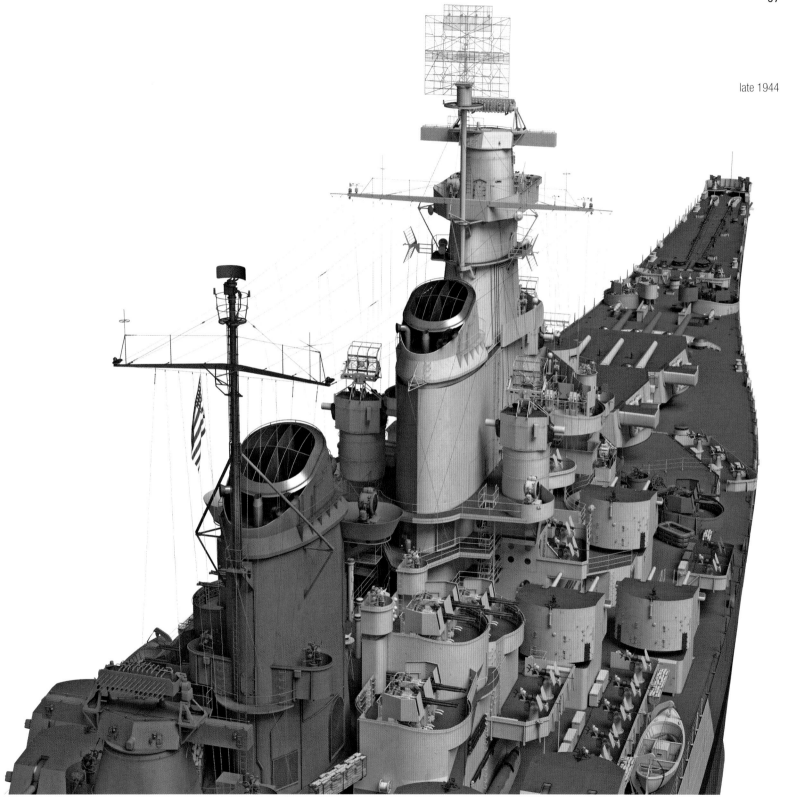

EARLY 1945, SAN FRANCISCO. The battleship is wearing Measure 22 camouflage again, but this time applied differently than in 1943 (note the colours of wooden decks, small steel horizontal surfaces and the stern).

1947, prior to the battleship's first deactivation.

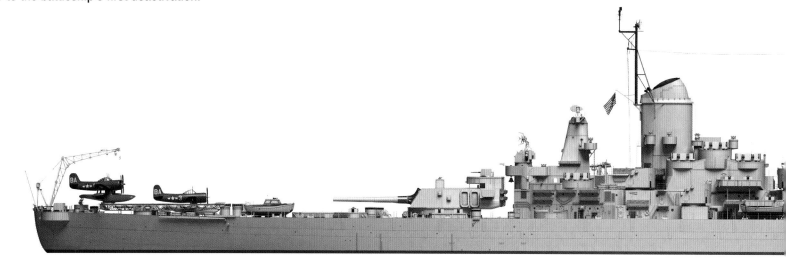

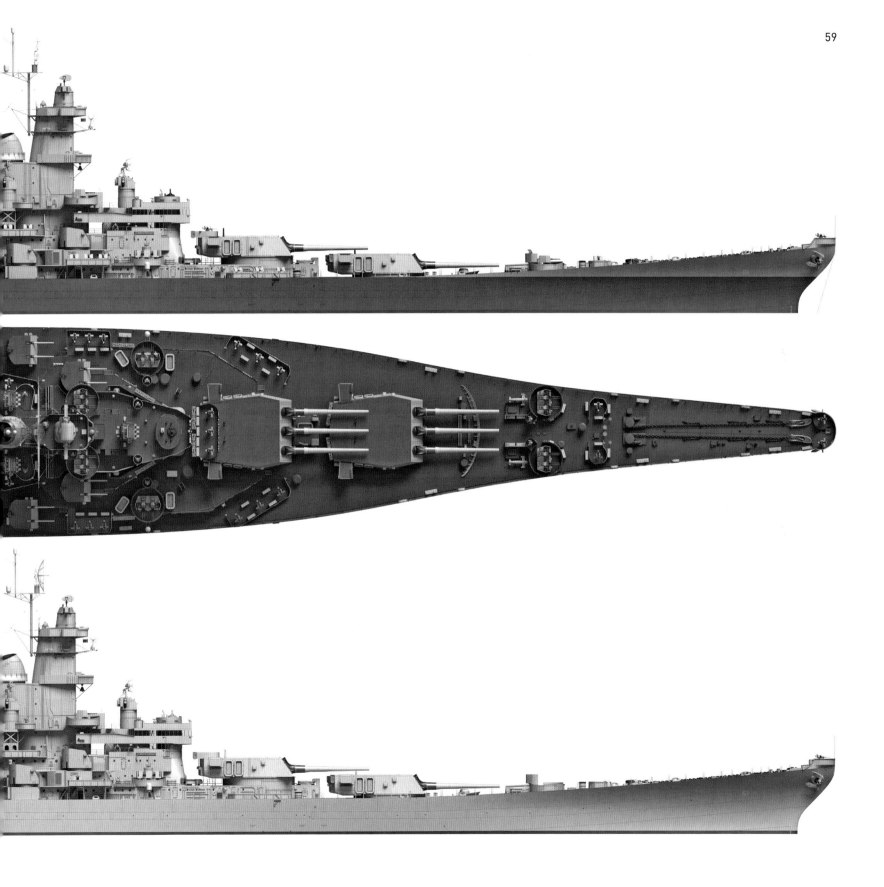

1947, prior to the battleship's first deactivation.

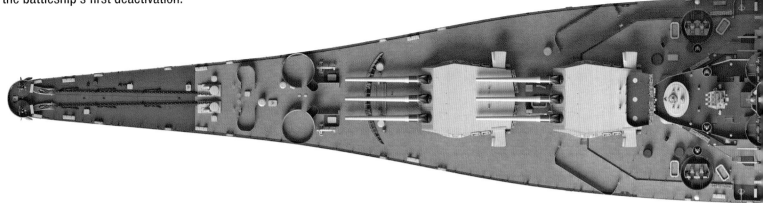

MID-1952, KOREAN WATERS. Air recognition markings include a large number '61' on the roof of main artillery turret no. 1 and a painted US flag on the roof of turret no. 2.

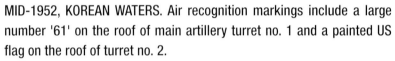

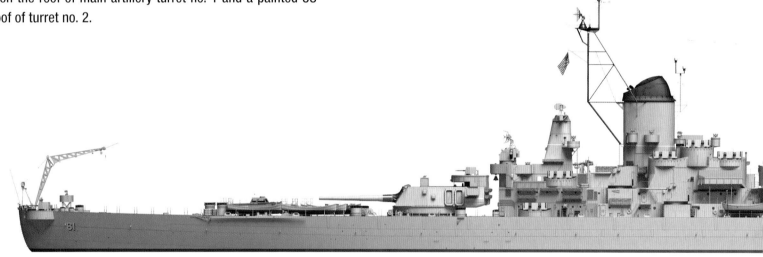

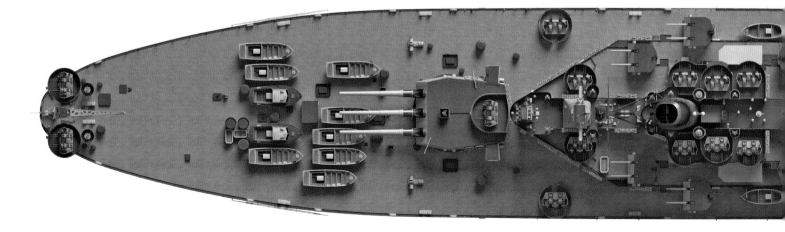

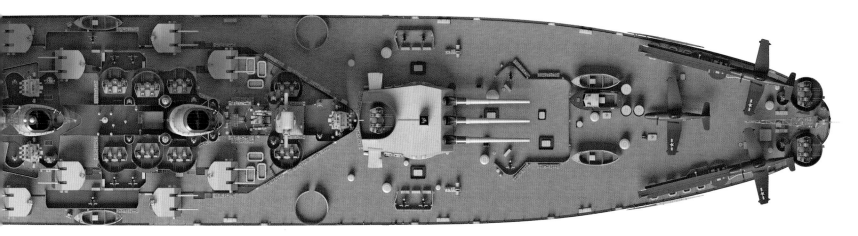

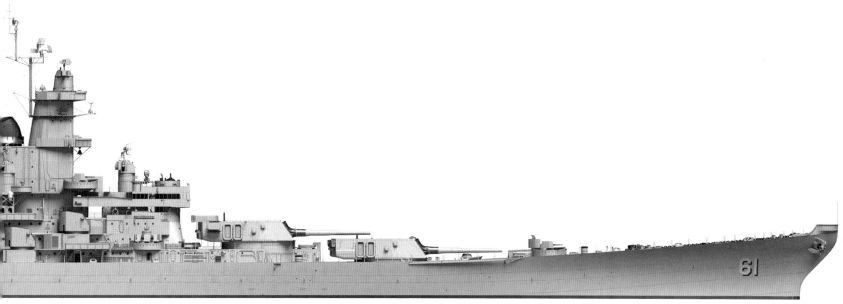

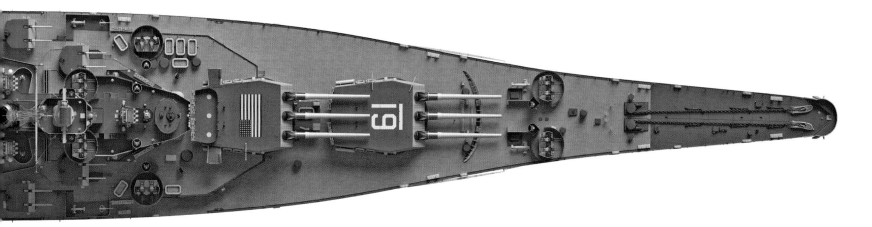

1945

1945

1945

1945

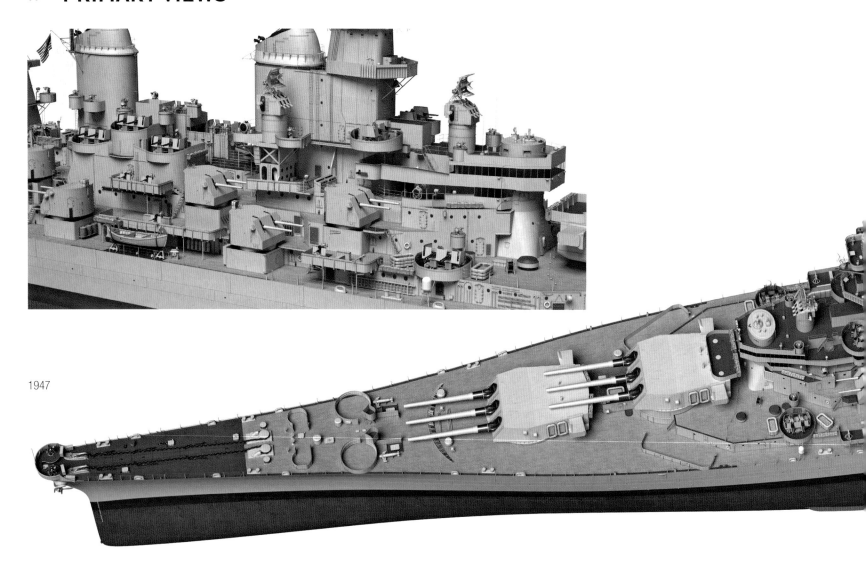

1947

1952

1952

LATE 1955, following the last major overhaul before the battleship's second deactivation.

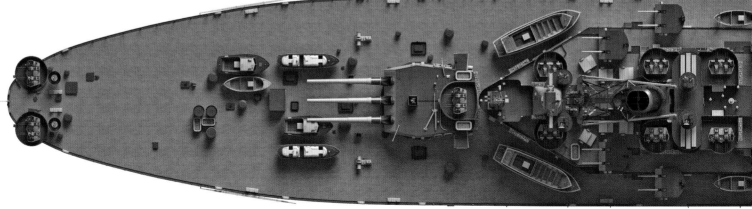

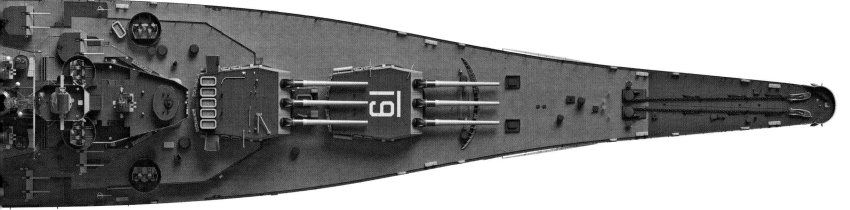

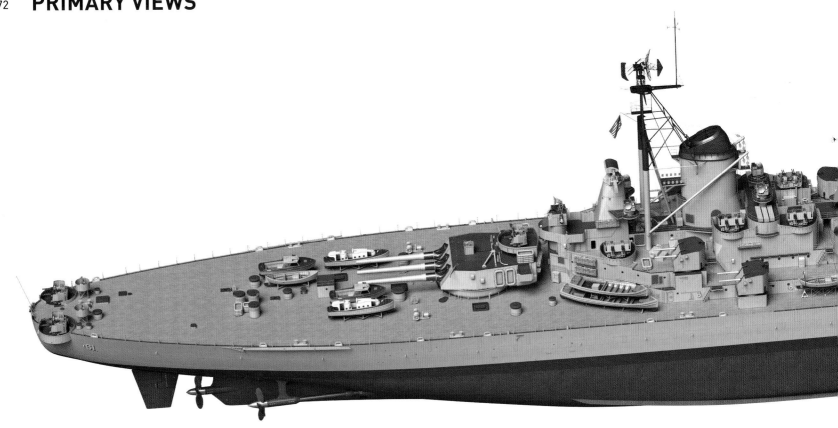

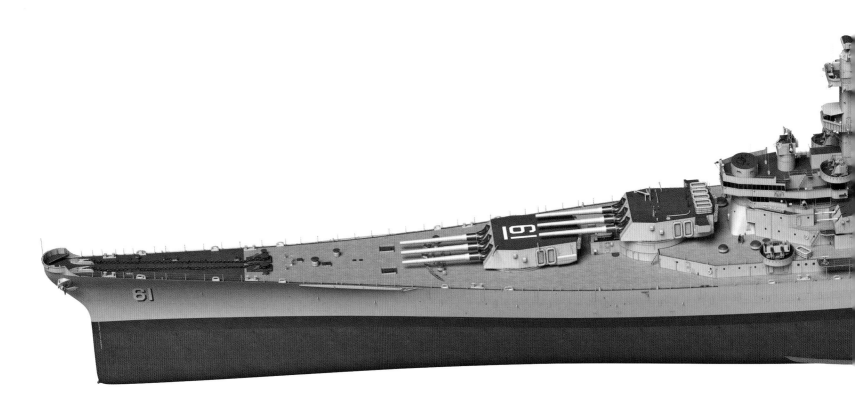

1955

1955

MID-1984, during training cruises following a major refit.

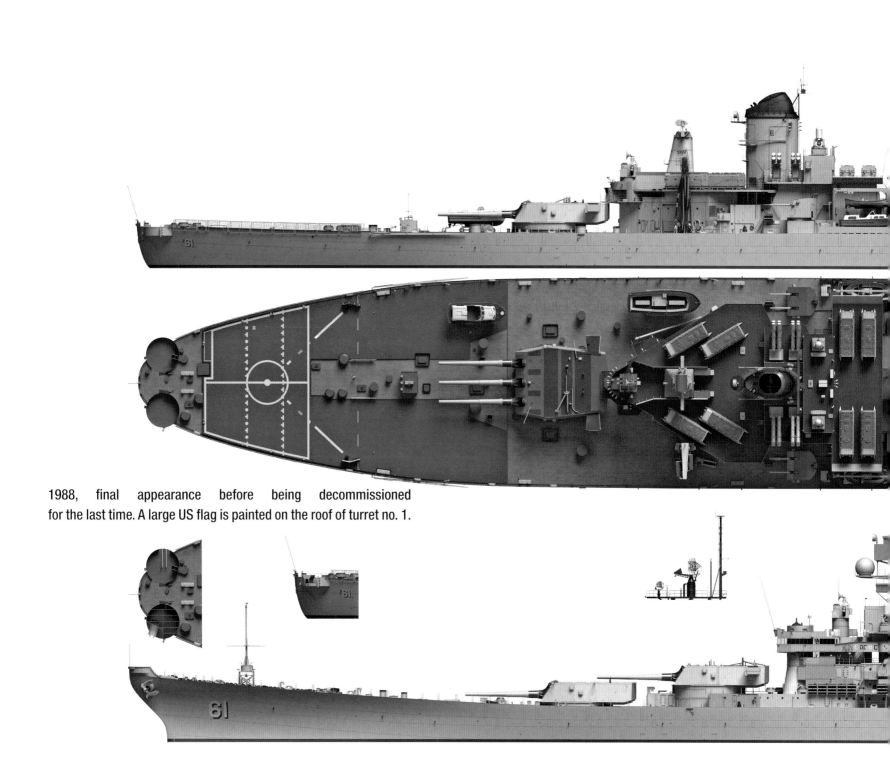

1988, final appearance before being decommissioned for the last time. A large US flag is painted on the roof of turret no. 1.

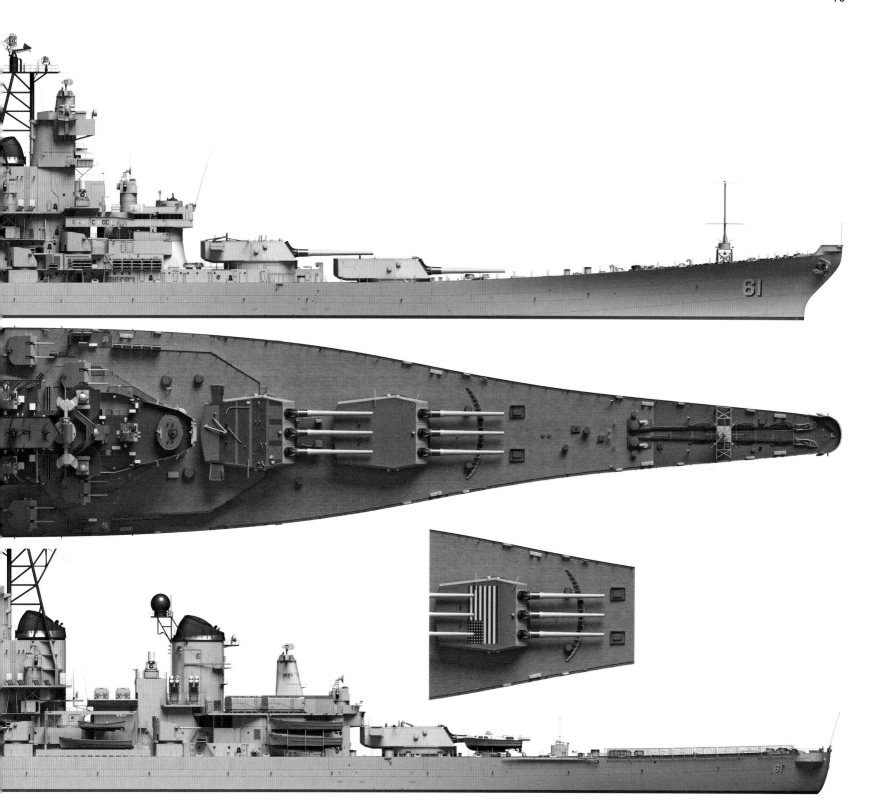

mid-1984

mid-1984

late 1986

late 1986

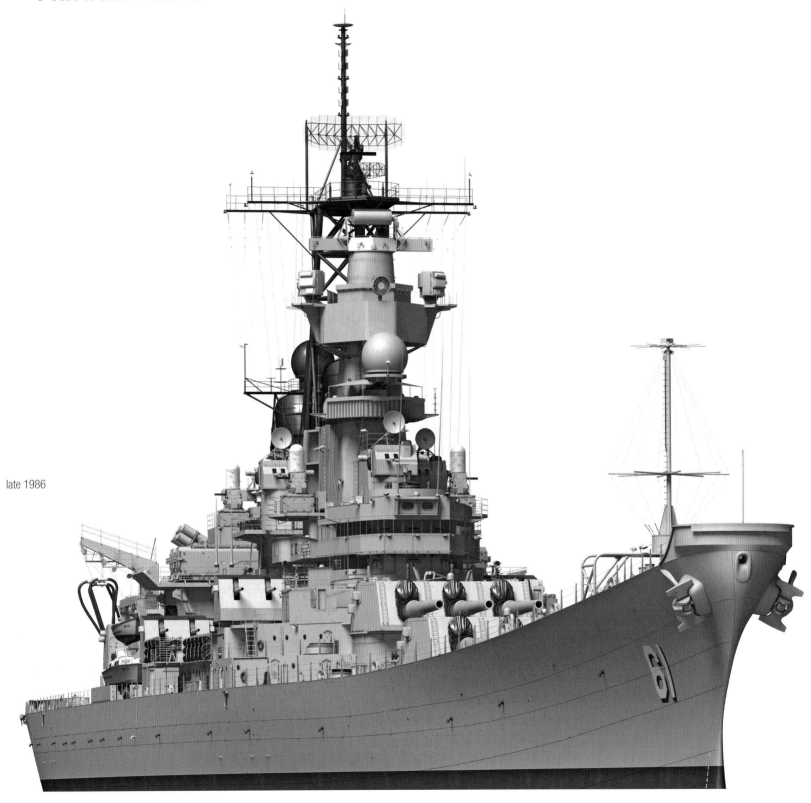

late 1986

EARLY 1944

1988

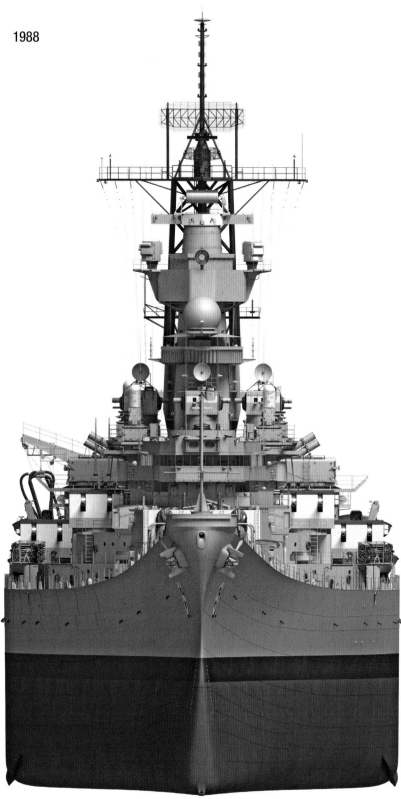

EARLY 1944

1988

**A GENERAL ARRANGEMENTS**

EXTERNAL VIEWS (1/600 SCALE)

A1/1 RIGHT PROFILE, SPRING 1943

A1/2 PLAN, SPRING 1943

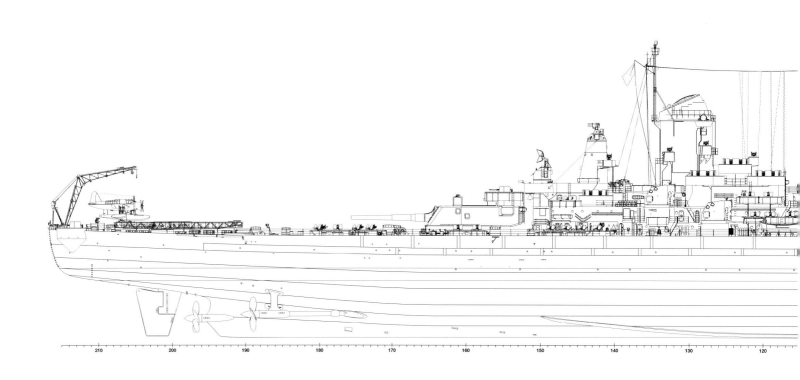

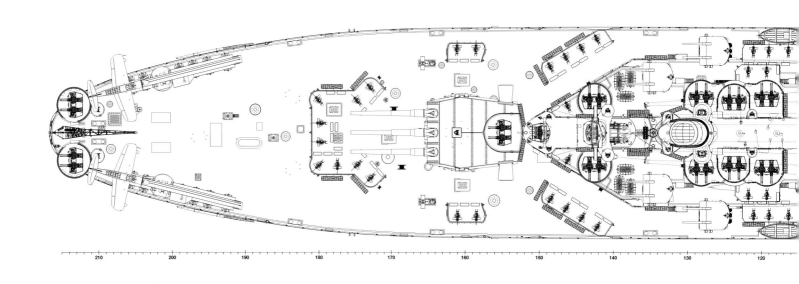

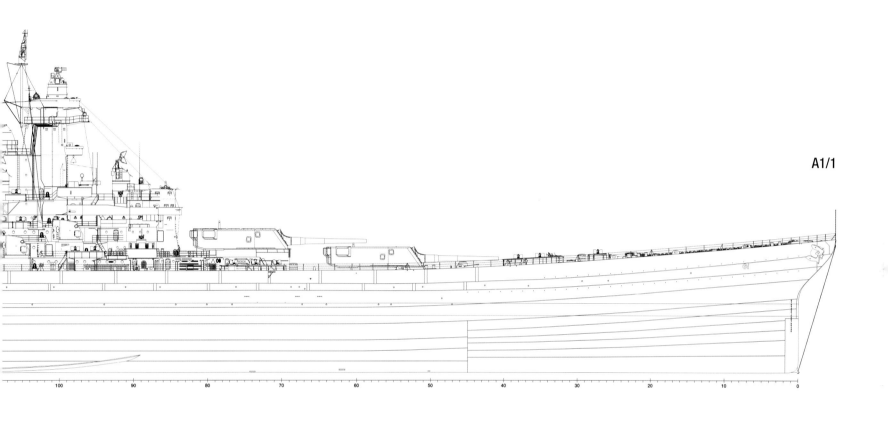

A1/1

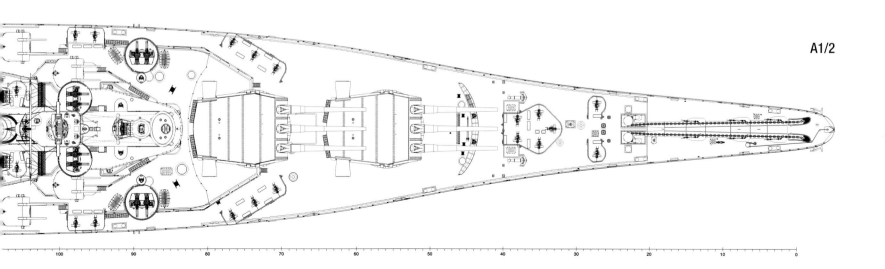

A1/2

**A GENERAL ARRANGEMENTS**

EXTERNAL VIEWS (1/600 SCALE)

A1/3 RIGHT PROFILE, LATE 1944

A1/4 PLAN, LATE 1944

A1/5 LEFT PROFILE, LATE 1944

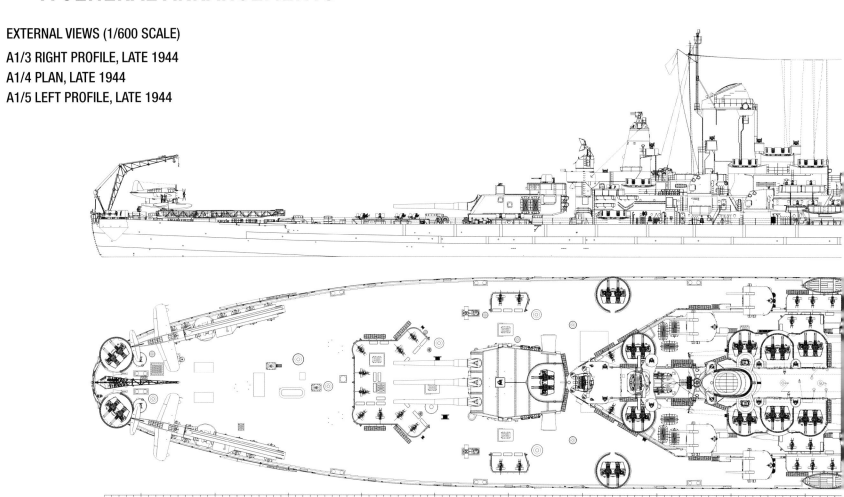

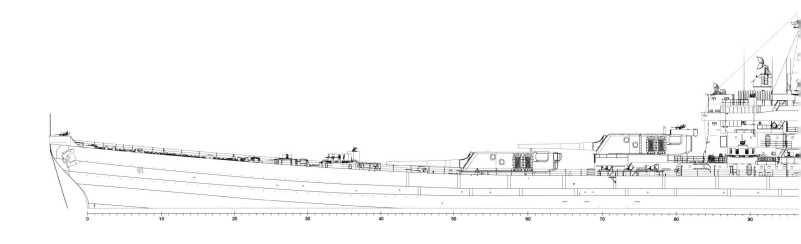

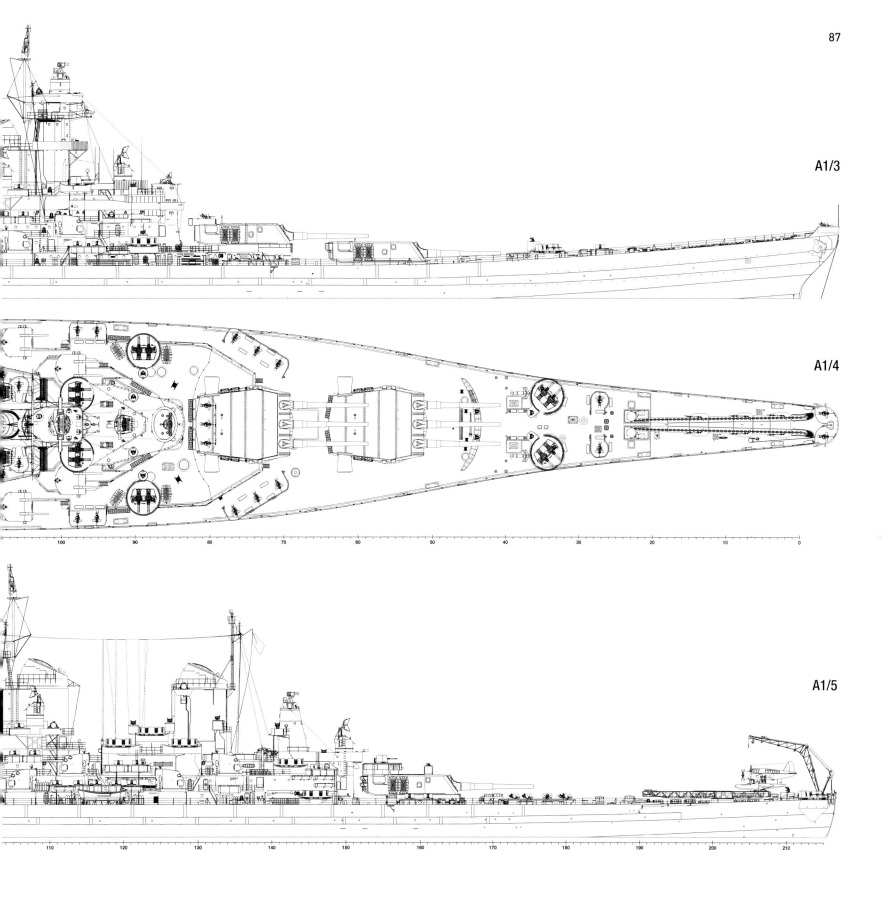

A1/3

A1/4

100 · 90 · 80 · 70 · 60 · 50 · 40 · 30 · 20 · 10 · 0

A1/5

110 · 120 · 130 · 140 · 150 · 160 · 170 · 180 · 190 · 200 · 210

**A GENERAL ARRANGEMENTS**

EXTERNAL VIEWS (1/600 SCALE)

A1/6 RIGHT PROFILE, EARLY 1945

A1/7 PLAN, EARLY 1945

A1/8 LEFT PROFILE, EARLY 1945

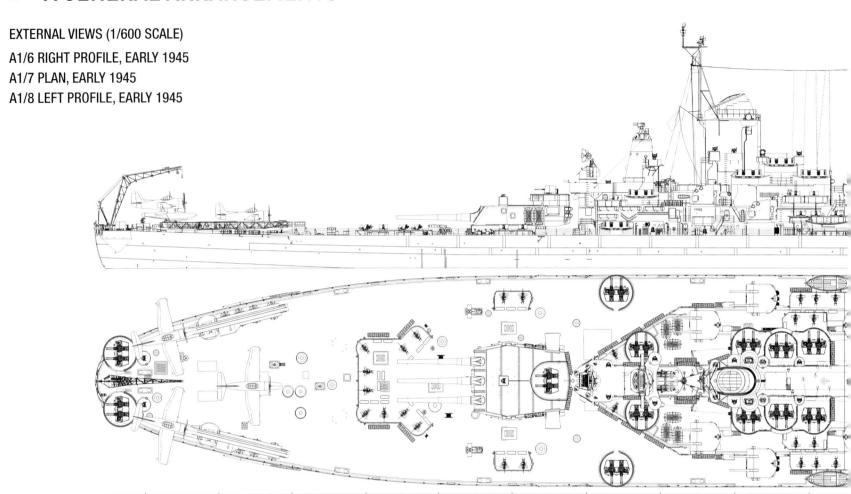

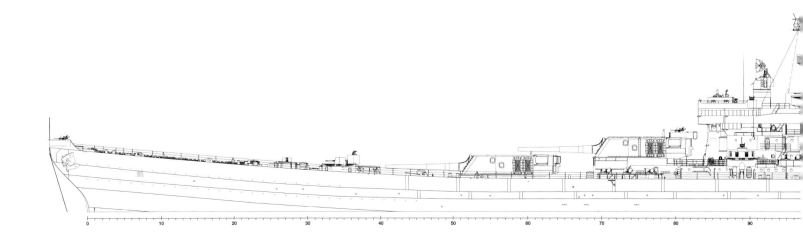

A1/6

A1/7

A1/8

# A GENERAL ARRANGEMENTS

EXTERNAL VIEWS (1/600 SCALE)

A1/9 RIGHT PROFILE, 1947

A1/10 PLAN, 1947

A1/11 LEFT PROFILE, 1947

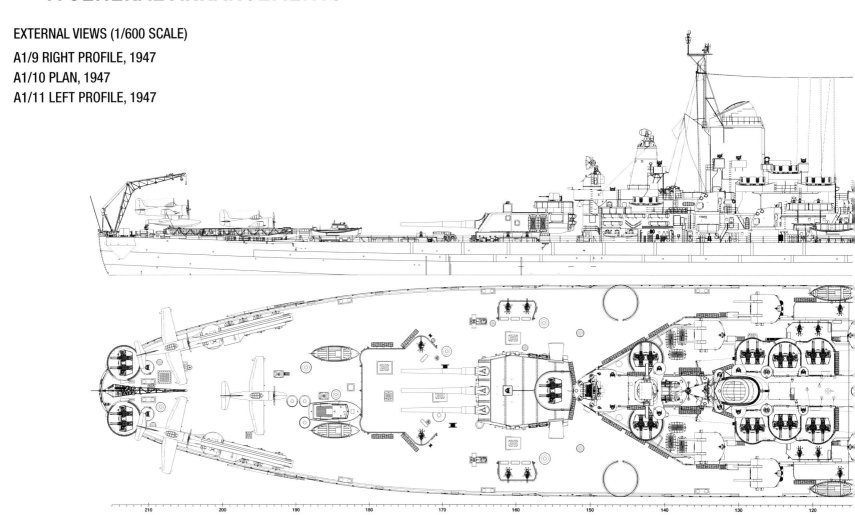

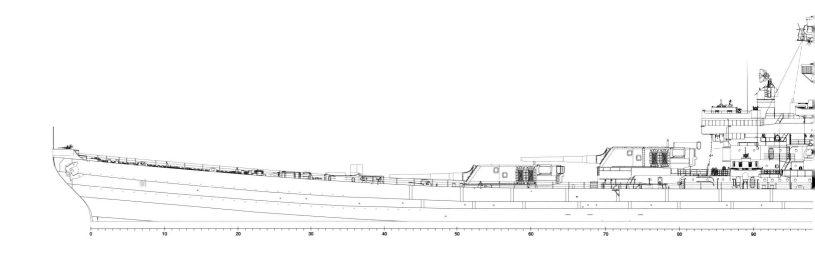

A1/9

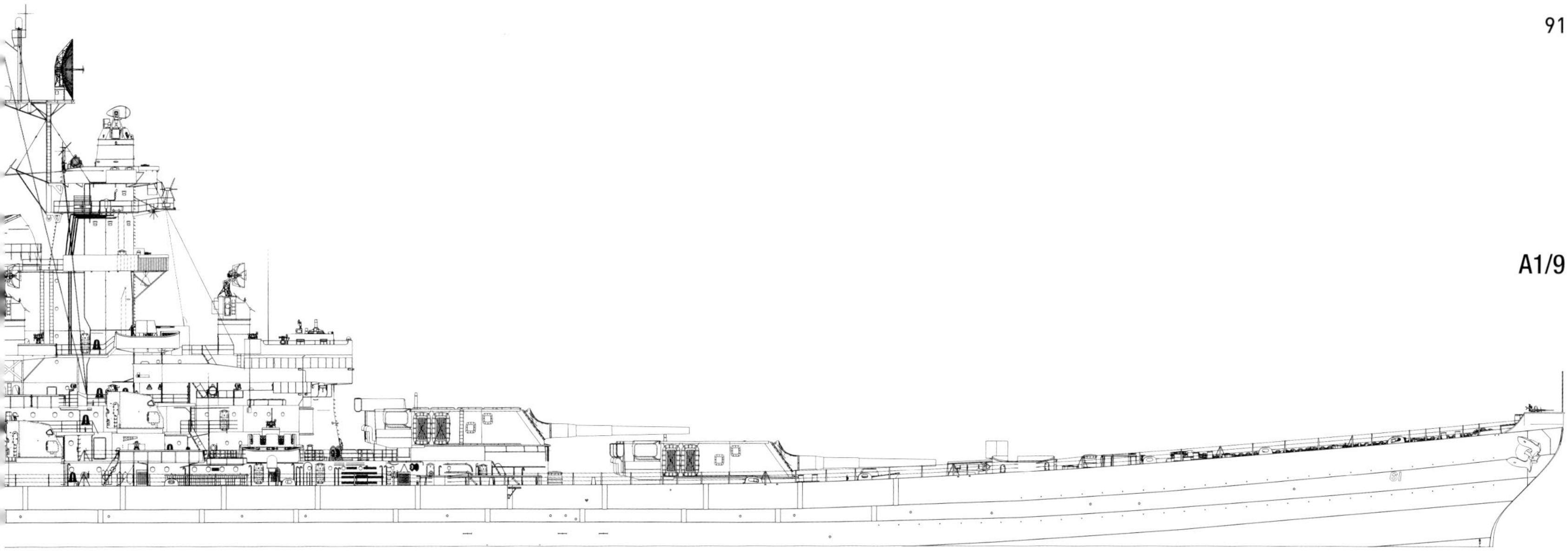

A1/10

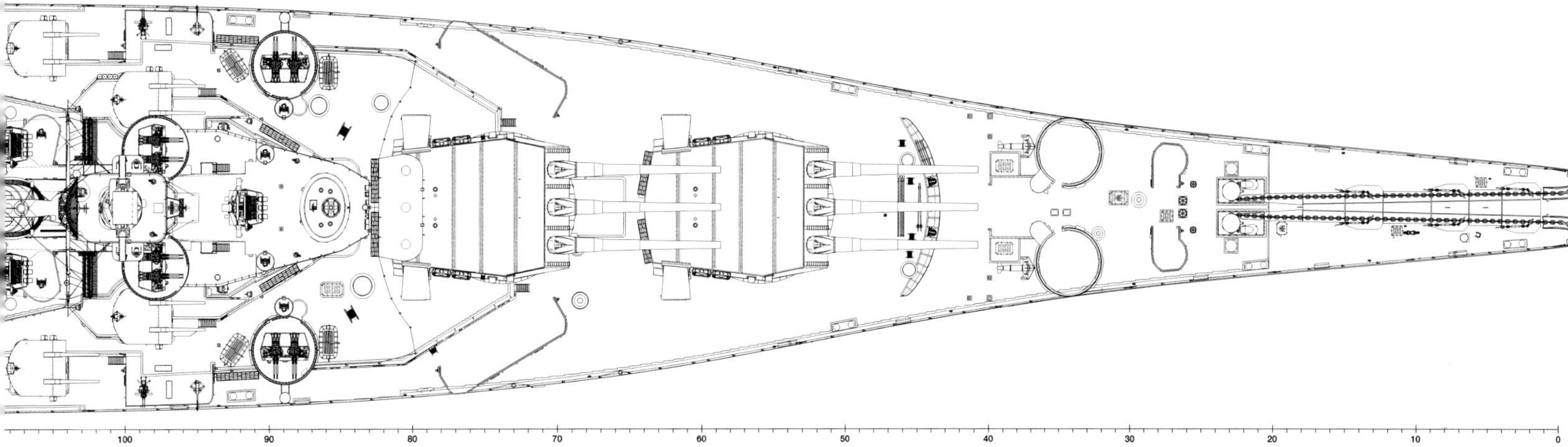

A1/11

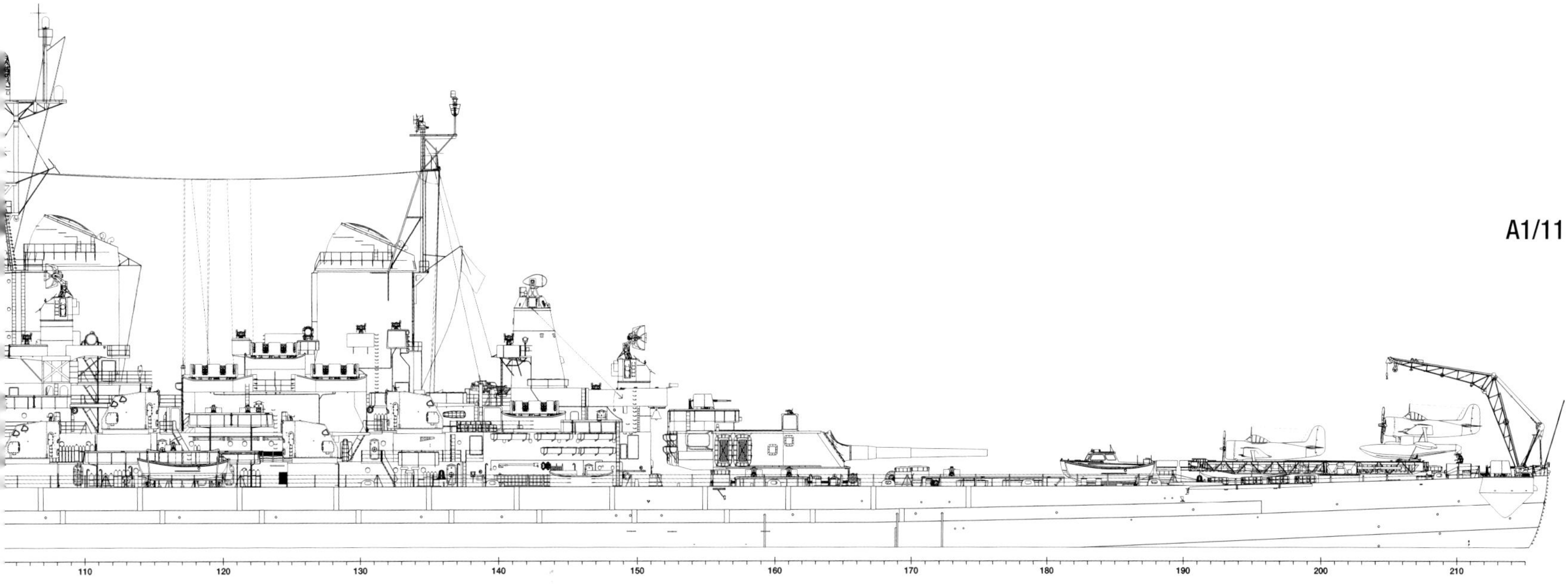

100  90  80  70  60  50  40  30  20  10  0

110  120  130  140  150  160  170  180  190  200  210

EXTERNAL VIEWS (1/600 SCALE)

A1/12 RIGHT PROFILE, MID-1952

A1/13 PLAN, MID-1952

A1/14 LEFT PROFILE, MID-1952

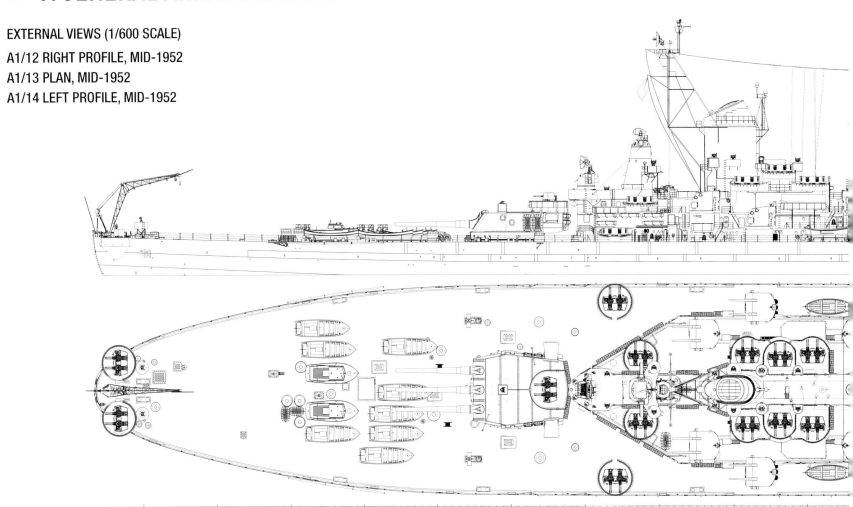

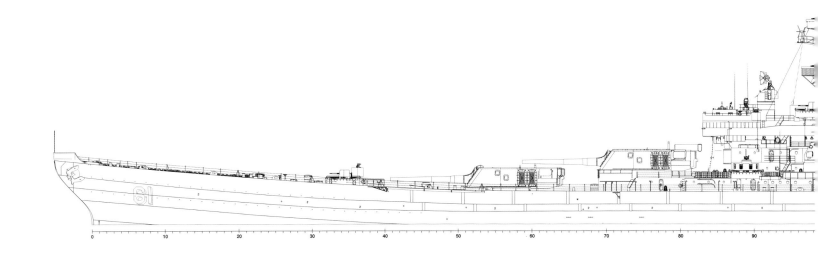

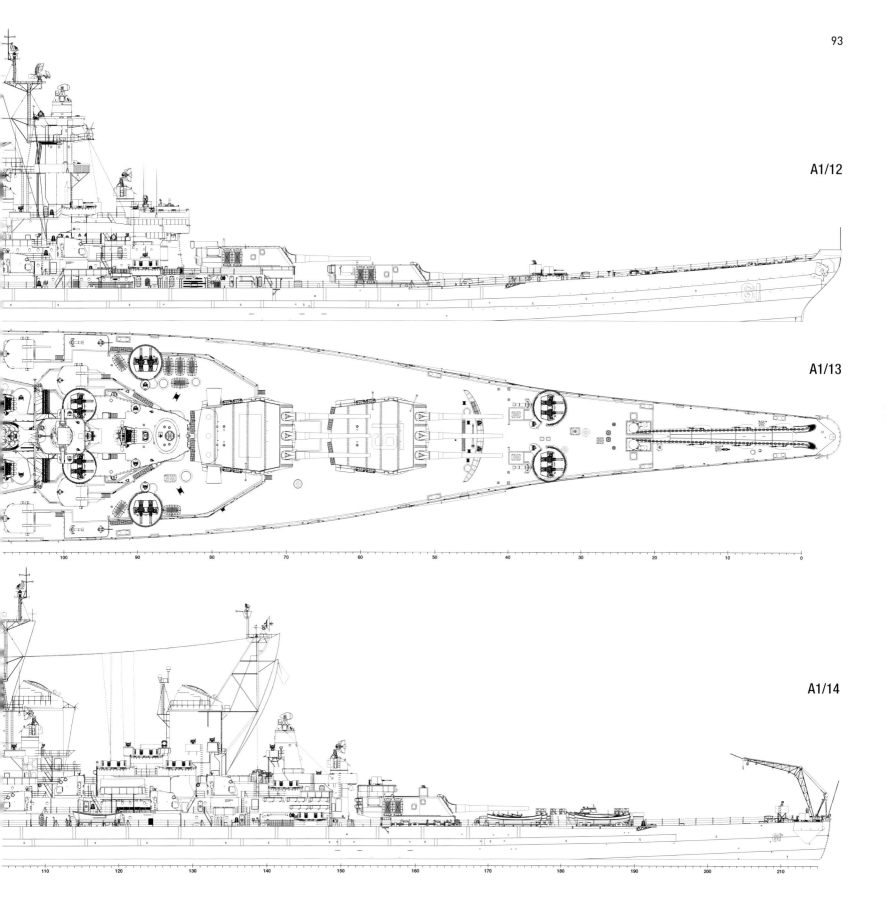

A1/12

A1/13

A1/14

**A GENERAL ARRANGEMENTS**

EXTERNAL VIEWS (1/600 SCALE)

A1/15 RIGHT PROFILE, LATE 1955

A1/16 PLAN, LATE 1955

A1/17 LEFT PROFILE, LATE 1955

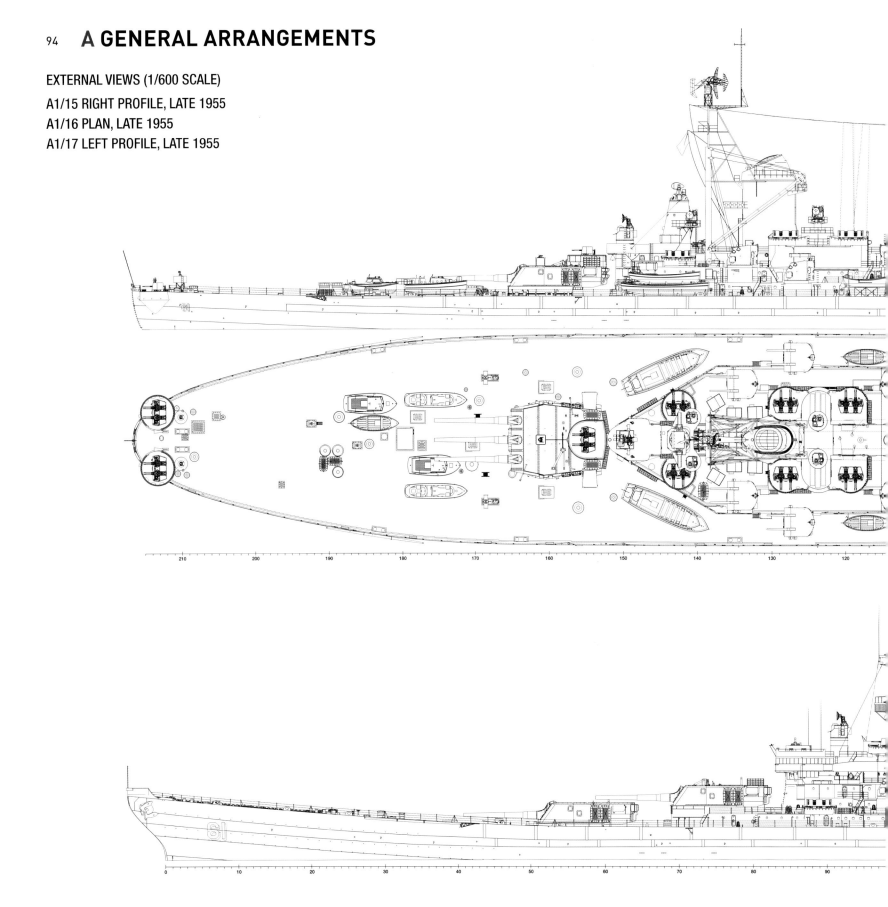

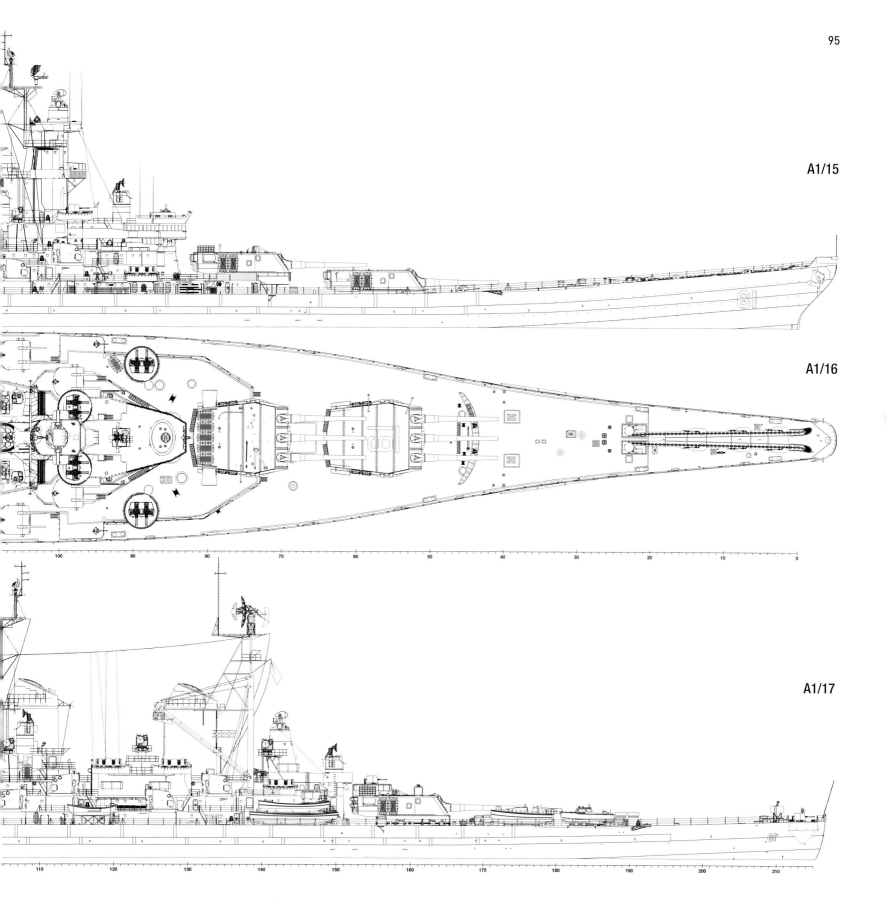

A1/15

A1/16

A1/17

EXTERNAL VIEWS (1/600 SCALE)

A1/18 RIGHT PROFILE, LATE 1986

A1/19 PLAN, LATE 1986

A1/20 LEFT PROFILE, LATE 1986

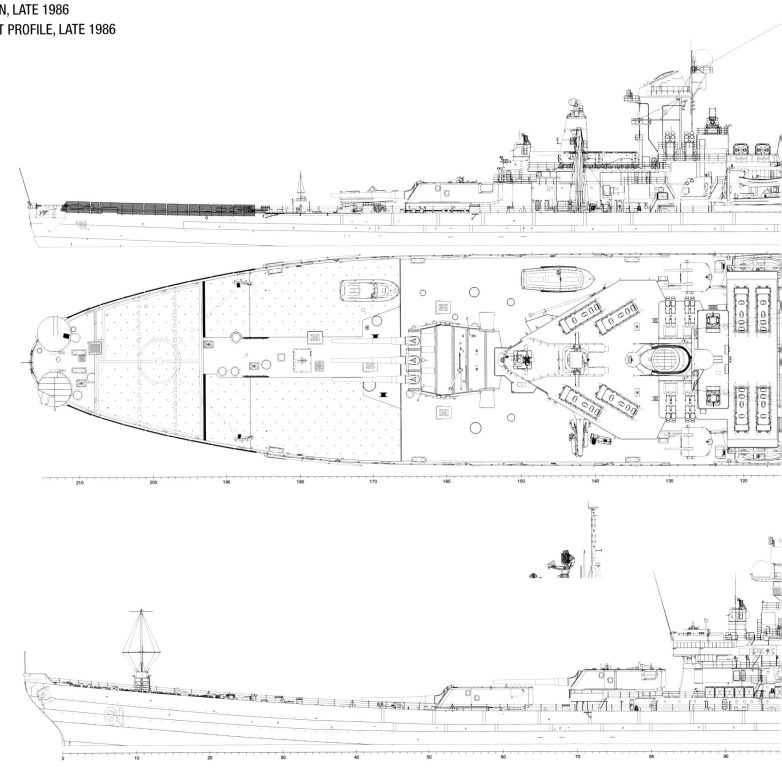

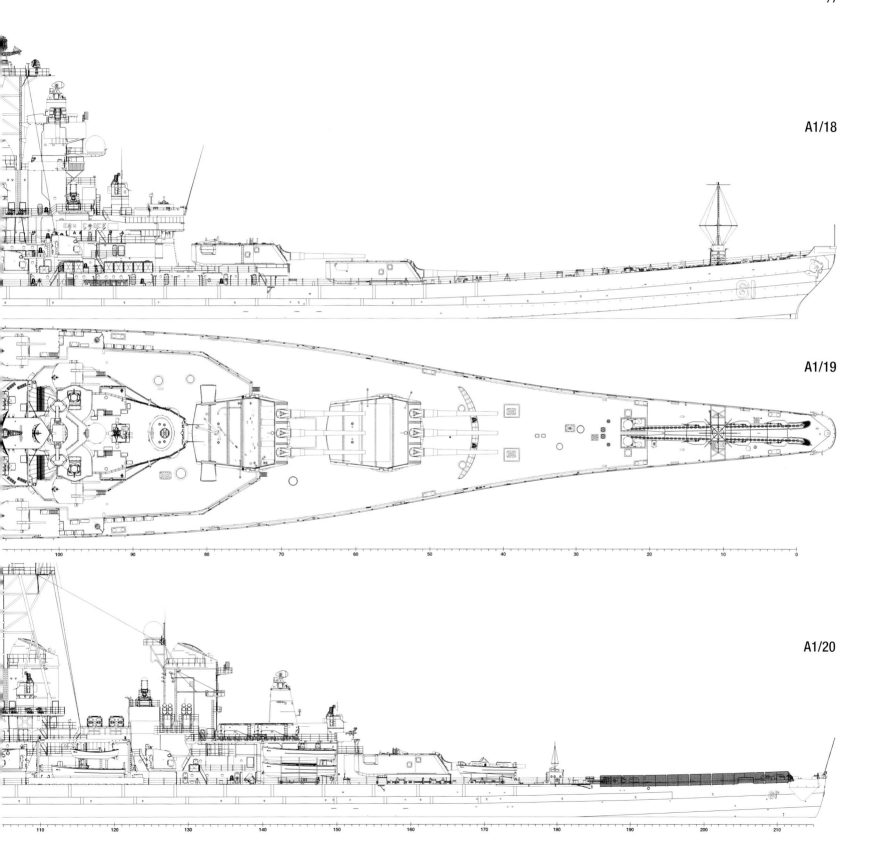

A1/18

A1/19

A1/20

EXTERNAL VIEWS (1/300 SCALE)

A1/21 FRONT VIEW, LATE 1944

A1/22 FRONT VIEW, LATE 1986

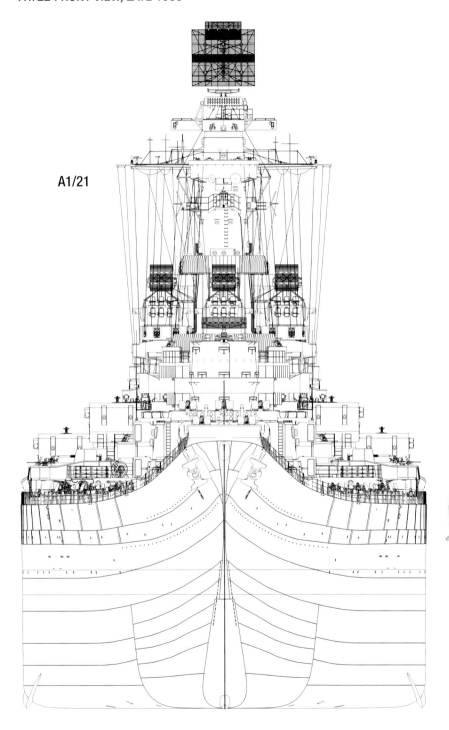

A1/21

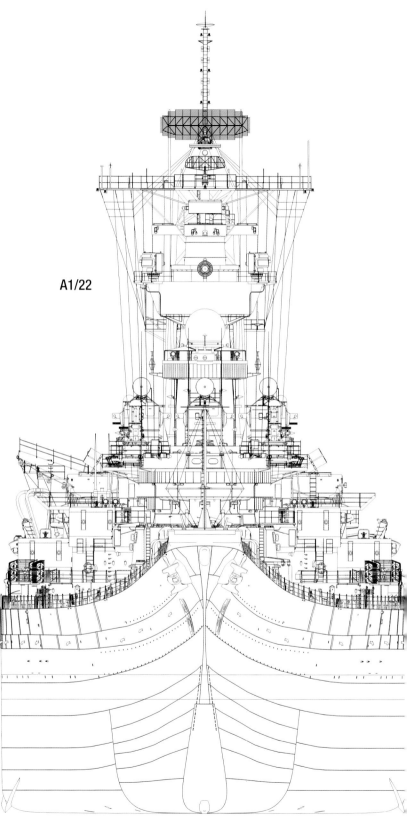

A1/22

A1/23 BACK VIEW, LATE 1944
A1/24 BACK VIEW, LATE 1986

A1/23

A1/24

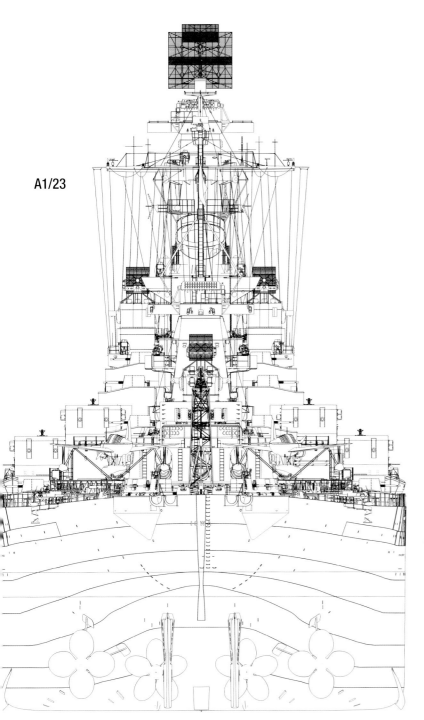

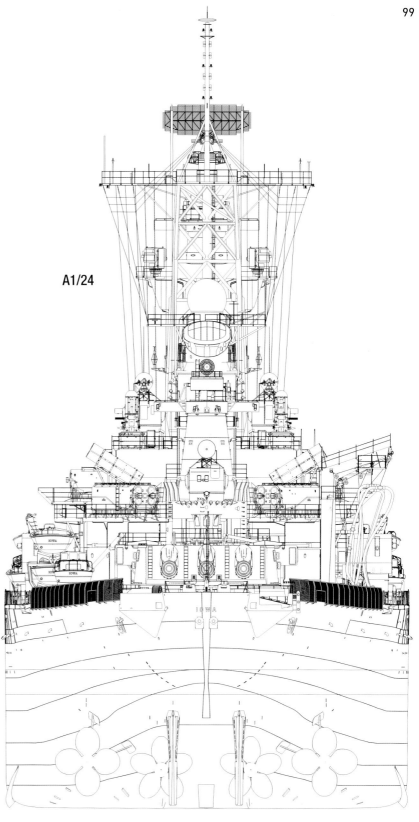

INTERNAL VIEWS (1/600 SCALE)

**A2/1 INTERNAL PROFILE, 1944**
1 Main deck
2 Second deck
3 Third deck
4  First platform
5 Second platform
6 Third platform
7 Hold

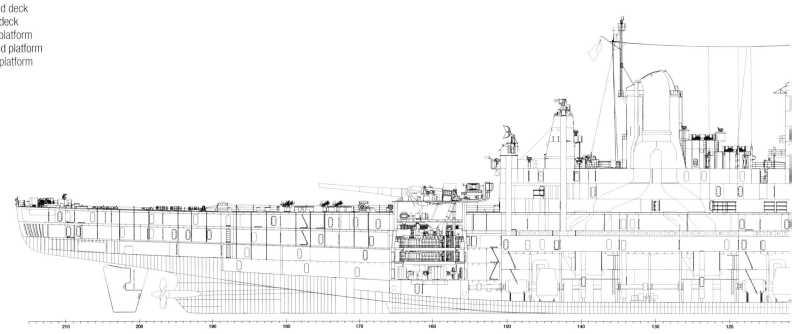

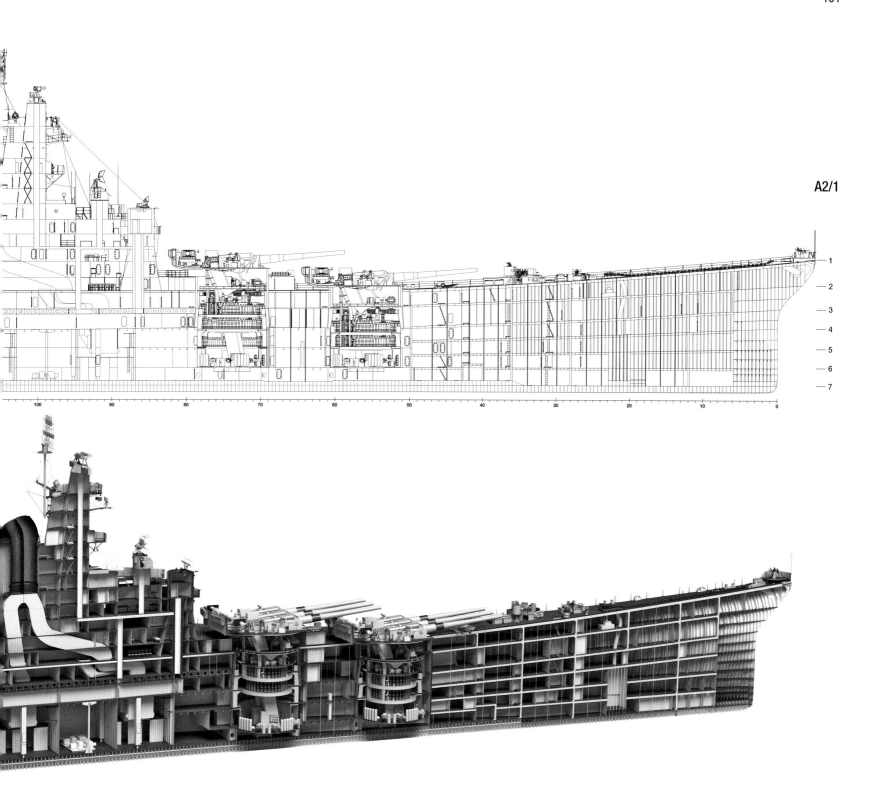

A2/1

INTERNAL VIEWS

A2/2 INTERNAL PROFILE WITH ARMOUR LAYOUT (1/600 SCALE)

A2/3 TRANSVERSE SECTION WITH ARMOUR LAYOUT, FRAME 119
(1/400 SCALE)

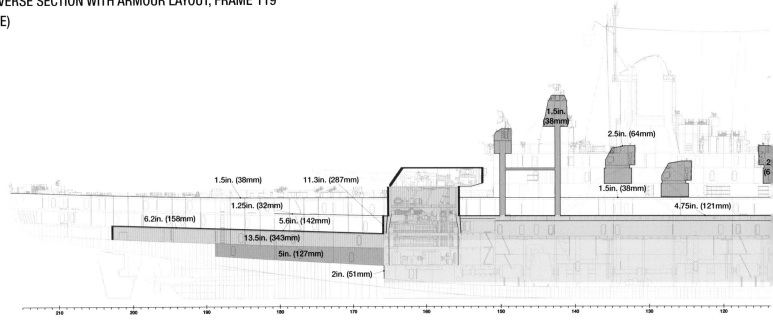

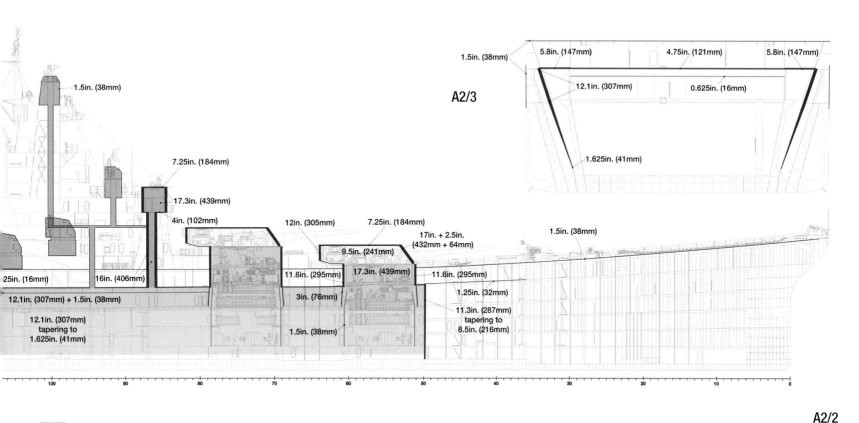

1.5in. (38mm)

5.8in. (147mm)   4.75in. (121mm)   5.8in. (147mm)

A2/3

12.1in. (307mm)   0.625in. (16mm)

1.625in. (41mm)

1.5in. (38mm)

7.25in. (184mm)

17.3in. (439mm)

4in. (102mm)

12in. (305mm)   7.25in. (184mm)

9.5in. (241mm)   17in. + 2.5in.
(432mm + 64mm)

1.5in. (38mm)

25in. (16mm)   16in. (406mm)   11.6in. (295mm)   17.3in. (439mm)   11.6in. (295mm)

12.1in. (307mm) + 1.5in. (38mm)   3in. (76mm)   1.25in. (32mm)

12.1in. (307mm)
tapering to
1.625in. (41mm)   1.5in. (38mm)   11.3in. (287mm)
tapering to
8.5in. (216mm)

A2/2

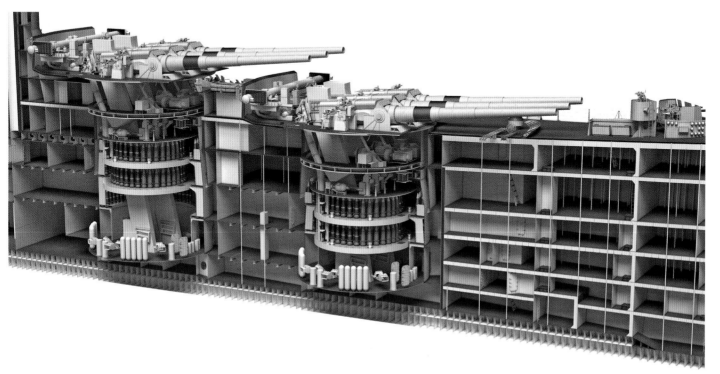

HULL EXTERNAL VIEWS (1/600 SCALE)

B1/1 RIGHT PROFILE, 1944

B1/2 BOTTOM VIEW (FRAGMENT)

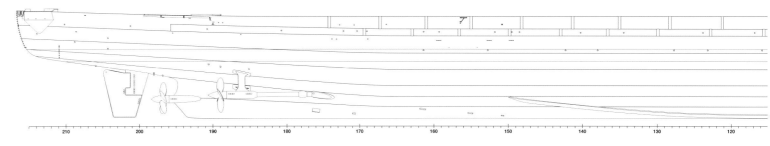

B1/1

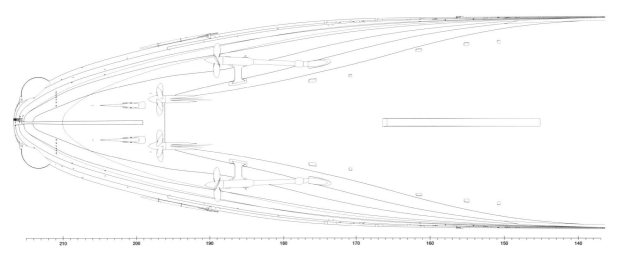

B1/2

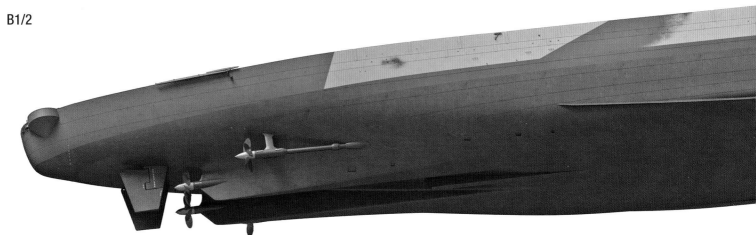

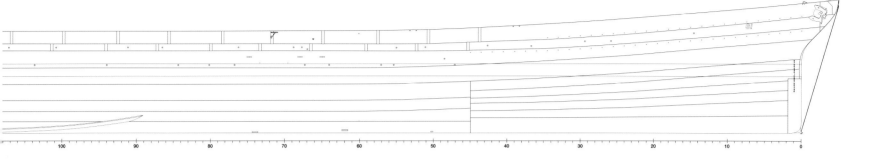

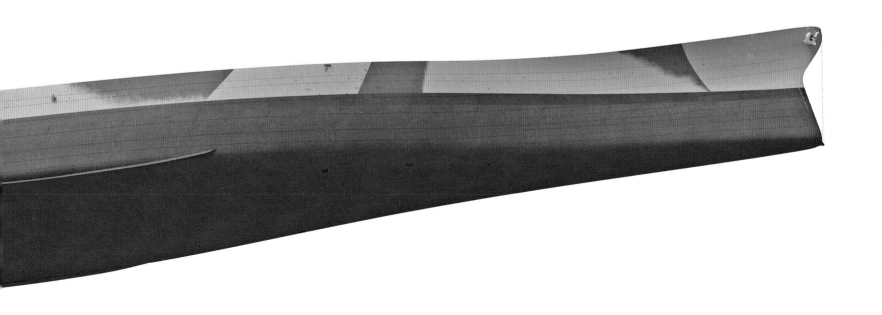

HULL EXTERNAL VIEWS (1/200 SCALE)

B1/3 FRONT VIEW, 1944

B1/4 BACK VIEW, 1944

B1/3

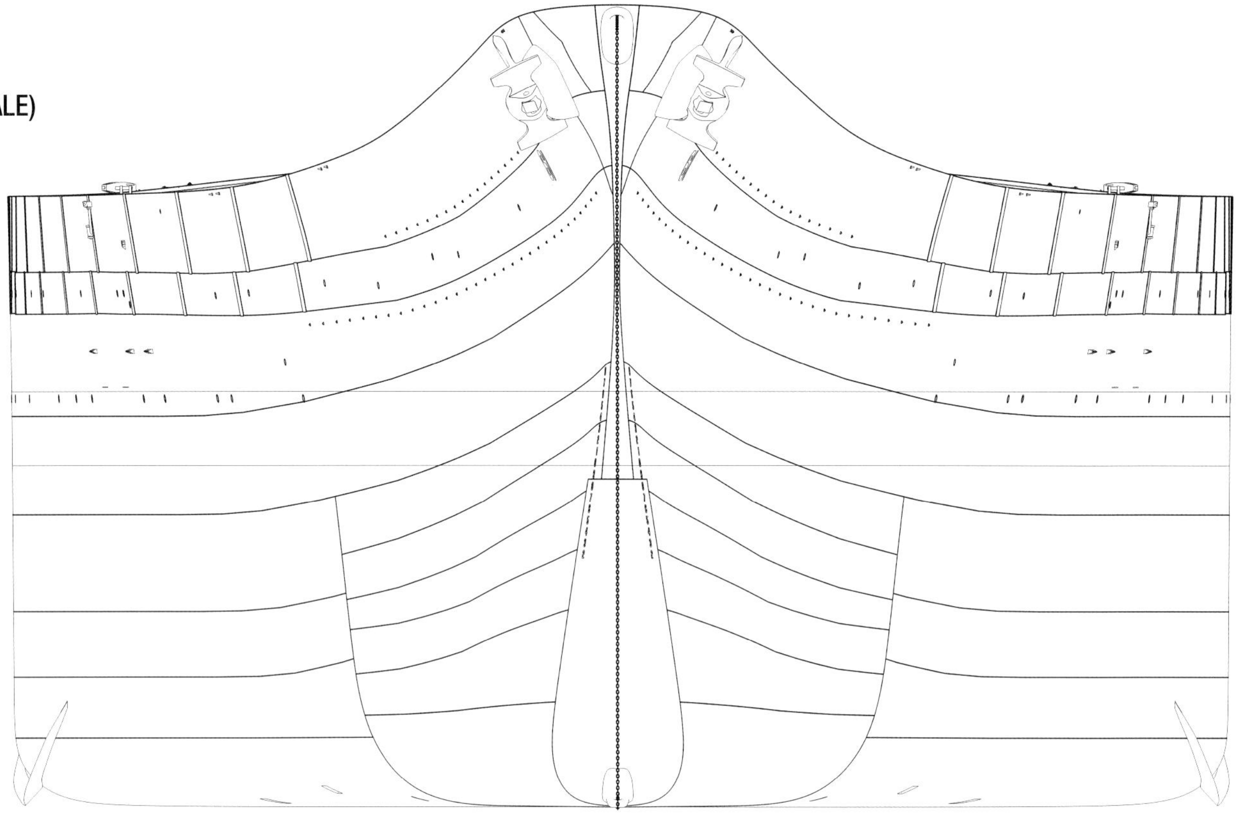

B1/4

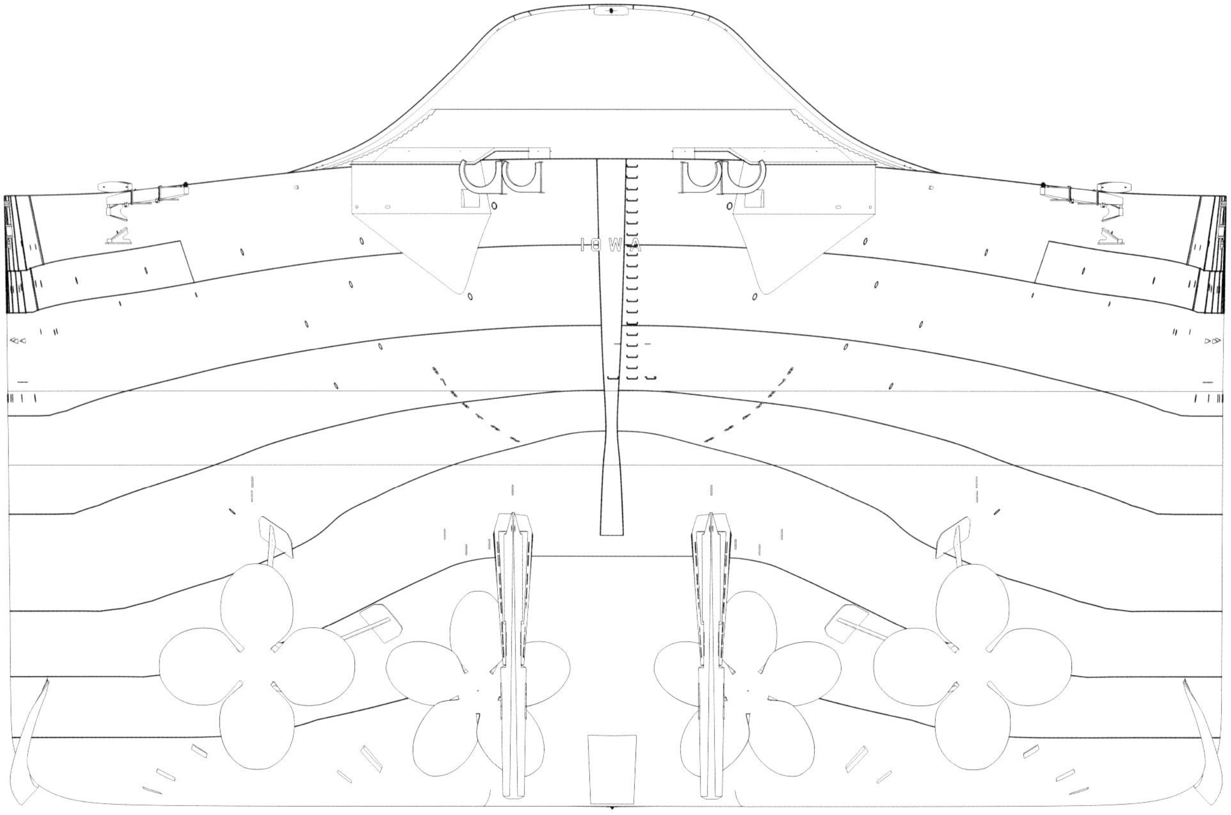

HULL LINES AND BODY PLANS (1/200 SCALE)

B1/5 BODY PLANS

B1/5

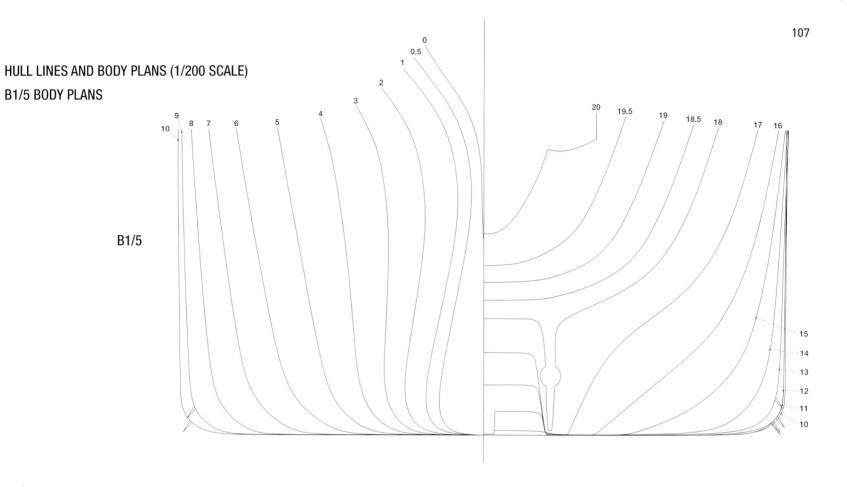

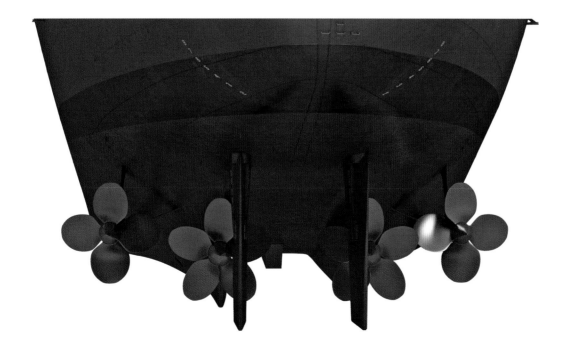

HULL LINES AND BODY PLANS (1/600 SCALE)

B1/6 SHEER ELEVATION

B1/7 WATERLINE PLAN

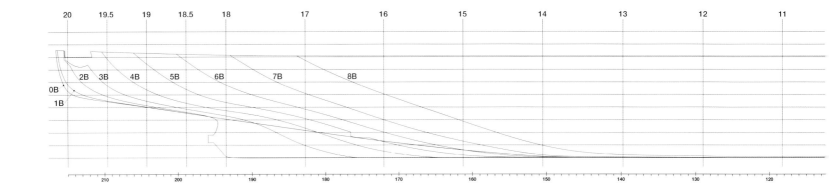

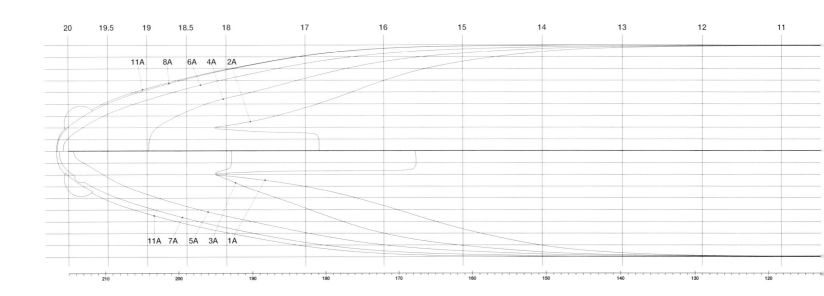

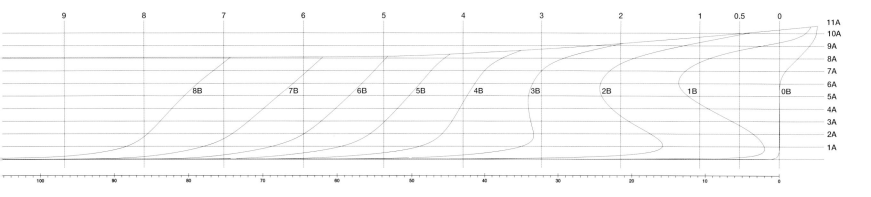

**B1/6**

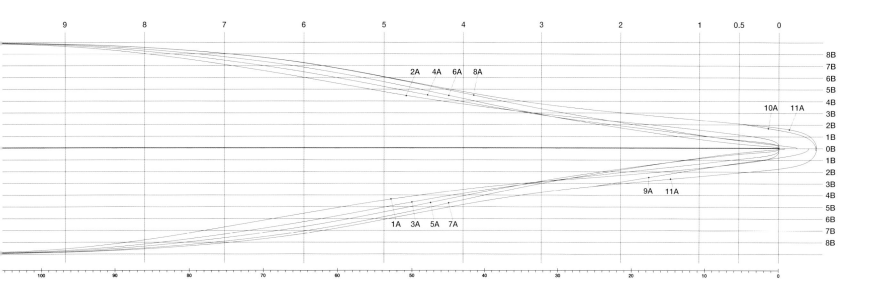

**B1/7**

## DECK PLANS (1/600 SCALE)

### B2/1 SECOND DECK, 1944

1 Airplane crane rotating machinery
2 40mm empty shells stowage
3 CPO storeroom
4 Passage
5 40mm ammunition ready service room
6 CPO quarters
7 WC
8 Washroom
9 Showers
10 CPO Lounge
11 Book stowage
12 Library
13 CPO galley
14 CPO mess room
15 Ship's service store
16 Crew's recreation room
17 Crew's mess
18 Hatchway
19 Winch hatchway
20 Garbage grinder room
21 20mm ammunition ready service room
22 Scullery annex
23 Scullery
24 Pipe and bar stowage
25 Athletic gear locker
26 Provision issue room
27 Barbette no. 3
28 Vegetable stowage
29 Vegetable preparing room
30 Master of arms office
31 Crew's galley
32 Crew's quarters
33 Butcher
34 Storeroom
35 Trash burner room
36 40mm hoist
37 Secondary artillery director tube
38 Main artillery director tube
39 Bakery
40 Bread room
41 Bakery stroreroom
42 Master of arms storeroom
43 Electrical tool issue room
44 Uptake no. 4
45 Carpenter

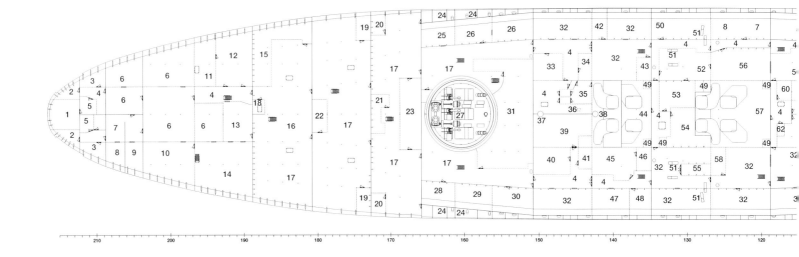

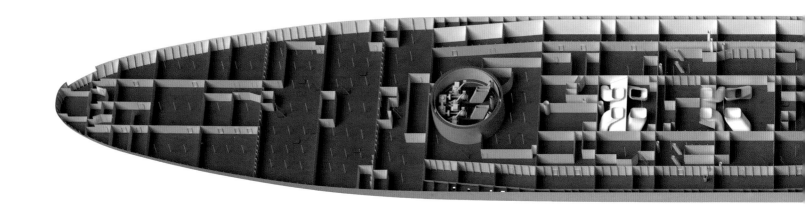

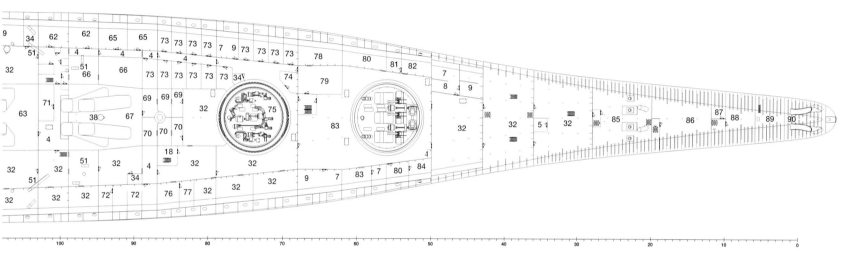

B2/1

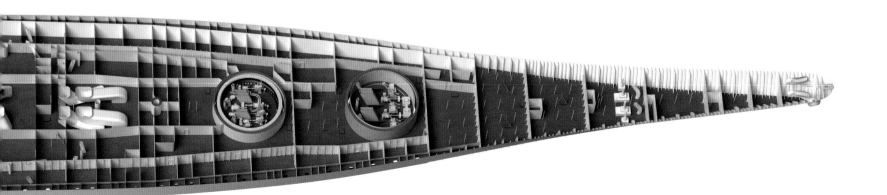

DECK PLANS (1/600 SCALE)

B2/2 SPLINTER DECK, 1944

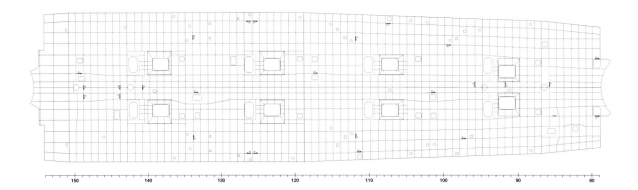

B2/2

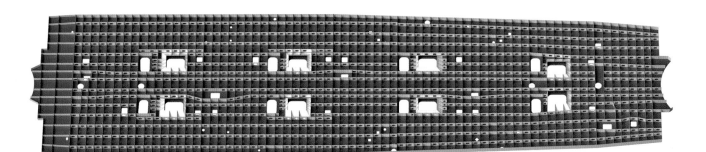

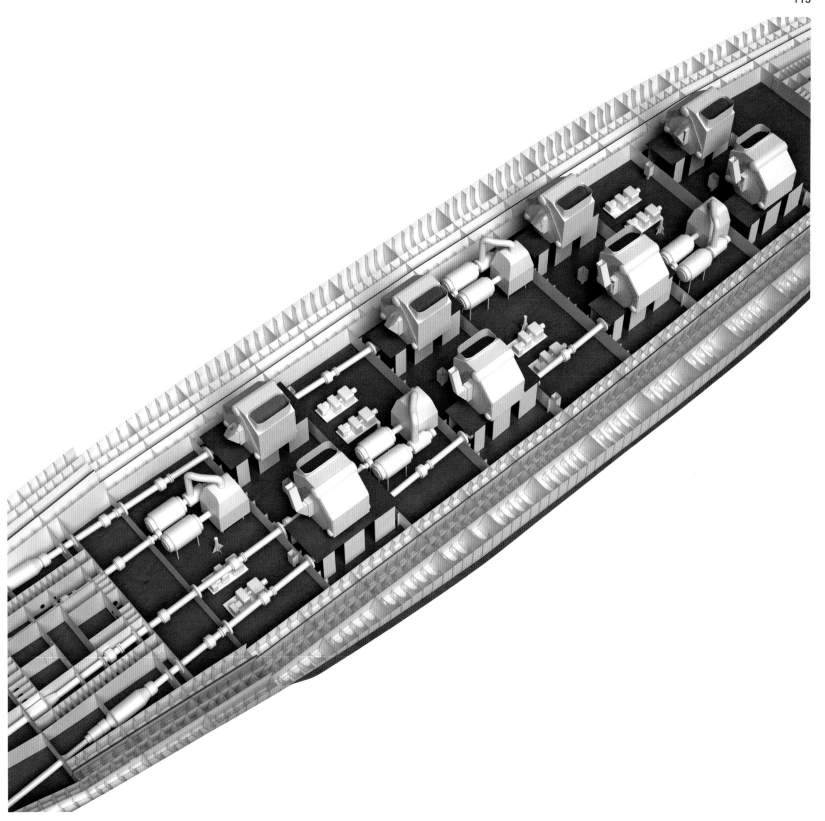

## DECK PLANS (1/600 SCALE)

### B2/3 THIRD DECK, 1944

1 Airplane crane hoisting machinery
2 Storeroom
3 Ordnance storeroom
4 Aviation storeroom
5 Aviation spare parts
6 Laundry
7 Laundry receiving room
8 Prison
9 Detention cell
10 Lucky bag

11 Barber shop
12 Passage
13 Washroom
14 WC
15 Crew's quarters
16 Vestibule
17 Laundry issue room
18 Tailor shop
19 Clobber shop
20 Clothing stores issue room
21 Printing shop
22 Dark room
23 Void

24 Fuel oil and ballast
25 Radio storeroom
26 Magazine cooling unit
27 Motor generator room
28 Main artillery plotting room
29 Combat information centre
30 Air cooling equipment
31 Secondary artillery plotting room
32 Radio room
33 40mm ammunition magazine
34 Repair locker
35 Repair station
36 Passage ('Broadway')

37 Testing lab
38 Telephone exchange room
39 Radar storeroom
40 Engine storeroom
41 Boiler no. 1
42 Boiler no. 2
43 Boiler no. 3
44 Boiler no. 4
46 Boiler no. 5
46 Boiler no. 6
47 Boiler no. 7
48 Boiler no. 8
49 5in. projectiles and handling room

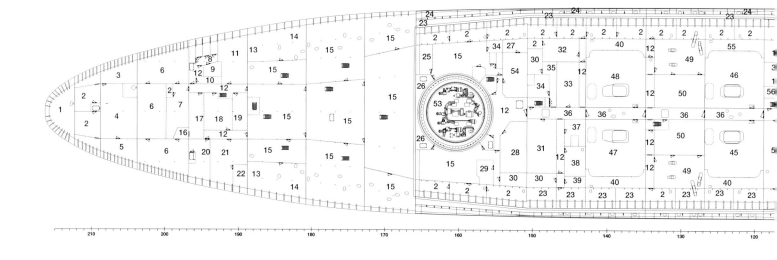

50 5in. powder magazine
51 Barbette no. 1
52 Barbette no. 2
53 Barbette no. 3
54 Interior communication room
55 Boiler workshop
56 Battle dressing stores
57 Radio transmitter room
58 Damage control station
59 Coding room
60 Main communication station
61 Central station
62 Radio central

63 Medical storeroom
64 Clinic
65 Doctor's office
66 Bath
67 Isolation ward
68 Clerical office
69 Dispensary
70 Navigator's storeroom
71 Sick bay
72 Surgical dressing room
73 Operating room
74 Sterilizing room
75 Pantry

76 Chemical warfare materials
77 40mm ammunition ready service room
78 Main issue room
79 Canvas awning storeroom
80 Alcohol stowage
81 Paint room
82 Acid locker

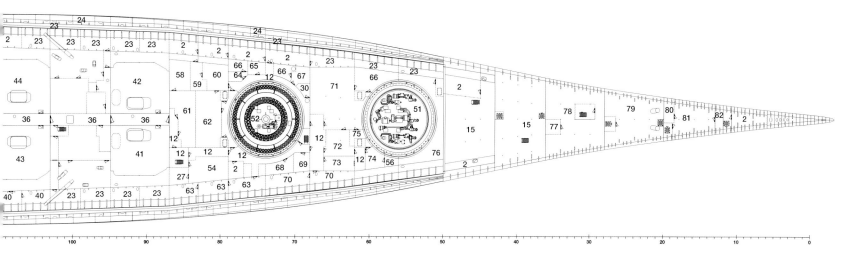

B2/3

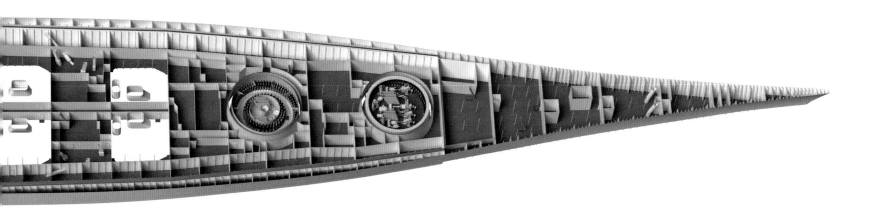

## DECK PLANS (1/600 SCALE)

### B2/4 FIRST PLATFORM, 1944

1 Void
2 Fuel oil and ballast
3 Storeroom
4 Gasoline tank
5 Steering gear room no. 1
6 Steering gear room no. 2
7 Steering gear power and control room no. 1
8 Steering gear power and control room no. 2
9 Provision storeroom

10 Ice machine room
11 Meat storeroom
12 Fruit and vegetable storeroom
13 Thawing room
14 Butter and eggs storeroom
15 40mm ammunition magazine
16 Catapult charges magazine
17 Ordnance storeroom
18 16in. powder magazine
19 Bomb fuze magazine
20 Fire bomb magazine
21 Engine room no. 1

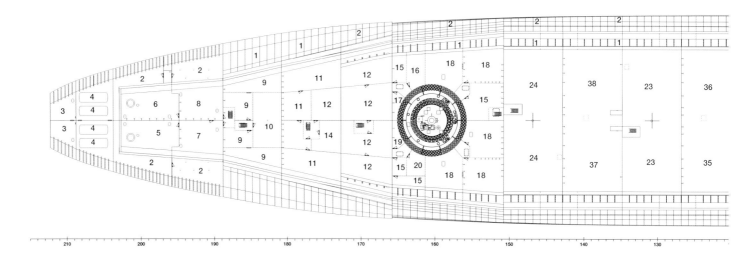

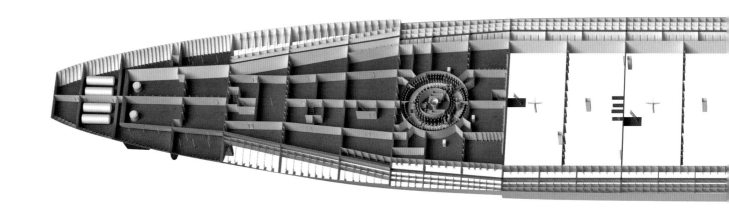

22 Engine room no. 2
23 Engine room no. 3
24 Engine room no. 4
25 Secondary artillery plotting station
26 Main artillery plotting station
27 Air cooling equipment
28 Combat information centre
29 Magazine cooling unit
30 20mm ammunition magazine

31 Boiler no. 1
32 Boiler no. 2
33 Boiler no. 3
34 Boiler no. 4
36 Boiler no. 5
36 Boiler no. 6
37 Boiler no. 7
38 Boiler no. 8
39 Paint storeroom

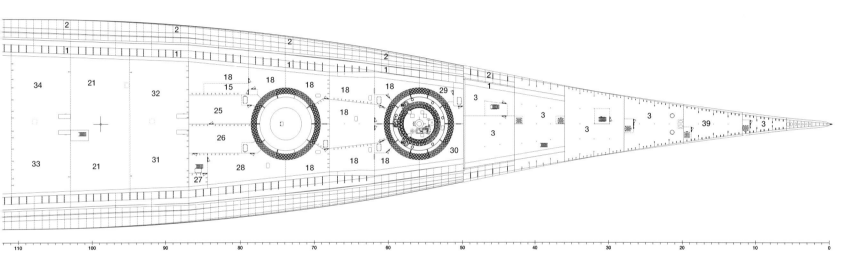

B2/4

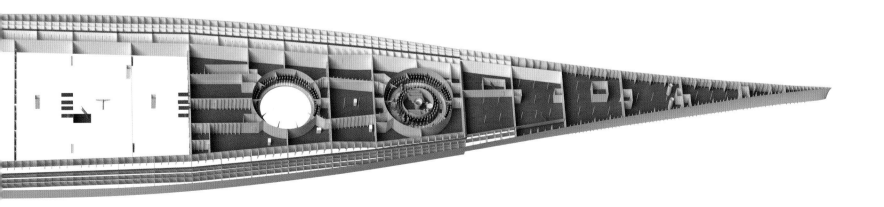

## DECK PLANS (1/600 SCALE)

### B2/5 SECOND PLATFORM, 1944

**1** Boiler no. 1
**2** Boiler no. 2
**3** Boiler no. 3
**4** Boiler no. 4
**6** Boiler no. 5
**6** Boiler no. 6
**7** Boiler no. 7

**8** Boiler no. 8
**9** Void
**10** Fuel oil and ballast
**11** Engine room no. 1
**12** Engine room no. 2
**13** Engine room no. 3
**14** Engine room no. 4
**15** Fire room no. 1
**16** Fire room no. 2
**17** Fire room no. 3

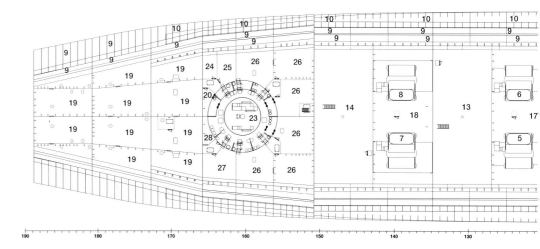

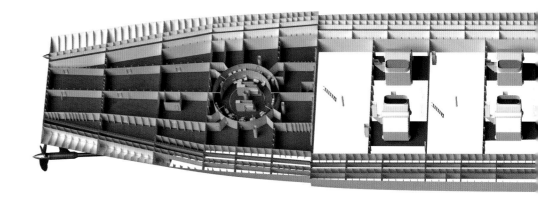

18 Fire room no. 4
19 Provision storeroom
20 Ordnance storeroom
21 Barbette no. 1
22 Barbette no. 2
23 Barbette no. 3
24 20mm ammunition magazine
25 Small arms magazine
26 16in. powder magazine
27 40mm ammunition magazine

28 Electrical booth
29 Emergency diesel generator room
30 Primer magazine
31 Storeroom
32 Landing force equipment storeroom
33 Electrical storeroom
34 Paint storeroom
35 Peak tank
36 Chain locker

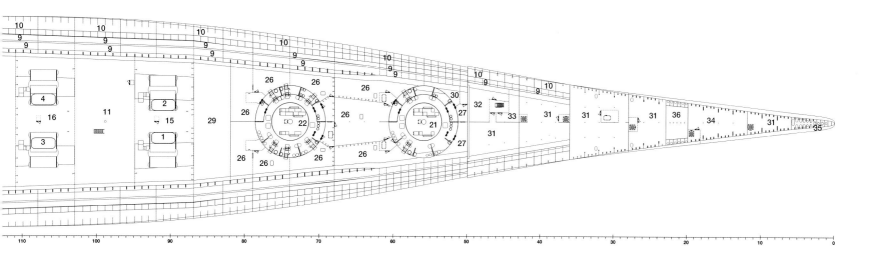

B2/5

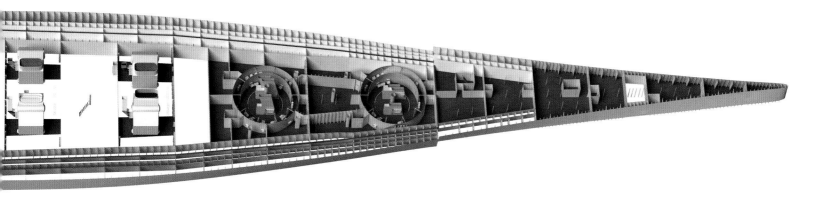

**DECK PLANS (1/600 SCALE)**

**B2/6 THIRD PLATFORM, 1944**

1 Void
2 Fuel oil and ballast
3 Marine quartermaster's storeroom
4 Warrant officer's storeroom
5 Storeroom
6 Officer's trunk room
7 Admiral's storeroom
8 Wardroom storeroom
9 Pyrotechnic locker
10 Ordnance storeroom
11 Chain locker
12 Peak tank
13 Fuel oil overflow

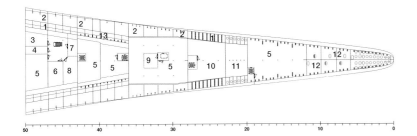

B2/6

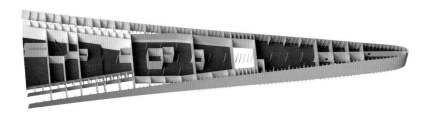

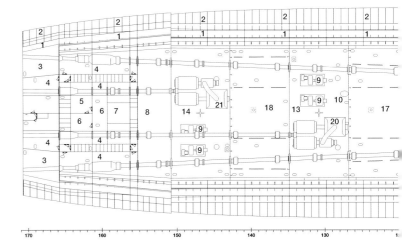

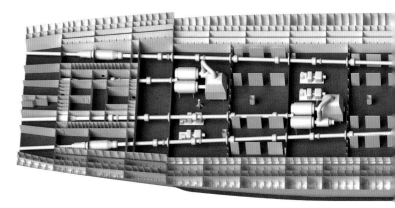

## B2/7 HOLD, 1944

1 Void
2 Fuel oil and ballast
3 Provisions storeroom
4 Shaft alley
5 Electrical booth
6 Wiring trunk
7 Ordnance storeroom
8 Emergency diesel generator room
9 Turbogenerator
10 Main engine control station and boiler central control station
11 Engine room no. 1
12 Engine room no. 2
13 Engine room no. 3
14 Engine room no. 4

15 Fire room no. 1
16 Fire room no. 2
17 Fire room no. 3
18 Fire room no. 4
19 Geared turbine set no. 1
20 Geared turbine set no. 2
21 Geared turbine set no. 3
22 Geared turbine set no. 4
23 Pump room
24 Storeroom
25 Marines storeroom
26 Chain locker
27 Peak tank

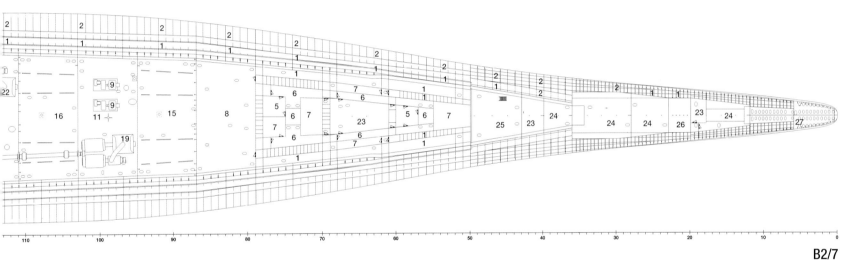

B2/7

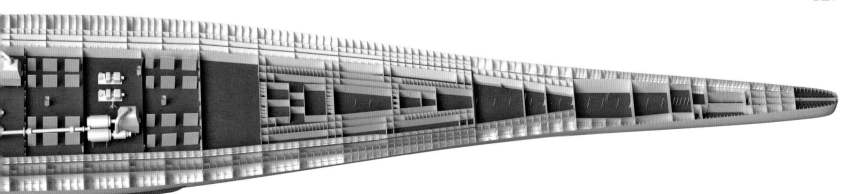

## TRANSVERSE SECTIONS (1/300 SCALE)

### B3/1 FRAME 212, 1944

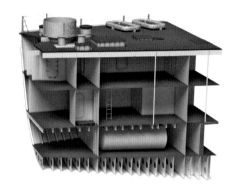

B3/1

### B3/2 FRAME 202, 1944

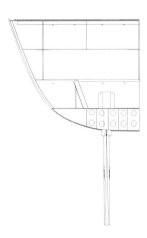

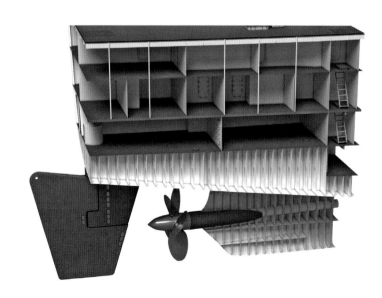

B3/2

B3/3 FRAME 187, 1944

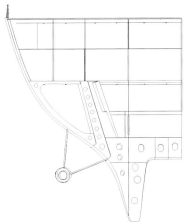

B3/3

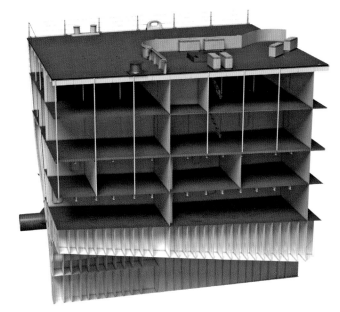

B3/4 FRAME 172, 1944

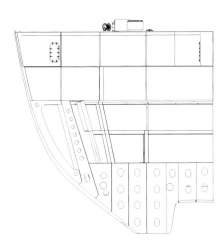

B3/4

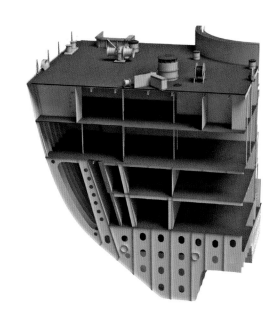

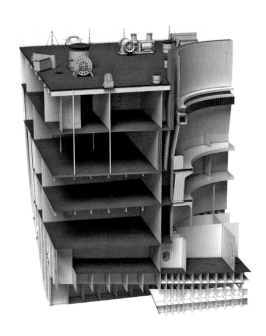

TRANSVERSE SECTIONS (1/300 SCALE)

B3/5 FRAME 160, 1944

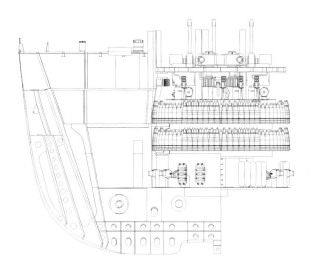

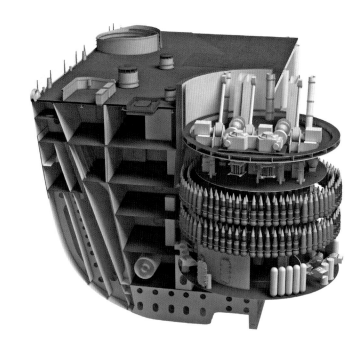

B3/5

**B3/6 FRAME 140, 1944**

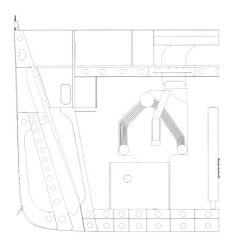

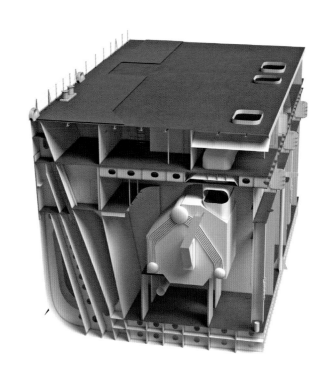

**B3/6**

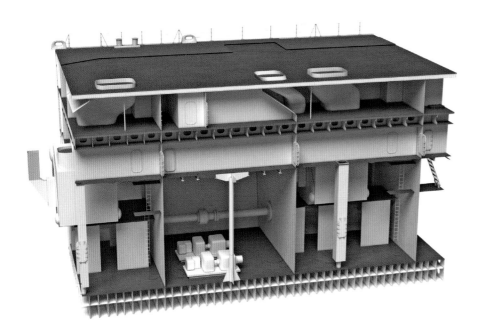

**B HULL**

TRANSVERSE SECTIONS (1/300 SCALE)

B3/7 FRAME 117, 1944

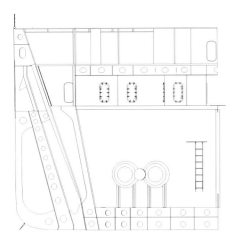

B3/7

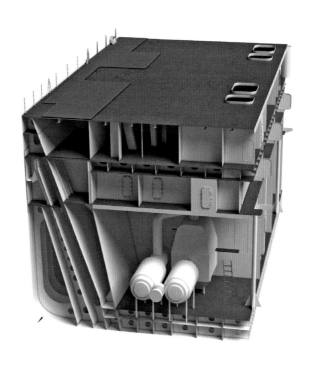

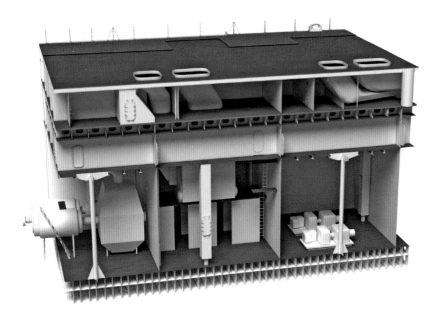

**B3/8 FRAME 94, 1944**

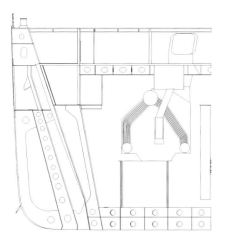

**B3/8**

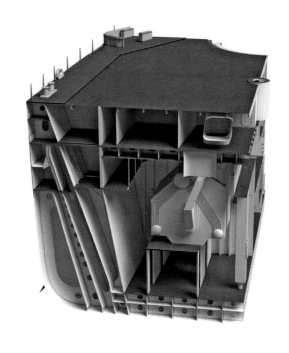

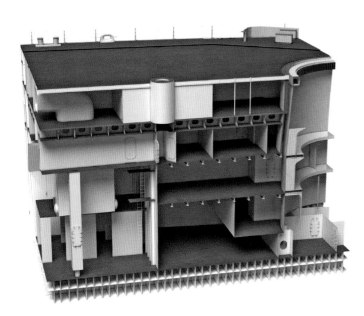

TRANSVERSE SECTIONS (1/300 SCALE)

B3/9 FRAME 74, 1944

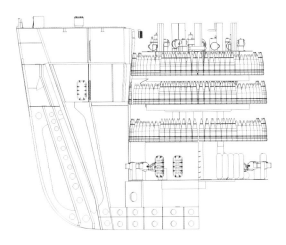

B3/9

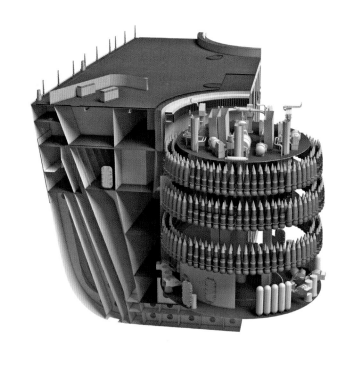

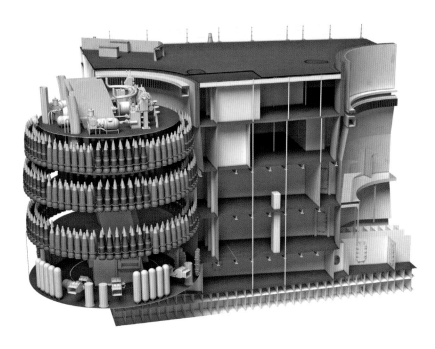

**B3/10 FRAME 55, 1944**

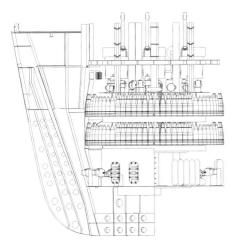

**B3/10**

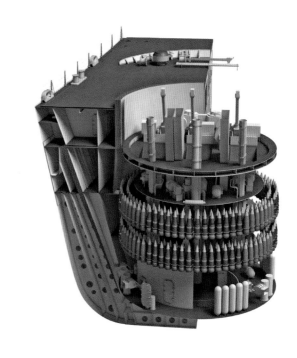

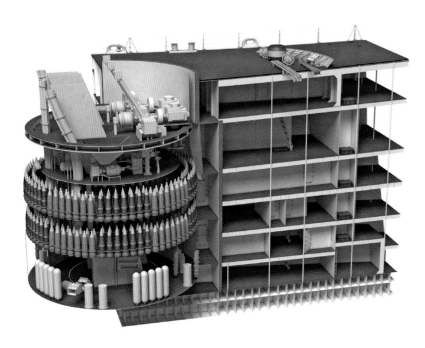

## TRANSVERSE SECTIONS (1/300 SCALE)

### B3/11 FRAME 39, 1944

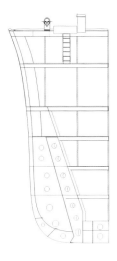

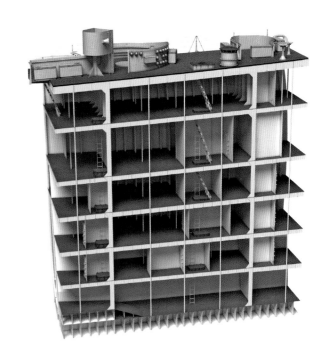

B3/11

### B3/12 FRAME 25, 1944

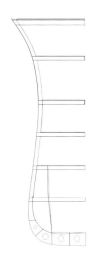

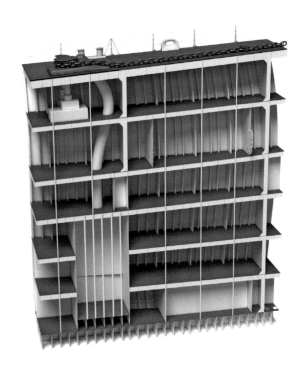

B3/12

**B3/13 FRAME 11, 1944**

**B3/13**

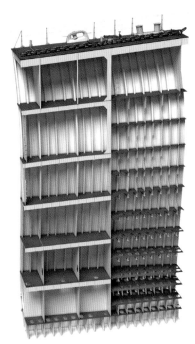

**B3/14 FRAME 2, 1944**

**B3/14**

SUPERSTRUCTURE, LATE 1944 (1/200 SCALE)

C1/1 RIGHT PROFILE, 5IN. MOUNTS OMITTED FOR CLARITY

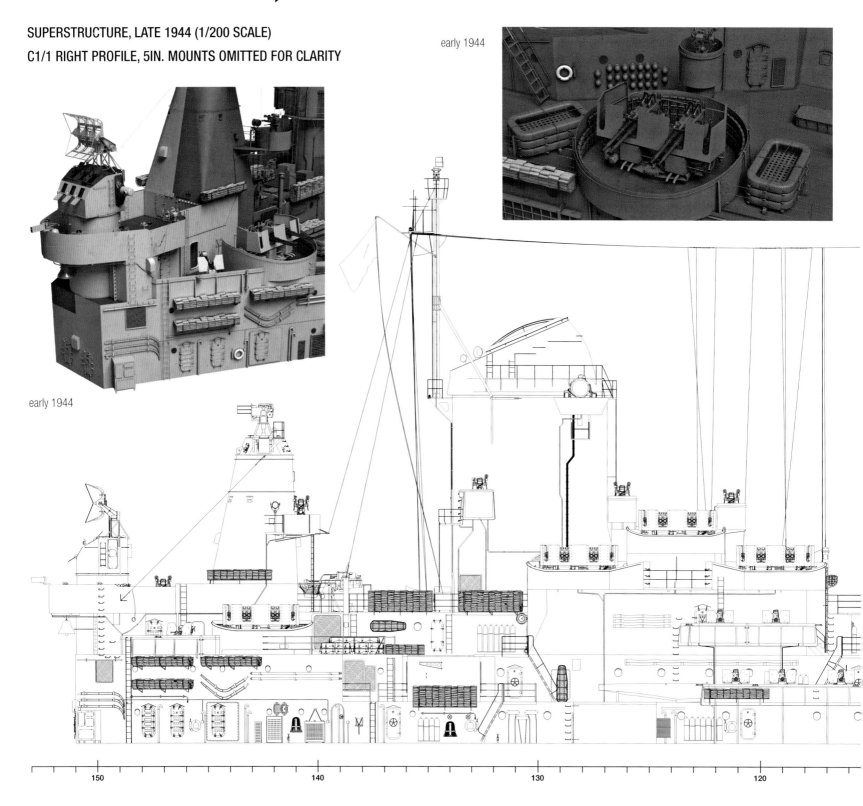

early 1944

early 1944

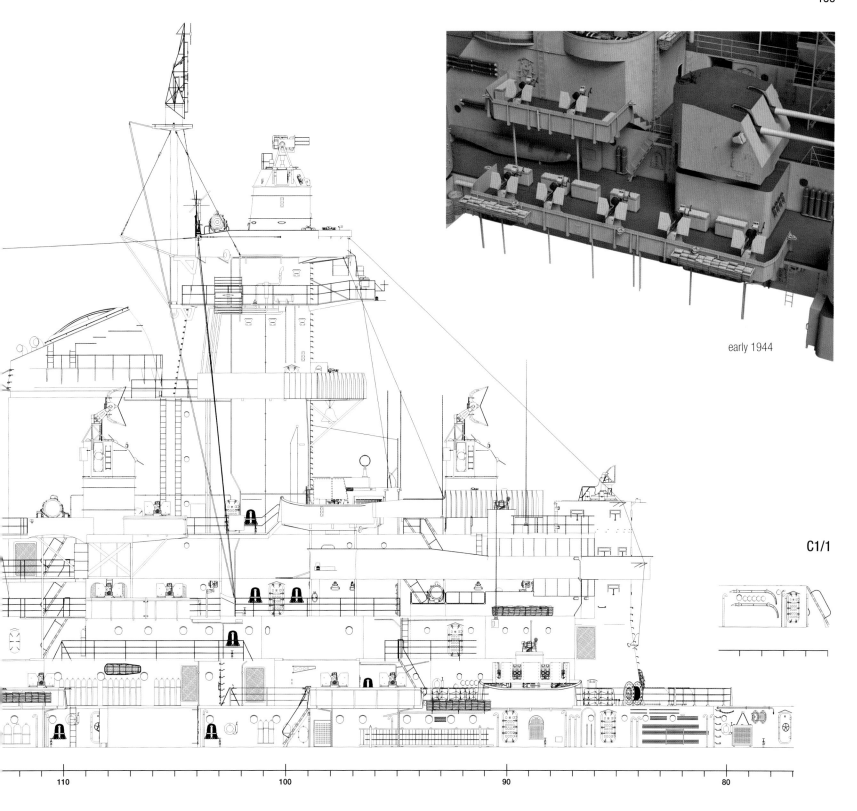

early 1944

C1/1

SUPERSTRUCTURE, LATE 1944 (1/200 SCALE)

C1/2 LEFT PROFILE, 5IN. MOUNTS OMITTED FOR CLARITY

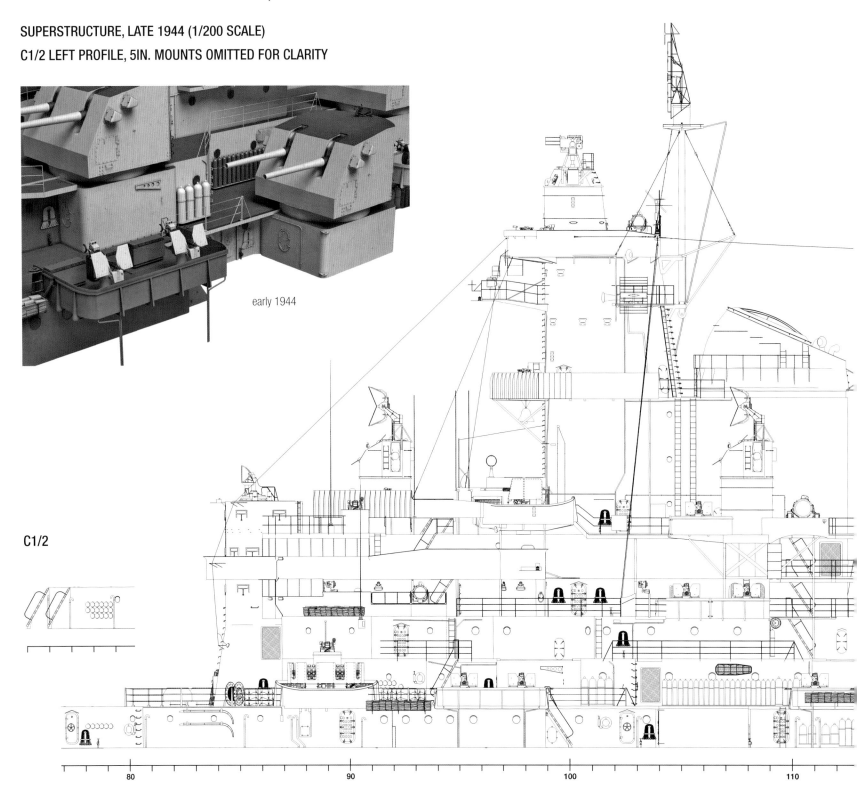

early 1944

C1/2

80                    90                    100                    110

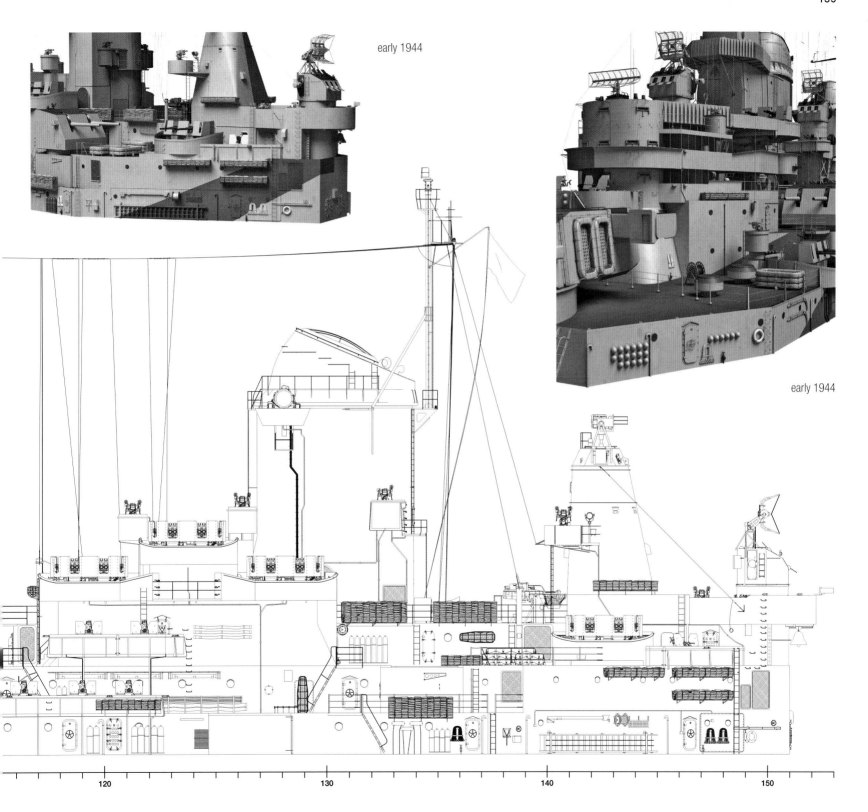

early 1944

early 1944

120     130     140     150

## SUPERSTRUCTURE, LATE 1944 (1/200 SCALE)

### C1/3 FRONT VIEW, 5IN. MOUNTS OMITTED FOR CLARITY

1 Main deck level
2 First superstructure deck level
3 Second superstructure deck level
4 Flag bridge level
5 Navigating bridge level
6 Pilot house top level
7 First level above pilot house top
8 Second level above pilot house top
9 Primary conning station level
10 Forward surface lookout station level
11 Whistle and siren platform level
12 Forward air defence station

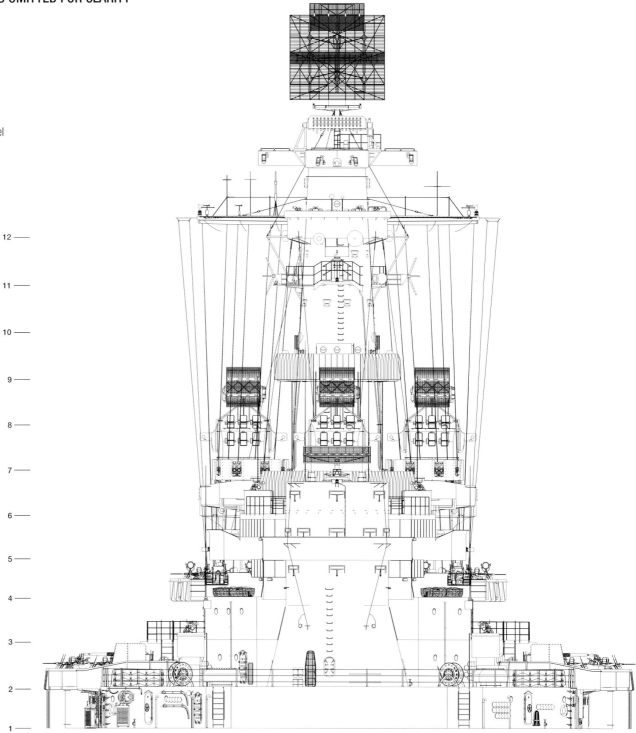

C1/3

C1/4 BACK VIEW, 5IN. MOUNTS OMITTED FOR CLARITY

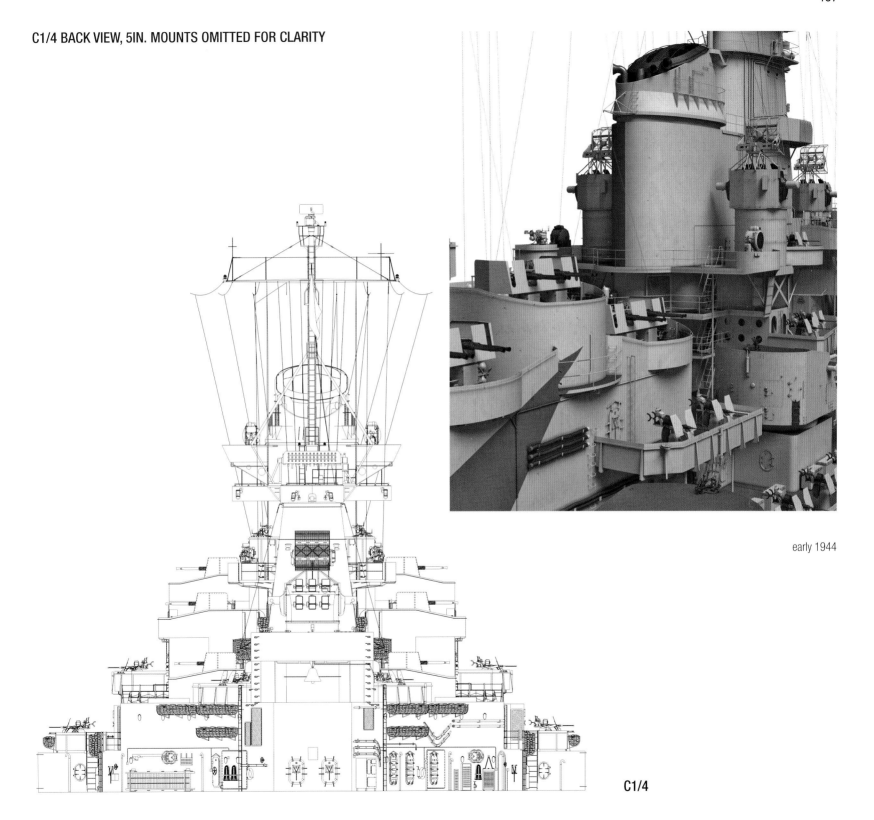

early 1944

C1/4

## SUPERSTRUCTURE, LATE 1944 (1/200 SCALE)

### C1/5 MAIN DECK LEVEL – PLAN

1 Davits (stowed)
2 Fire plug
3 Hose reel
4 Accommodation ladder (stowed)
5 Life ring
6 Goose vent
7 Deck gear locker
8 Gas bottles
9 Oerlikon platform support
10 Drain pipe
11 Ladder rung
12 Electrical boxes
13 Vertical ladder
14 Floater net basket
15 Fire hose rack
16 40mm ammunition passing scuttle
17 Ammunition handling boom
18 Fenders (stowed)
19 Davit support
20 Helmets (stowed)
21 Fire hose applicator
22 Vent
23 Steam cutoff
24 Phone locker
25 Secondary artillery director tube
26 Crew's WC
27 After deck office
28 First aid station
29 Office
30 Repair locker
31 40mm ammunition trunk
32 Main artillery director tube

C1/5

33 Crew's bathroom
  and decontamination station
34 Air intake
35 Uptake
36 Storage room
37 Passage
38 Crew's quarters

39 Gun tube
40 Secondary artillery upper handling room
41 5in. ammunition hoist
42 Captain's office
43 Flag office
44 Executive officer's office
45 Chaplain's office

46 Damage control office
47 Mess attendant's messing
48 Fan room
49 Wardroom pantry
50 Wardroom
51 40mm ammunition magazine
52 Conning tower armoured tube

53 Armory
54 Repair shop
55 WC
56 Officer's cabin
57 Vent trunk
58 Executive officer's work room
59 Executive officer's cabin
60 Forward deck office
61 Supply trunk

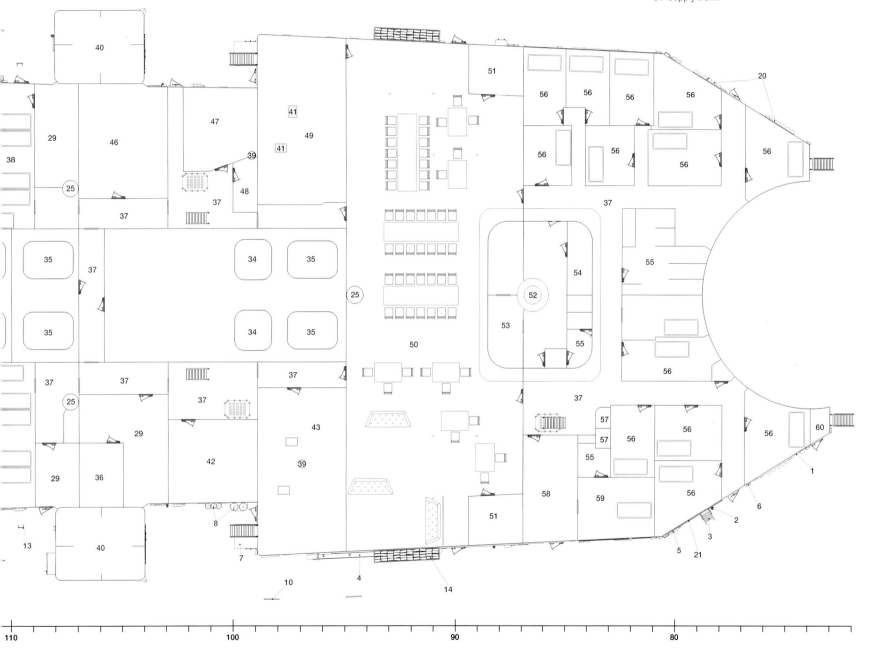

SUPERSTRUCTURE, LATE 1944 (1/200 SCALE)

C1/6 MAIN DECK LEVEL – VIEW FROM FRAME 100 TOWARDS
THE BOW, STARBOARD SIDE
C1/7 MAIN DECK LEVEL – VIEW FROM FRAME 100 TOWARDS
THE BOW, PORT SIDE
C1/8 MAIN DECK LEVEL – VIEW FROM FRAME 104 TOWARDS
THE STERN, STARBOARD SIDE
C1/9 MAIN DECK LEVEL – VIEW FROM FRAME 104 TOWARDS
THE STERN, PORT SIDE
C1/10 MAIN DECK LEVEL – VIEW FROM FRAME 108 TOWARDS
THE BOW, STARBOARD SIDE
C1/11 MAIN DECK LEVEL – VIEW FROM FRAME 108 TOWARDS
THE BOW, PORT SIDE
C1/12 MAIN DECK LEVEL – VIEW FROM FRAME 124 TOWARDS
THE STERN, STARBOARD SIDE (PORT SIDE SYMMETRICAL)
C1/13 MAIN DECK LEVEL – VIEW FROM FRAME 129 TOWARDS
THE BOW, STARBOARD SIDE (PORT SIDE SYMMETRICAL)

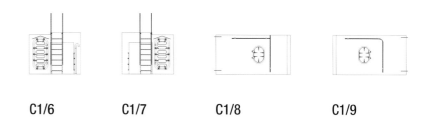

C1/6     C1/7     C1/8     C1/9

C1/10     C1/11     C1/12     C1/13

early 1944

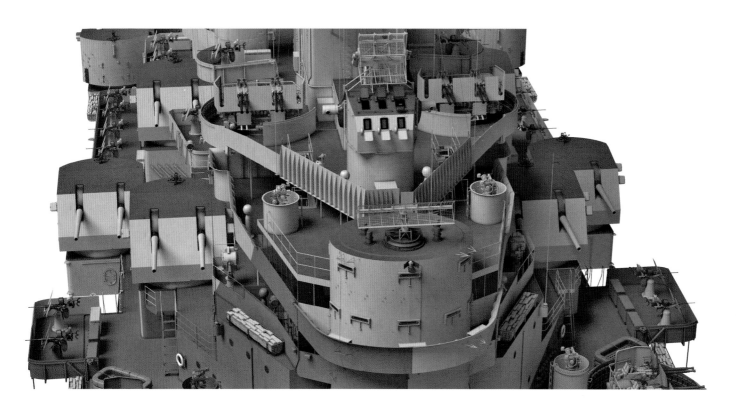

early 1944

early 1944

## SUPERSTRUCTURE, LATE 1944 (1/200 SCALE)

### C1/14 FIRST SUPERSTRUCTURE DECK LEVEL – PLAN

1  Waterway
2  Mushroom vent
3  Wire cable reel
4  Deck hatch
5  Life rafts
6  Quadruple Bofors mount tub
7  Tie down rod
8  40mm ammunition ring rack
9  40mm ammunition cupola
10 Empty shell chute

11 Bofors director tub
12 Helmets (stowed)
13 Single Oerlikon mount
14 20mm ammunition locker
15 20mm magazine loading frame
16 Spare barrel tube
17 Gas bottles
18 Stokes stretcher
19 Floater net basket
20 Fire plug

21 Spare float for OS2U floatplane
22 Vent hood
23 Screened vent
24 Oil hoses (stowed)
25 Bofors mount no. 43
26 Bofors mount no. 44
27 5in. mount no. 53

28 5in. mount no. 54
29 5in. mount no. 57
30 5in. mount no. 58
31 Secondary artillery director tube
32 Main artillery director tube
33 Vent trunk
34 Fan room

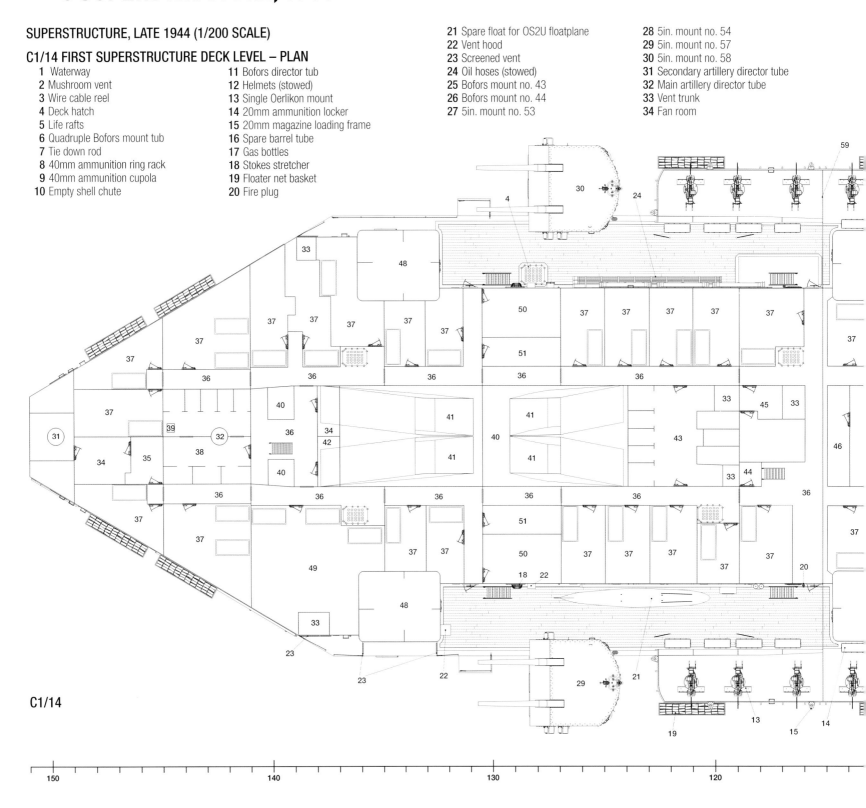

C1/14

143

35 Officer's barber shop
36 Passage
37 Officer's cabin
38 Officer's WC and showers
39 40mm ammunition hoist
40 Air intake
41 Uptake

42 Uptake linen locker
43 Officer's WC, showers and decontamination station
44 Linen locker
45 Radio broadcast station
46 Lighting booth
47 Air conditioning machine room

48 Secondary artillery upper handling room
49 Bunkroom
50 20mm ammunition storage and clipping room
51 Ordnance storage room
52 Captain's stateroom

53 Captain's bathroom
54 Captain's cabin
55 Vestibule
56 Captain's pantry
57 Conning tower armoured tube
58 Storage room
59 Expansion joint

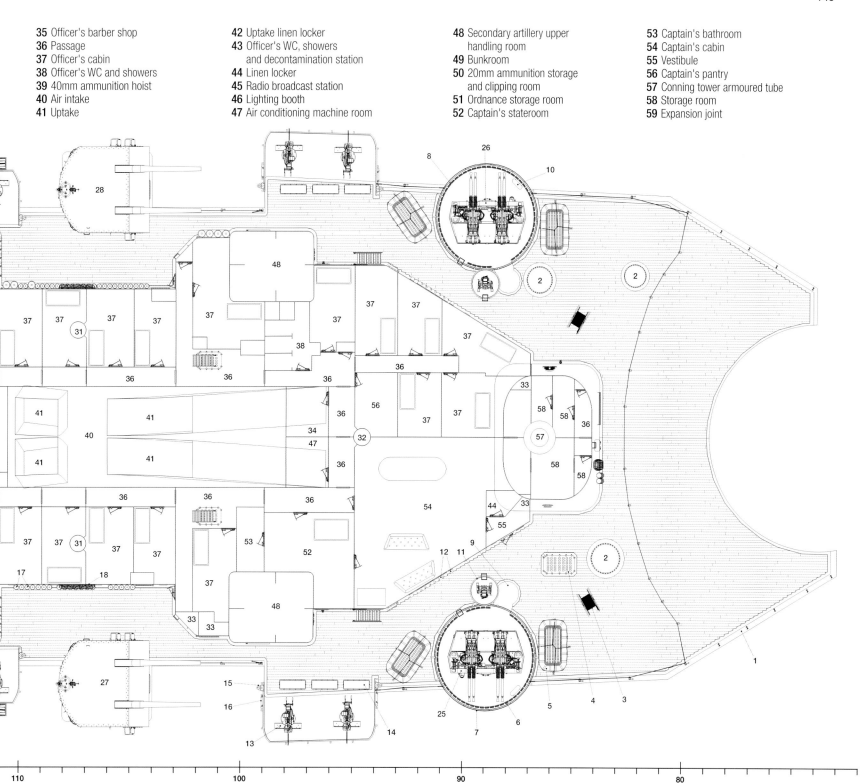

**C SUPERSTRUCTURE, 1944**

SUPERSTRUCTURE, LATE 1944 (1/200 SCALE)

C1/15 FIRST SUPERSTRUCTURE DECK LEVEL – UNDERSIDE OF STARBOARD SIDE OERLIKON TUB AT FRAME 95

C1/16 FIRST SUPERSTRUCTURE DECK LEVEL – UNDERSIDE OF STARBOARD SIDE OERLIKON TUB AT FRAME 115

C1/17 FIRST SUPERSTRUCTURE DECK LEVEL – STARBOARD SIDE ELEVATION FRAGMENT AT FRAME 90 WITH BOFORS GUN TUB OMITTED FOR CLARITY

C1/18 FIRST SUPERSTRUCTURE DECK LEVEL – PORT SIDE ELEVATION FRAGMENT AT FRAME 90 WITH BOFORS GUN TUB OMITTED FOR CLARITY

C1/19 FIRST SUPERSTRUCTURE DECK LEVEL – VIEW FROM FRAME 97 TOWARDS THE STERN, STARBOARD SIDE (PORT SIDE SYMMETRICAL)

C1/20 FIRST SUPERSTRUCTURE DECK LEVEL – VIEW FROM FRAME 103 TOWARDS THE BOW, STARBOARD SIDE

C1/21 FIRST SUPERSTRUCTURE DECK LEVEL – VIEW FROM FRAME 103 TOWARDS THE BOW, PORT SIDE

C1/22 FIRST SUPERSTRUCTURE DECK LEVEL – VIEW FROM FRAME 111 TOWARDS THE STERN, STARBOARD SIDE (PORT SIDE SYMMETRICAL)

C1/23 FIRST SUPERSTRUCTURE DECK LEVEL – VIEW FROM FRAME 115 TOWARDS THE BOW, STARBOARD SIDE (PORT SIDE SYMMETRICAL)

C1/24 FIRST SUPERSTRUCTURE DECK LEVEL – VIEW FROM FRAME 132 TOWARDS THE STERN, STARBOARD SIDE

C1/25 FIRST SUPERSTRUCTURE DECK LEVEL – VIEW FROM FRAME 132 TOWARDS THE STERN, PORT SIDE

C1/26 FIRST SUPERSTRUCTURE DECK LEVEL – VIEW FROM FRAME 136 TOWARDS THE BOW, STARBOARD SIDE

early 1944

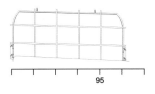

C1/15

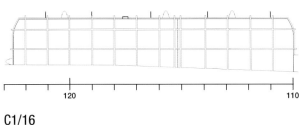

C1/16

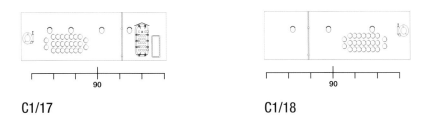

C1/17      C1/18

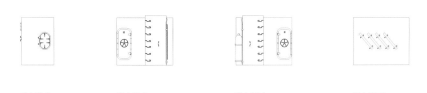

C1/19      C1/20      C1/21      C1/22

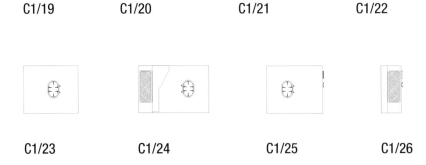

C1/23      C1/24      C1/25      C1/26

early 1944

early 1944

## SUPERSTRUCTURE, LATE 1944 (1/200 SCALE)

### C1/27 SECOND SUPERSTRUCTURE DECK LEVEL – PLAN

1 Ladder rung
2 Antenna outrigger
3 Antenna lead-in
4 Screened vent
5 Whip antenna
6 Drain pipe
7 Fire plug
8 Gas bottles
9 Vertical ladder
10 Oil hoses (stowed)
11 Hose reel
12 Life rafts
13 Single Oerlikon mount
14 20mm ammunition locker
15 20mm magazine loading frame

16 Spare barrel tube
17 Floater net basket
18 Stokes stretcher
19 Phone box
20 Hand rail
21 Ship's bell
22 Secondary artillery director foundation
23 Step up
24 Empty shell bin
25 Waterway
26 Bofors mount no. 413
27 Bofors mount no. 414
28 5in. mount no. 51
29 5in. mount no. 52
30 5in. mount no. 55
31 5in. mount no. 56
32 5in. mount no. 59
33 5in. mount no. 510

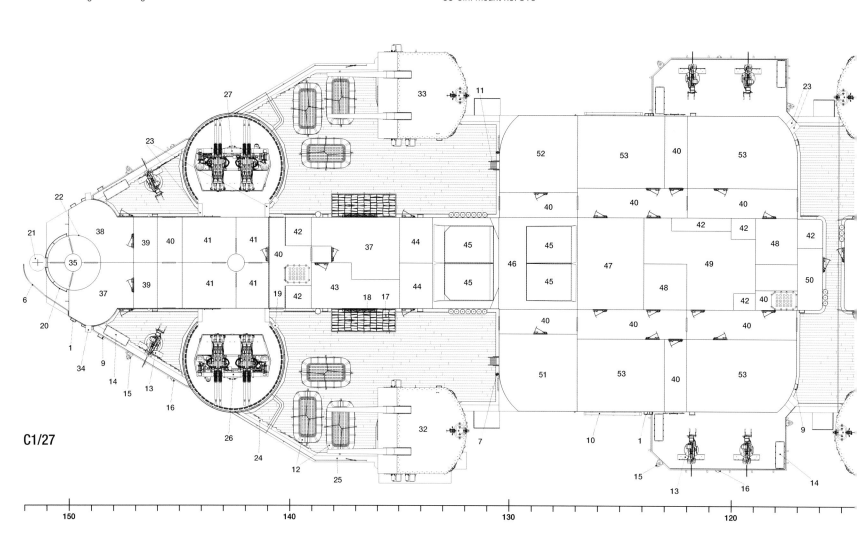

C1/27

**34** Vent hood
**35** Secondary artillery director tube
**36** Main artillery director tube
**37** Radio room
**38** Optical shop
**39** Film locker
**40** Passage
**41** 40mm ammunition storage
**42** Vent trunk
**43** Radar room
**44** Storage room
**45** Uptake
**46** Air intake
**47** Battery charging station
**48** 20mm ammunition storage
**49** Repair shop
**50** Crew's WC and showers
**51** Radar repair shop

**52** Fire control shop
**53** Classroom
**54** Gun repair locker
**55** Photo lab
**56** Officer's cabin
**57** Admiral's pantry
**58** Lobby
**59** Chief of staff's stateroom
**60** Bathroom
**61** Admiral's cabin
**62** Chief of staff's cabin
**63** Chart house
**64** Admiral's stateroom
**65** Conning tower armoured tube
**66** Plenum chamber

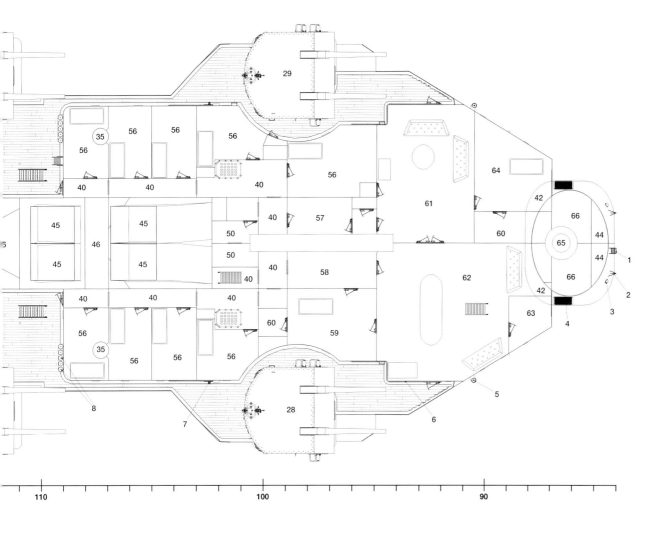

# C SUPERSTRUCTURE, 1944

SUPERSTRUCTURE, LATE 1944 (1/200 SCALE)

C1/28 SECOND SUPERSTRUCTURE DECK LEVEL – UNDERSIDE
OF STARBOARD SIDE OERLIKON TUB AT FRAME 120

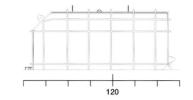

C1/28

120

## C1/29 FLAG BRIDGE LEVEL – PLAN

1 Peep hole
2 Drain pipe
3 Window wiper motor
4 Floater net basket
5 Metal grating
6 12in. signal lamp
7 Support stanchion
8 Waterway
9 Escape scuttle
10 Flag bag
11 24in. searchlight
12 Pelorus
13 Locker
14 Fire hose rack
15 Fire plug
16 Screened vent
17 Secondary artillery director tube
18 Single Oerlikon mount
19 20mm ammunition locker
20 Vertical ladder

21 Spare barrel tube
22 Antenna trunk
23 Step
24 Vent hood
25 Helmets (stowed)
26 Ladder rung
27 Empty shell chute
28 Empty shell bin
29 Quadruple Bofors mount tub
30 Tie down rod
31 40mm ammunition ring rack
32 Support beam
33 Drill ammunition locker
34 Hatch
35 Painted safety line

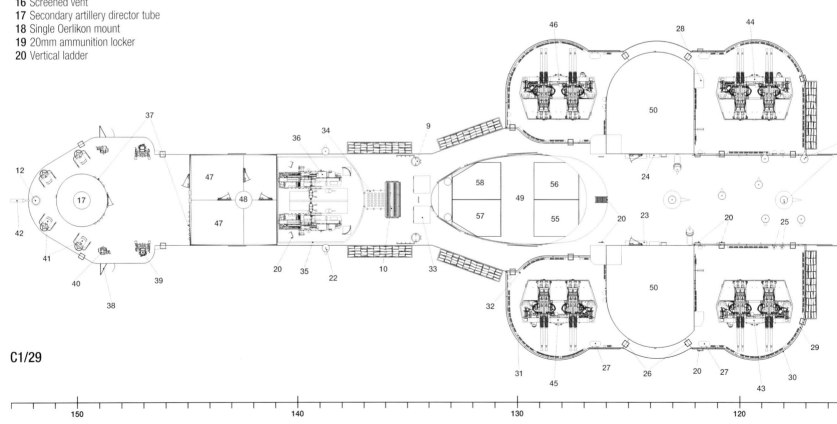

C1/29

150     140     130     120

149

36 Twin 5in. practice loading machine
37 Electrical switches
38 Antenna outrigger
39 Mk51 director
40 Target designator
41 Sky lookout
42 Speed light
43 Bofors mount no. 47
44 Bofors mount no. 48
45 Bofors mount no. 411
46 Bofors mount no. 412
47 Radar room
48 Main artillery director tube
49 Air intake
50 40mm ammunition magazine and handling room

51 Flue boiler no. 1
52 Flue boiler no. 2
53 Flue boiler no. 3
54 Flue boiler no. 4
55 Flue boiler no. 5
56 Flue boiler no. 6
57 Flue boiler no. 7
58 Flue boiler no. 8
59 Crew's WC
60 Vent
61 Passage
62 Signal shelter
63 Storage room
64 Classroom
65 40mm ammunition hoist
66 Flag radio room
67 Flag conning
68 Conning tower tube
69 Captain's chair

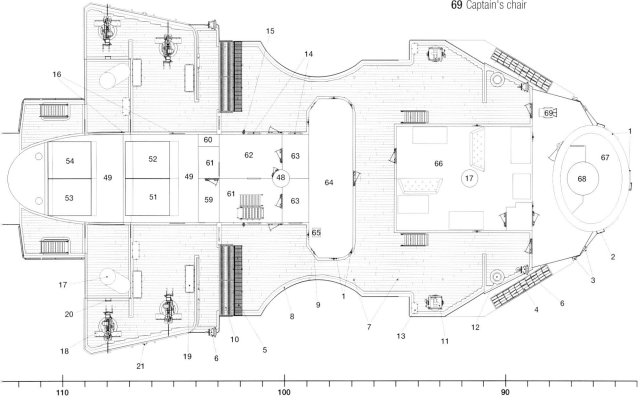

**C SUPERSTRUCTURE, 1944**

SUPERSTRUCTURE, LATE 1944 (1/200 SCALE)

C1/30 FLAG BRIDGE TO NAVIGATING BRIDGE LEVEL – VIEW FROM FRAME 102 TOWARDS THE STERN, STARBOARD SIDE

C1/31 FLAG BRIDGE LEVEL TO CAP OF FUNNEL NO. 1 – VIEW FROM FRAME 115 TOWARDS THE BOW

C1/32 AMIDSHIPS BOFORS GUN TUBS – VIEW FROM THE CENTRE LINE TOWARDS STARBOARD SIDE

C1/33 AMIDSHIPS BOFORS GUN TUBS – FRONT VIEW

C1/34 AMIDSHIPS BOFORS GUN TUBS – BACK VIEW

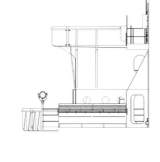

C1/30

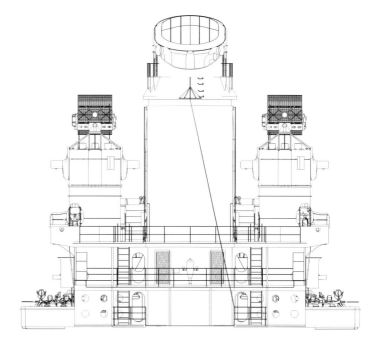

C1/31

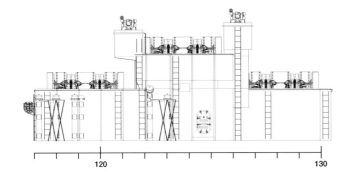

C1/32

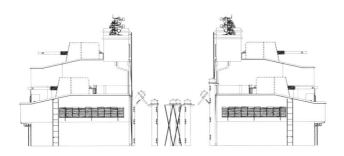

C1/33

C1/34

C1/35 FUNNEL NO. 2 – RIGHT PROFILE (FRAGMENT)
C1/36 FUNNEL NO. 2 – FRONT VIEW
C1/37 FUNNEL NO. 2 – BACK VIEW
C1/38 AFT DIRECTOR TOWER – FRONT VIEW
C1/39 AFT DIRECTOR TOWER – BACK VIEW

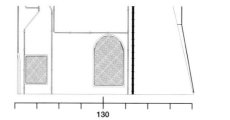

C1/35

130

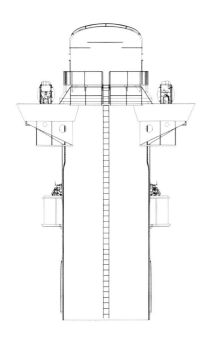

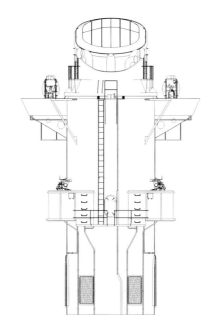

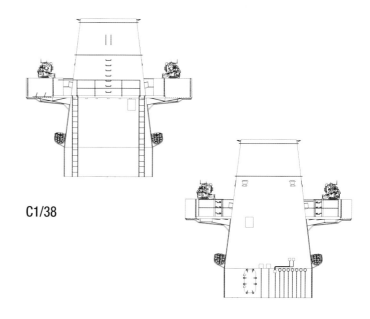

C1/38

C1/36

C1/37

C1/39

early 1944

**SUPERSTRUCTURE, LATE 1944 (1/200 SCALE)**

**C1/40 NAVIGATING BRIDGE LEVEL, FRAMES 83–115 – PLAN**

1 Antenna outrigger
2 Portable windshield
3 Peep hole
4 Side light
5 Fairlead for signal halyards
6 Support stanchion
7 Fire plug
8 Pelorus
9 Hinged searchlight service platform
10 Compass
11 Screened vent
12 Secondary artillery director tube
13 Flue boiler no. 1
14 Flue boiler no. 2

15 Flue boiler no. 3
16 Flue boiler no. 4
17 Air intake
18 Crew's WC
19 Passage
20 40mm ammunition hoist
21 Radar room
22 Storage room
23 Navigator's sea cabin
24 Charthouse
25 Captain's sea cabin
26 Aerological lab
27 Light lock
28 Ship conning station
29 Pilot house
30 Armoured conning tower

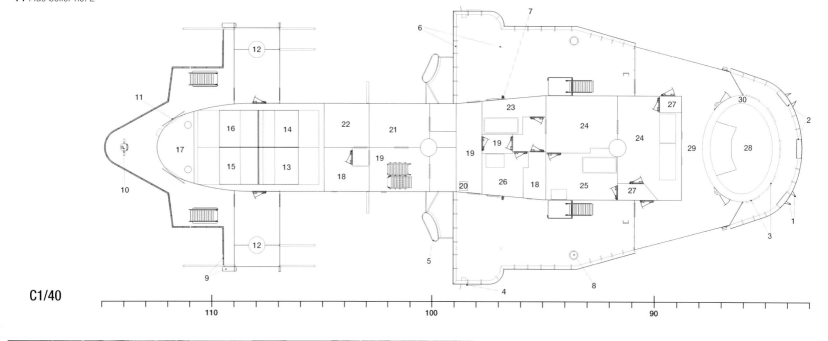

C1/40

early 1944

## C1/41 NAVIGATING BRIDGE LEVEL, FRAMES 120–127 – PLAN

**1** Empty shell scuttle
**2** Helmets (stowed)
**3** Mk51 director
**4** Bofors mount no. 49
**5** Bofors mount no. 410

## C1/42 NAVIGATING BRIDGE LEVEL, FRAMES 140–145 – PLAN

## C1/43 PILOT HOUSE TOP LOWER LEVEL – PLAN

**1** Mk51 director
**2** Mk37 director foundation
**3** Whip antenna
**4** Support stanchion
**5** Armoured conning tower
**6** Peep hole
**7** Masthead light
**8** Antenna outrigger
**9** Fire control station

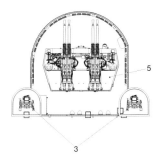
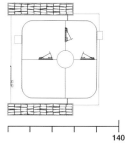
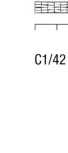

**C1/42**

140

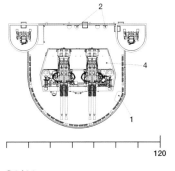

**C1/41**

120

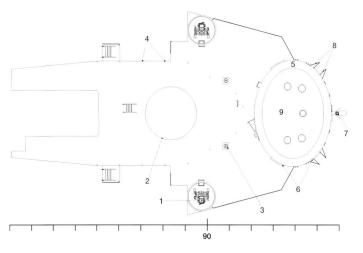

**C1/43**

90

early 1944

**SUPERSTRUCTURE, LATE 1944 (1/200 SCALE)**

**C1/44 PILOT HOUSE TOP LEVEL, FRAMES 84–113 – PLAN**
1 Mk40 director
2 Mk3 (FC) radar antenna
3 Conning tower armoured roof
4 Pelorus
5 Target designator
6 Chart table
7 Pennant locker
8 Halyard tie rod
9 Fire plug
10 Single Oerlikon mount
11 Foot and hand rail
12 Mk37 director foundation
13 36in. searchlight
14 Bofors mount no. 45
15 Bofors mount no. 46
16 Flue boiler no. 1
17 Flue boiler no. 2
18 Flue boiler no. 3
19 Flue boiler no. 4
20 Officer's cabin
21 Passage
22 Radar room
23 40mm ammunition
   storage room
24 Secondary artillery
   director tube
25 Main artillery director tube
26 40mm ammunition hoist
27 Fighting lights

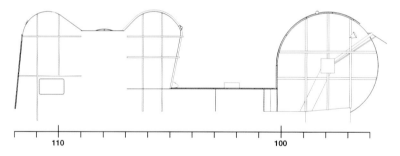

C1/44

**C1/45 PILOT HOUSE TOP LEVEL, FRAMES 94–113 – UNDERSIDE (FRAGMENT)**

**C1/46 PILOT HOUSE TOP LEVEL, FRAMES 126–135 – PLAN**
1 Mk51 director
2 Phone box
3 Vertical ladder
4 Flue boiler no. 5
5 Flue boiler no. 6
6 Flue boiler no. 7
7 Flue boiler no. 8

C1/45

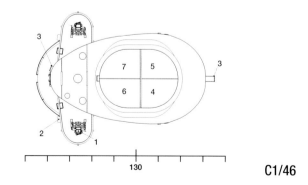

C1/46

## C1/47 PILOT HOUSE TOP LEVEL, FRAMES 139–144 – PLAN

**1** Mk 51 director
**2** Antenna outrigger
**3** 12in. signal lamp
**4** Phone box
**5** Hand and foot rail
**6** Peep hole
**7** Hatch
**8** Main artillery director tube
**9** After surface lookout

## C1/48 FIRST LEVEL ABOVE PILOT HOUSE TOP – PLAN

**1** Radio direction finder loop
**2** Antenna lead-in
**3** Crew's WC
**4** Passage
**5** Radar room
**6** Storage room
**7** Main artillery director tube

## C1/49 SECOND LEVEL ABOVE PILOT HOUSE TOP, FRAMES 99–112 – PLAN

**1** Ship's bell
**2** Ladder rung
**3** Drain pipe
**4** Steam pipe
**5** Officer's cabin
**6** Passage
**7** Radar room

## C1/50 SECOND LEVEL ABOVE PILOT HOUSE TOP, FRAMES 127–135 – PLAN

**1** Hatch
**2** 36in. searchlight
**3** Mainmast foundation

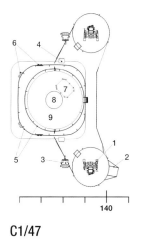

C1/47

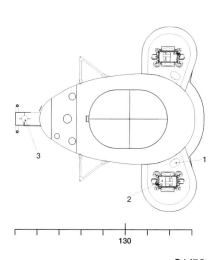

C1/50

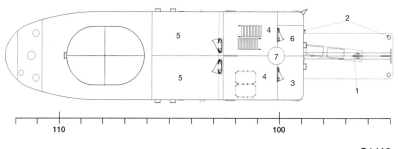

C1/48

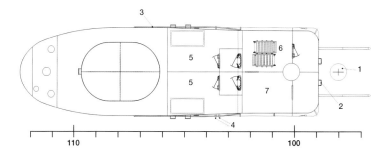

early 1944

C1/49

**C SUPERSTRUCTURE, 1944**

## SUPERSTRUCTURE, LATE 1944 (1/200 SCALE)

### C1/51 PRIMARY CONNING STATION LEVEL – PLAN
1 Wind deflector
2 Chart table
3 Target designator
4 Pelorus
5 Steam pipes
6 Walkway
7 Handrails
8 Outrigger
9 Officer's WC
10 Passage
11 Captain's sea cabin
12 Charthouse
13 Steering station
14 Main artillery director tube
15 Cap of funnel no. 1

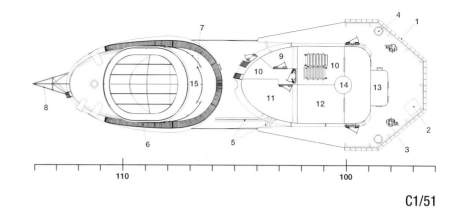

C1/51

### C1/52 PRIMARY CONNING STATION LEVEL – UNDERSIDE (FRAGMENT)

### C1/53 CAP OF FUNNEL NO. 2 – PLAN

### C1/54  PRIMARY CONNING STATION LEVEL UPWARDS – VIEW FROM FRAME 105 TOWARDS THE BOW

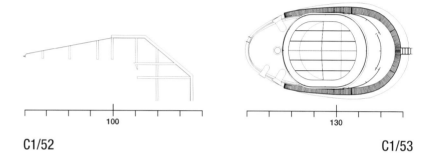

C1/52

C1/53

### C1/55 FORWARD SURFACE LOOKOUT STATION LEVEL – PLAN
1 Peep hole
2 Radio room
3 Forward surface lookout station
4 Main artillery director tube

### C1/56 WHISTLE AND SIREN PLATFORM LEVEL – PLAN
1 SG radar antenna
2 BK antenna
3 Range light
4 Siren
5 Small whistle
6 Whip antenna
7 Foundation of foremast
8 Large whistle
9 Brace
10 Passage
11 Radar room
12 Main artillery director tube
13 TDY antenna (fitted in the second half of 1944)

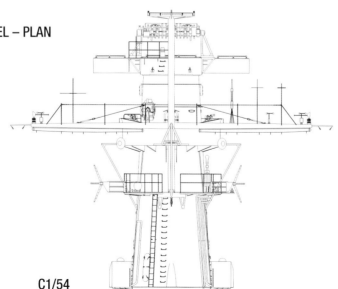
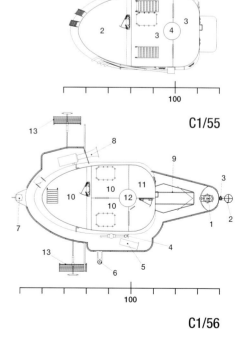

C1/54

C1/55

C1/56

## C1/57 WHISTLE AND SIREN PLATFORM LEVEL – UNDERSIDE

## C1/58 FORWARD AIR DEFENCE STATION – PLAN
  **1** Wind baffle
  **2** Target designator
  **3** Sky lookout
  **4** Outrigger for mast's forestay
  **5** Outrigger for mast's backstay
  **6** Phone box
  **7** 24in. searchlight on a platform
  **8** Peep hole
  **9** Yardarm
  **10** Yardarm stay
  **11** TBS antenna
  **12** Wind indicator
  **13** BK antenna
  **14** Outrigger
  **15** Yard blinker light
  **16** Lookout station
  **17** Hatch
  **18** Antenna outrigger
  **19** Fighting lights
  **20** Foot and hand rail
  **21** AS-56 antenna

## C1/59 FORWARD AIR DEFENCE STATION – UNDERSIDE (FRAGMENT)
  **1** Drain pipe
  **2** AS-37 antenna

## C1/60 SK RADAR SERVICE PLATFORM ON TOP OF FOREMAST – PLAN
  **1** SK radar foundation
  **2** Jacob's ladder

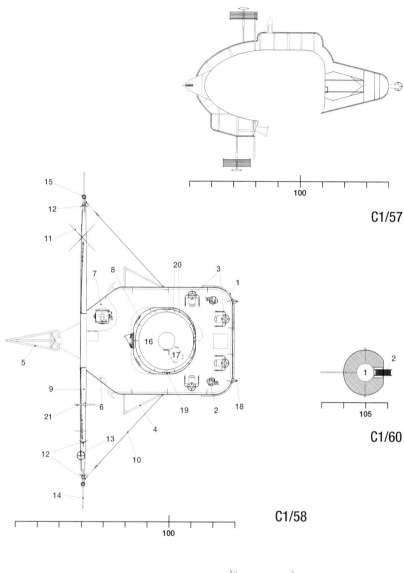

C1/57

C1/60

C1/58

early 1944

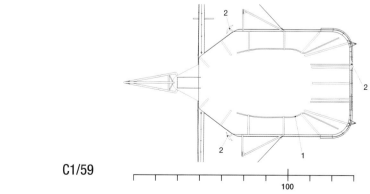

C1/59

## SUPERSTRUCTURE, LATE 1944 (1/200 SCALE)

### C1/61 MAINMAST – PLAN
1 BK antenna
2 TBS antenna
3 Blinker light
4 SG radar antenna

### C1/62 MAINMAST – BACK VIEW
1 Wave guide
2 Support brace

### C1/63 MAIN DECK HOUSE IN FRONT OF BARBETTE NO. 2 – RIGHT PROFILE
### C1/64 MAIN DECK HOUSE IN FRONT OF BARBETTE NO. 2 – LEFT PROFILE
### C1/65 MAIN DECK HOUSE IN FRONT OF BARBETTE NO. 2 – FRONT VIEW

### C1/66 MAIN DECK HOUSE IN FRONT OF BARBETTE NO. 2 – PLAN
1 20mm ammunition clipping room
2 Passage
3 Vent trunk
4 Hose reel
5 Fire plug
6 Locker

### C1/67 ROOF OF MAIN DECK HOUSE IN FRONT OF BARBETTE NO. 2 – PLAN
1 Vent
2 Life rafts

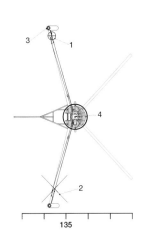
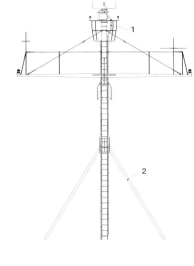

C1/61

135

C1/62

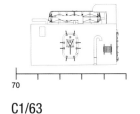

C1/63

C1/64

70

70

C1/65

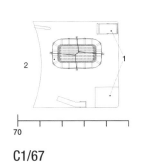

C1/66

70

C1/67

70

early 1944

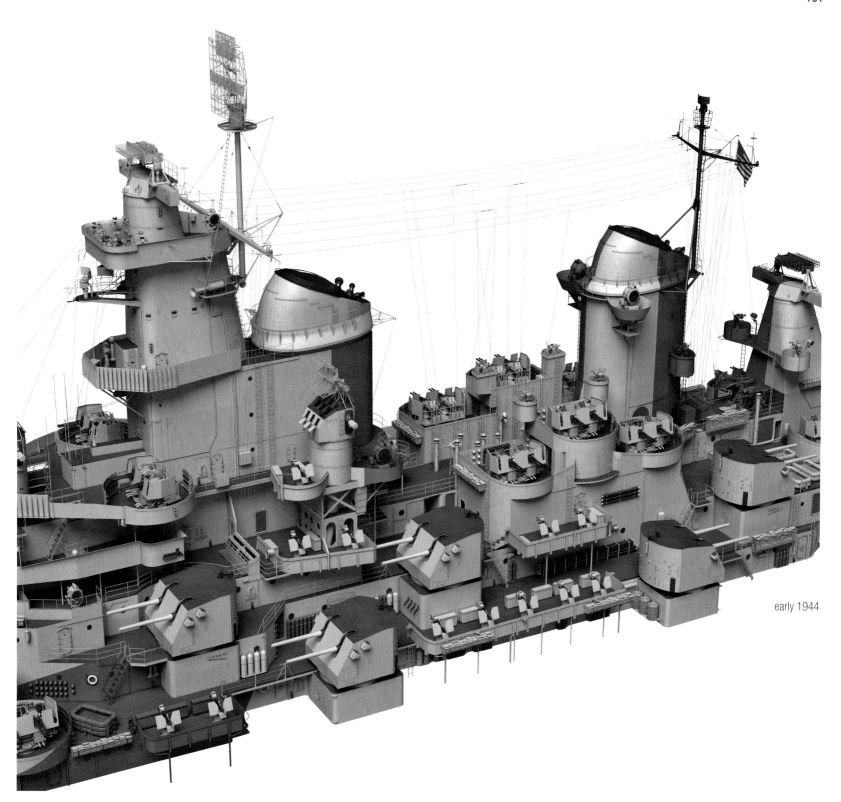

early 1944

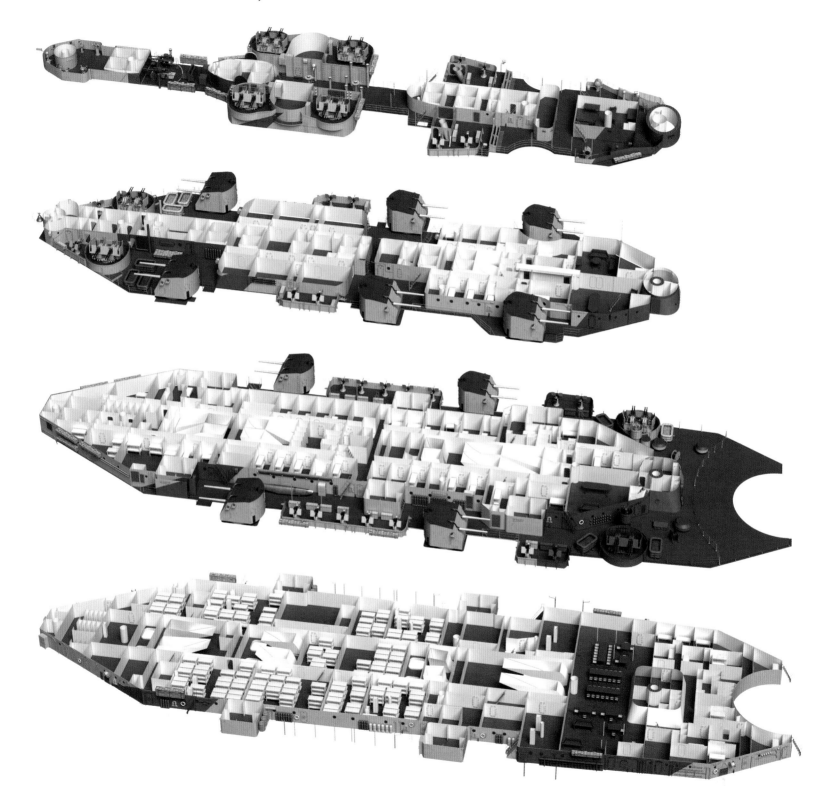

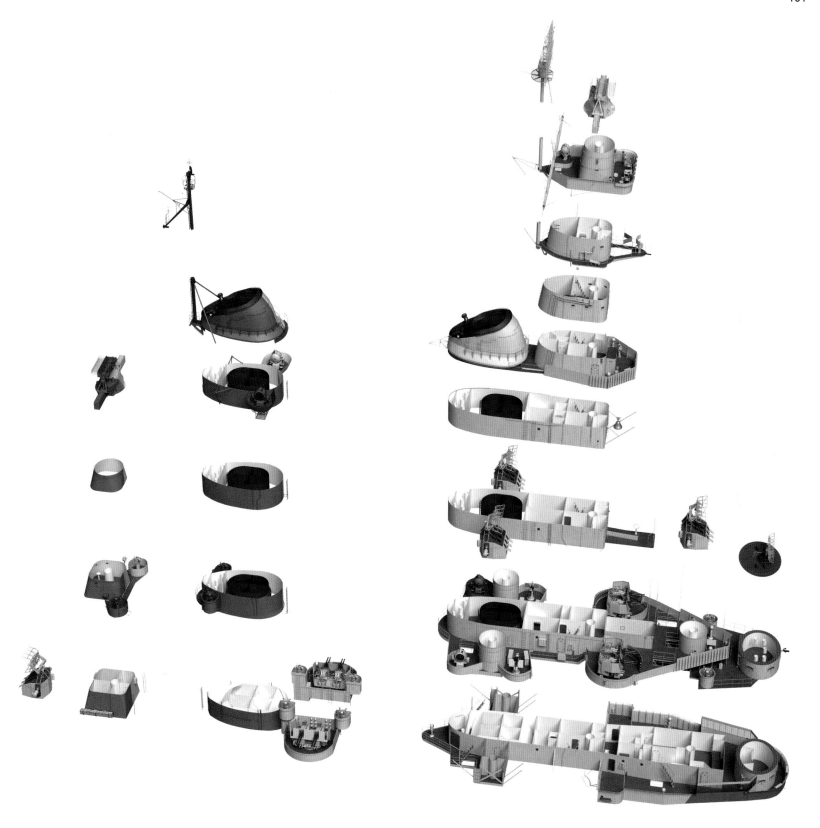

SUPERSTRUCTURE, EARLY 1943 (1/200 SCALE)

ARROWS MARK AREAS MODIFIED BEFORE
THE BATTLESHIP'S DEPLOYMENT TO THE PACIFIC IN EARLY 1944

C2/1 RIGHT PROFILE (FRAGMENTS), 5IN. MOUNTS OMITTED
FOR CLARITY

C2/2 FRONT VIEW (FRAGMENT)

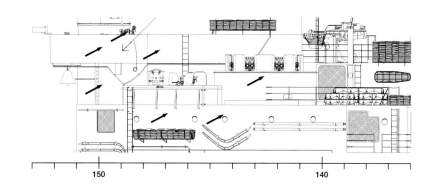

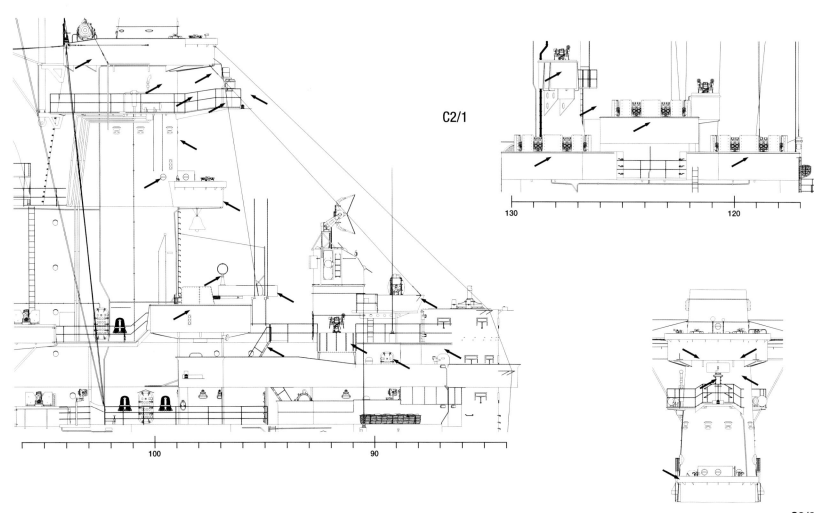

C2/1

C2/2

C2/3 FLAG BRIDGE LEVEL – PLAN (FRAGMENT)
C2/4 NAVIGATING BRIDGE LEVEL – PLAN (FRAGMENT)
C2/5 PILOT HOUSE TOP LEVEL – PLAN (FRAGMENTS)
C2/6 PRIMARY CONNING STATION LEVEL – PLAN (FRAGMENT)

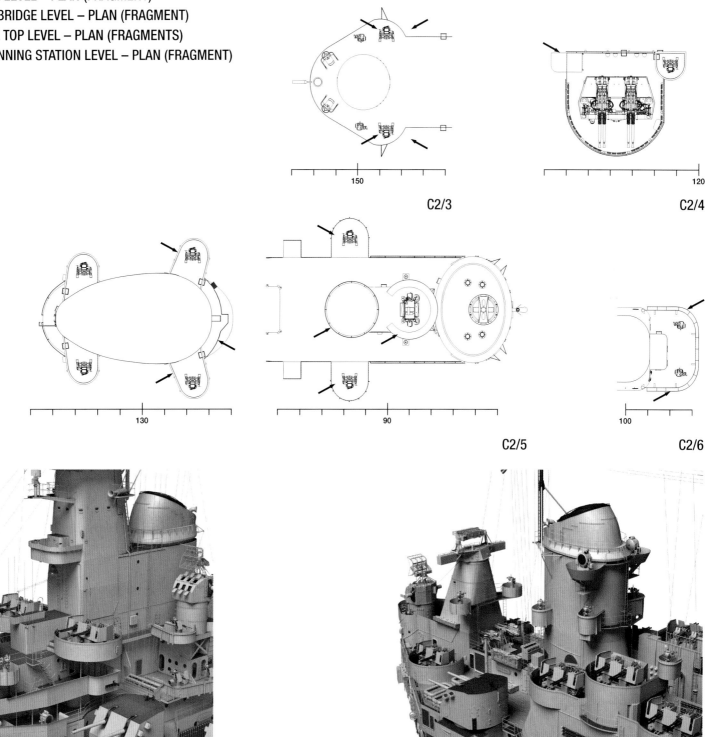

150

C2/3

120

C2/4

130

90

100

C2/5

C2/6

early 1943

**C SUPERSTRUCTURE MODIFICATIONS, 1943–1958**

SUPERSTRUCTURE, MID 1945 (1/200 SCALE)

ARROWS MARK AREAS MODIFIED DURING THE BATTLESHIP'S REFIT
IN EARLY 1945

C2/7 RIGHT PROFILE (FRAGMENTS),
5IN. MOUNTS OMITTED FOR CLARITY

C2/7

## C2/8 FRONT VIEW (FRAGMENT)

**1** Mk13 radar antenna (fitted in early 1945)
**2** TDY antenna (fitted in early 1945)
**3** ECM antenna (fitted in early 1945)
**4** Mk12/22 radar antennas (fitted in early 1945 on all Mk37 directors)

## C2/9 FIRST SUPERSTRUCTURE DECK LEVEL – PLAN (FRAGMENT)

**1** ECM antenna radome (1945–1949)

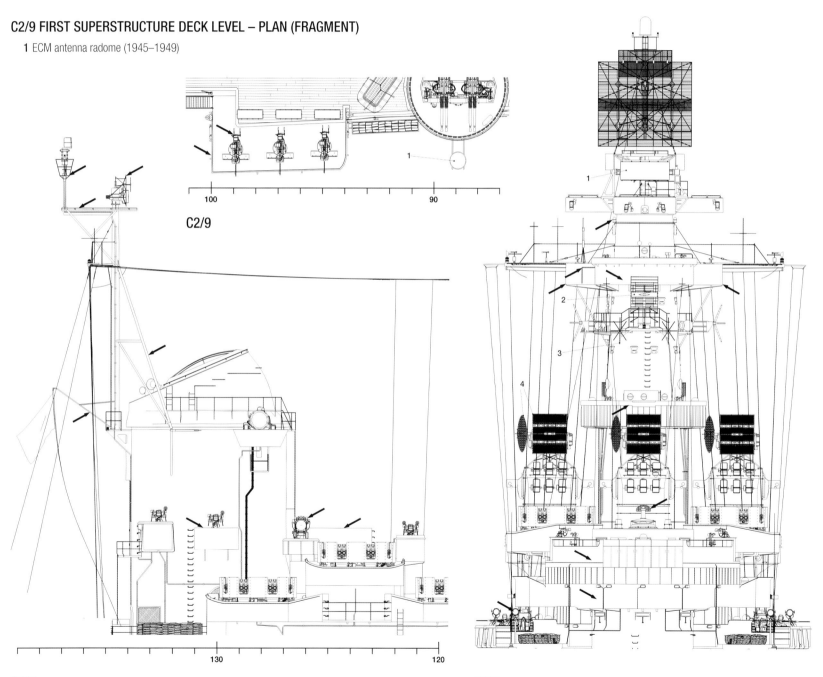

C2/9

C2/7

C2/8

SUPERSTRUCTURE, MID 1945 (1/200 SCALE)

ARROWS MARK AREAS MODIFIED DURING THE BATTLESHIP'S REFIT
IN EARLY 1945

C2/10 FLAG BRIDGE LEVEL – PLAN (FRAGMENT)
C2/11 NAVIGATING BRIDGE LEVEL – PLAN (FRAGMENT)
   1 Mk57 director (fitted in early 1945)
   2 Mk51 director (moved to a new platform in early 1945)
   3 Structure with observation platform on top (added in early 1945)

C2/12 CENTRE LINE STRUCTURE BETWEEN FRAMES 122 AND 126,
FLAG BRIDGE LEVEL UPWARDS – FRONT VIEW
C2/13 NAVIGATING BRIDGE LEVEL – UNDERSIDE (FRAGMENT)
C2/14 PILOT HOUSE TOP LEVEL – PLAN (FRAGMENT)
   1 Mk27 radar antenna (fitted in early 1945)

C2/15 FORWARD AIR DEFENCE STATION – PLAN (FRAGMENT)
   1 AS-56 antenna (fitted in early 1945)

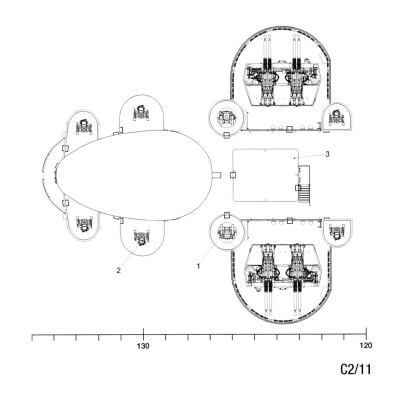

C2/11

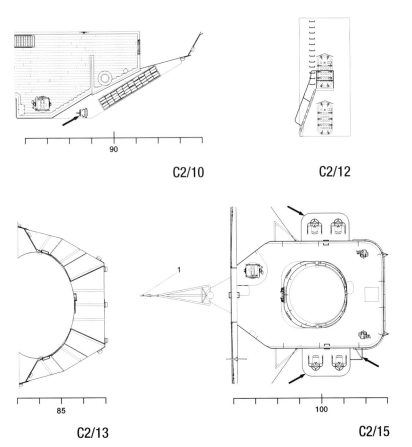

C2/10

C2/12

C2/13

C2/15

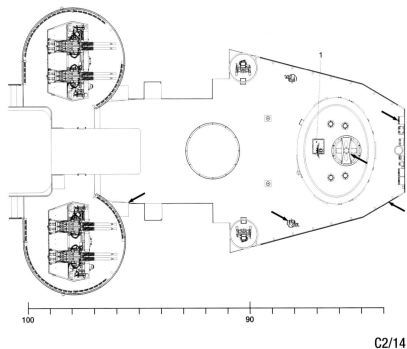

C2/14

## C2/16 RADAR SERVICE PLATFORM ON TOP OF FOREMAST – PLAN
**1** SK radar foundation (relocated early 1945)
**2** SU radome (fitted early 1945)
**3** DBA radome (fitted early 1945)

## C2/17 RADAR SERVICE PLATFORM ON TOP OF FOREMAST – BACK VIEW

## C2/18 MAINMAST – PLAN
**1** SR radar (fitted early 1945)
**2** SG radar (relocated early 1945)

## C2/19 MAINMAST – BACK VIEW

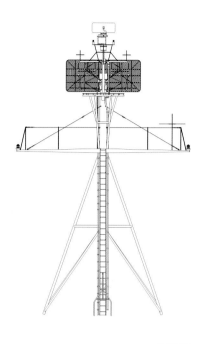

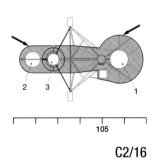

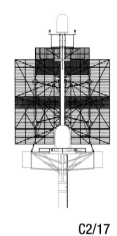

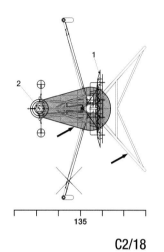

105

135

C2/16

C2/17

C2/18

C2/19

mid-1945

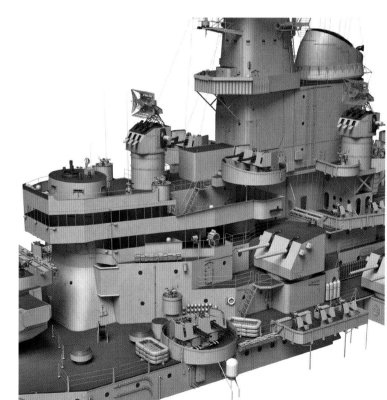

SUPERSTRUCTURE, 1947 (1/200 SCALE)

ARROWS MARK AREAS MODIFIED FROM 1946 TO 1947

C2/20 RIGHT PROFILE (FRAGMENTS)

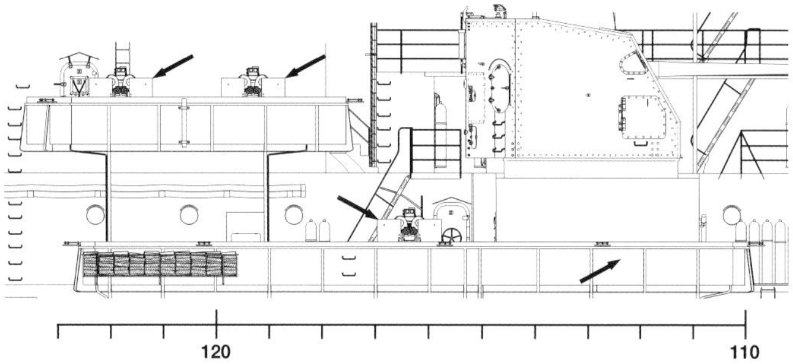

mid-1945

120                                                    110

C2/20

150                        140                        130

C2/20

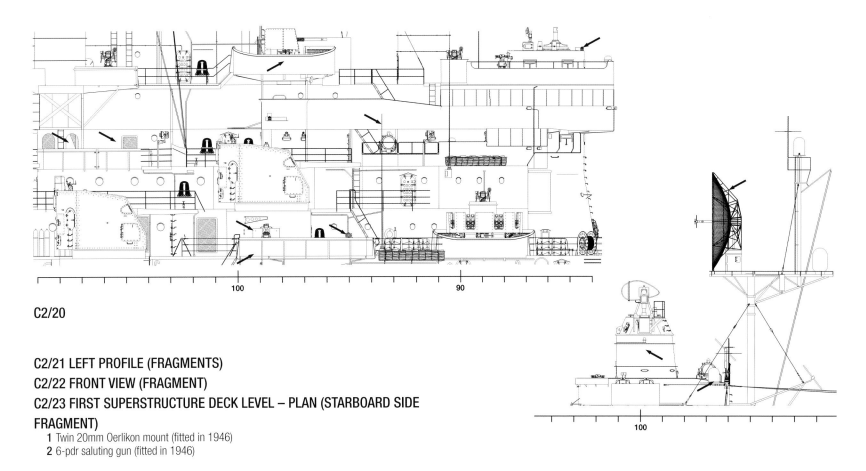

C2/20

**C2/21 LEFT PROFILE (FRAGMENTS)**
**C2/22 FRONT VIEW (FRAGMENT)**
**C2/23 FIRST SUPERSTRUCTURE DECK LEVEL – PLAN (STARBOARD SIDE FRAGMENT)**

**1** Twin 20mm Oerlikon mount (fitted in 1946)
**2** 6-pdr saluting gun (fitted in 1946)

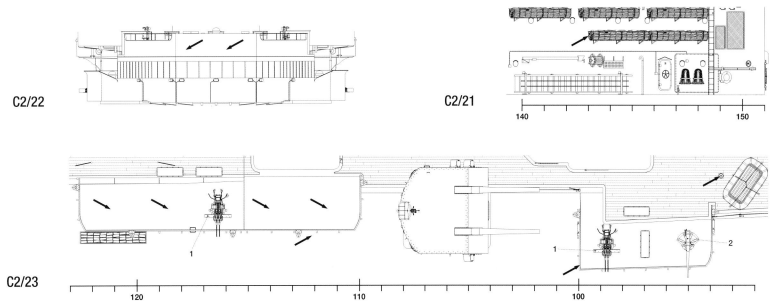

C2/22

C2/21

C2/23

SUPERSTRUCTURE, 1947 (1/200 SCALE)

ARROWS MARK AREAS MODIFIED FROM 1946 TO 1947

**C2/24 SECOND SUPERSTRUCTURE DECK LEVEL – PLAN (STARBOARD SIDE FRAGMENTS)**
  **1** Twin 20mm Oerlikon mount (fitted in 1946)

**C2/25 FLAG BRIDGE LEVEL – PLAN (STARBOARD SIDE FRAGMENT)**

**C2/26 FORWARD AIR DEFENCE STATION AND FOREMAST – BACK VIEW (FRAGMENT)**
  **1** SK-2 radar antenna (fitted in 1946)
  **2** ECM antenna radome (fitted in 1946)

**C2/27 FORWARD AIR DEFENCE STATION AND FOREMAST – PLAN (FRAGMENT)**
  **1** SK-2 radar antenna (fitted in 1946)
  **2** ECM antenna radome (fitted in 1946)

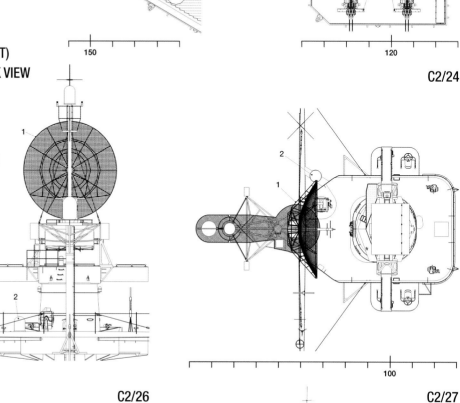

C2/24

C2/26

C2/27

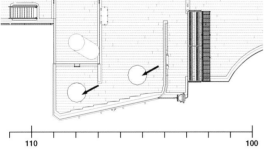

C2/25

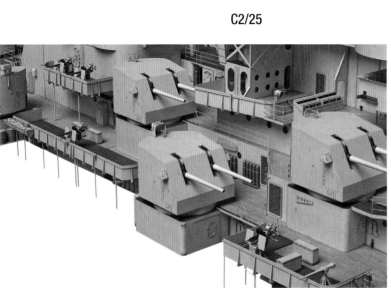

1947

1952

**C SUPERSTRUCTURE MODIFICATIONS, 1943–1958**

SUPERSTRUCTURE, 1952 (1/200 SCALE)

ARROWS MARK AREAS MODIFIED BEFORE THE BATTLESHIP'S
REACTIVATION FOR KOREAN DEPLOYMENT

C2/28 RIGHT PROFILE

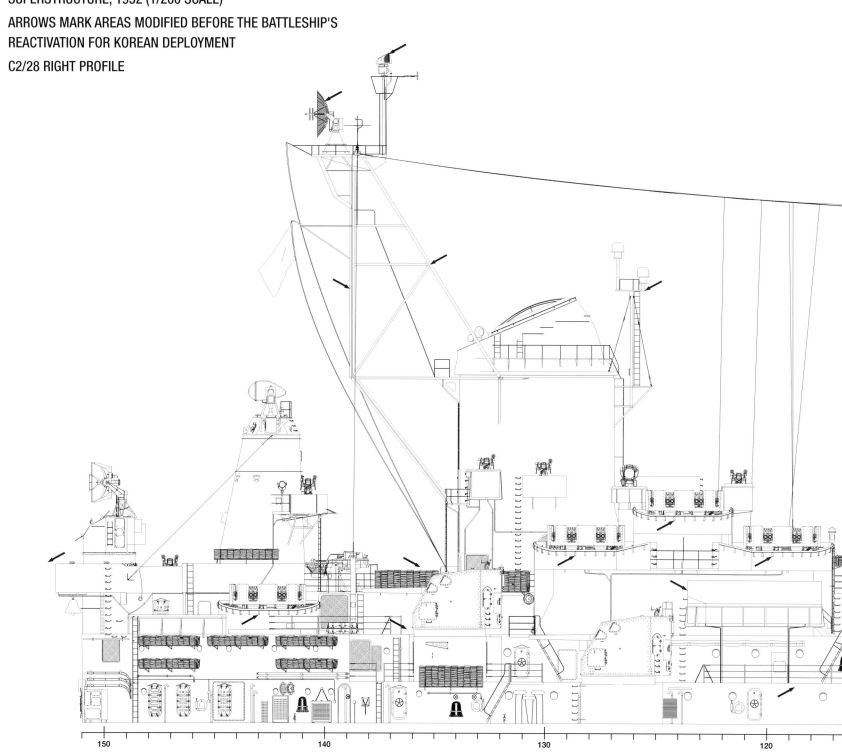

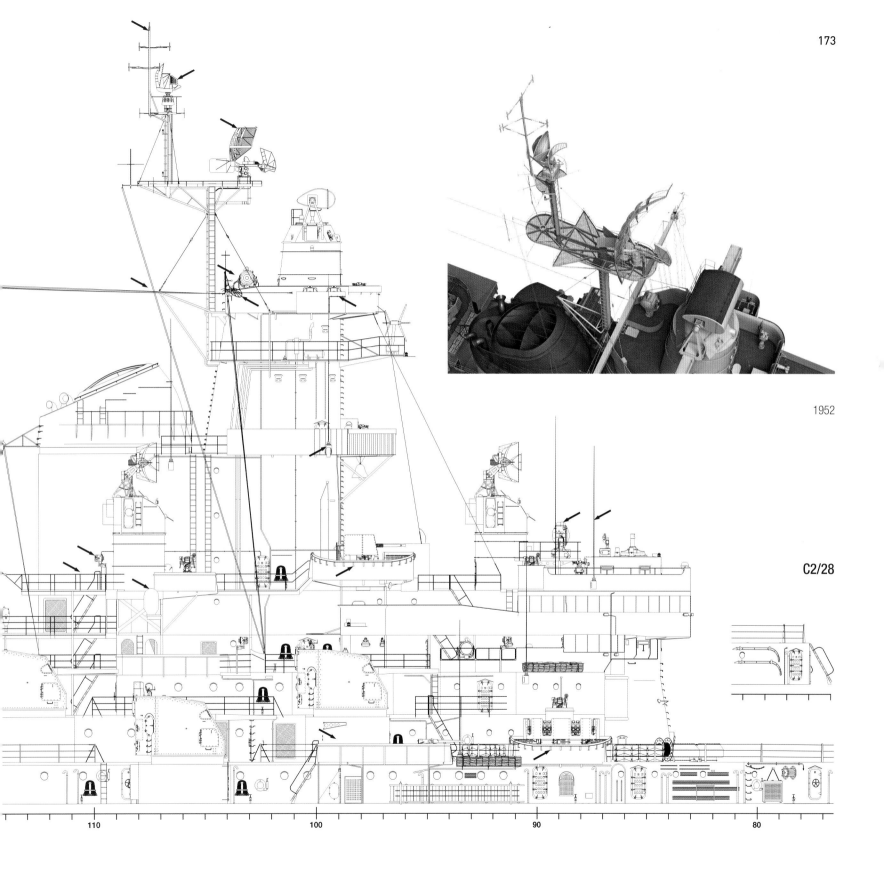

1952

C2/28

SUPERSTRUCTURE, 1952 (1/200 SCALE)

ARROWS MARK AREAS MODIFIED BEFORE THE BATTLESHIP'S REACTIVATION FOR KOREAN DEPLOYMENT

C2/29 FIRST SUPERSTRUCTURE DECK LEVEL – PLAN (STARBOARD SIDE FRAGMENT)

C2/30 FIRST SUPERSTRUCTURE DECK LEVEL – PLAN (PORT SIDE FRAGMENT)

C2/31 SECOND SUPERSTRUCTURE DECK LEVEL – FRONT VIEW (STARBOARD SIDE FRAGMENT)

C2/32 PILOT HOUSE TOP LEVEL – PLAN (FRAGMENTS)

1 ECM antenna radome (fitted in 1951)

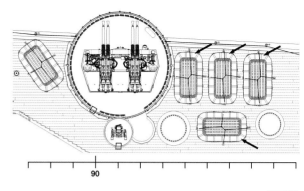

C2/30

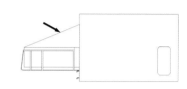

C2/31

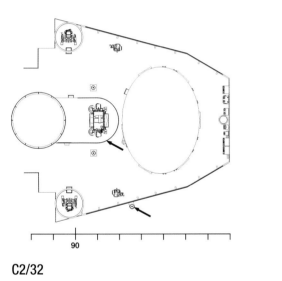

C2/32

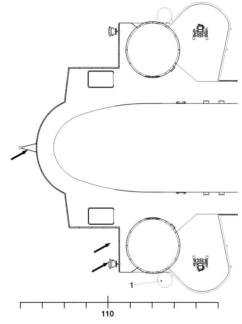

C2/29

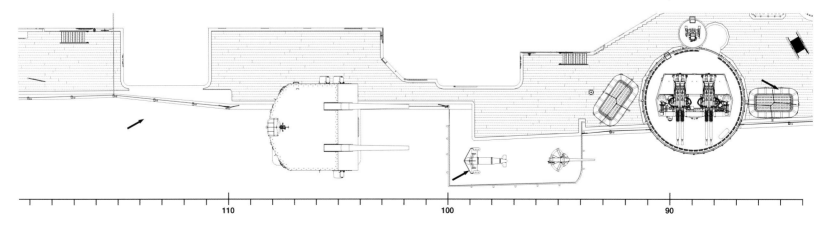

## SUPERSTRUCTURE, 1952 (1/200 SCALE)

## ARROWS MARK AREAS MODIFIED BEFORE THE BATTLESHIP'S REACTIVATION FOR KOREAN DEPLOYMENT

### C2/33 PRIMARY CONNING STATION LEVEL – PLAN
  **1** "Sword" ECM antenna (fitted in 1951)

### C2/34 PRIMARY CONNING STATION LEVEL UPWARDS – FRONT VIEW

### C2/35 FORWARD AIR DEFENCE STATION – PLAN
  **1** "Sword" ECM antenna (fitted in 1951)
  **2** "Derby" ECM antenna (fitted in 1951)

### C2/36 FOREMAST – PLAN

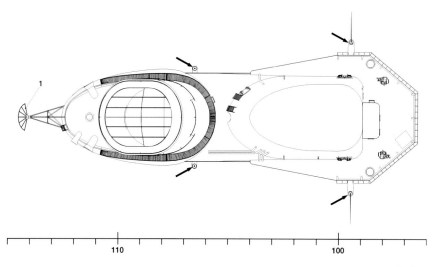

C2/33

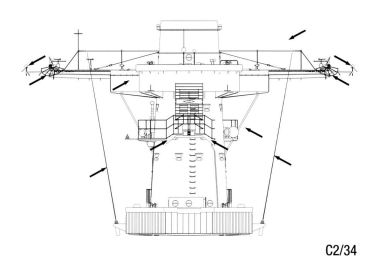

C2/34

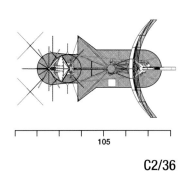

C2/36

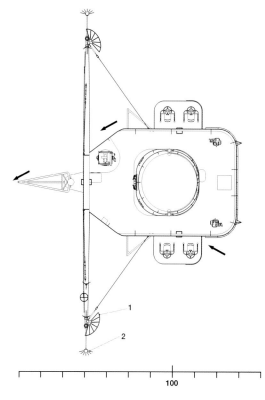

C2/35

SUPERSTRUCTURE, 1952 (1/200 SCALE)

ARROWS MARK AREAS MODIFIED BEFORE THE BATTLESHIP'S
REACTIVATION FOR KOREAN DEPLOYMENT

C2/37 FOREMAST – FRONT VIEW (FRAGMENT)

   **1** SPS-6 radar antenna (fitted in 1951)
   **2** SG-6 radar antenna (fitted in 1948)
   **3** AT-150 TBS antenna (fitted in 1948)

C2/38 FOREMAST – BACK VIEW (FRAGMENT)
C2/39 FUNNEL NO. 2 AND MAINMAST – PLAN

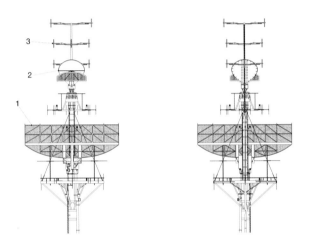

C2/37　　　　　　C2/38

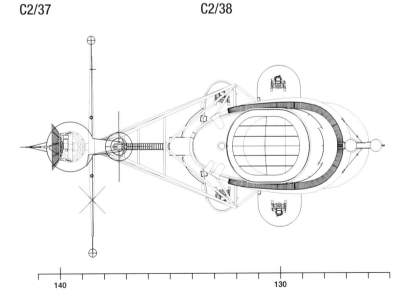

C2/39

C2/40  FUNNEL NO. 2 AND MAINMAST – FRONT VIEW

   **1** SG-1b radar antenna (fitted in 1948)
   **2** AT-150 TBS antenna (fitted in 1948)
   **3** SP radar antenna (fitted in 1948)
   **4** DBM radar direction finder (fitted in 1948)

C2/41  FUNNEL NO. 2 AND MAINMAST – BACK VIEW

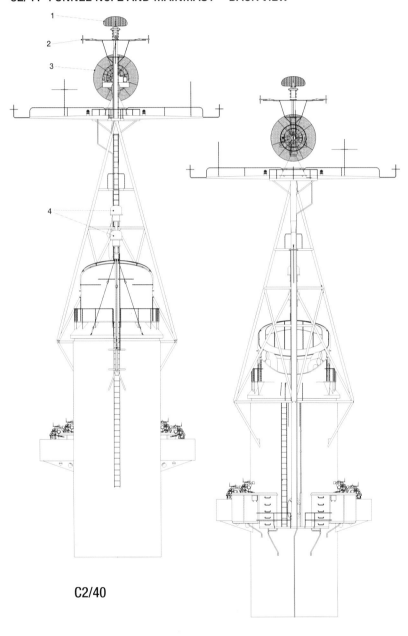

C2/40　　　　　　　　　　　　C2/41

1952

1955

SUPERSTRUCTURE, 1955 (1/200 SCALE)

ARROWS MARK AREAS MODIFIED DURING THE BATTLESHIP'S REFIT
IN LATE 1955

C2/42 RIGHT PROFILE
C2/43 LEFT PROFILE (FRAGMENT)

C2/43

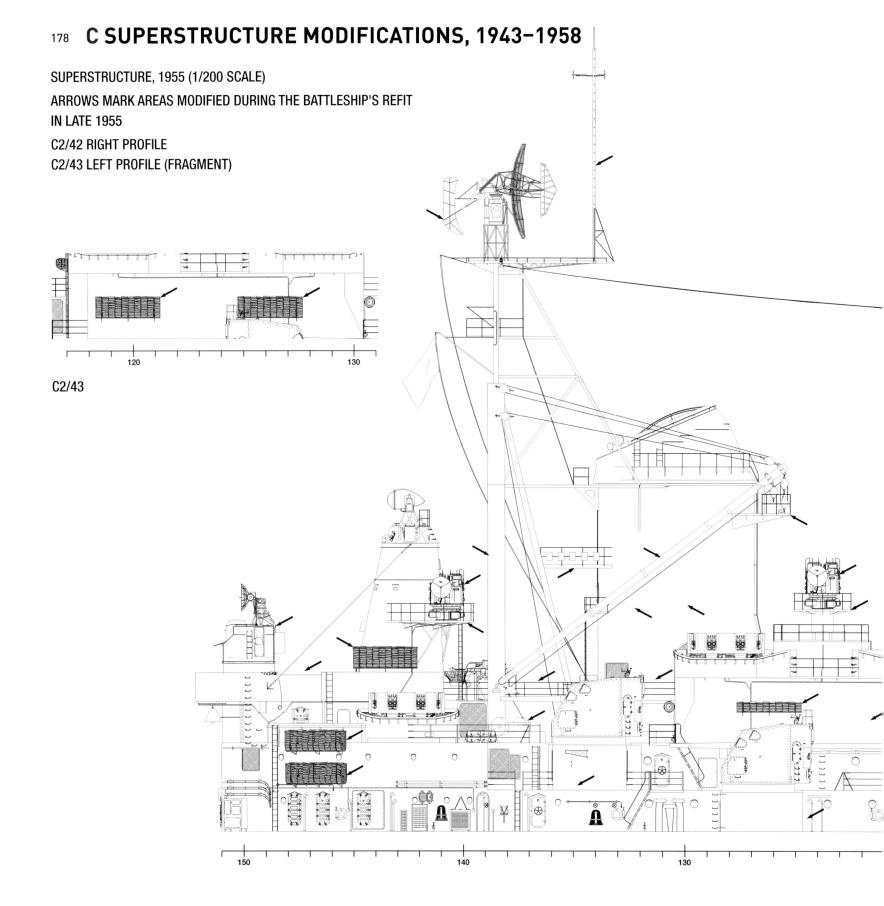

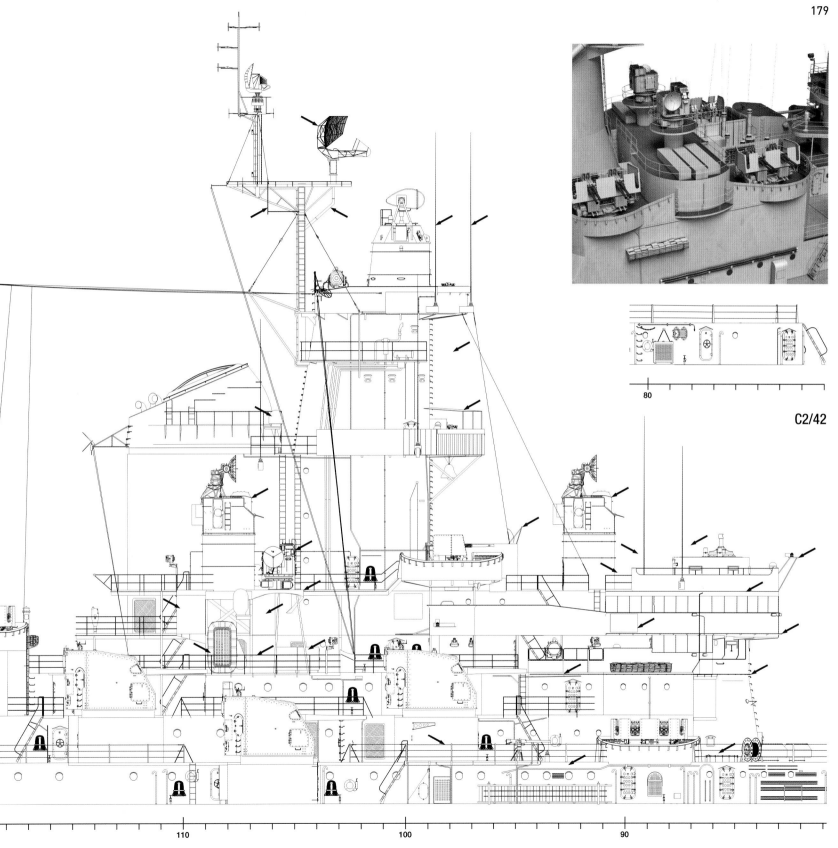

C2/42

80

110                   100                   90

SUPERSTRUCTURE, 1955 (1/200 SCALE)

ARROWS MARK AREAS MODIFIED DURING THE BATTLESHIP'S REFIT IN LATE 1955

**C2/44 SECOND SUPERSTRUCTURE DECK LEVEL – PLAN (STARBOARD SIDE FRAGMENTS)**
  **1** Winch for loading boom

**C2/45 FLAG BRIDGE LEVEL – PLAN (FRAGMENTS)**
  **1** New form of Mk37 director with Mk25 radar antenna (fitted in 1955)

**C2/46 NAVIGATING BRIDGE LEVEL – PLAN (FRAGMENTS)**
  **1** Mk 56 director (fitted in 1955)

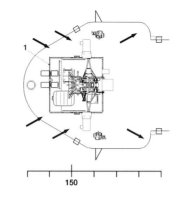

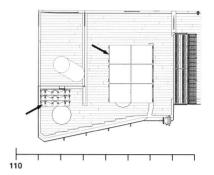

C2/45

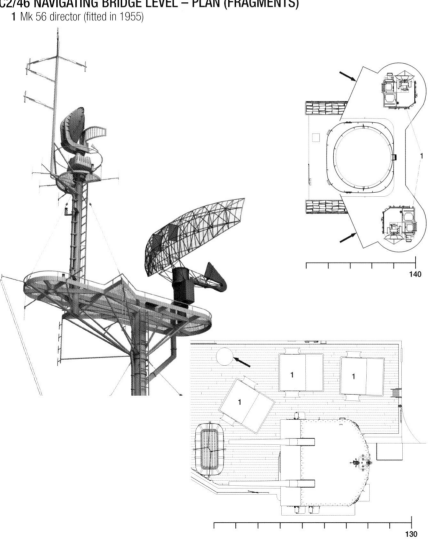

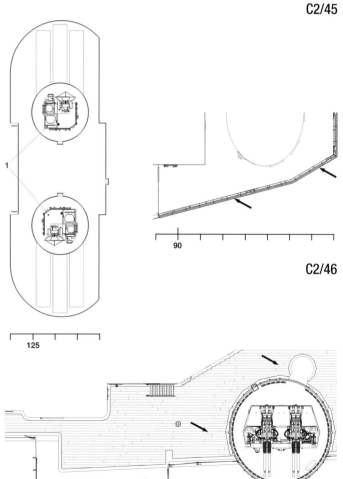

C2/46

C2/44

## C2/47 PILOT HOUSE TOP LEVEL – PLAN (FRAGMENTS)
**1** New form of Mk37 director with Mk25 radar antenna (fitted in 1955)
**2** Mk 56 director (fitted in 1955)

## C2/48 PRIMARY CONNING STATION LEVEL – PLAN (FRAGMENT)
**1** ECM antenna radome (fitted in 1955)

## C2/49 FORWARD AIR DEFENCE STATION – PLAN (FRAGMENT)

## C2/50 FOREMAST – FRONT VIEW (FRAGMENT)
**1** SPS-12 radar antenna (fitted in 1955)

## C2/51 FUNNEL NO. 2 AND MAINMAST – PLAN
**1** SPS-8 radar antenna (fitted in 1955)
**2** Loading boom

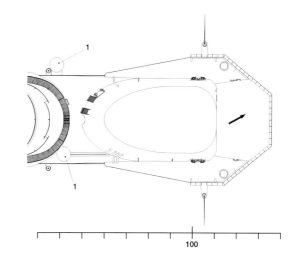

C2/48

100

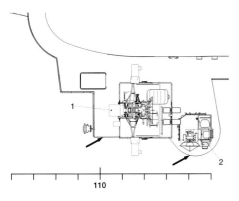

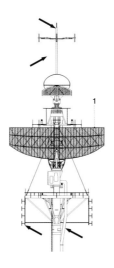

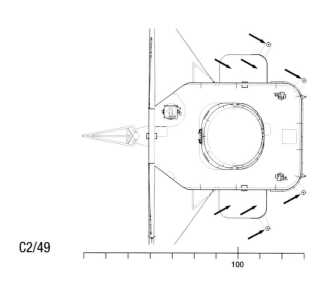

C2/47

110

C2/50

C2/49

100

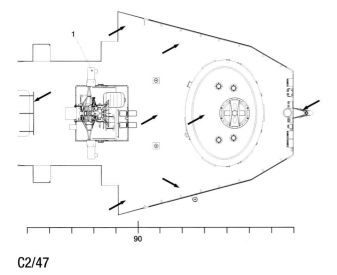

90

C2/47

C2/51

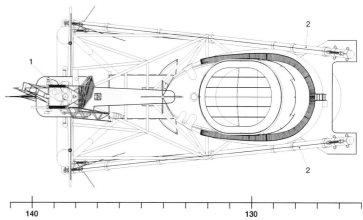

140

130

SUPERSTRUCTURE, 1955 (1/200 SCALE)

C2/52 FUNNEL NO. 2 AND MAINMAST – FRONT VIEW

C2/53 FUNNEL NO. 2 AND MAINMAST – BACK VIEW

1955

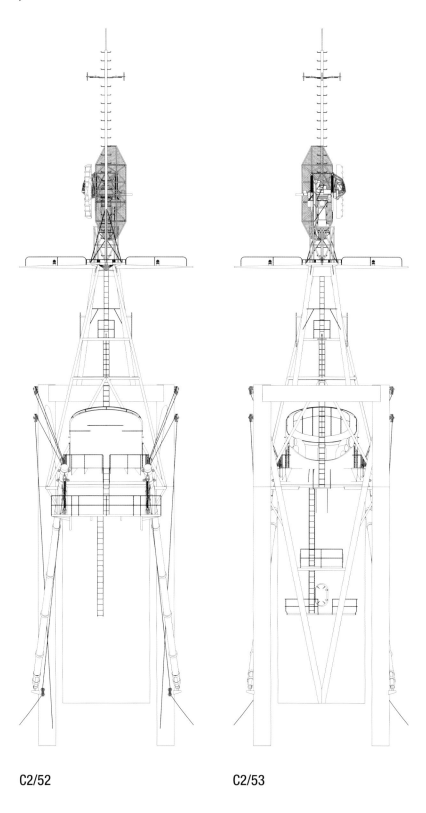

C2/52                    C2/53

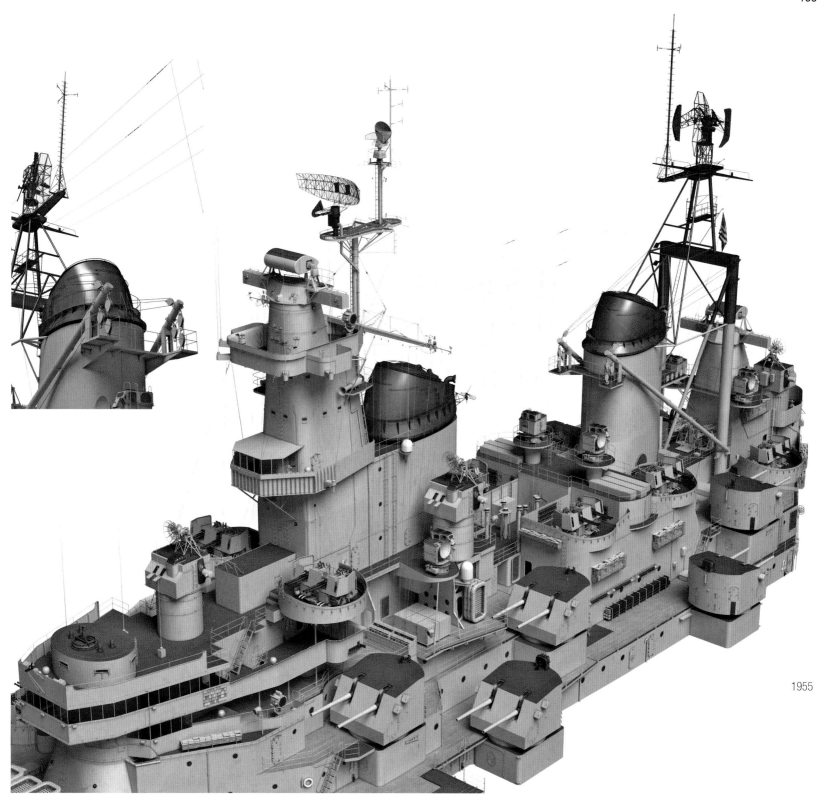

1955

**C SUPERSTRUCTURE, 1984–1990**

SUPERSTRUCTURE, 1984 (1/200 SCALE)

C3/1 RIGHT PROFILE

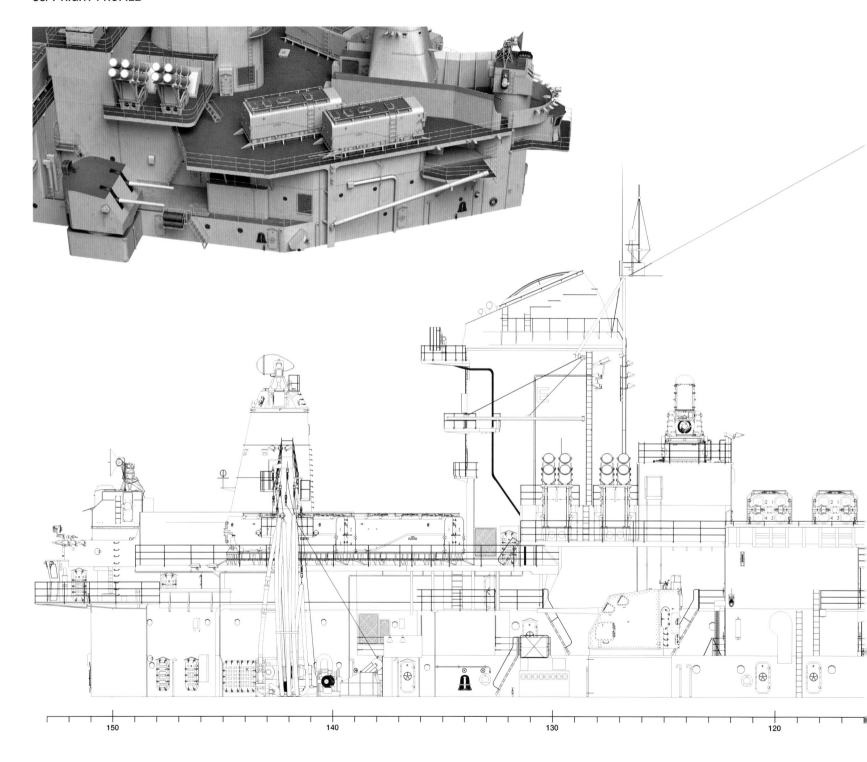

150                    140                    130                    120

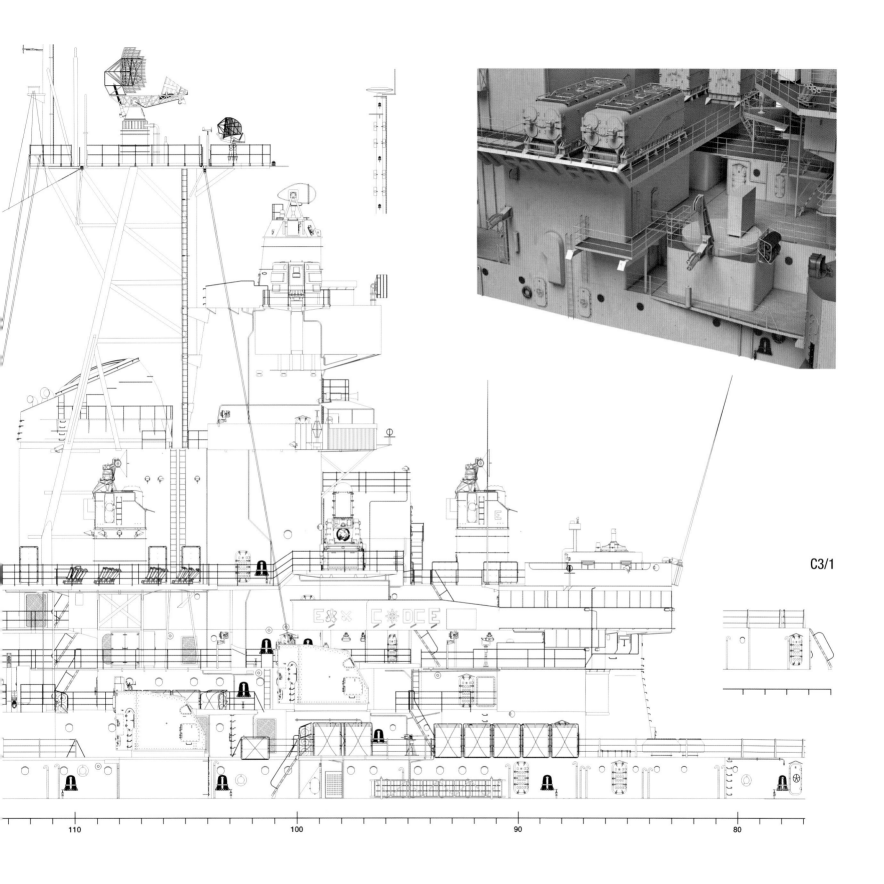

C3/1

**C SUPERSTRUCTURE, 1984–1990**

SUPERSTRUCTURE, 1984 (1/200 SCALE)

C3/2 LEFT PROFILE (FRAGMENT)

C3/3 FRONT VIEW

C3/4 BACK VIEW

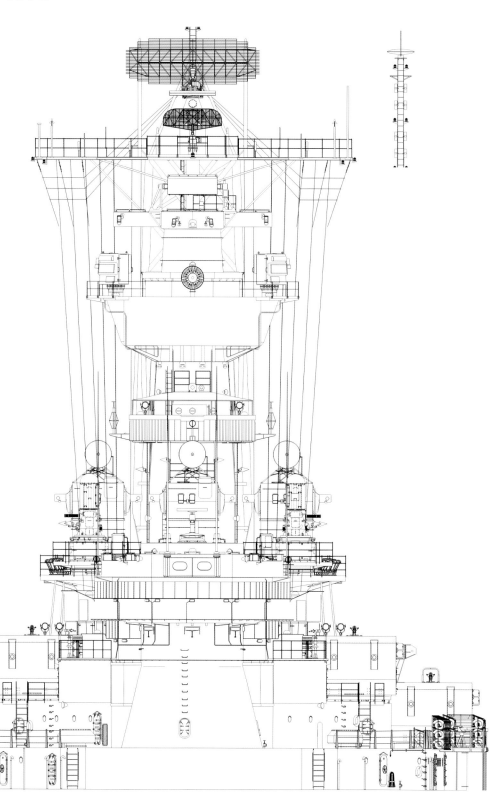

C3/3

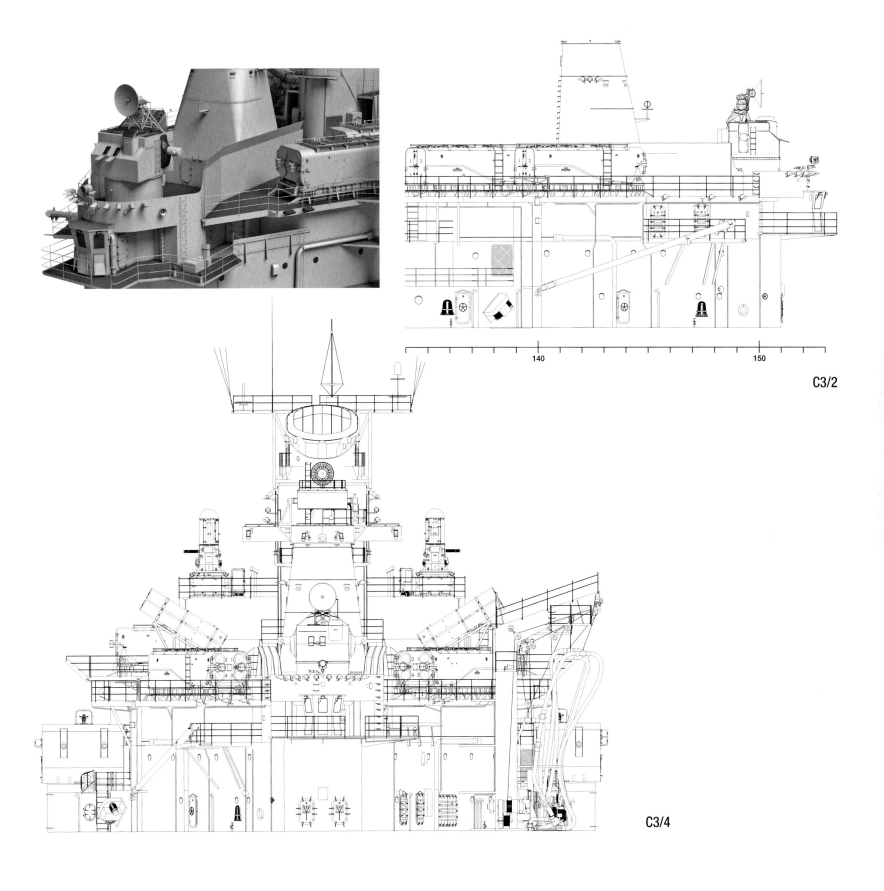

C3/2

C3/4

SUPERSTRUCTURE, LATE 1944 (1/200 SCALE)

### C3/5 MAIN DECK LEVEL – PLAN (STARBOARD SIDE FRAGMENT)
**1** Replenishment at sea (RAS) king post
**2** Winch

### C3/6 FIRST SUPERSTRUCTURE DECK LEVEL – PLAN (STARBOARD SIDE FRAGMENT)
**1** RAS king post
**2** Stowed $CO_2$ life rafts (2 pieces)
**3** Stowed $CO_2$ life rafts (3 pieces)
**4** 40mm saluting gun

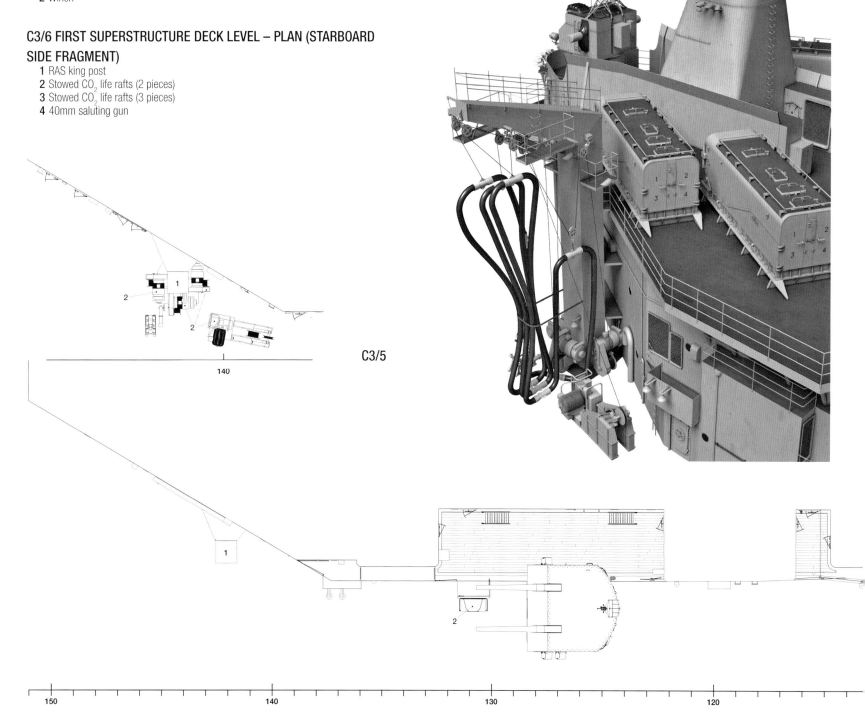

C3/5

140

150     140     130     120

C3/6

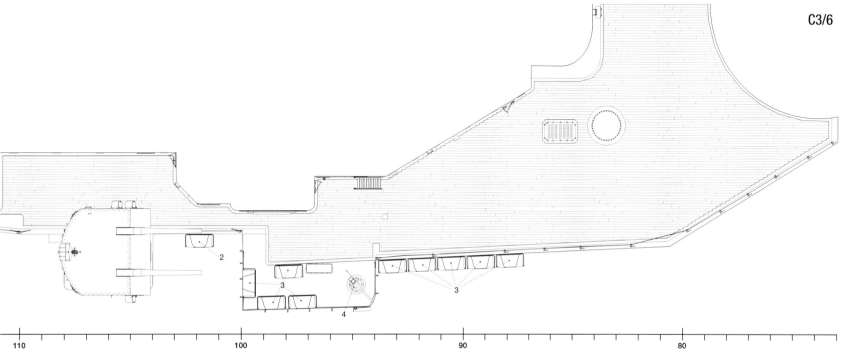

2

3

3

4

110     100     90     80

SUPERSTRUCTURE, LATE 1984 (1/200 SCALE)

**C3/7 FIRST SUPERSTRUCTURE DECK LEVEL – PLAN (PORT SIDE FRAGMENT)**
**1** Boat boom

**C3/8 SECOND SUPERSTRUCTURE DECK LEVEL – PLAN**
**1** Stowed $CO_2$ life rafts (2 pieces)
**2** Helicopter control station
**3** Boat cradle
**4** Boat king post cradle

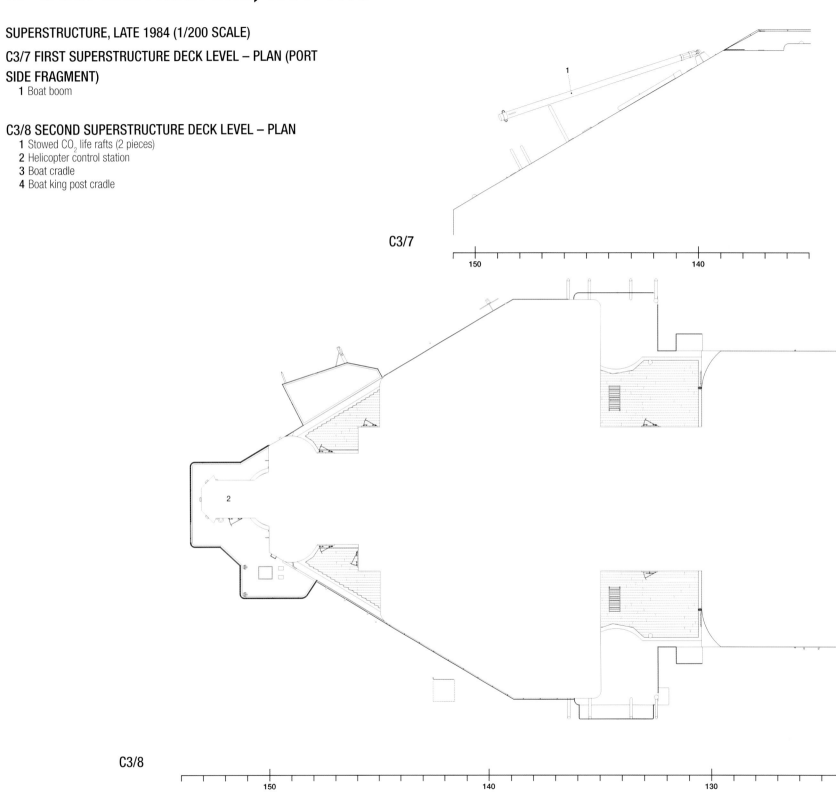

C3/7

C3/8

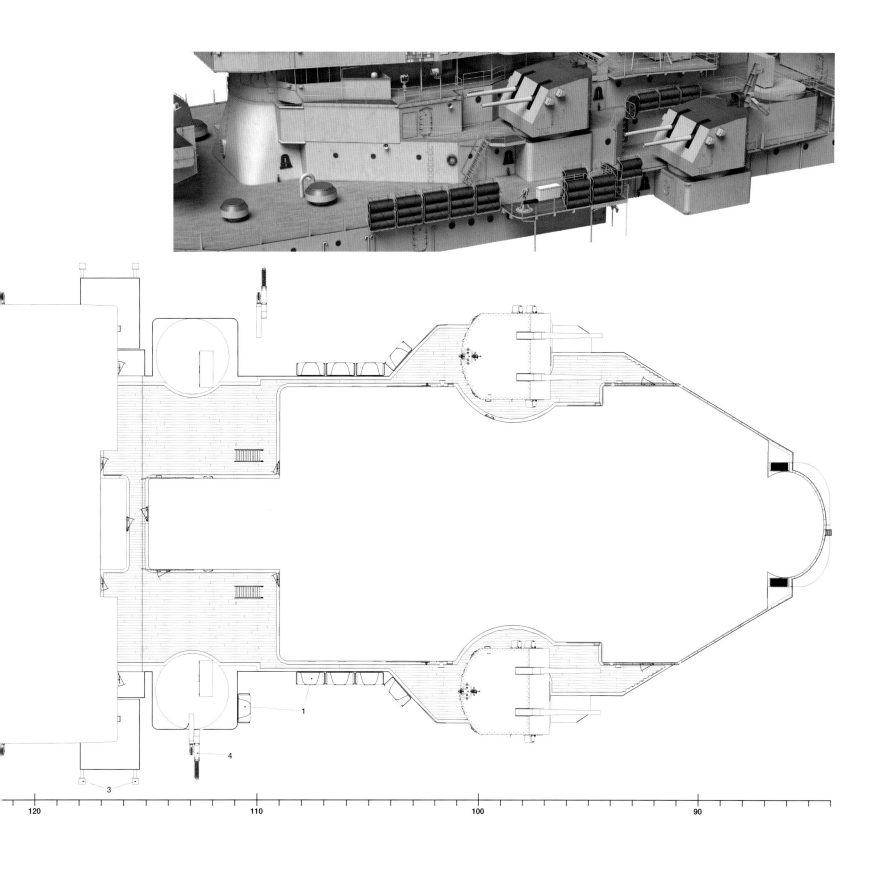

120                     110                          100                           90

**C SUPERSTRUCTURE, 1984–1990**

SUPERSTRUCTURE, LATE 1984 (1/200 SCALE)

C3/9 SECOND SUPERSTRUCTURE DECK LEVEL – UNDERSIDE
(FRAGMENT)

C3/10 FLAG BRIDGE LEVEL – PLAN
1 ABL no. 1
2 ABL no. 2
3 ABL no. 3
4 ABL no. 4
5 ABL no. 5
6 ABL no. 6
7 ABL no. 7
8 ABL no. 8
9 Harpoon launcher no. 1
10 Harpoon launcher no. 2
11 Harpoon launcher no. 3
12 Harpoon launcher no. 4

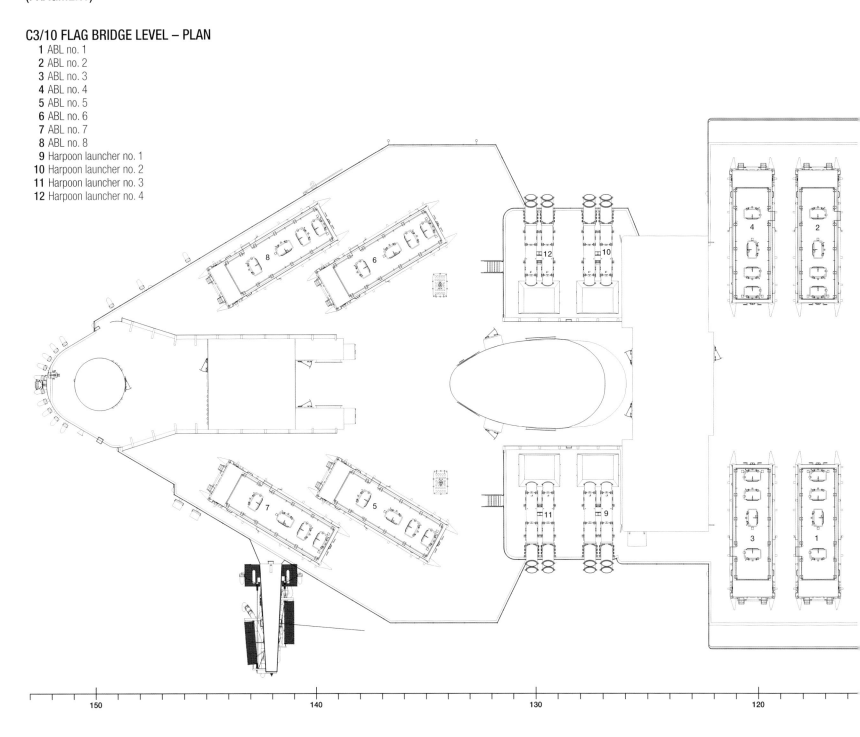

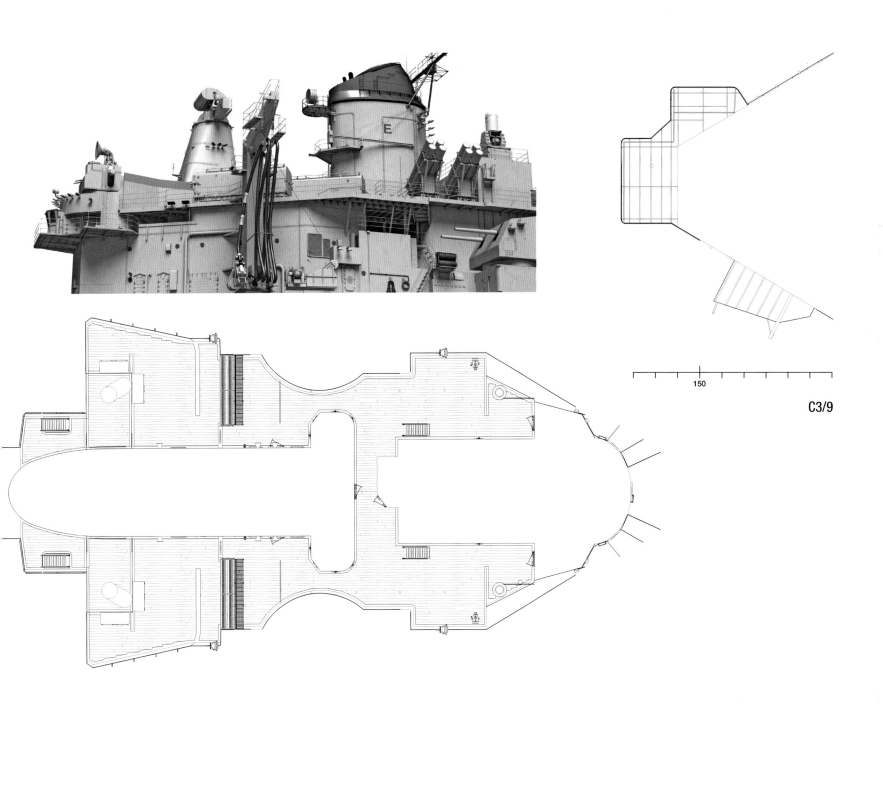

C3/9

150

C3/10

110                    100                    90

SUPERSTRUCTURE, LATE 1984 (1/200 SCALE)

C3/11 FLAG BRIDGE LEVEL – UNDERSIDE (STARBOARD SIDE FRAGMENT)

C3/12 FLAG BRIDGE LEVEL UPWARDS – VIEW FROM FRAME 115

TOWARDS THE STERN

C3/13 FUNNEL NO. 2 – FRONT VIEW

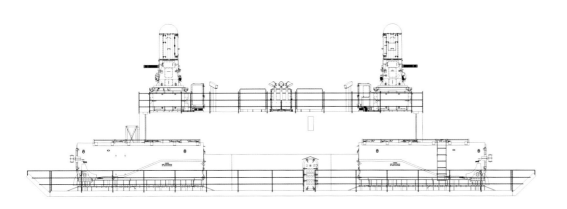

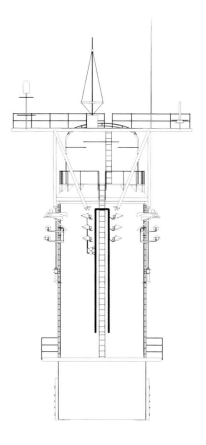

C3/12

C3/13

C3/11

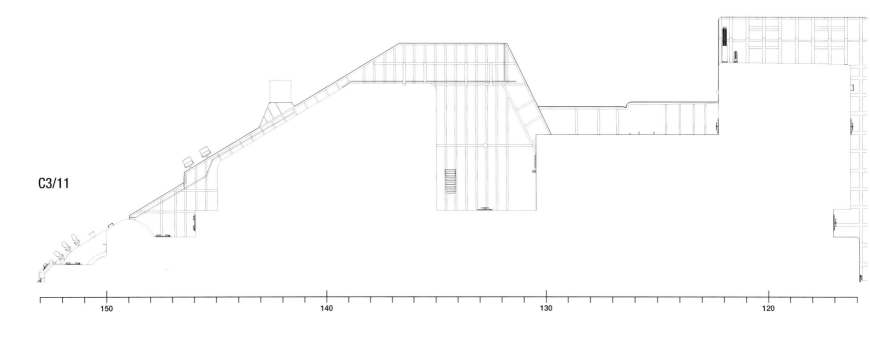

150        140        130        120

C3/14 FUNNEL NO. 2 – BACK VIEW
C3/15 FLAG BRIDGE LEVEL UPWARDS – VIEW FROM FRAME 138 TOWARDS THE STERN
C3/16 NAVIGATING BRIDGE LEVEL, FRAMES 83–115 – PLAN (STARBOARD SIDE FRAGMENT)
C3/17 NAVIGATING BRIDGE LEVEL, FRAMES 122–134 – PLAN

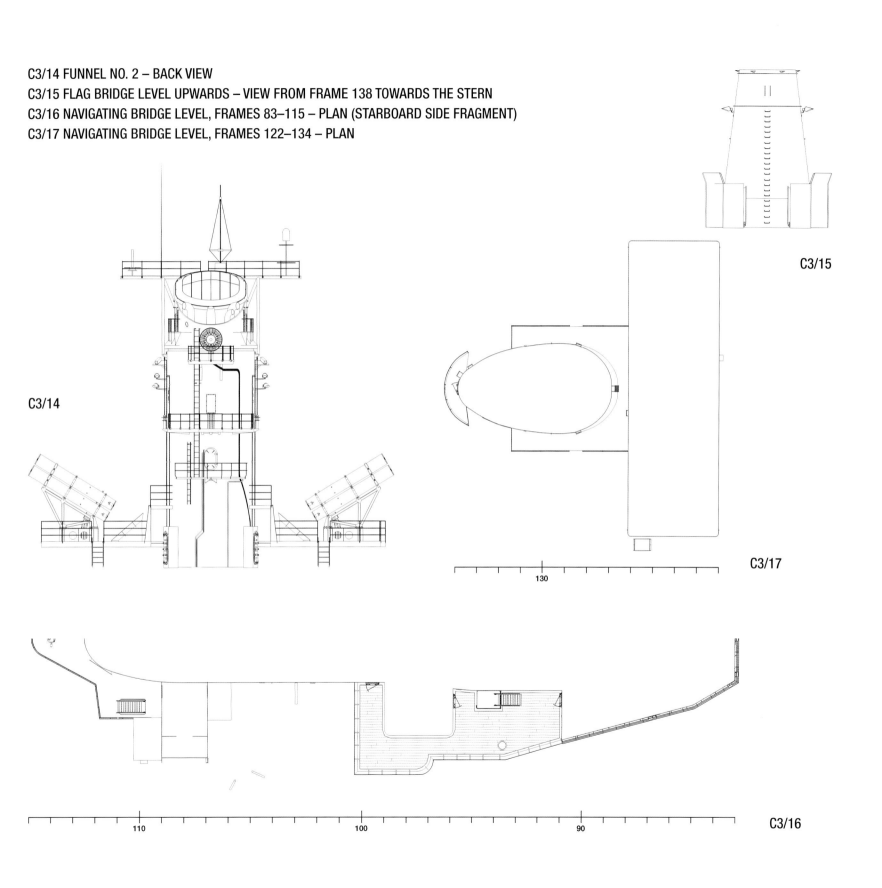

C3/15

C3/14

C3/17

130

110 100 90

C3/16

## SUPERSTRUCTURE, LATE 1984 (1/200 SCALE)

### C3/18 PILOT HOUSE TOP LEVEL, FRAMES 80–114 – PLAN

1 SSR-1 antenna
2 Whip antenna
3 SPS-64 radar antenna
4 Phalanx CIWS mount no. 21
5 Phalanx CIWS mount no. 22
6 Phalanx CIWS ammunition locker
7 SRBOC chaff launcher
8 Chaff locker

### C3/19 PILOT HOUSE TOP LEVEL – UNDERSIDE (FRAGMENT)

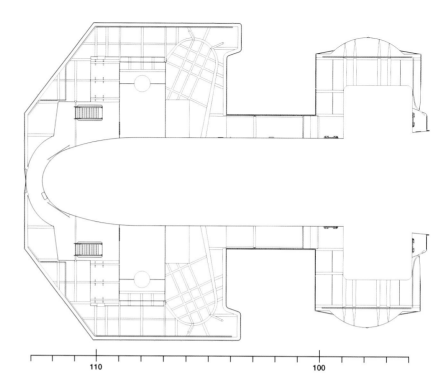

C3/19

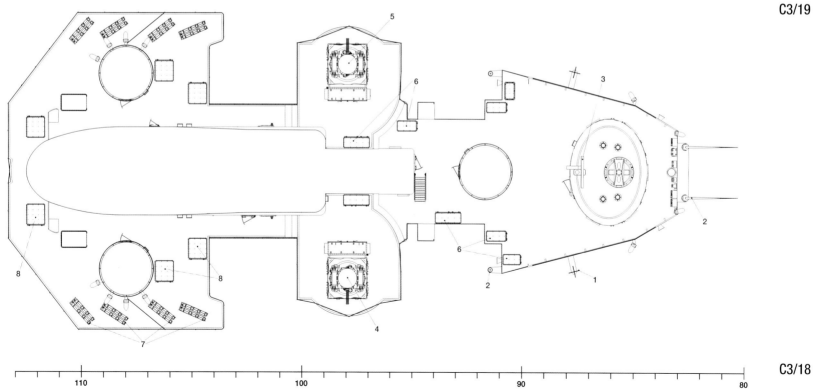

C3/18

## C3/20 PILOT HOUSE TOP LEVEL, FRAMES 122–135 – PLAN

**1** Phalanx CIWS mount no. 23
**2** Phalanx CIWS mount no. 24
**3** Phalanx CIWS ammunition locker
**4** Derrick

## C3/21 FIRST LEVEL ABOVE PILOT HOUSE TOP – PLAN

## C3/22 SECOND LEVEL ABOVE PILOT HOUSE TOP – PLAN

## C3/23 PRIMARY CONNING STATION LEVEL – PLAN

**1** SSR-1 antenna (removed in 1988)

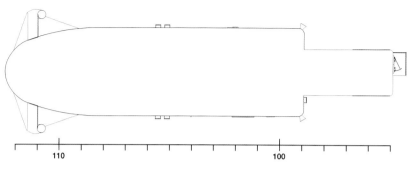

C3/21

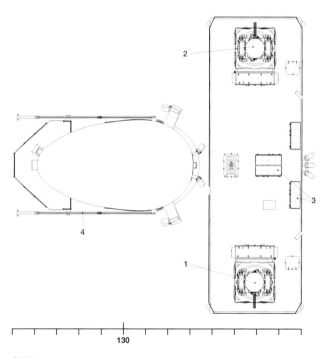

C3/20

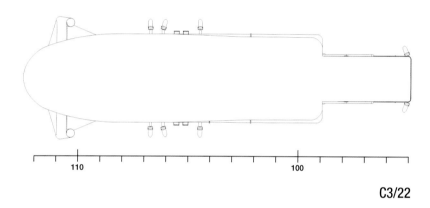

C3/22

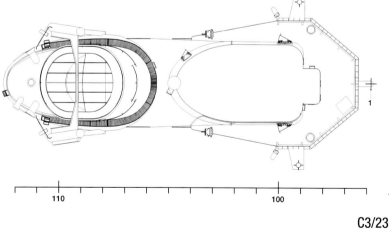

C3/23

SUPERSTRUCTURE, LATE 1984 (1/200 SCALE)

C3/24  PRIMARY CONNING STATION LEVEL UPWARDS – VIEW FROM
FRAME 105 TOWARDS THE BOW

C3/25 CAP OF FUNNEL NO. 2 – PLAN
  **1** OE-8 antenna
  **2** CCTV antenna
  **3** Trussed whip antenna

C3/26 FORWARD SURFACE LOOKOUT STATION LEVEL – PLAN

C3/27 ELECTRONIC WARFARE ROOM LEVEL – PLAN

C3/28 ELECTRONIC WARFARE ROOM LEVEL – UNDERSIDE (FRAGMENT)

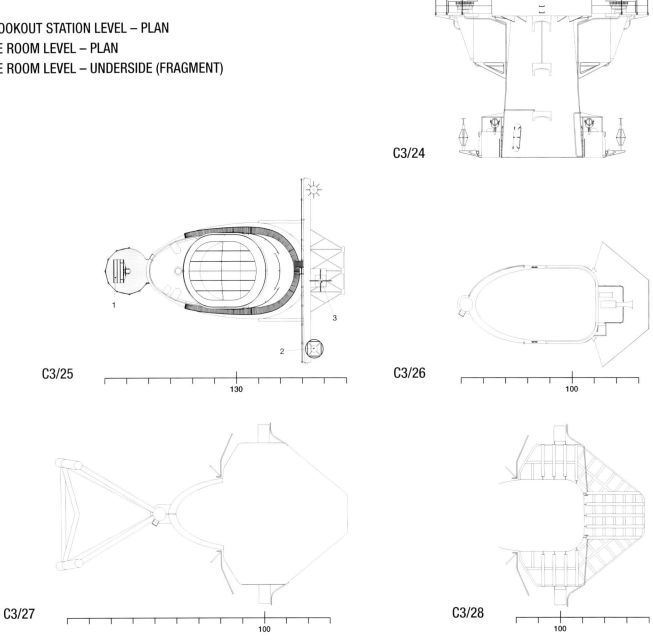

C3/24

C3/25    130

C3/26    100

C3/27    100

C3/28    100

## C3/29 FORWARD AIR DEFENCE STATION – PLAN
**1** OE-8 antenna
**2** SLQ-32 antenna
**3** SLQ-32 antenna base (antenna omitted for clarity)
**4** SLQ-32 antenna service platform (unfolded)

## C3/30 FORWARD AIR DEFENCE STATION – PLAN (FRAGMENT)
**1** SLQ-32 antenna service platform (folded)

## C3/31 FOREMAST PLATFORM – PLAN
**1** SPS-10 radar antenna
**2** SPS-49 radar antenna
**3** Wind speed and direction indicator
**4** Masthead light
**5** Blinker light
**6** AT-150 antenna
**7** Network box

## C3/32 FOREMAST PLATFORM – UNDERSIDE

C3/29

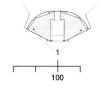

C3/30

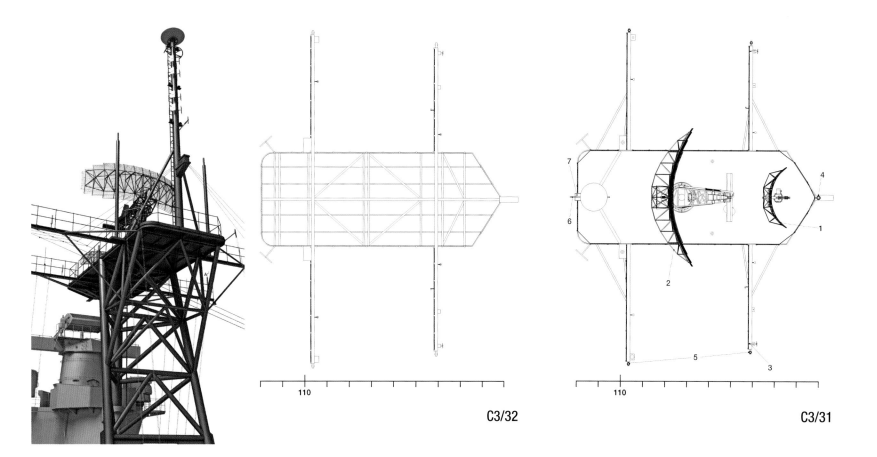

C3/32

C3/31

SUPERSTRUCTURE, LATE 1984 (1/200 SCALE)

**C3/33 FOREMAST – BACK VIEW**
   **1** Red lights
   **2** White lights
   **3** URN-25 antenna
   **4** Lightning rod

**C3/34 FOREMAST PLATFORM – VIEW FROM FRAME 105 TOWARDS THE BOW**

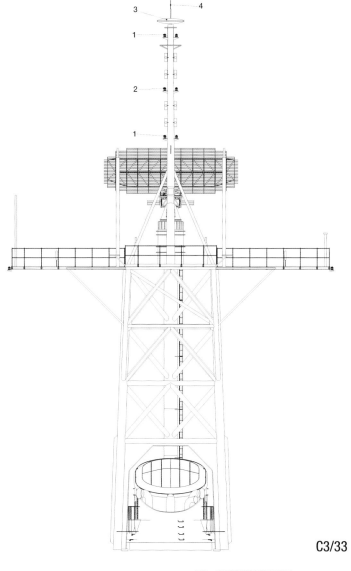

C3/34

C3/33

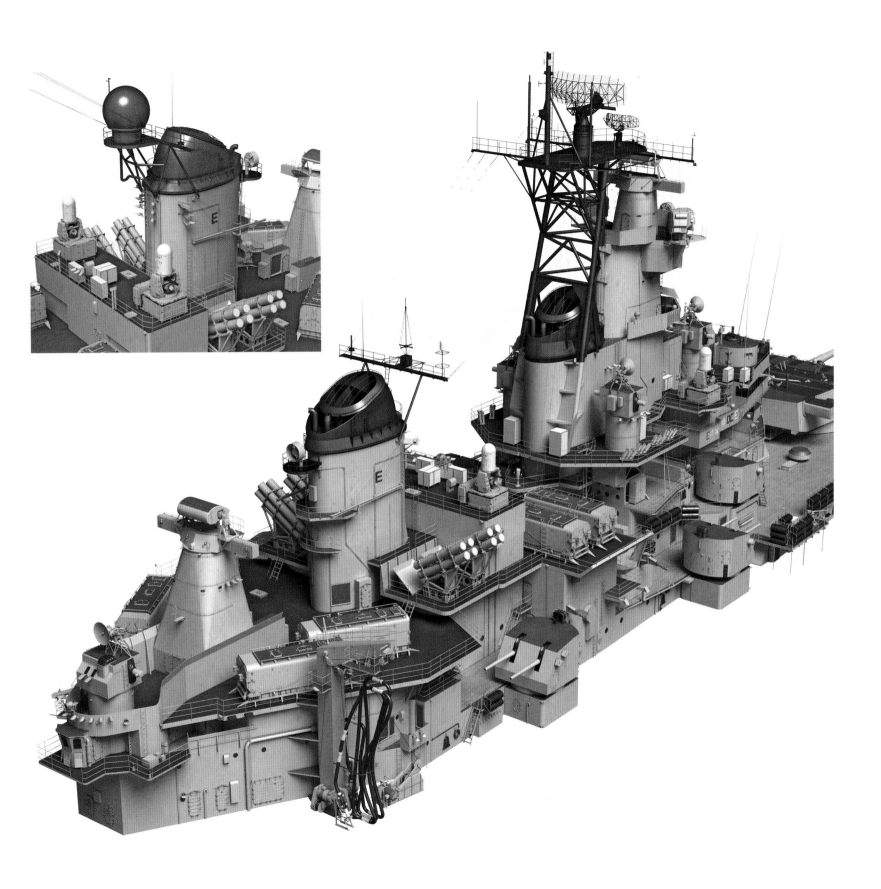

## SUPERSTRUCTURE, 1988 (1/200 SCALE)

### C3/35 RIGHT PROFILE (FRAGMENTS)
1 Radar antenna for controlling RPVs (fitted in 1986)
2 WLR-1 antenna (fitted in 1987)
3 Radar antenna for controlling RPVs (fitted in 1988)

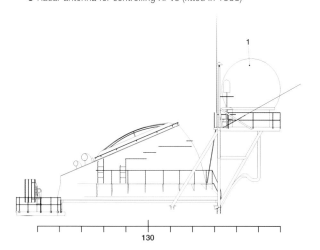
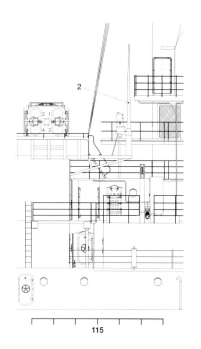
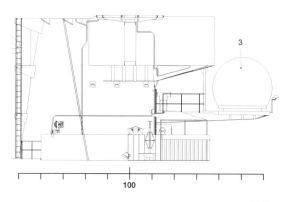

130

115

100

C3/35

## C3/36 SECOND SUPERSTRUCTURE DECK TO PILOT HOUSE TOP LEVEL – VIEW FROM FRAME 113 TOWARDS THE STERN

**1** WLR-1 antenna (fitted in 1987)

## C3/37 FUNNEL NO. 2 – FRONT VIEW (FRAGMENT)

**1** Radar antenna for controlling RPVs (fitted in 1986)

## C3/38 FORWARD SURFACE LOOKOUT STATION LEVEL – PLAN (FRAGMENT)

**1** Radar antenna for controlling RPVs (fitted in 1988)

## C3/39 FORWARD SURFACE LOOKOUT STATION LEVEL – UNDERSIDE (FRAGMENT)

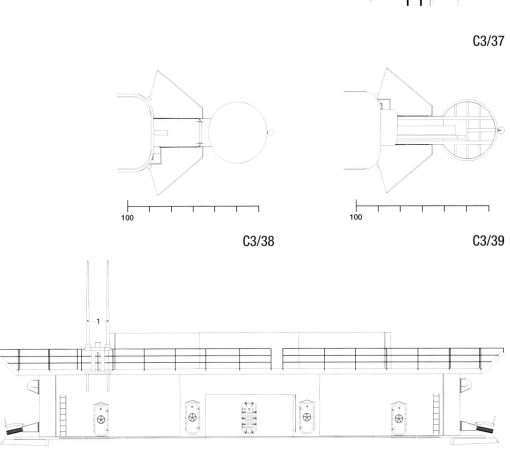

C3/37

100

C3/38

100

C3/39

C3/36

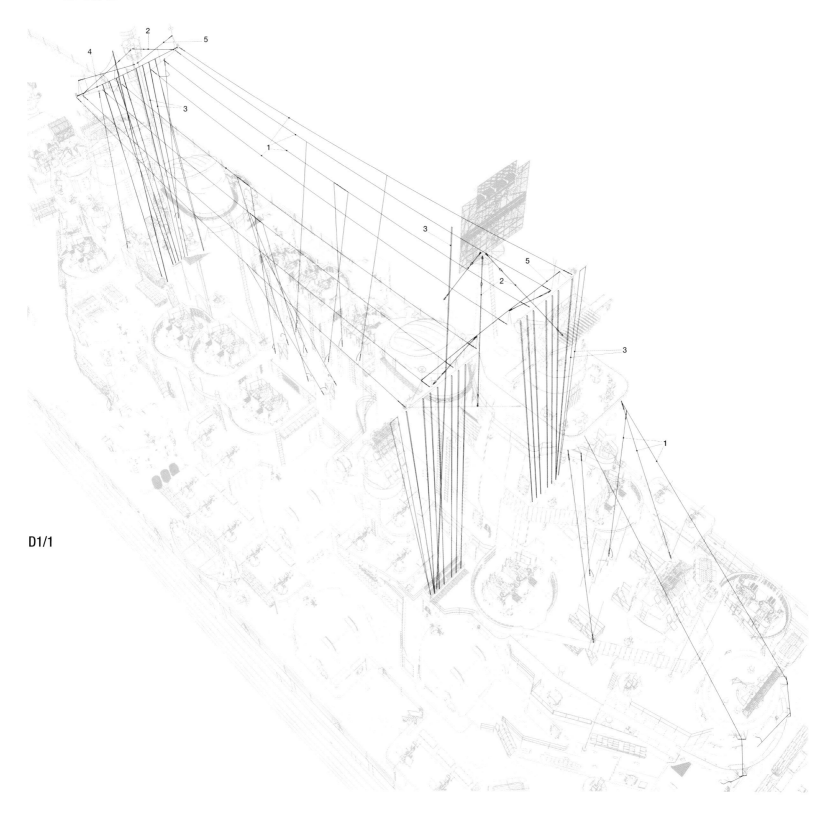

D1/1

SHIP'S RIG (NO SCALE)

D1/1 AXONOMETRIC VIEW, 1944

D1/2 AXONOMETRIC VIEW, 1988

**D1/1–2 SHIP'S RIG**
1 Wire antenna
2 Stay
3 Halyard
4 Halyard status line
5 Lifeline

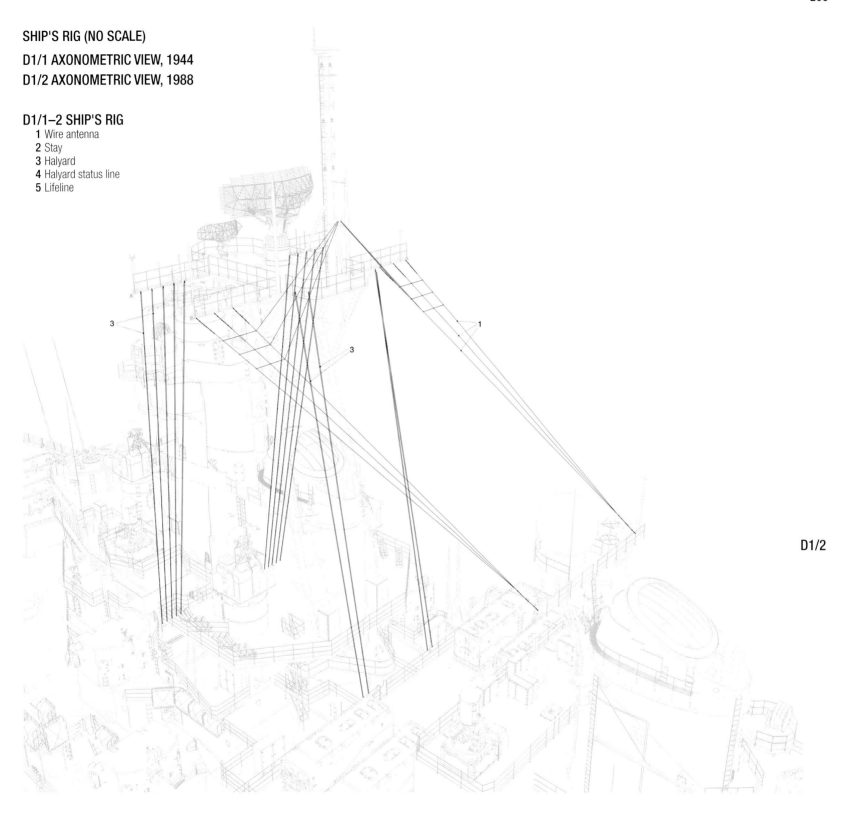

D1/2

SHIP'S RIG (NO SCALE)

D1/3 WIRE ANTENNA TOWERS (1/50 SCALE)

D1/4 WIRE ANTENNA INSULATOR (1/12.5 SCALE)

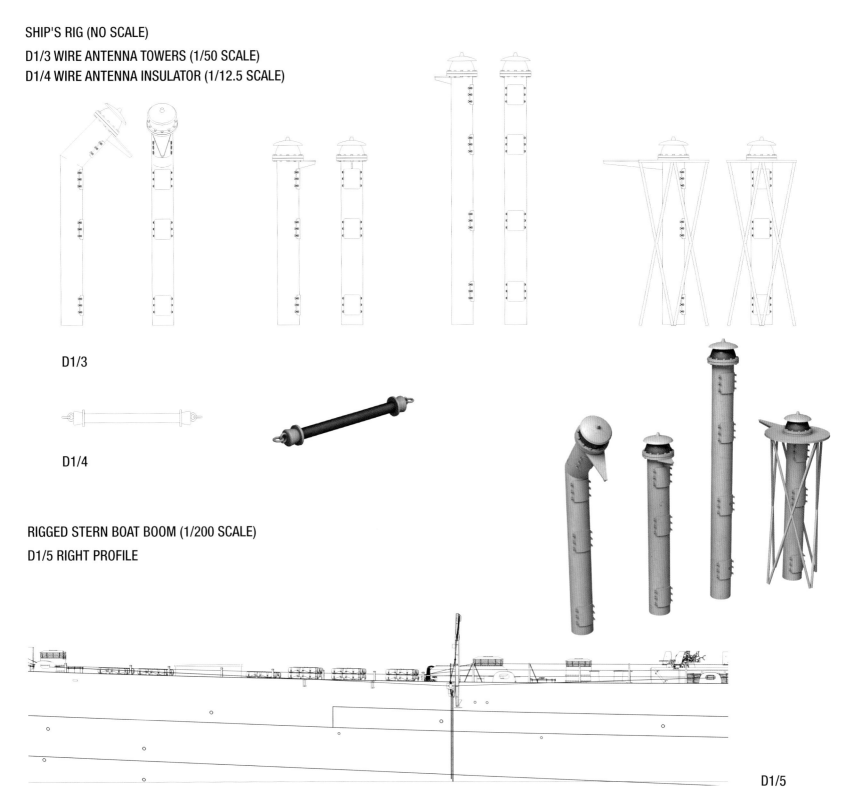

D1/3

D1/4

RIGGED STERN BOAT BOOM (1/200 SCALE)

D1/5 RIGHT PROFILE

D1/5

D1/6 FRONT VIEW
D1/7 PLAN

D1/7

D1/6

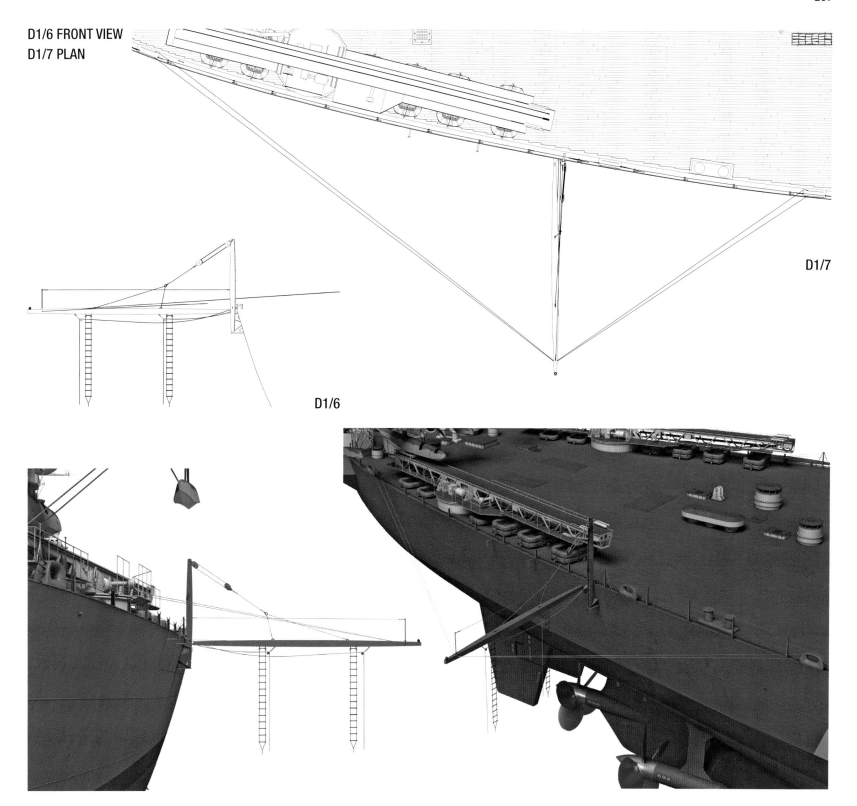

RIGGED ACCOMMODATION LADDER (1/100 SCALE)

D1/8 RIGHT PROFILE

D1/9 FRONT VIEW

D1/10 PLAN

D1/10

D1/8

D1/9

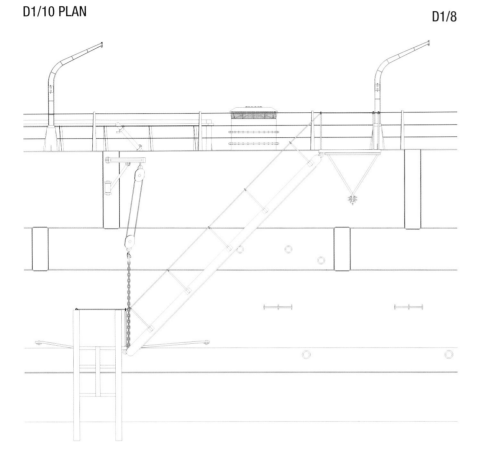
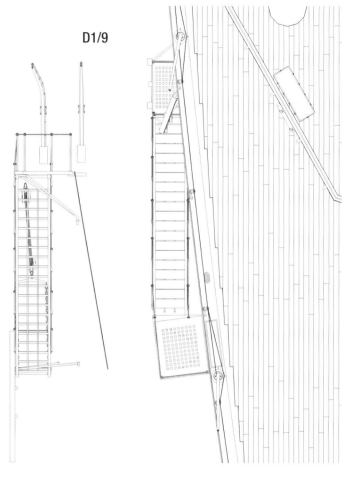

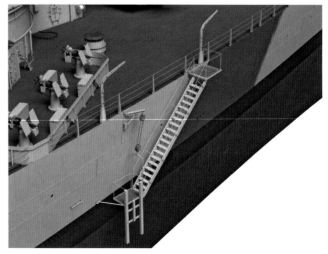

26FT MOTOR WHALEBOAT DAVIT, 1943–1949 (1/100 SCALE)

D1/11 RIGHT PROFILE
D1/12 FRONT VIEW
D1/13 BACK VIEW
D1/14 PLAN

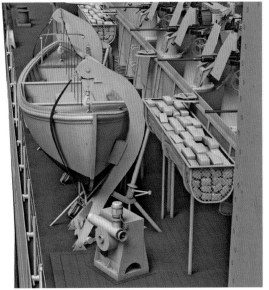

26FT MOTOR WHALEBOAT DAVIT, 1952–1958 (1/100 SCALE)

D1/15 RIGHT PROFILE
D1/16 BACK VIEW

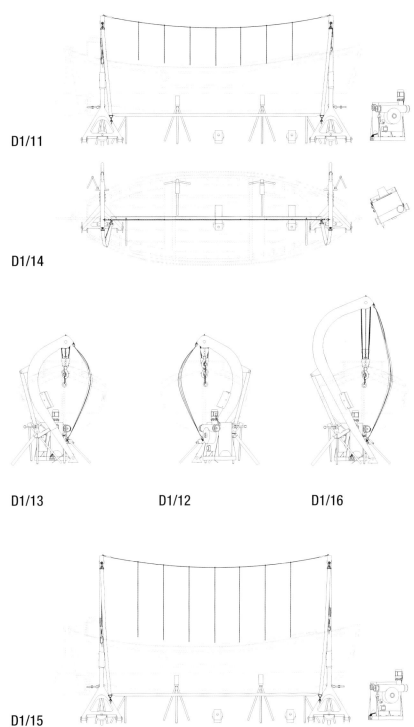

D1/11

D1/14

D1/13          D1/12          D1/16

D1/15

STARBOARD SIDE BOAT DAVIT,
1984–1990 (1/125 SCALE)

D1/17 RIGHT PROFILE
D1/18 FRONT VIEW
D1/19 BACK VIEW
D1/20 PLAN

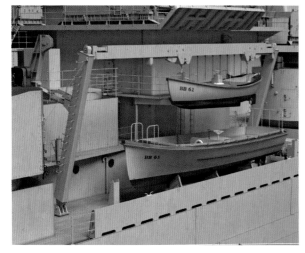

PORT SIDE BOAT DAVIT BEAM, 1984–1990 (1/125 SCALE)

D1/21 RIGHT PROFILE

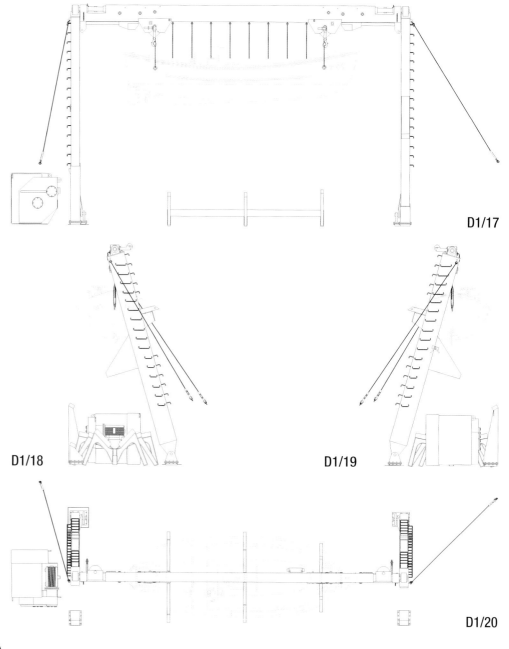

D1/17

D1/18

D1/19

D1/20

D1/21

STERN CRANE, 1943–1949 (1/150 SCALE)

D1/22 RIGHT PROFILE
D1/23 FRONT VIEW
D1/24 BACK VIEW
D1/25 PLAN

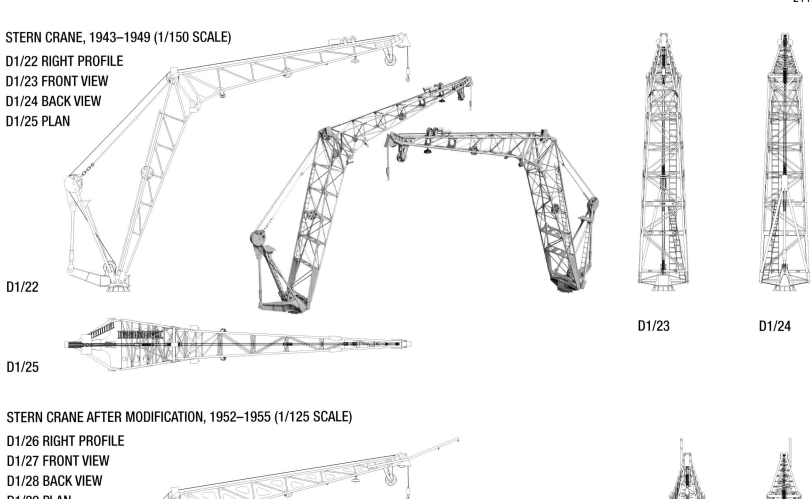

D1/22

D1/25

D1/23

D1/24

STERN CRANE AFTER MODIFICATION, 1952–1955 (1/125 SCALE)

D1/26 RIGHT PROFILE
D1/27 FRONT VIEW
D1/28 BACK VIEW
D1/29 PLAN

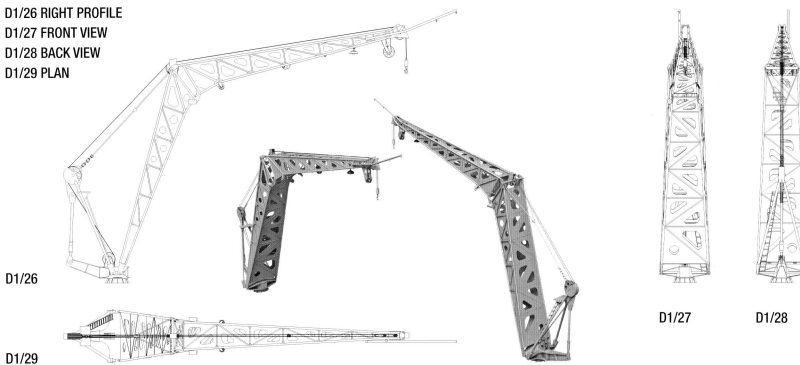

D1/26

D1/29

D1/27

D1/28

## 16IN./50 MK7 GUNS IN THE TRIPLE TURRET (1/150 SCALE)

## E1/1 TURRET NO. 1, APRIL 1943 – RIGHT PROFILE
## E1/2 TURRET NO. 1, APRIL 1943 – FRONT VIEW
## E1/3 TURRET NO. 1, APRIL 1943 – BACK VIEW

### E1/1-35 16INCH TRIPLE TURRET

1 Barbette
2 Ladder
3 Barrel
4 Barrel at elevation of +30°
5 Removable blast bag
6 Trainer's sight under protective hood
7 Pointer's sight under protective hood
8 Periscope under protective cover
9 Rangefinder arm hood
10 Access hatch
11 Floater net basket
12 Vent duct
13 Platform under access hatch (Turret No. 2 only)
14 Guard rail (Turret No. 2 only)
15 Towing cable stowage brackets

16 Mk51 director behind four hinged shields
17 Quadruple Bofors mount
18 Ready-to-use ammunition clips
19 Balsa life raft (fitted on all turrets in the summer of 1943)
20 Ladder (added in 1944, Turret No. 2 only)
21 Single Oerlikon mount (added in the summer of 1943)
22 Floater net basket (moved upwards in the summer of 1943)
23 Ammunition magazine loading frame
24 Spare barrel tube
25 Stowed helmet
26 Ammunition locker
27 Floater net basket added and Bofors shield shortened (from summer of 1943)
28 Additional vent shield (added on all turrets in early 1945)
29 Sealed hole after removal of rangefinder (from January 1948, only Turret No. 1)
30 Removable main artillery ammunition loading beam (from 1952 usually kept fitted at all times)
31 Guard rail (present on all turrets from 1958)
32 Derrick (added in 1958)
33 Life rafts (replaced Oerlikon tub in 1954; Oerlikon mounts removed around 1947)
34 Life rafts (added in 1954)
35 DR 810 muzzle velocity meter Doppler radar (fitted on all turrets in 1984)
36 Anti slip surfaces (on Turrets Nos. 2 and 3 from 1984)
37 Awning attachment bar and eye plates (only on Turret No. 2 from 1984)
38 Modified vent duct (on all turrets from 1984)

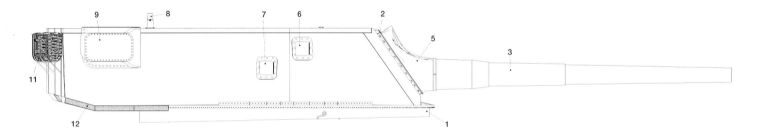

E1/1

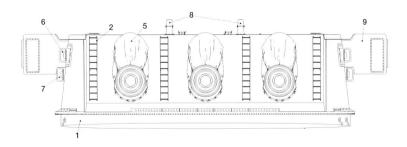

E1/2

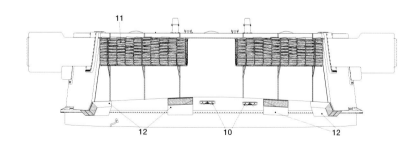

E1/3

E1/4 TURRET NO. 1, APRIL 1943 – PLAN

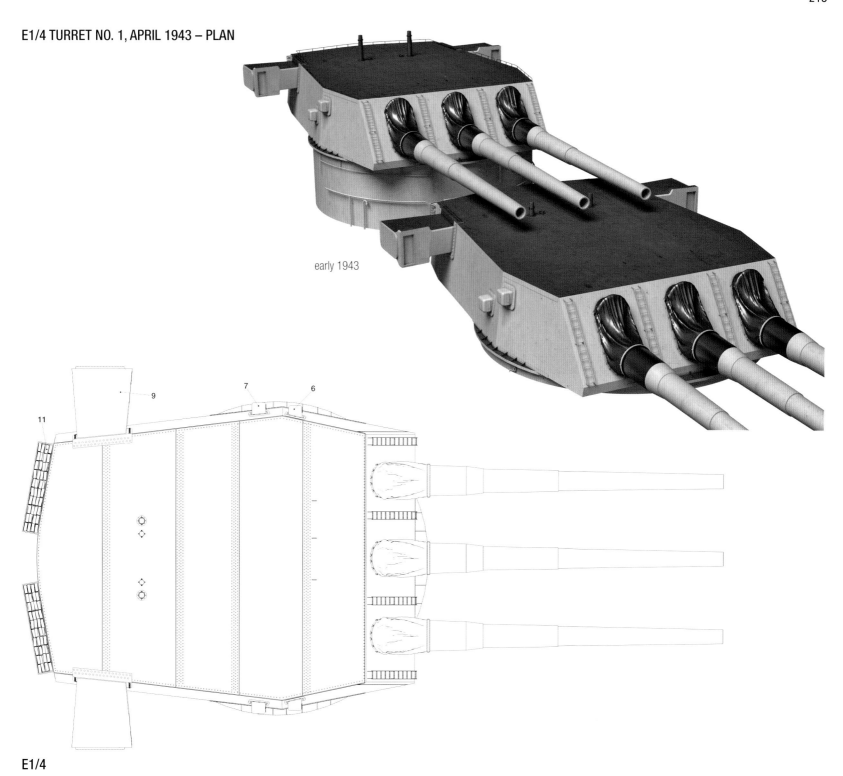

early 1943

E1/4

**E ARMAMENT – 16IN GUNS**

16IN./50 MK7 GUNS IN THE TRIPLE TURRET (1/150 SCALE)

E1/5  TURRET NO. 1 – BOTTOM VIEW (FRAGMENT)

E1/6 BARBETTE OF TURRET NO. 1 – LEFT PROFILE

E1/7 TURRET NO. 2, APRIL 1943 – RIGHT PROFILE (FRAGMENT)

E1/8 TURRET NO. 2, APRIL 1943 – LEFT PROFILE

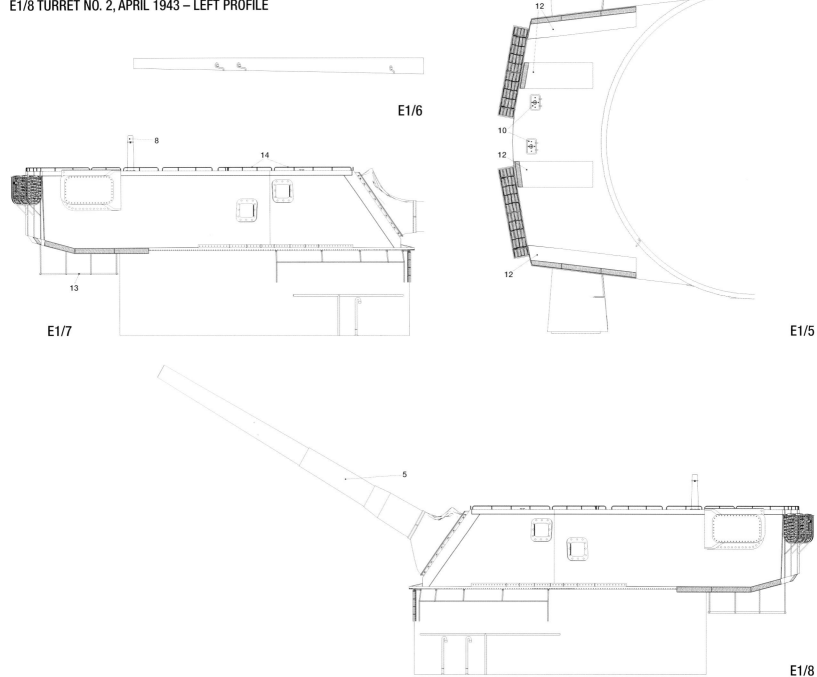

E1/6

E1/7

E1/5

E1/8

E1/9 TURRET NO. 2, APRIL 1943 – BACK VIEW
E1/10 TURRET NO. 3, APRIL 1943 – LEFT PROFILE (FRAGMENT)

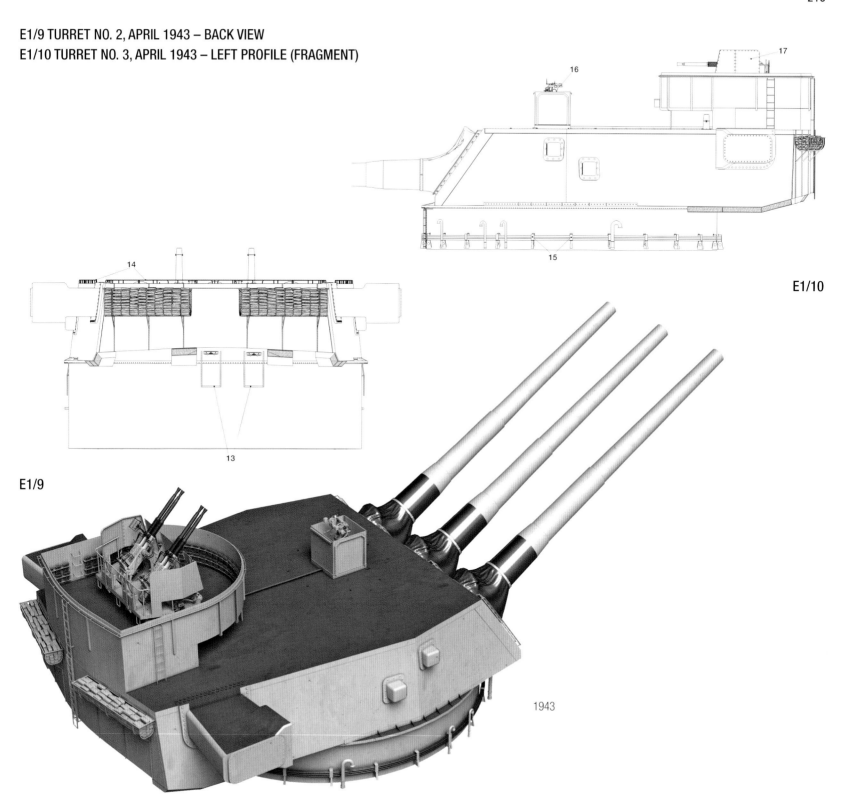

E1/10

E1/9

1943

16IN./50 MK7 GUNS IN THE TRIPLE TURRET (1/150 SCALE)

E1/11 TURRET NO. 3, APRIL 1943 – FRONT VIEW

E1/12 TURRET NO. 3, APRIL 1943 – BACK VIEW

E1/13 TURRET NO. 3, APRIL 1943 – PLAN (FRAGMENT)

E1/14 BARBETTE OF TURRET NO. 3 – RIGHT PROFILE

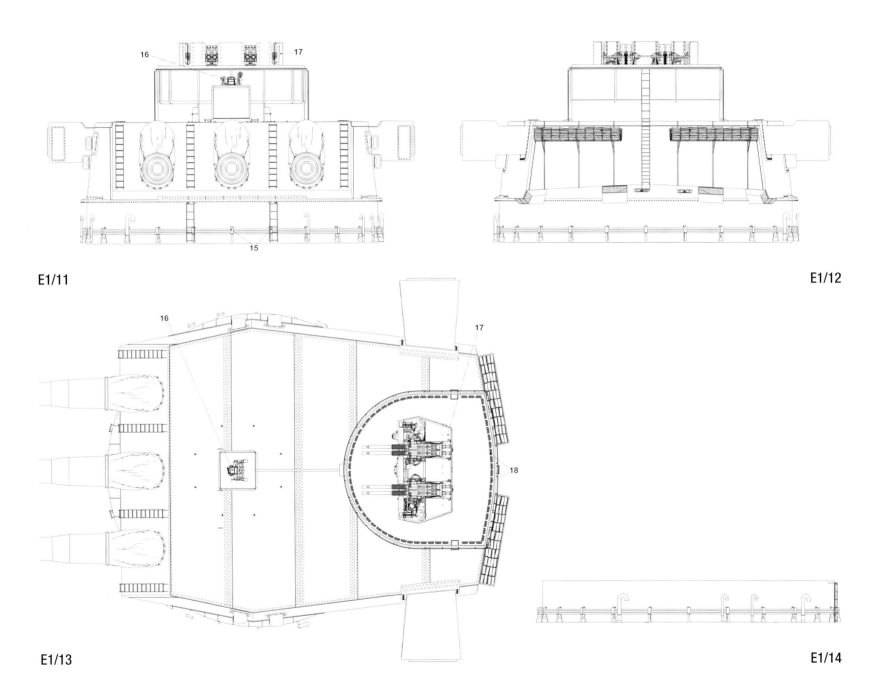

E1/11

E1/12

E1/13

E1/14

E1/15 TURRET NO. 2, 1944 – RIGHT PROFILE (FRAGMENT)

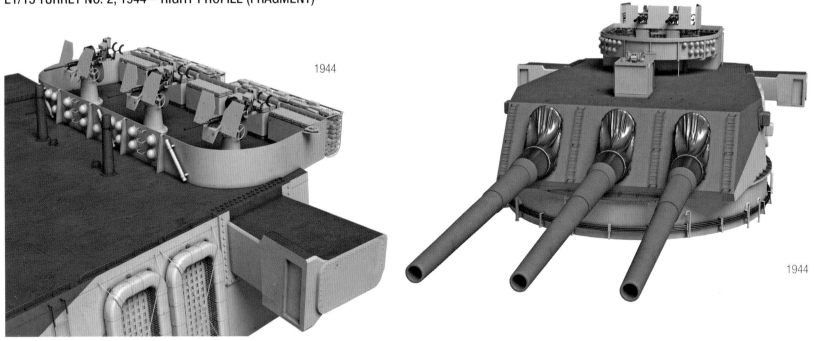

1944

1944

22    21

19    20

E1/15

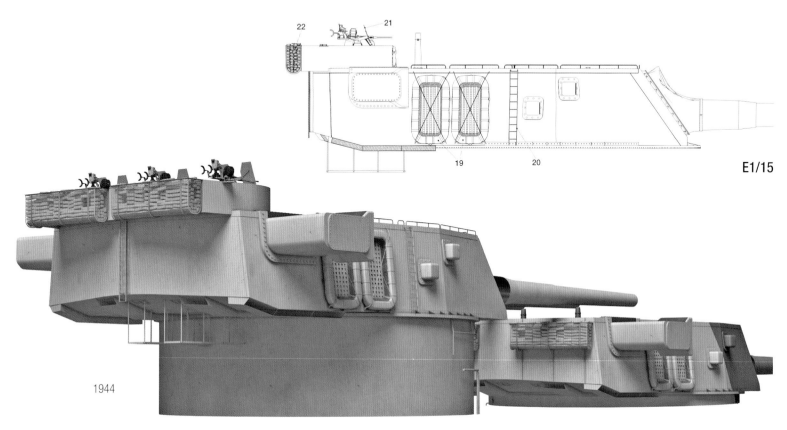

1944

**E ARMAMENT – 16IN GUNS**

16IN./50 MK7 GUNS IN THE TRIPLE TURRET (1/150 SCALE)

E1/16 TURRET NO. 2, 1944 – FRONT VIEW

E1/17 TURRET NO. 2, 1944 – BACK VIEW

E1/18 TURRET NO. 2, 1944 – PLAN (FRAGMENT)

E1/19 TURRET NO. 3, 1944 – BACK VIEW

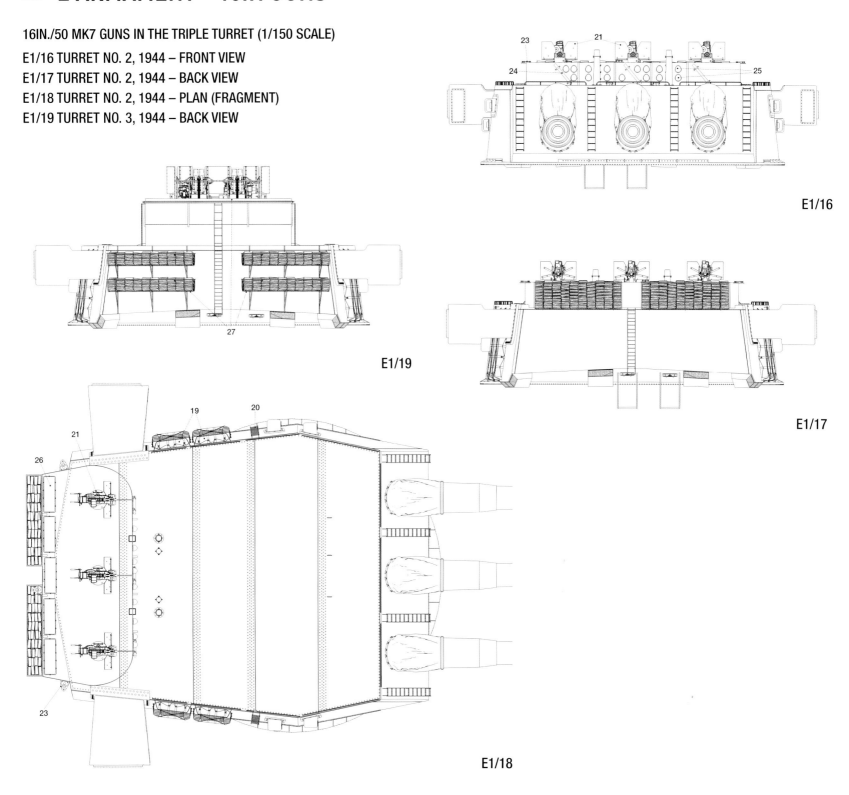

E1/16

E1/19

E1/17

E1/18

E1/20 TURRET NO. 1, 1945 – RIGHT PROFILE (FRAGMENT)
E1/21 TURRET NO. 1, 1945 – BACK VIEW
E1/22 TURRET NO. 1, 1945 – PLAN (FRAGMENT)

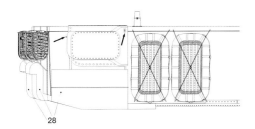

28

E1/20

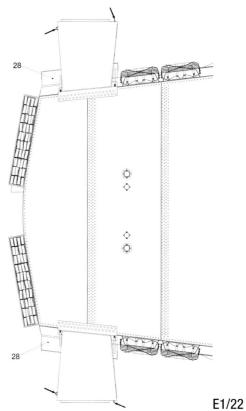

28

28

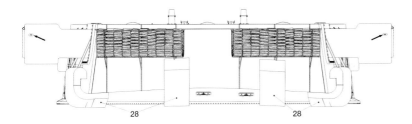

28

28

E1/21

E1/22

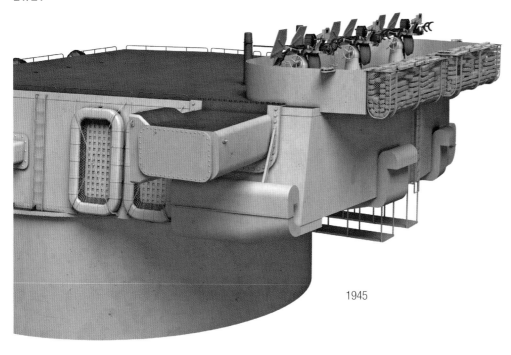

1945

**E ARMAMENT – 16IN GUNS**

16IN./50 MK7 GUNS IN THE TRIPLE TURRET (1/150 SCALE)

E1/23 TURRET NO. 1, 1958 – RIGHT PROFILE (FRAGMENT)

E1/24 TURRET NO. 1, 1958 – FRONT VIEW

E1/25 TURRET NO. 1, 1958 – PLAN (FRAGMENT)

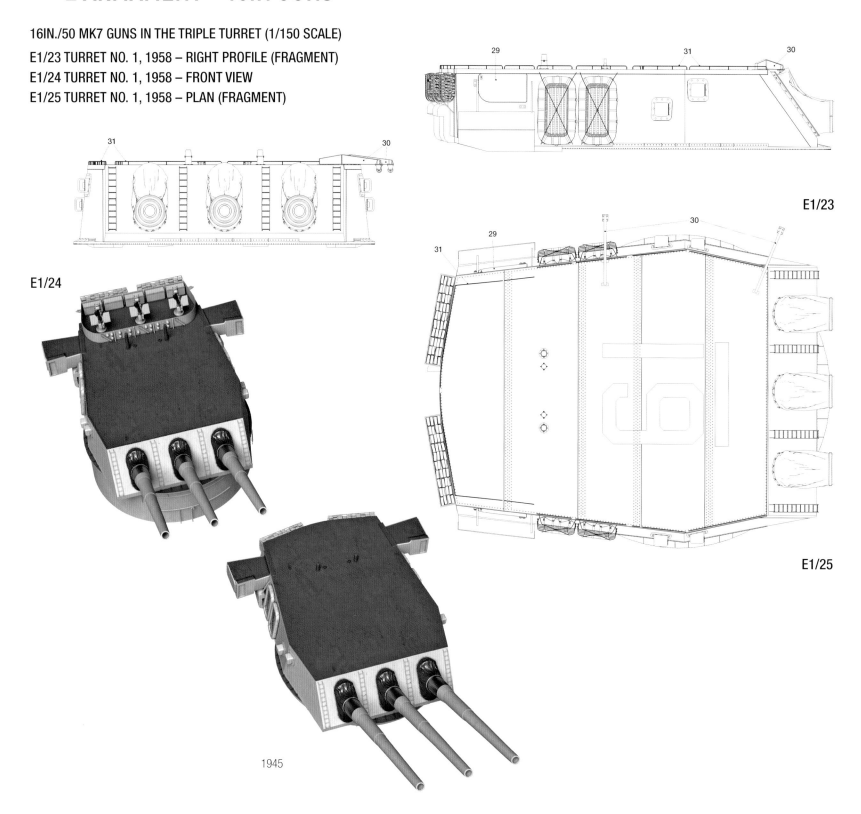

E1/23

E1/24

E1/25

1945

E1/26 TURRET NO. 2, 1958 – RIGHT PROFILE (FRAGMENT)
E1/27 TURRET NO. 2, 1958 – FRONT VIEW
E1/28 TURRET NO. 2, 1958 – PLAN (FRAGMENT)

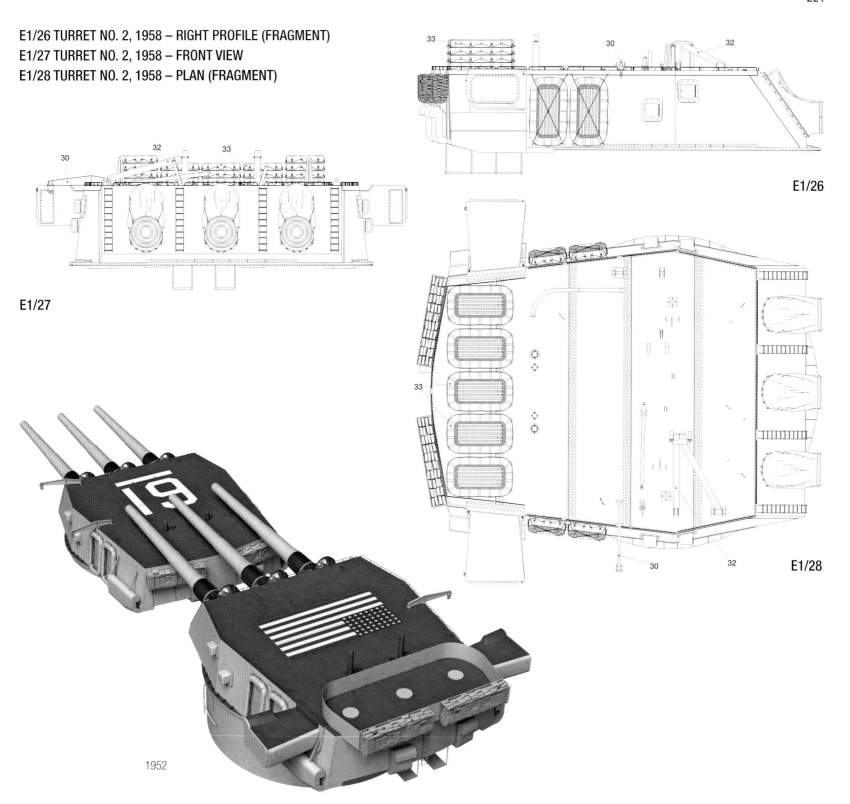

E1/26

E1/27

E1/28

1952

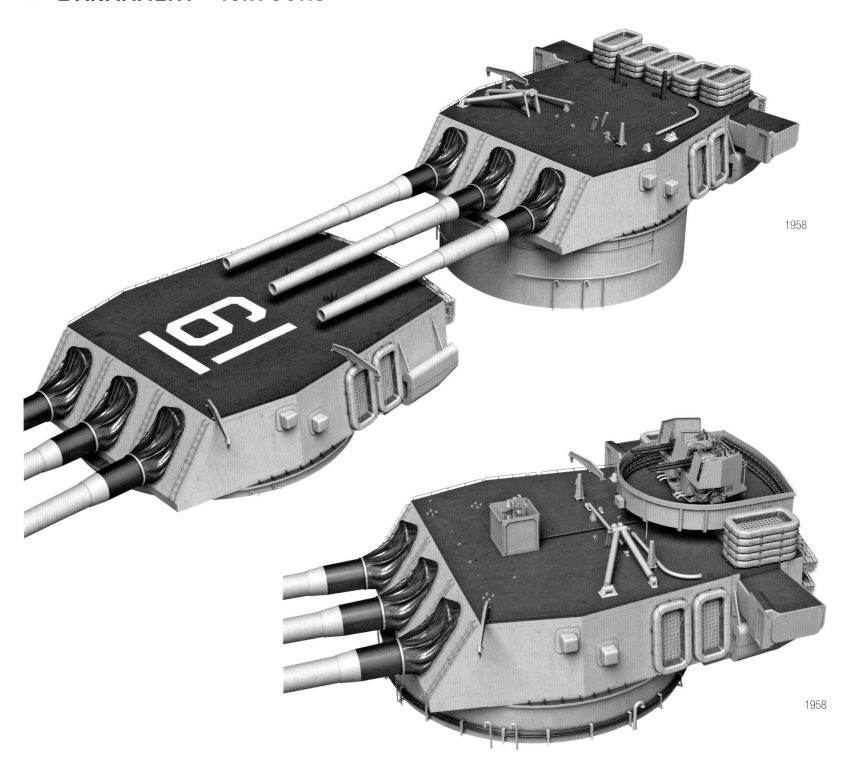

1958

1958

16IN./50 MK7 GUNS IN THE TRIPLE TURRET (1/150 SCALE)

E1/29 TURRET NO. 3, 1958 – RIGHT PROFILE (FRAGMENT)

E1/30 TURRET NO. 3, 1958 – FRONT VIEW

E1/31 TURRET NO. 3, 1958 – PLAN (FRAGMENT)

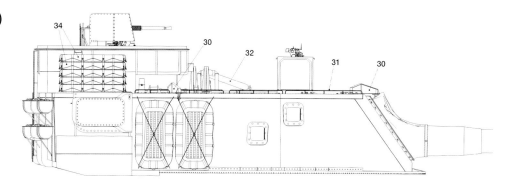

E1/29

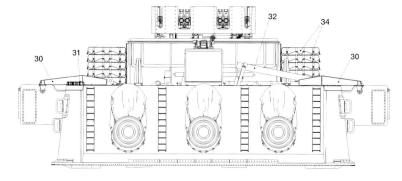

E1/30

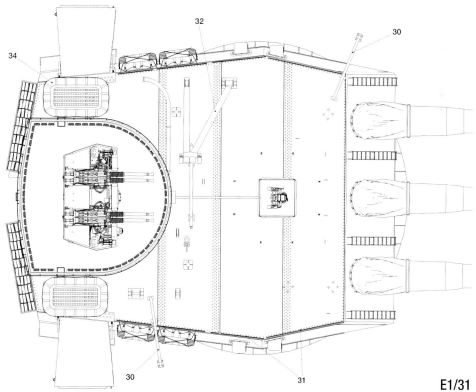

E1/31

16IN./50 MK7 GUNS IN THE TRIPLE TURRET (1/150 SCALE)

E1/32 TURRET NO. 2, 1984 – RIGHT PROFILE (FRAGMENT)

E1/33 TURRET NO. 2, 1984 – FRONT VIEW

E1/34 TURRET NO. 2, 1984 – BACK VIEW

E1/35 TURRET NO. 2, 1984 – PLAN (FRAGMENT)

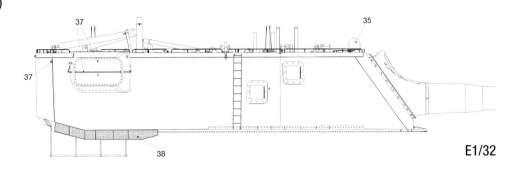

E1/32

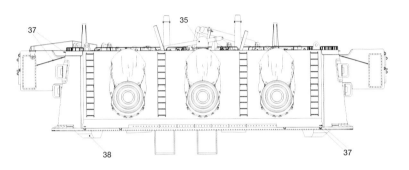

E1/33

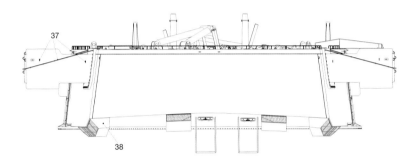

E1/34

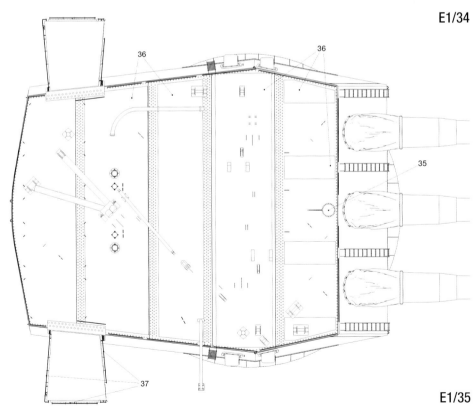

E1/35

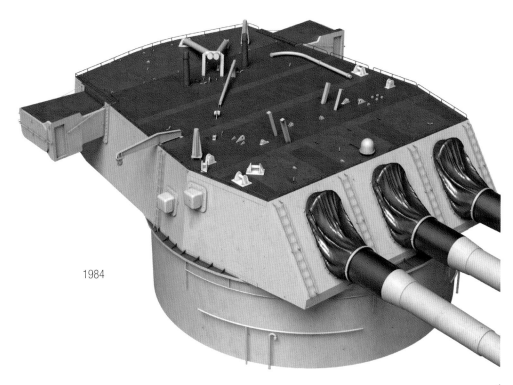

1984

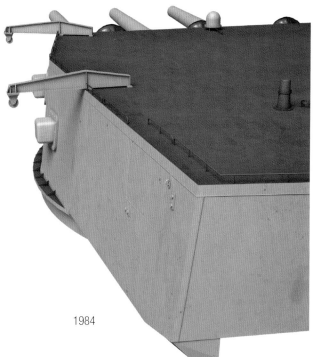

1984

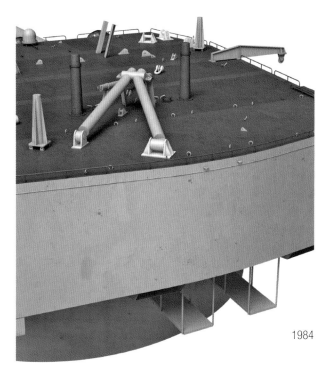

1984

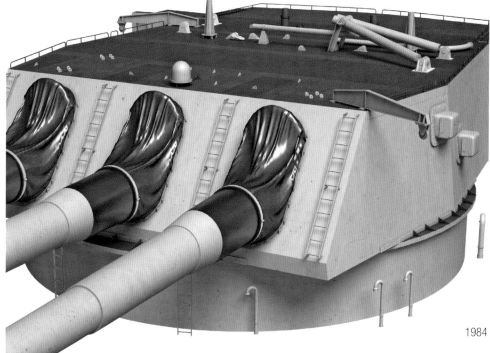

1984

## 16IN./50 MK7 GUNS IN THE TRIPLE TURRET – SECTIONS (1/150 SCALE)

### E1/36 TURRET NO. 1 – RIGHT PROFILE

### E1/37 TURRET NO. 1 – FRONT VIEW

### E1/38 TURRET NO. 1 – BACK VIEW

### E1/36-45 16IN. TRIPLE TURRET – SECTIONS
1 Gun (elevated to loading angle of +5°)
2 Barbette
3 Gunhouse level
4 Pan floor
5 Machinery floor
6 Upper projectile stowage and handling floor
7 Lower projectile stowage and handling floor
8 Powder handling room level
9 Rangefinder arm
10 Gas seal sleeve
11 Rangefinder rail bracket
12 Rangefinder trainer's seat
13 Rangefinder pointer's seat
14 Rangefinder operator's seat
15 Trunnion
16 Trainer's telescope
17 Pointer's telescope
18 Sight setter's station
19 Left powder trunk
20 Centre powder trunk
21 Right powder trunk
22 Powder door operator's station
23 Powder hoist door

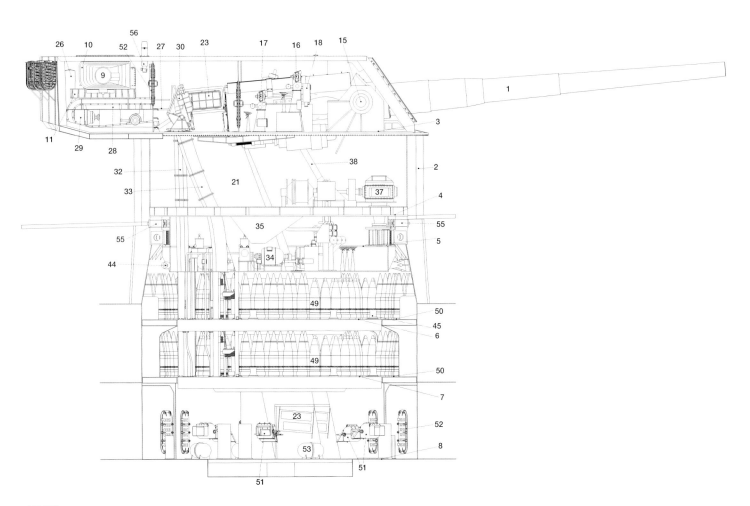

E1/36

24 Powder hoist motor
25 Loader's platform
26 Sprinkling tanks
27 Rammer operator's platform
28 Rammer chain casing
29 Rammer electric motor
30 Projectile cradle
31 Left projectile hoist
32 Centre projectile hoist
33 Right projectile hoist
34 Projectile hoist electric motor
35 Gun pocket
36 Training gear electric motor
37 Training gear wormwheel and pinion bracket
38 Elevating screw
39 Elevating gear motor

40 Train reduction gear
41 Turret trainer's handwheels
42 Gun layer's handwheels
43 Projectile hoist reduction gear
44 Train buffer
45 Parbuckling gear capstan
46 Projectile ring drive
47 Projectile ring electric motor
48 Parbuckling gear electric motor
49 Rotating projectile stowage
50 Fixed projectile stowage
51 Powder passing scuttle
52 Access door
53 Immersion tank
54 Air flask
55 Roller path
56 Periscope
57 Powder hoist operator's station

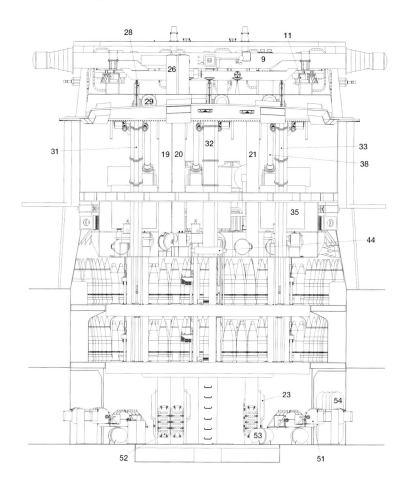

E1/37

E1/38

# E ARMAMENT – 16IN GUNS

16IN./50 MK7 GUNS IN THE TRIPLE TURRET – SECTIONS (1/150 SCALE)

E1/39 TURRET NO. 1 – BACK VIEW (SECTION OF GUNHOUSE
AT TRANSVERSE BULKHEAD)

E1/40 TURRET NO. 1 – BACK VIEW (SECTION OF GUNHOUSE
AT PROJECTILE CRADLES)

E1/39

E1/40

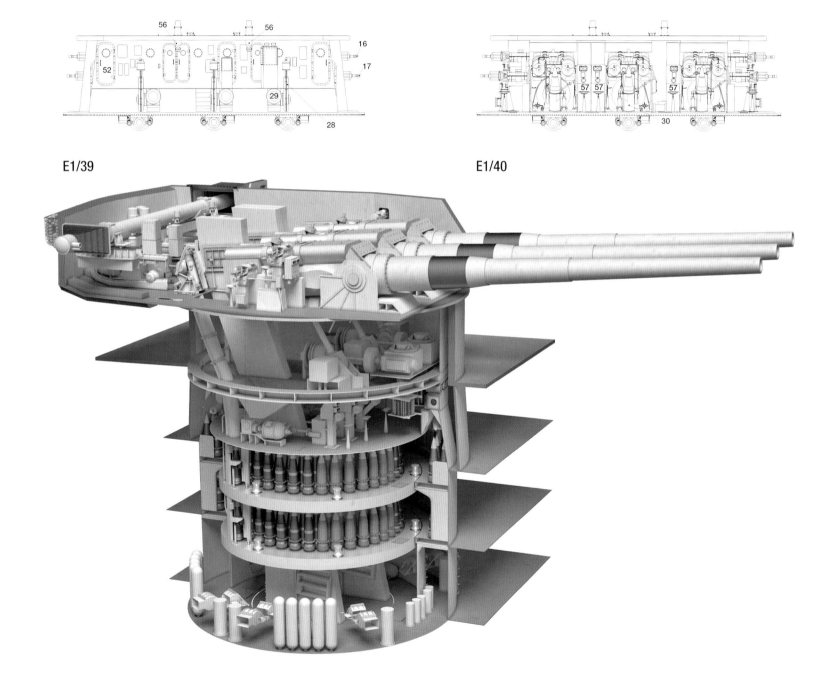

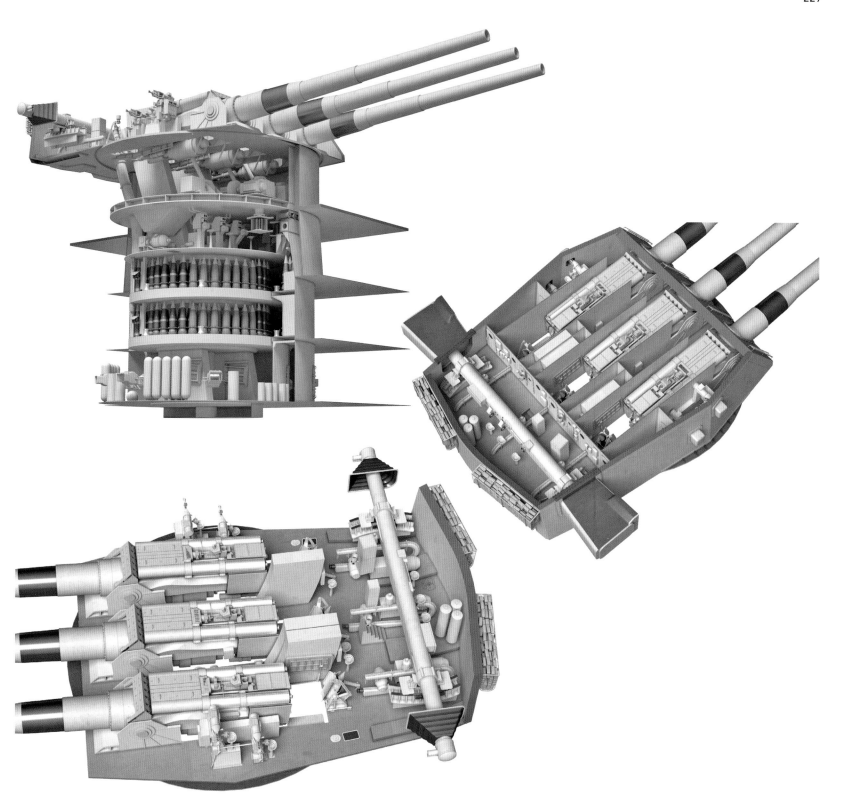

# E ARMAMENT – 16IN GUNS

16IN./50 MK7 GUNS IN THE TRIPLE TURRET – SECTIONS (1/150 SCALE)

E1/41 TURRET NO. 1, GUNHOUSE LEVEL – PLAN

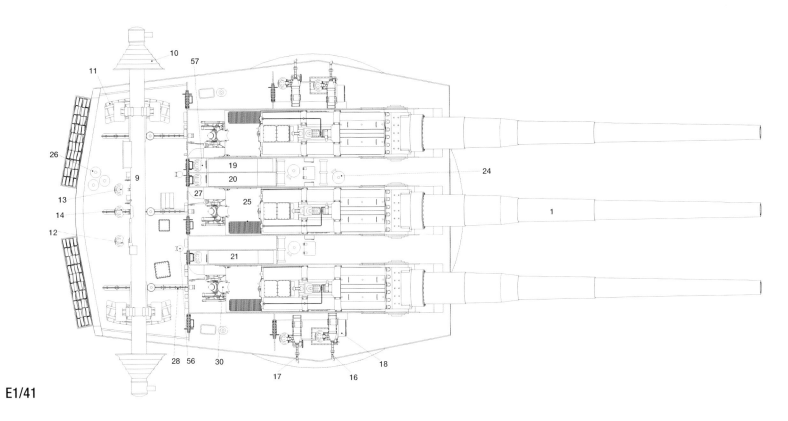

E1/41

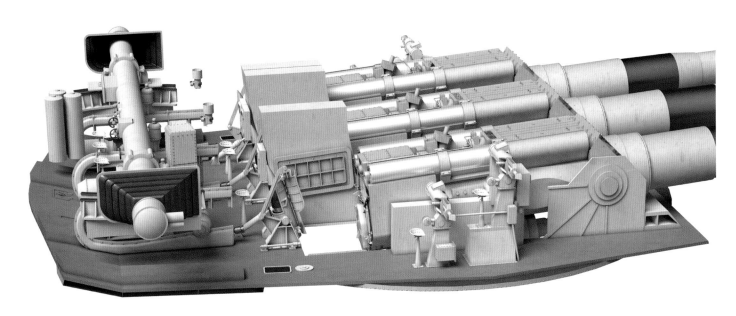

16IN./50 MK7 GUNS IN THE TRIPLE TURRET – SECTIONS (1/150 SCALE)

E1/42 TURRET NO. 1, PAN FLOOR – PLAN

E1/43 TURRET NO. 1, MACHINERY FLOOR – PLAN

E1/44 TURRET NO. 1, UPPER PROJECTILE STOWAGE AND HANDLING
FLOOR – PLAN

E1/45 TURRET NO. 1, POWDER HANDLING ROOM – PLAN

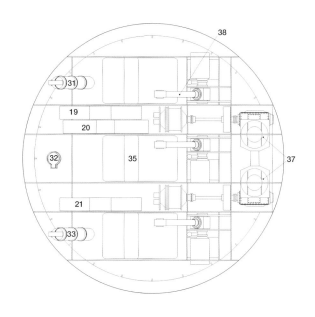

E1/42

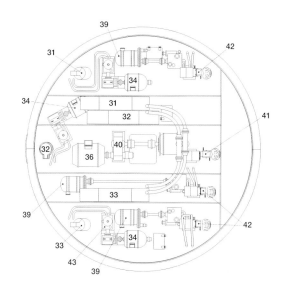

E1/43

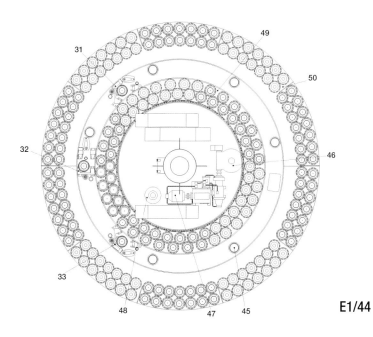

E1/44

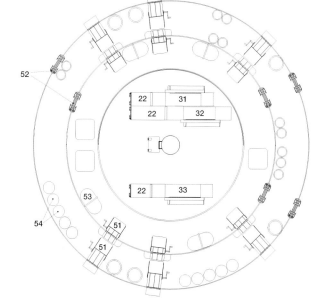

E1/45

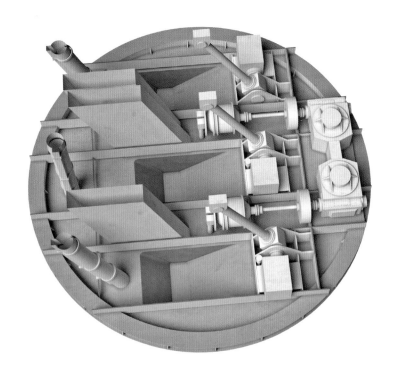

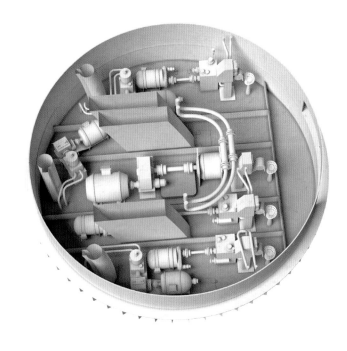

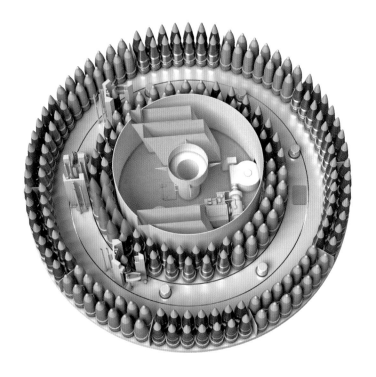

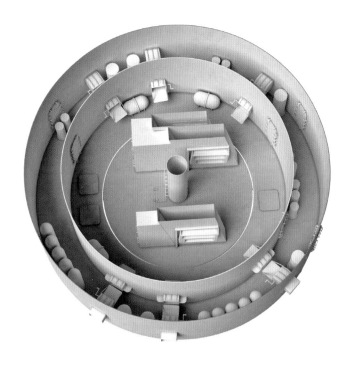

16IN./50 MK7 GUN (1/150 SCALE)

E1/46 RIGHT PROFILE
E1/47 LEFT PROFILE (FRAGMENT)
E1/48 FRONT VIEW (FRAGMENT)
E1/49 BACK VIEW (FRAGMENT)
E1/50 PLAN (FRAGMENT)

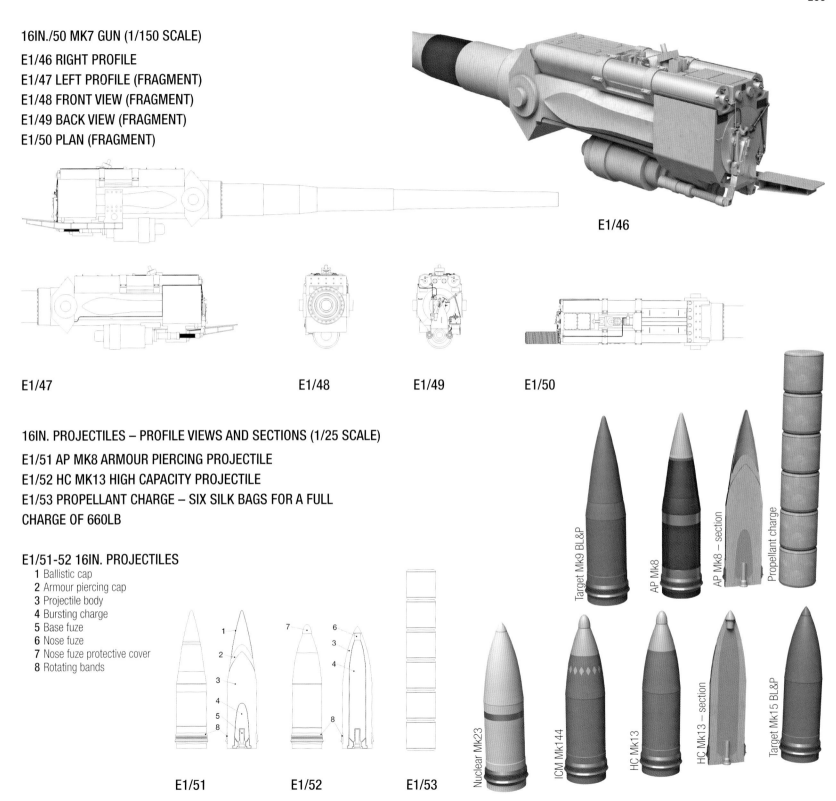

E1/46

E1/47          E1/48          E1/49          E1/50

16IN. PROJECTILES – PROFILE VIEWS AND SECTIONS (1/25 SCALE)

E1/51 AP MK8 ARMOUR PIERCING PROJECTILE
E1/52 HC MK13 HIGH CAPACITY PROJECTILE
E1/53 PROPELLANT CHARGE – SIX SILK BAGS FOR A FULL
CHARGE OF 660LB

E1/51-52 16IN. PROJECTILES
  1 Ballistic cap
  2 Armour piercing cap
  3 Projectile body
  4 Bursting charge
  5 Base fuze
  6 Nose fuze
  7 Nose fuze protective cover
  8 Rotating bands

E1/51          E1/52          E1/53

Target Mk9 BL&P    AP Mk8    AP Mk8 – section    Propellant charge

Nuclear Mk23    ICM Mk144    HC Mk13    HC Mk13 – section    Target Mk15 BL&P

## 5IN./38 MK12 GUNS IN THE MK28 MOD2 ENCLOSED TWIN MOUNT (1/50 SCALE)

## E2/1 RIGHT PROFILE
## E2/2 LEFT PROFILE

### E2/1-11 5IN. GUNS IN ENCLOSED TWIN MOUNT
1 Barrel
2 Gun port seal
3 Side access door
4 Access cover latch
5 Step iron (present only on inboard side of each mount)
6 Trainer's sight

7 Pointer's sight
8 Checker's sight
9 Rear access door
10 Empty case ejection port
11 Auxiliary empty case ejection port
12 Mount captain's sight
13 Mount captain's hatch
14 Roof hatch counter balance
15 Periscope with a removable cover (shifted to the right off mount's centerline; removed shortly after commissioning)
16 Guard rail (fitted on inboard side of each mount; removed shortly after commissioning)
17 Sub-caliber mounting bracket (fitted on inboard side of each mount; removed shortly after commissioning)
18 Mount captain's blast hood (fitted in early 1945 only to the four mounts on superstructure deck level 01)
19 Water deflector (added in early 1945)

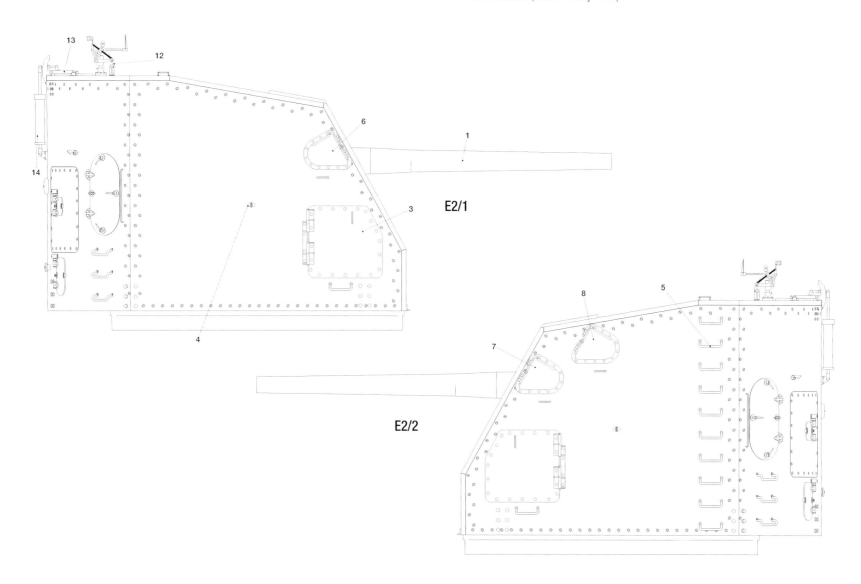

**E2/3 FRONT VIEW**
**E2/4 BACK VIEW**

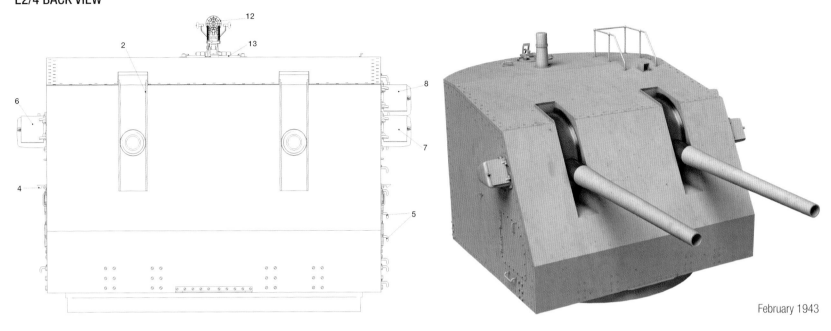

E2/3

February 1943

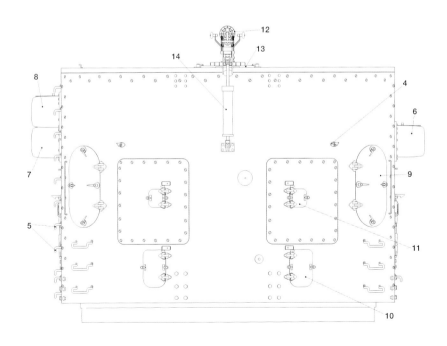

E2/4

1944

**E ARMAMENT – 5IN GUNS**

5IN./38 MK12 GUNS IN THE MK28 MOD2 ENCLOSED TWIN MOUNT
(1/50 SCALE)

E2/5 PLAN

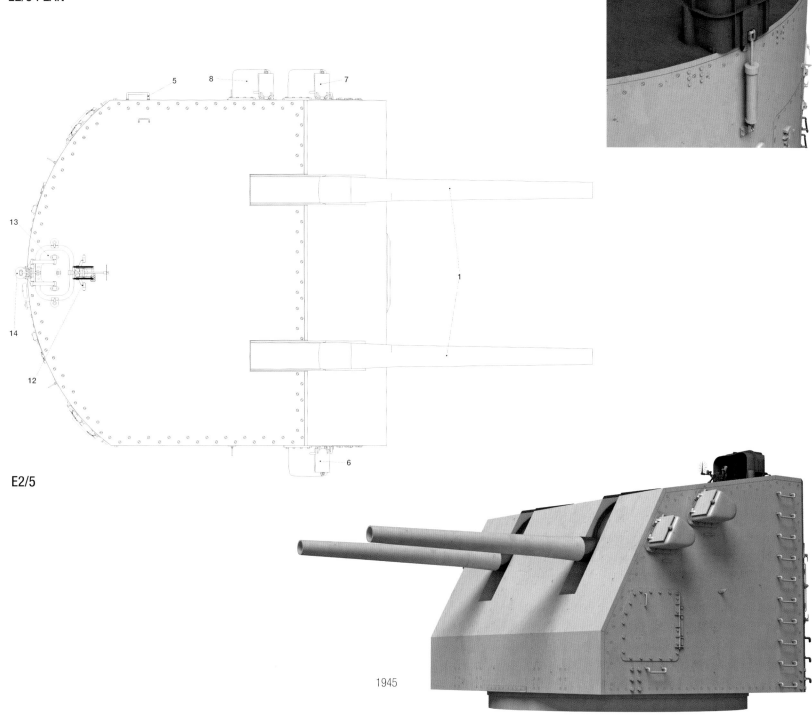

E2/5

1945

E2/6 RIGHT PROFILE (FRAGMENT) – APPEARANCE AT COMMISSIONING
IN FEBRUARY 1943
E2/7 FRONT VIEW (FRAGMENT) – APPEARANCE AT COMMISSIONING
IN FEBRUARY 1943
E2/8 PLAN (FRAGMENT) – APPEARANCE AT COMMISSIONING
IN FEBRUARY 1943

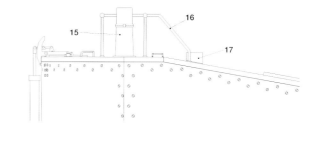

E2/6

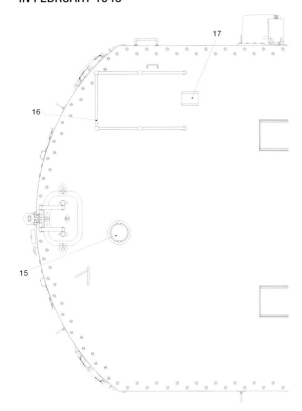

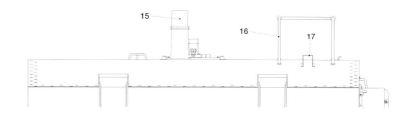

E2/7

E2/8

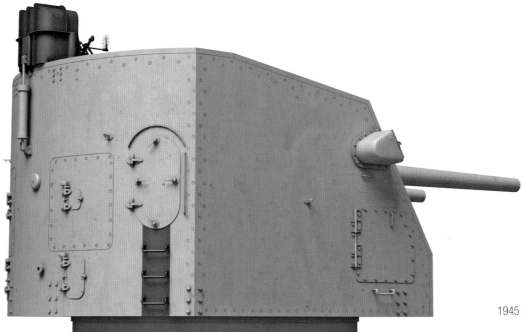

1945

**E ARMAMENT – 5IN GUNS**

5IN./38 MK12 GUNS IN THE MK28 MOD2 ENCLOSED TWIN MOUNT
(1/50 SCALE)

E2/9 RIGHT PROFILE (FRAGMENT) – AFTER MODIFICATIONS IN EARLY 1945
E2/10 BACK VIEW (FRAGMENT) – AFTER MODIFICATIONS IN EARLY 1945
E2/11 PLAN (FRAGMENT) – AFTER MODIFICATIONS IN EARLY 1945

1944

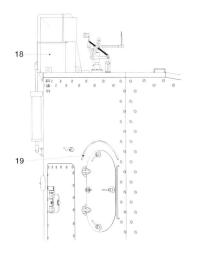

E2/9

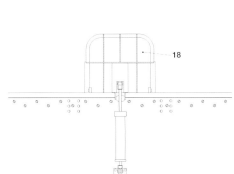

E2/10

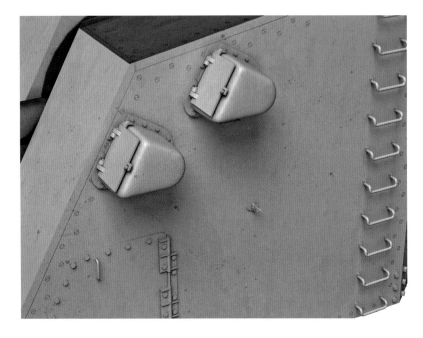

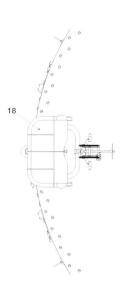

E2/11

E2/12 MOUNT CAPTAIN'S SIGHT – RIGHT PROFILE (1/25 SCALE)
E2/13 MOUNT CAPTAIN'S SIGHT – BACK VIEW (1/25 SCALE)
E2/14 MOUNT CAPTAIN'S SIGHT – PLAN (1/25 SCALE)

  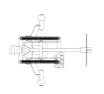 

E2/12          E2/13          E2/14

TWIN 5IN. PRACTICE LOADING MACHINE (1/50 SCALE)

E2/15 RIGHT PROFILE
E2/16 LEFT PROFILE OF THE RIGHT-HAND MACHINE

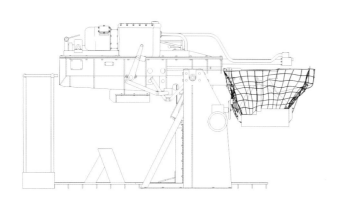 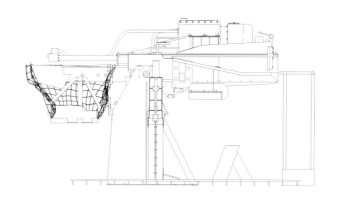

E2/15                                                              E2/16

TWIN 5IN. PRACTICE LOADING MACHINE, 1943–1958 (1/50 SCALE)

E2/17 FRONT VIEW

E2/18 BACK VIEW

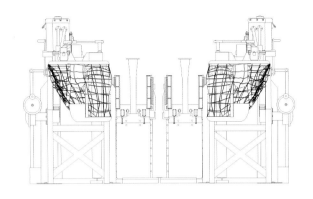

E2/17                    E2/18

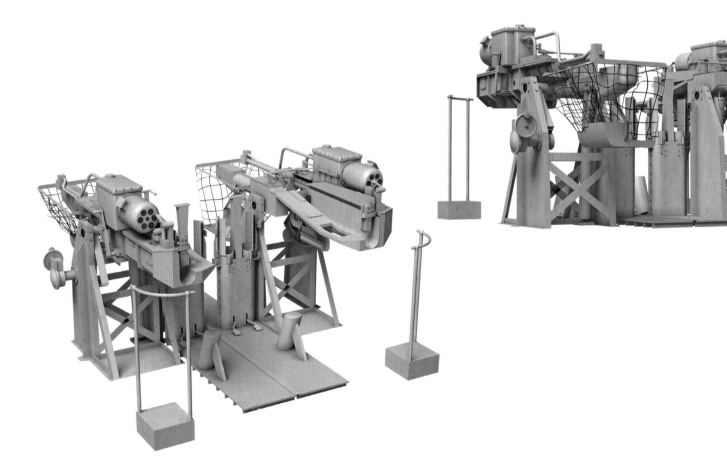

**E2/19 PLAN**

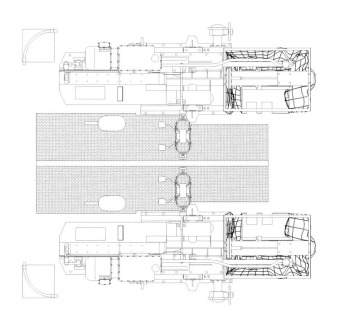

**E2/19**

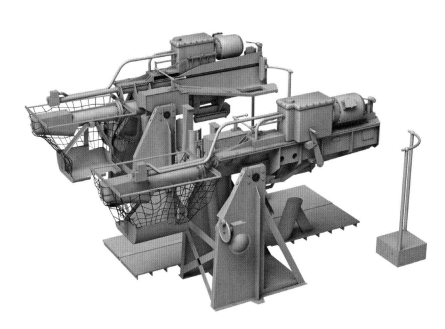

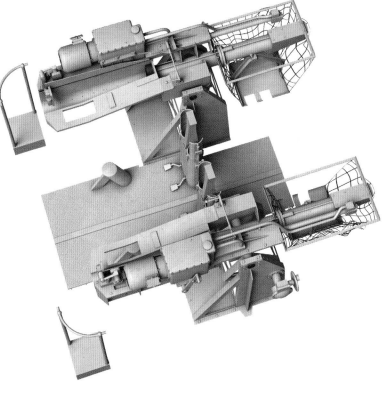

BOFORS 40MM/56 MK1, MK2 GUNS IN THE MK2 QUADRUPLE MOUNT,
1943–1958 (1/25 SCALE)

E3/1 RIGHT PROFILE

**E3/1-9 BOFORS 40MM**
**QUADRUPLE MOUNT**

1 Shield
2 Carriage
3 Mount stand
4 Barrel
5 Elevating sight
6 Training sight
7 Pointer's handwheel
8 Trainer's handwheel
9 Pointer's seat
10 Trainer's seat
11 Firing pedal
12 Elevation power drive
13 Train power drive
14 Starting switch (elevation drive)
15 Starting switch (train drive)
16 Firing motor starter
17 Case discharge chute
18 Coolant tank
19 Coolant pipe
20 Cooling pump motor
21 Loaders' platform
22 Guard rail
23 Training circle cover
24 Loader guides' protective cover

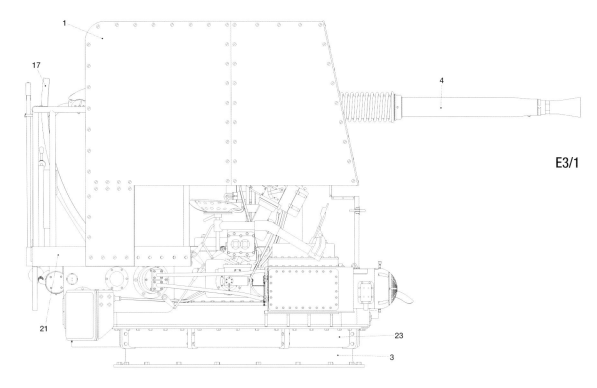

E3/1

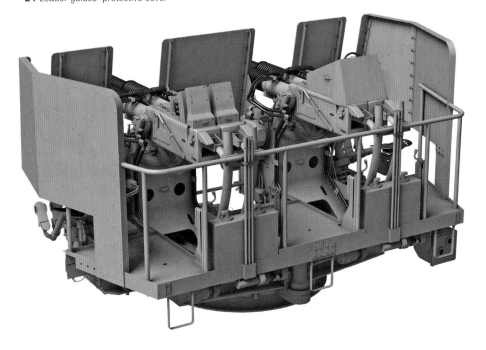

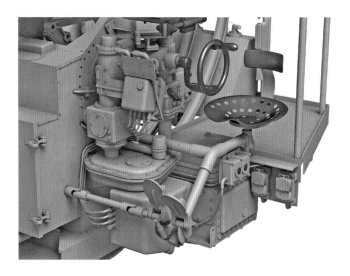

# E3/2 RIGHT PROFILE WITH SHIELD OMITTED FOR CLARITY

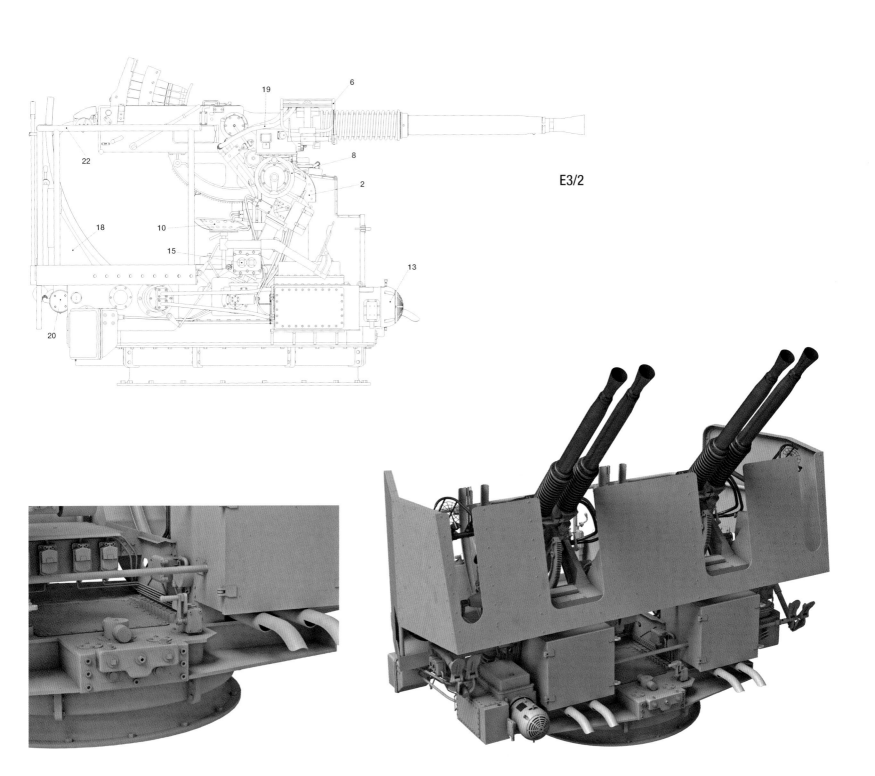

E3/2

BOFORS 40MM/56 MK1, MK2 GUNS IN THE MK2 QUADRUPLE MOUNT,
1943–1958 (1/25 SCALE)

E3/3 LEFT PROFILE

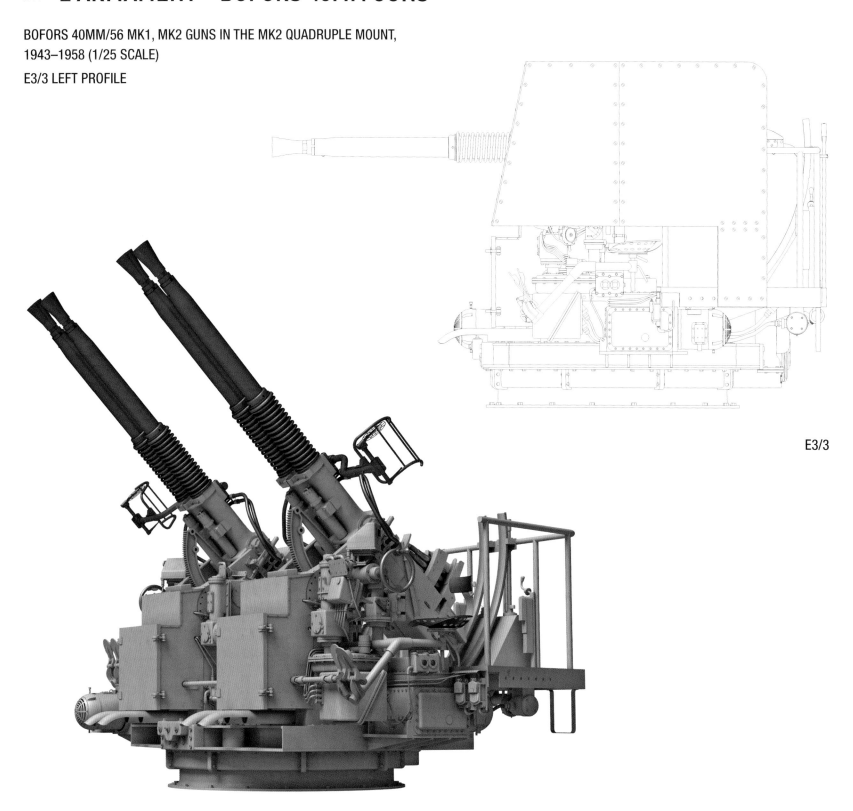

E3/3

E3/4 LEFT PROFILE WITH SHIELD OMITTED FOR CLARITY
AND GUNS ELEVATED TO +45°

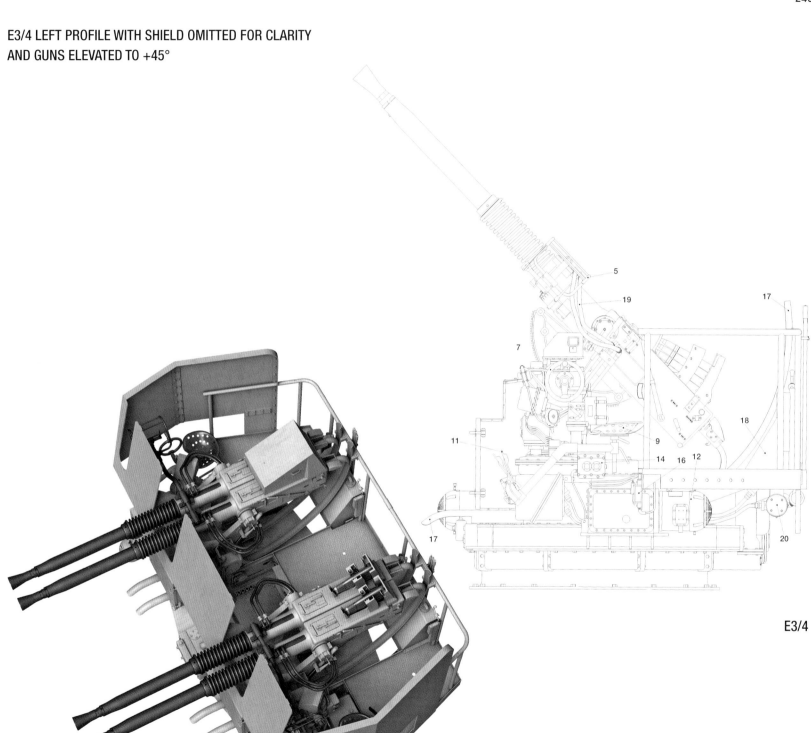

E3/4

# E ARMAMENT – BOFORS 40MM GUNS

BOFORS 40MM/56 MK1, MK2 GUNS IN THE MK2 QUADRUPLE MOUNT,
1943–1958 (1/25 SCALE)

## E3/5 FRONT VIEW

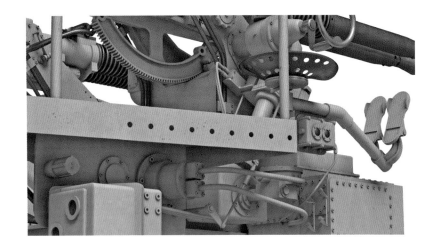

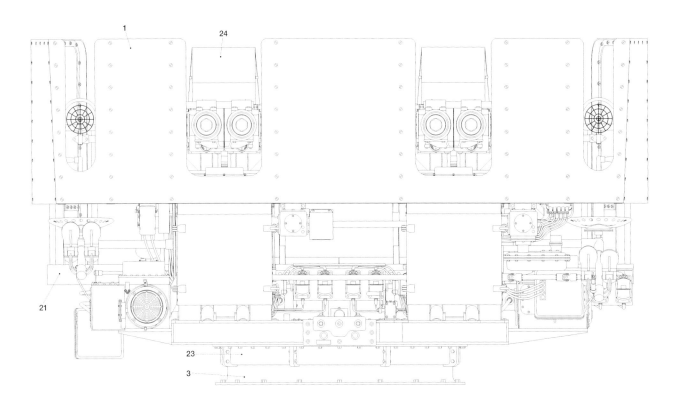

E3/5

**E3/6 FRONT VIEW WITH SHIELD OMITTED FOR CLARITY AND GUNS ELEVATED TO +45°**

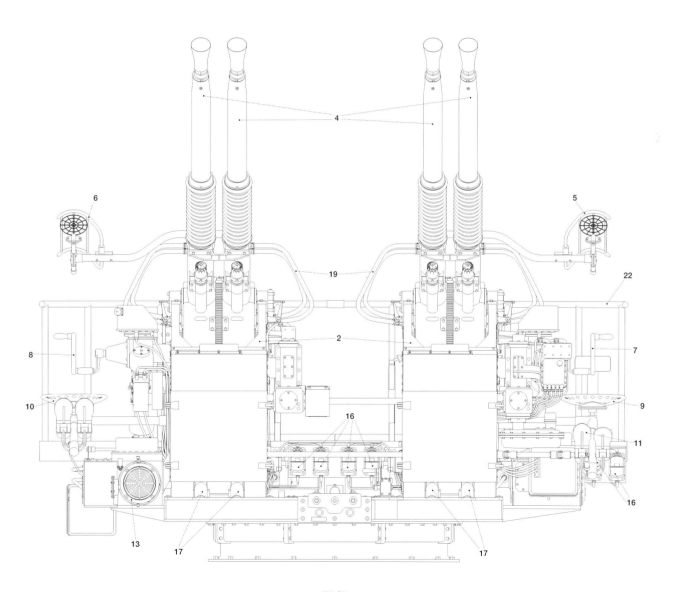

E3/6

# E ARMAMENT – BOFORS 40MM GUNS

BOFORS 40MM/56 MK1, MK2 GUNS IN THE MK2 QUADRUPLE MOUNT,
1943–1958 (1/25 SCALE)

### E3/7 BACK VIEW

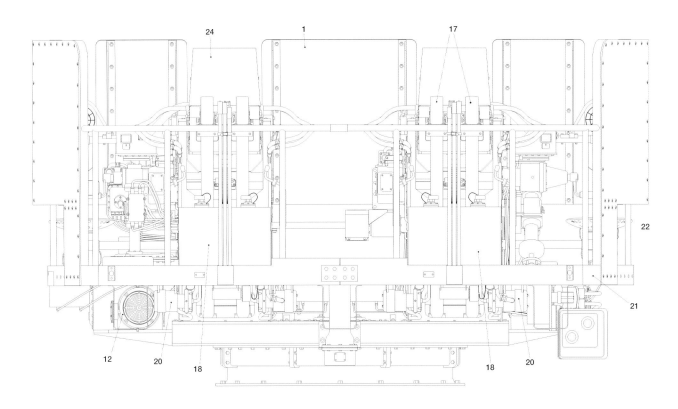

E3/7

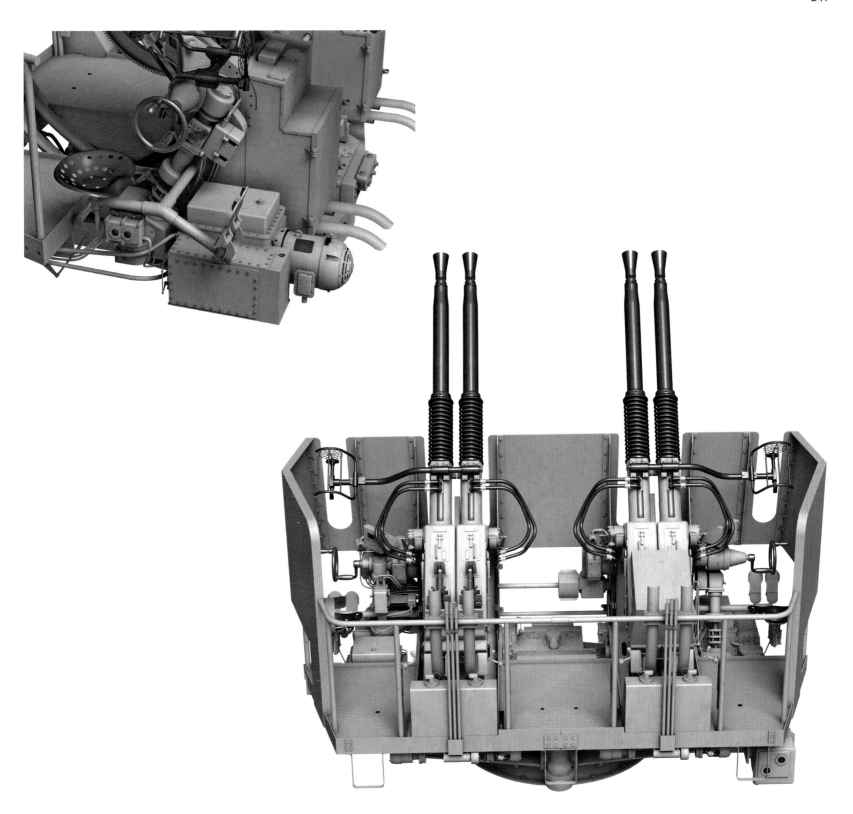

# E ARMAMENT – BOFORS 40MM GUNS

BOFORS 40MM/56 MK1, MK2 GUNS IN THE MK2 QUADRUPLE MOUNT,
1943–1958 (1/25 SCALE)

E3/8 PLAN WITH SHIELD OMITTED FOR CLARITY

E3/9 SHIELD – PLAN

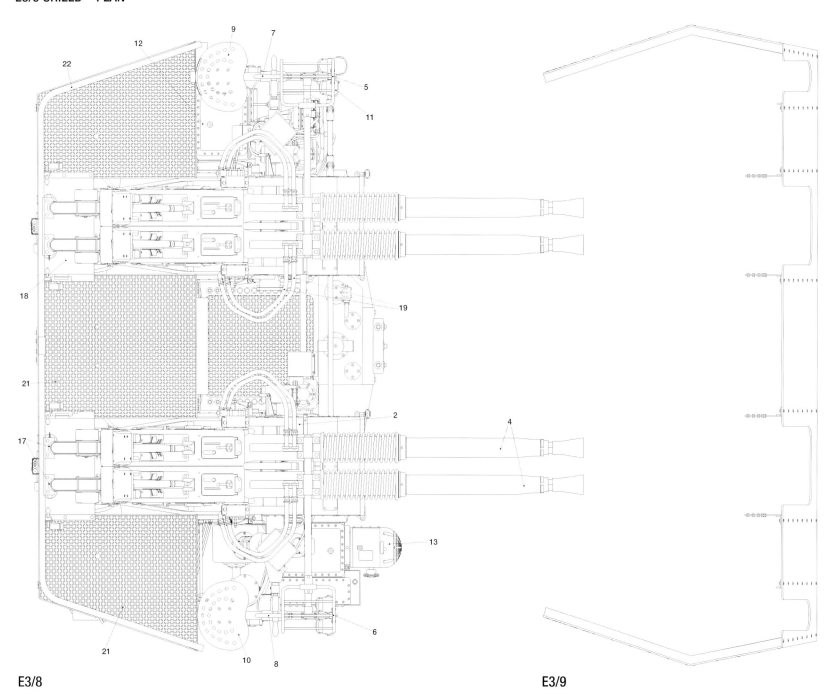

E3/8

E3/9

## PAIRED BOFORS 40MM/56 MK1 AND MK2 GUNS (1/25 SCALE)

E3/10 RIGHT PROFILE

E3/11 FRONT VIEW

E3/12 BACK VIEW

E3/13 PLAN

E3/14 BOTTOM VIEW

### E3/11–14 PAIRED MK1 AND MK2 GUNS

1 Flash guard
2 Water jacket on barrel
3 Recoil spring
4 Recoil cylinder
5 Firing plunger
6 Trunnion
7 Side door
8 Top door
9 Loader guide
10 Elevation arc
11 Ammunition clip chute
12 Hand operating lever
13 Firing selector lever
14 Feed control thumb lever
15 Case deflector
16 Mk1 gun (left-handed)
17 Mk2 gun (right-handed)

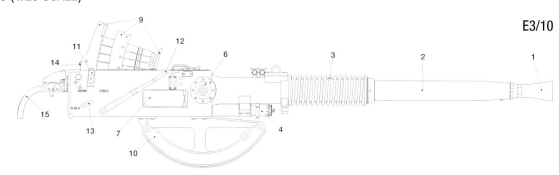

E3/10

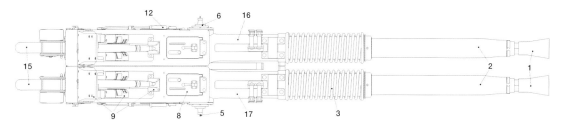

E3/13

E3/14

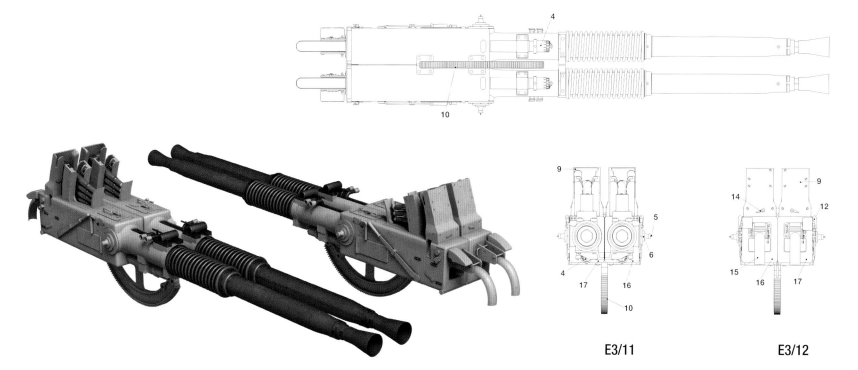

E3/11

E3/12

**E ARMAMENT – BOFORS 40MM GUNS**

FOUR-ROUND AMMUNITION CLIP (1/15 SCALE)

E3/15 PROFILE

E3/16 FRONT VIEW

E3/17 BACK VIEW

E3/18 PLAN

E3/19 40MM ROUND – PROFILE (1/15 SCALE)

E3/20 40MM ROUND – SECTION (1/15 SCALE)
 1 Primer
 2 Cartridge case
 3 Propellant charge
 4 Tracer
 5 Rotating band
 6 Bursting charge
 7 Fuze

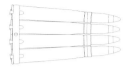

E3/15　　　　E3/16　　　E3/17

E3/18　　　　E3/19　　　　E3/20

E3/21 40MM HE-T-SD PROJECTILE (HIGH EXPLOSIVE-TRACER-SELF DESTROYING) – PROFILE (1/15 SCALE)

E3/21

E3/22 LOCATION OF BOFORS QUADRUPLE MOUNTS IN EARLY 1943
(15 MOUNTS) – PLAN (1/1500 SCALE)
E3/23 LOCATION OF BOFORS QUADRUPLE MOUNTS MID-1943 –
LATE 1946 AND 1952 – MID-1955 (19 MOUNTS) – PLAN (1/1500 SCALE)
E3/24 LOCATION OF BOFORS QUADRUPLE MOUNTS 1947 – 1951
(15 MOUNTS) – PLAN (1/1500 SCALE)
E3/25 LOCATION OF BOFORS QUADRUPLE MOUNTS MID-1955 – 1958
(13 MOUNTS) – PLAN (1/1500 SCALE)

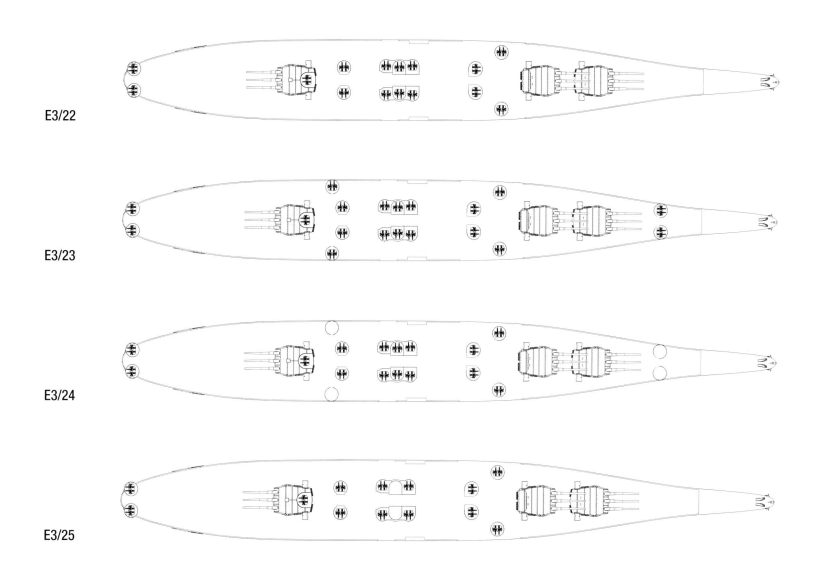

E3/22

E3/23

E3/24

E3/25

OERLIKON 20MM/70 MK4 GUN IN THE MK4 SINGLE MOUNT, 1943–1946
(1/25 SCALE)

E4/1 RIGHT PROFILE
E4/2 LEFT PROFILE

E4/1-5 OERLIKON 20MM SINGLE MOUNT
 1 Shield
 2 Barrel
 3 Barrel spring
 4 Trigger
 5 Magazine
 6 Mk14 gun sight
 7 Power unit bracket
 8 Electric cable and air hose
 9 Shoulder rests
 10 Harness
 11 Mount pedestal
 12 Elevation handwheel
 13 Cartridge case collecting bag

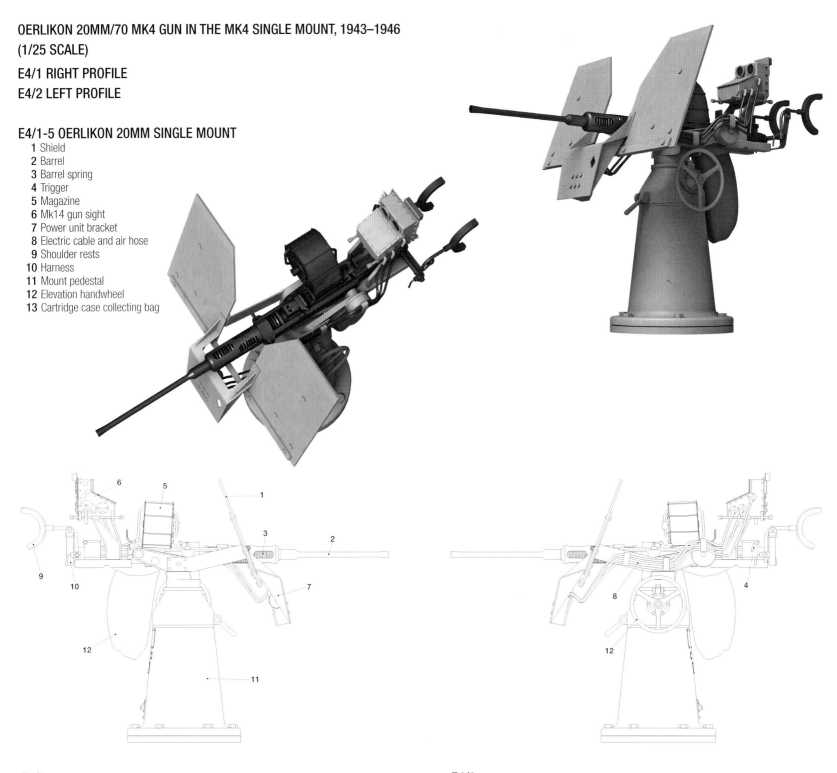

E4/1

E4/2

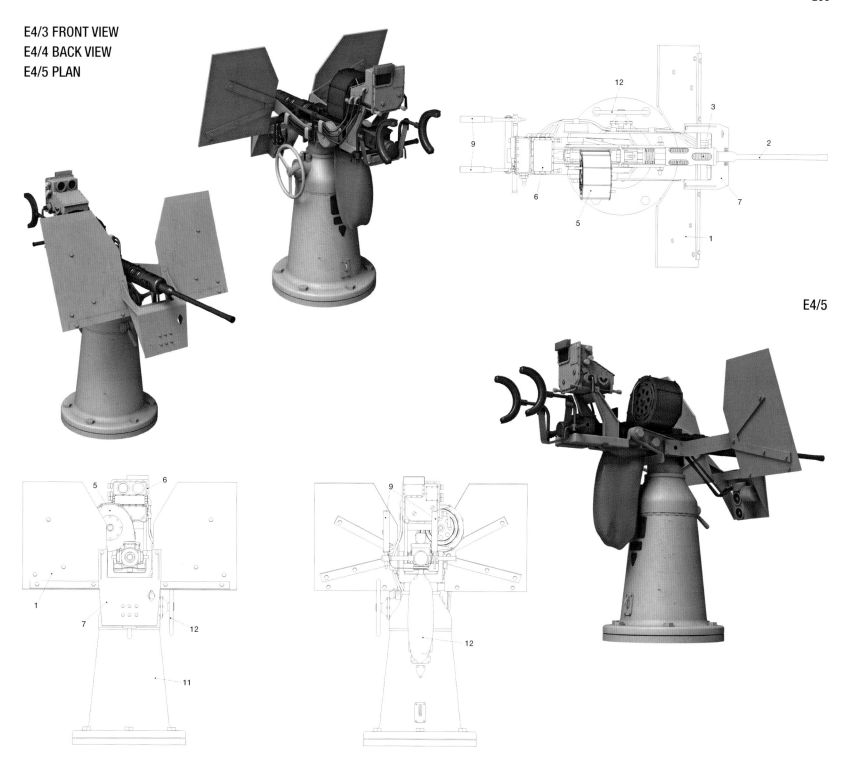

E4/3 FRONT VIEW
E4/4 BACK VIEW
E4/5 PLAN

E4/5

E4/3

E4/4

OERLIKON 20MM/70 MK4 GUN IN THE MK24 TWIN MOUNT, 1946 –1947
(1/25 SCALE)

E4/6 RIGHT PROFILE
E4/7 LEFT PROFILE
E4/8 FRONT VIEW
E4/9 BACK VIEW
E4/10 PLAN

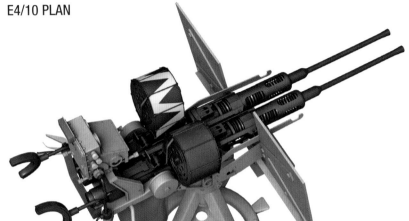

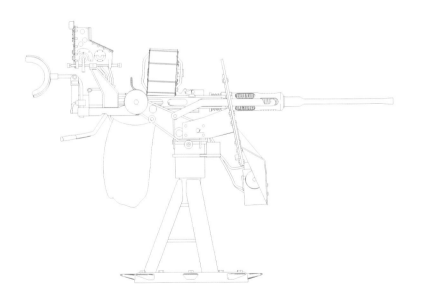

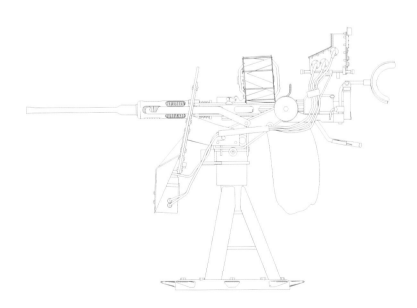

E4/6

E4/7

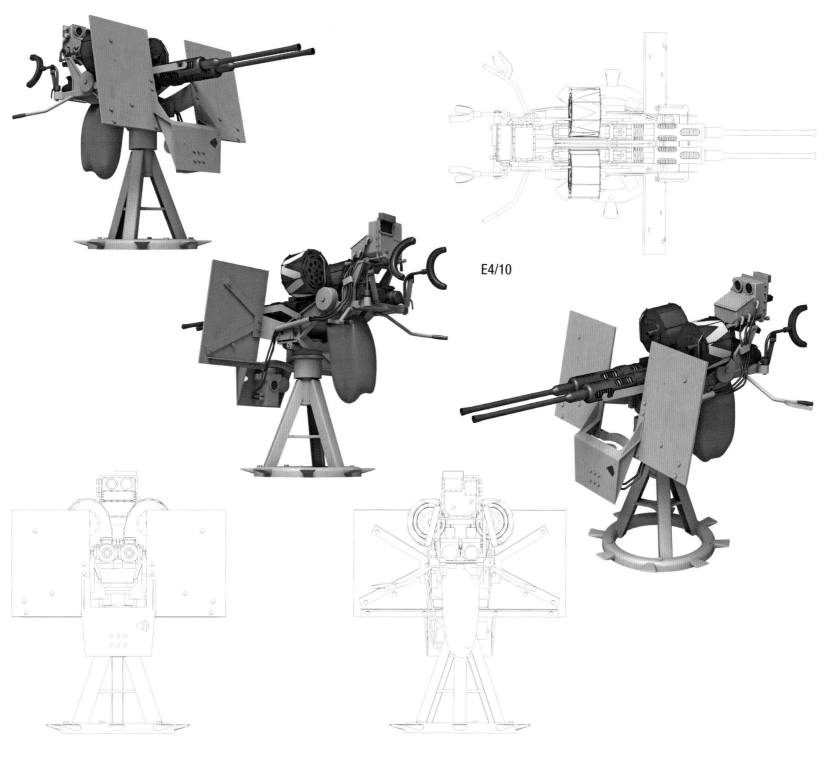

E4/10

E4/8

E4/9

OERLIKON 20MM/70 MK4 GUN (1/25 SCALE)

E4/11 RIGHT PROFILE

E4/12 LEFT PROFILE

E4/13 FRONT VIEW

E4/14 BACK VIEW

E4/15 PLAN

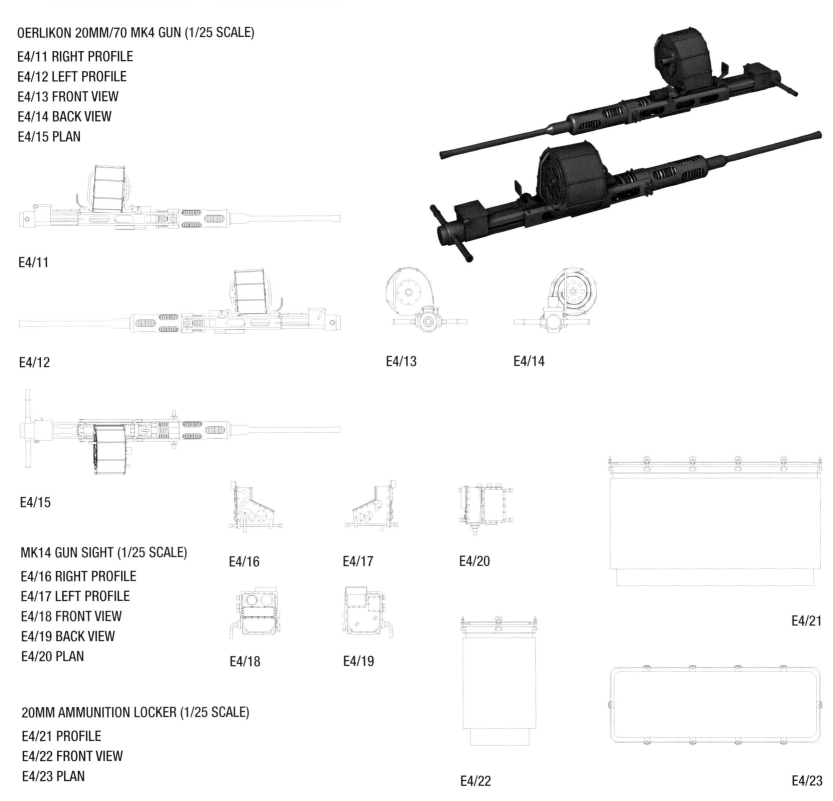

E4/11

E4/12

E4/13

E4/14

E4/15

MK14 GUN SIGHT (1/25 SCALE)

E4/16 RIGHT PROFILE

E4/17 LEFT PROFILE

E4/18 FRONT VIEW

E4/19 BACK VIEW

E4/20 PLAN

E4/16

E4/17

E4/20

E4/18

E4/19

E4/21

20MM AMMUNITION LOCKER (1/25 SCALE)

E4/21 PROFILE

E4/22 FRONT VIEW

E4/23 PLAN

E4/22

E4/23

20MM MAGAZINE LOADING FRAME (1/25 SCALE)

E4/24 PROFILE

E4/25 PLAN


SPARE BARREL TUBE (1/25 SCALE)

E4/26 PROFILE


E4/27 LOCATION OF OERLIKON MOUNTS IN EARLY 1943
(60 SINGLE MOUNTS) – PLAN (1/1500 SCALE)
E4/28 LOCATION OF OERLIKON MOUNTS MID-1943 – 1944
(52 SINGLE MOUNTS) – PLAN (1/1500 SCALE)
E4/29 LOCATION OF OERLIKON MOUNTS 1945–1946
(52 SINGLE MOUNTS)
E4/30 LOCATION OF OERLIKON MOUNTS IN 1947
(16 TWIN MOUNTS) – PLAN (1/1500 SCALE)

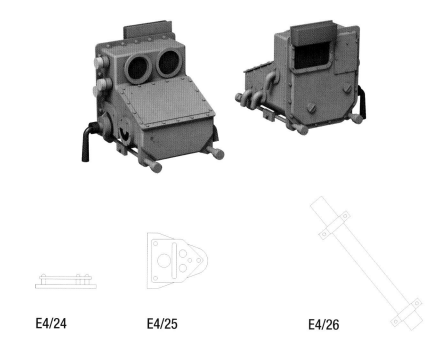

E4/24          E4/25          E4/26

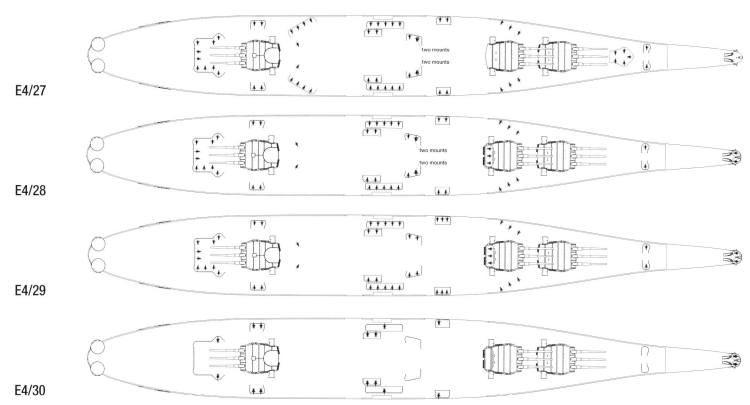

E4/27

E4/28

E4/29

E4/30

**E ARMAMENT – TOMAHAWK CRUISE MISSILES**

MK143 ABL (ARMORED BOX LAUNCHER) WITH FOUR BGM-109
TOMAHAWK MISSILES STORED INSIDE, 1984–1990 (1/50 SCALE)

E5/1 RIGHT PROFILE
E5/2 LEFT PROFILE

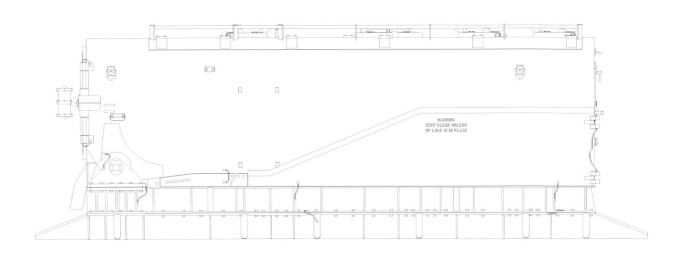

E5/1

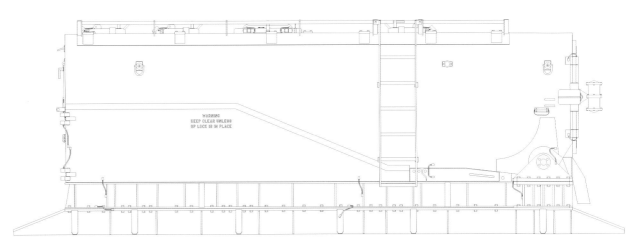

E5/2

E5/3 FRONT VIEW
E5/4 BACK VIEW

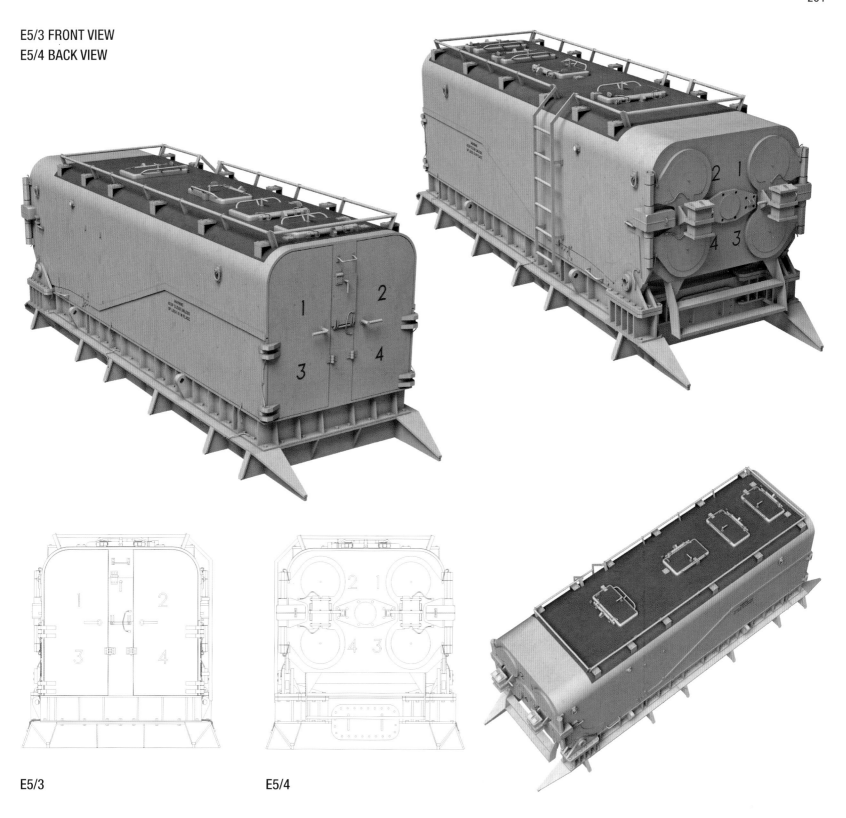

E5/3

E5/4

**E ARMAMENT – TOMAHAWK CRUISE MISSILES**

MK143 ABL (ARMORED BOX LAUNCHER) WITH FOUR BGM-109
TOMAHAWK MISSILES STORED INSIDE, 1984–1990 (1/50 SCALE)

E5/5 PLAN

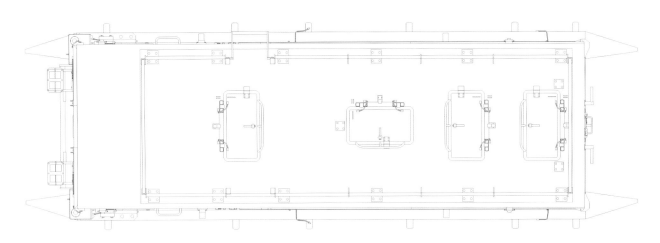

E5/5

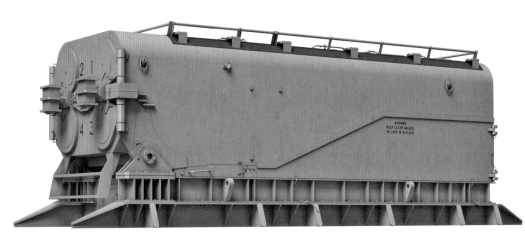

BGM-109 TOMAHAWK CRUISE MISSILE (1/50 SCALE)

E5/6 PROFILE

E5/7 FRONT VIEW

E5/8 PLAN

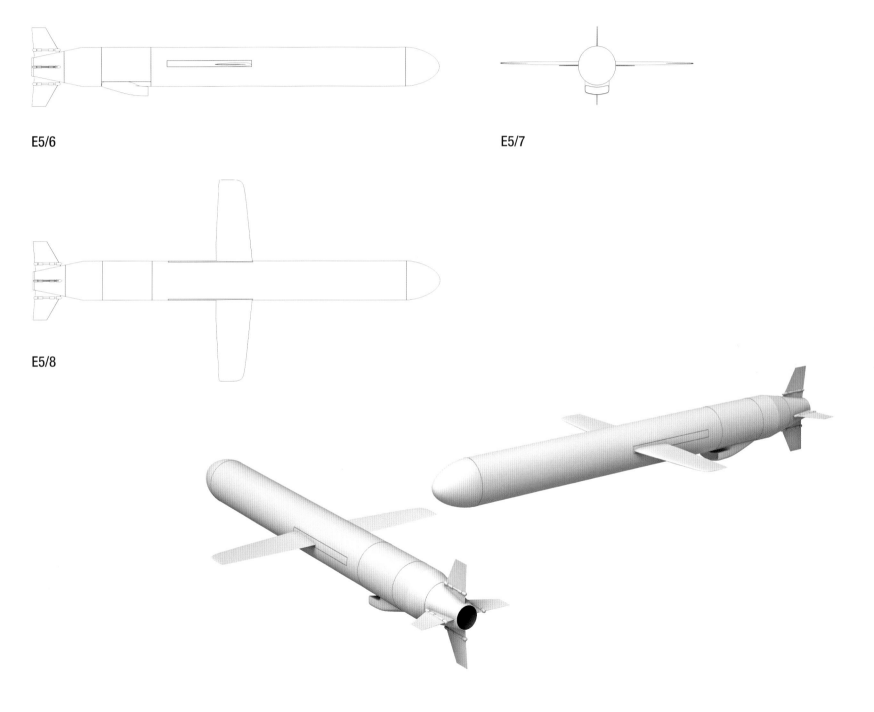

E5/6

E5/7

E5/8

263

**E ARMAMENT – HARPOON ANTI-SHIP MISSILES**

MK141 LAUNCHER WITH FOUR RGM-84 HARPOON MISSILES STORED
IN KEVLAR ARMOURED CANISTERS, 1984–1990 (1/50 SCALE)

E6/1 PROFILE
E6/2 FRONT VIEW
E6/3 BACK VIEW
E6/4 PLAN

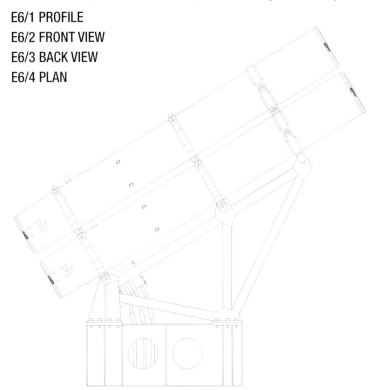

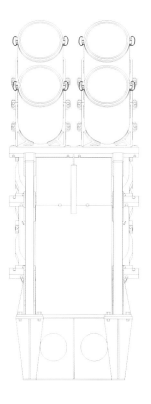

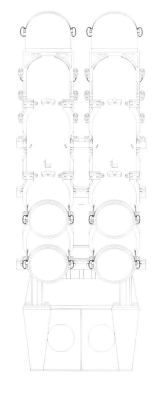

E6/1

E6/2

E6/3

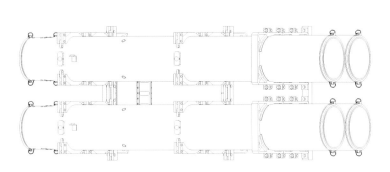

E6/4

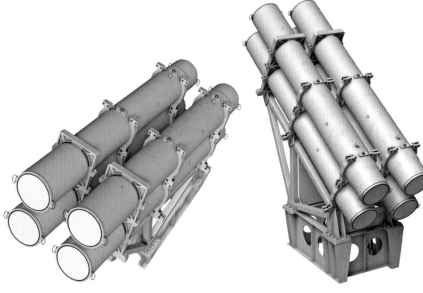

# RGM-84 HARPOON ANTI-SHIP MISSILE (1/50 SCALE)

E6/5 PROFILE
E6/6 FRONT VIEW
E6/7 PLAN
E6/8 BOTTOM VIEW

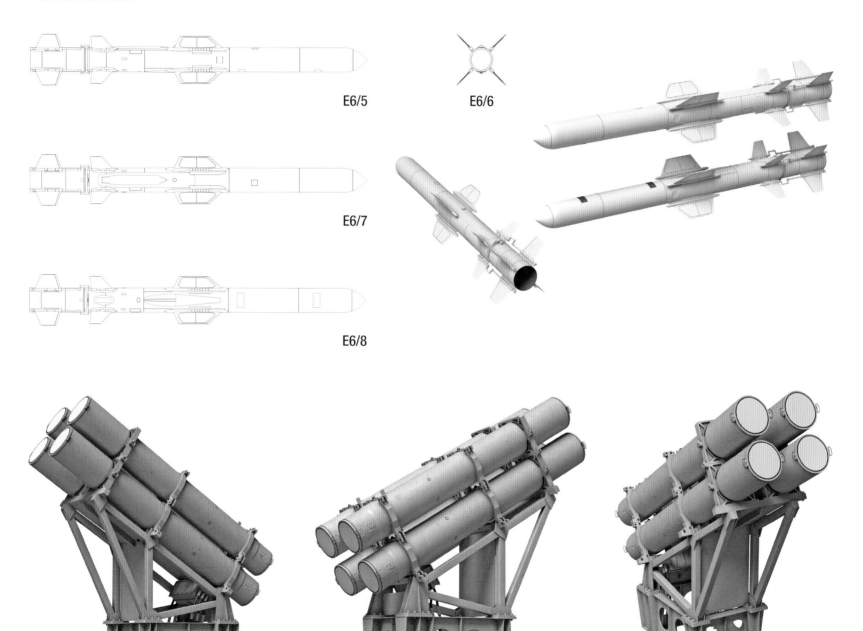

E6/5

E6/6

E6/7

E6/8

# E ARMAMENT – PHALANX CIWS (CLOSE-IN WEAPON SYSTEM)

MK15 PHALANX CIWS (CLOSE-IN WEAPON SYSTEM)
BLOCK 0 – 20MM/76 M61A1 VULCAN SIX-BARRELLED
GUN IN THE MK72 MOUNT, 1984–1990 (1/37.5 SCALE)

E7/1 RIGHT PROFILE
E7/2 LEFT PROFILE

E7/1-5 PHALANX CIWS BLOCK 0
   **1** Search radar housing
   **2** Tracking radar housing
   **3** 20mm/76 M61A1 Vulcan six-barrelled gun
   **4** Electronics compartment
   **5** Ammunition storage drum (989 rounds)

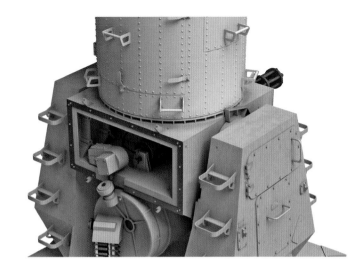

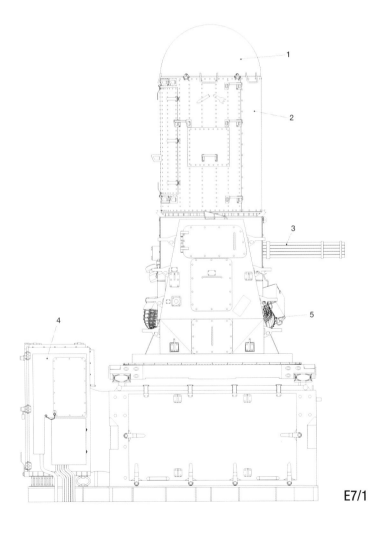

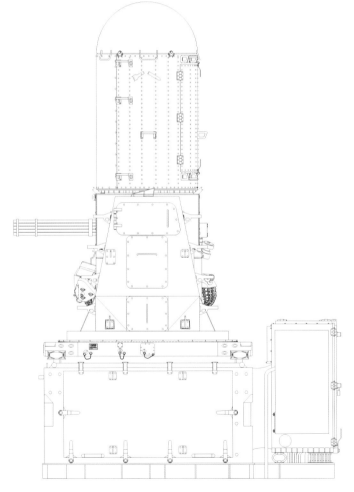

E7/1

E7/2

# E ARMAMENT – PHALANX CIWS (CLOSE-IN WEAPON SYSTEM)

MK15 PHALANX CIWS (CLOSE-IN WEAPON SYSTEM)
BLOCK 0 – 20MM/76 M61A1 VULCAN SIX-BARRELLED
GUN IN THE MK72 MOUNT, 1984–1990 (1/37.5 SCALE)

E7/3 FRONT VIEW
E7/4 BACK VIEW

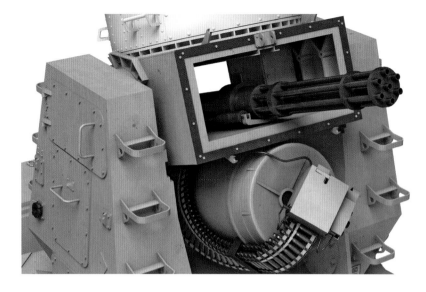

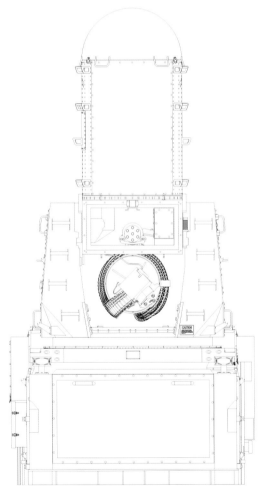

E7/3

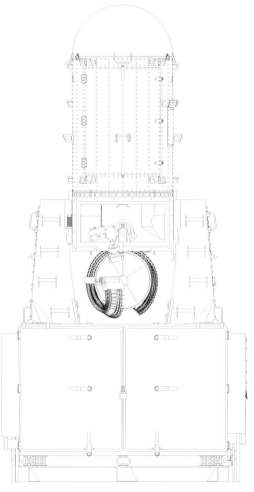

E7/4

**E7/5 PLAN**

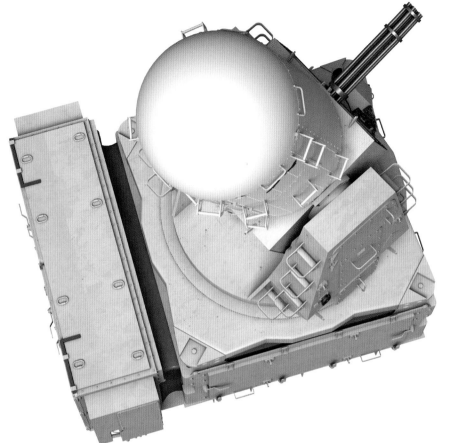

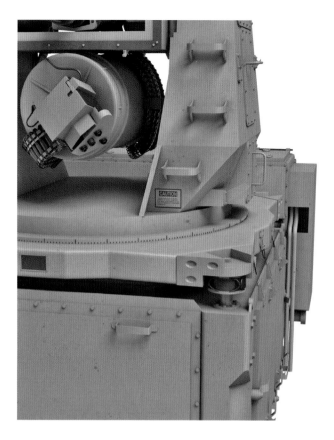

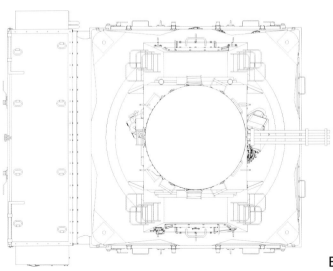

E7/5

MK36 SRBOC (SUPER RAPID BLOOMING OFFBOARD CHAFF) IN MK137
LAUNCHER, 1984–1990 (1/25 SCALE)

E8/1 PROFILE

E8/2 FRONT VIEW

E8/3 BACK VIEW

E8/4 PLAN

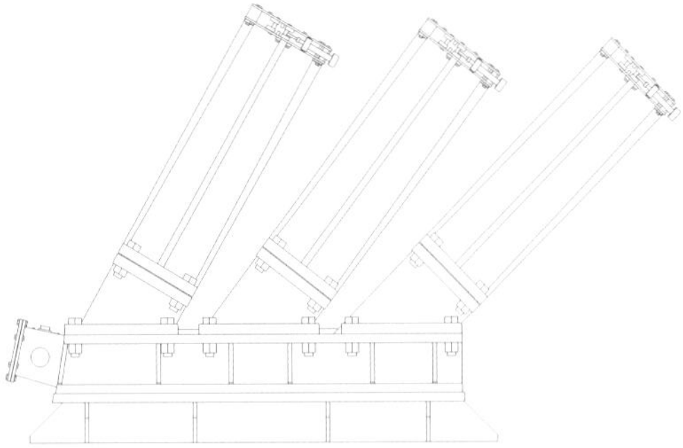

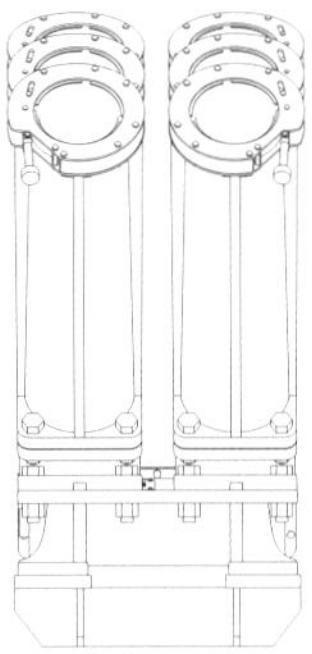

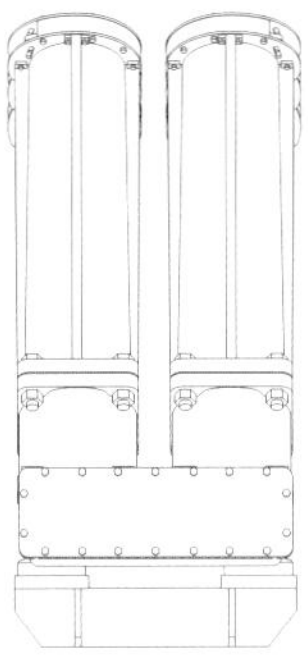

E8/1

E8/2

E8/3

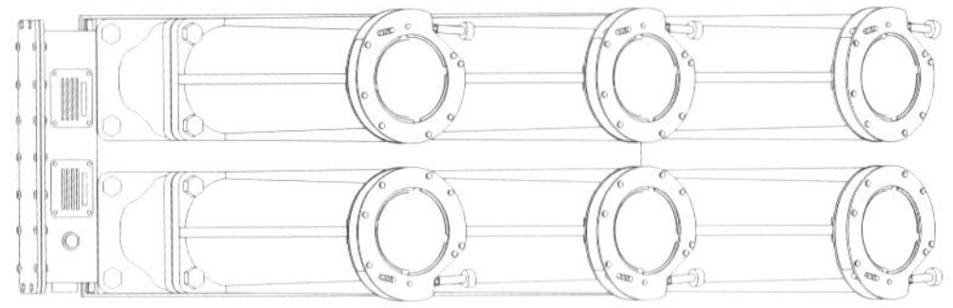

E8/4

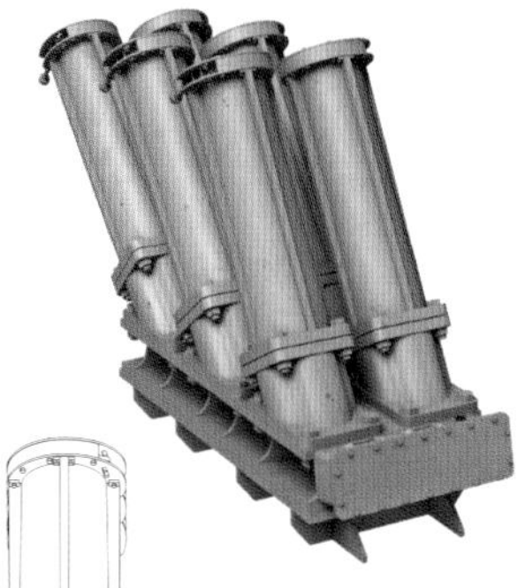

6-PDR SALUTING GUN, 1946–1958 (1/25 SCALE)

E8/5 PROFILE

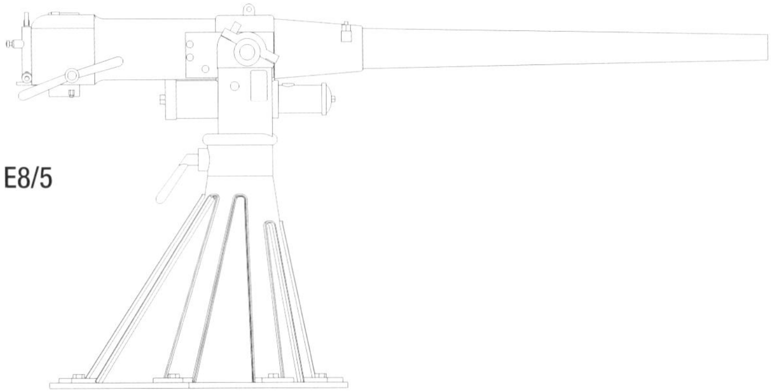

E8/5

E8/6 FRONT VIEW
E8/7 BACK VIEW
E8/8 PLAN

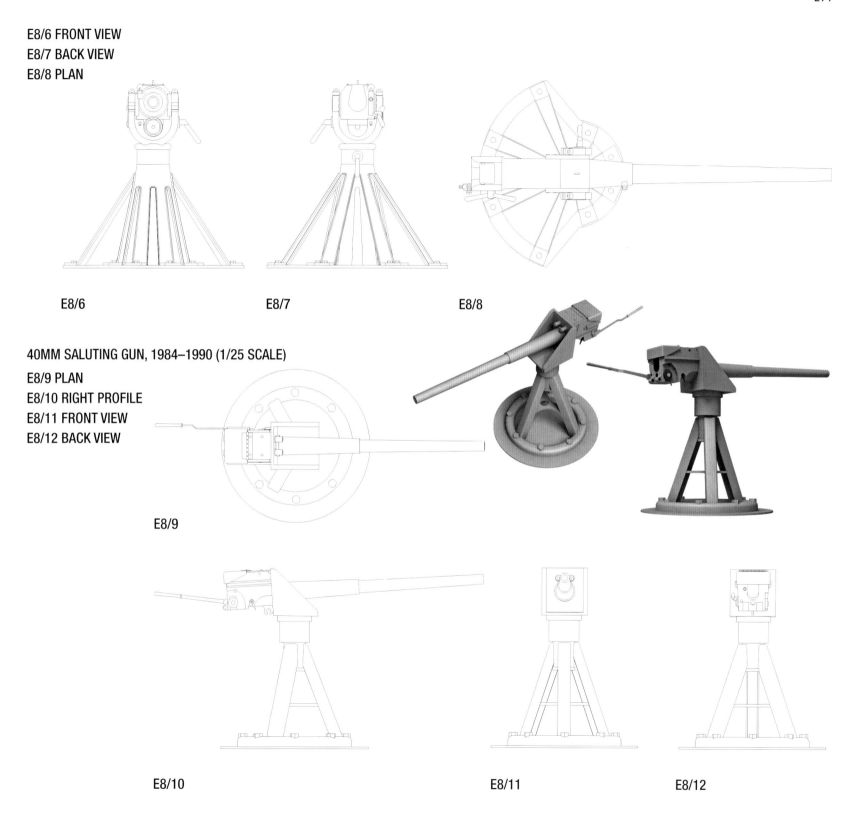

E8/6

E8/7

E8/8

40MM SALUTING GUN, 1984–1990 (1/25 SCALE)

E8/9 PLAN
E8/10 RIGHT PROFILE
E8/11 FRONT VIEW
E8/12 BACK VIEW

E8/9

E8/10

E8/11

E8/12

MK38 DIRECTOR WITH MK8 (FH) RADAR ANTENNA FITTED ON TOP,
1943–1946 (1/75 SCALE)

F1/1 RIGHT PROFILE
F1/2 LEFT PROFILE
F1/3 FRONT VIEW
F1/4 BACK VIEW
F1/5 PLAN

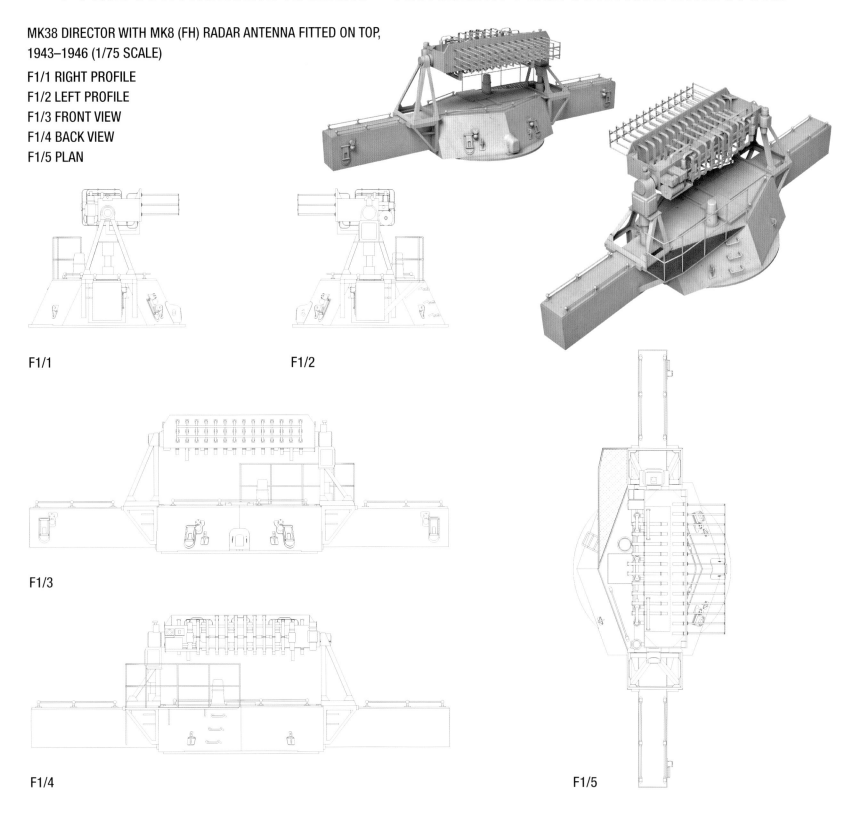

F1/1

F1/2

F1/3

F1/4

F1/5

273

MK13 RADAR ANTENNA THAT REPLACED THE MK8 ANTENNA ON TOP
OF FORE DIRECTOR IN 1945 AND AFT DIRECTOR IN 1946 (1/75 SCALE)

F1/6 PROFILE
F1/7 FRONT VIEW
F1/8 BACK VIEW
F1/9 PLAN

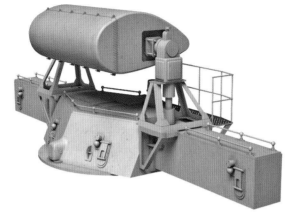

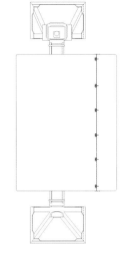

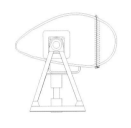
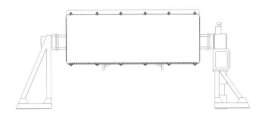
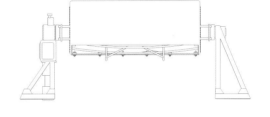

F1/6

F1/7

F1/8

F1/9

MK40 DIRECTOR ON THE ROOF OF THE CONNING TOWER (1/50 SCALE)

F1/10 PROFILE
F1/11 FRONT VIEW
F1/12 PLAN

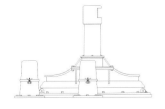

F1/10

F1/11

F1/12

MK3 (FC) RADAR ANTENNA FITTED ON MK40 DIRECTOR,
SUMMER 1943–1945 (1/50 SCALE)

F1/13 PROFILE
F1/14 FRONT VIEW
F1/15 PLAN

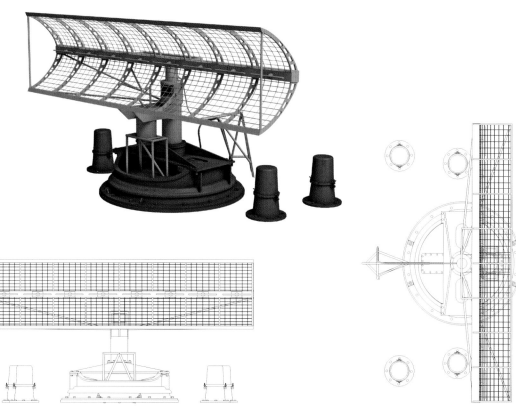

F1/13

F1/14

F1/15

MK27 RADAR ANTENNA, 1945–1955 (1/37.5 SCALE)

F1/16 PROFILE
F1/17 BACK VIEW
F1/18 PLAN

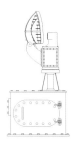

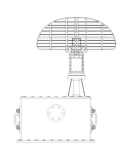

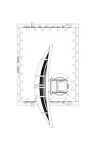

F1/16

F1/17

F1/18

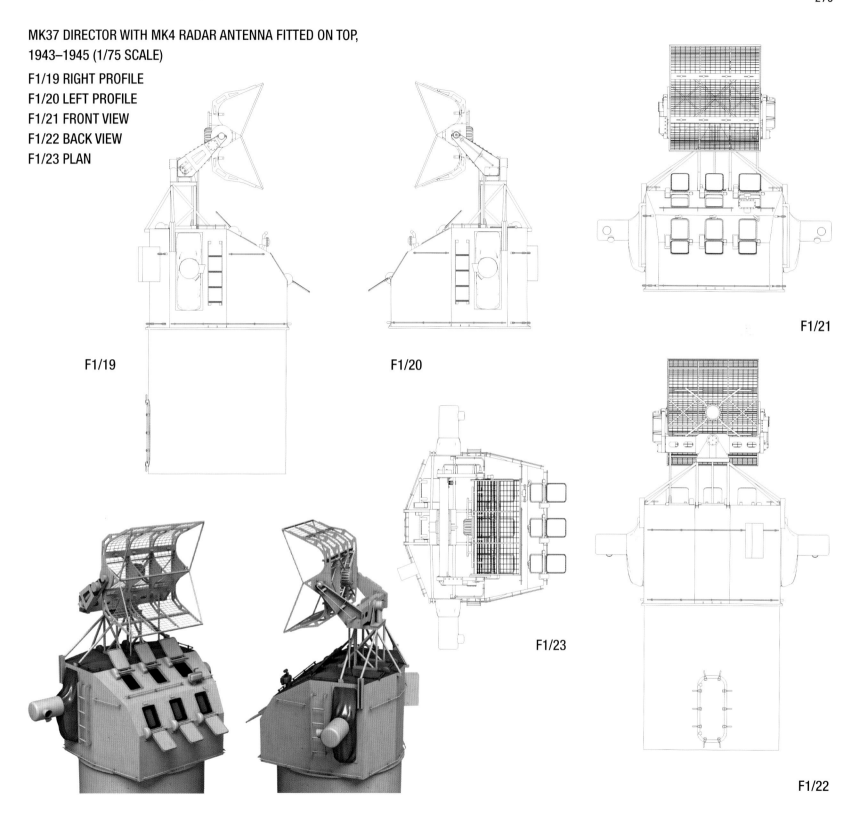

MK37 DIRECTOR WITH MK4 RADAR ANTENNA FITTED ON TOP,
1943–1945 (1/75 SCALE)

F1/19 RIGHT PROFILE
F1/20 LEFT PROFILE
F1/21 FRONT VIEW
F1/22 BACK VIEW
F1/23 PLAN

F1/19

F1/20

F1/21

F1/23

F1/22

MK37 DIRECTOR WITH MK12/22 RADAR ANTENNAS FITTED ON TOP,
1945–1955 (1/75 SCALE)

F1/24 RIGHT PROFILE
F1/25 LEFT PROFILE
F1/26 FRONT VIEW
F1/27 BACK VIEW
F1/28 PLAN

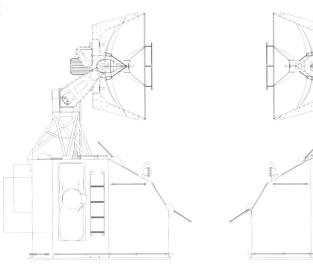

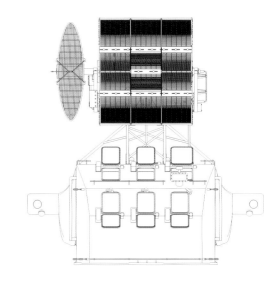

F1/24

F1/25

F1/26

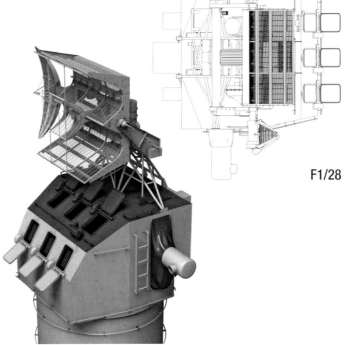

F1/28

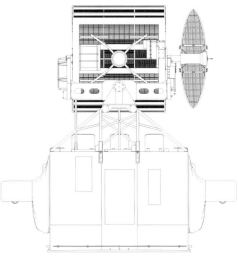

F1/27

MK37 DIRECTOR WITH REBUILT SHIELD AND MK25 RADAR ANTENNA
FITTED ON TOP, 1955–1990 (1/75 SCALE)

F1/29 RIGHT PROFILE
F1/30 FRONT VIEW
F1/31 BACK VIEW
F1/32 PLAN

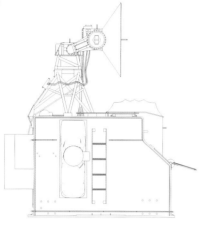

F1/29

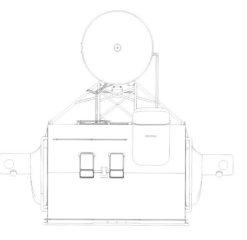

F1/30

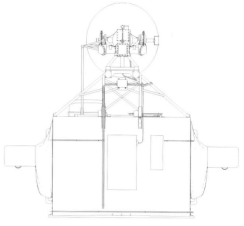

F1/31

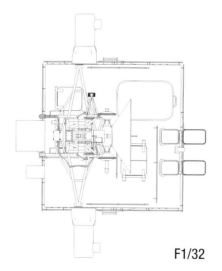

F1/32

ORIGINAL FORM OF THE MK25 ANTENNA, 1955-1958 (1/37.5 SCALE)

F1/33 RIGHT PROFILE

F1/34 FRONT VIEW

F1/35 BACK VIEW

F1/36 PLAN

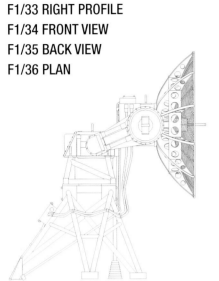

F1/33

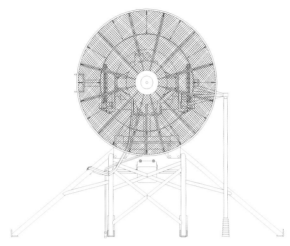

F1/34

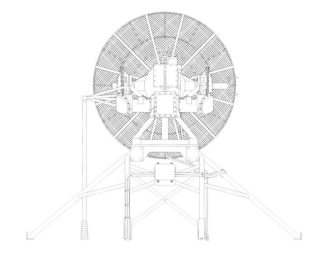

F1/35

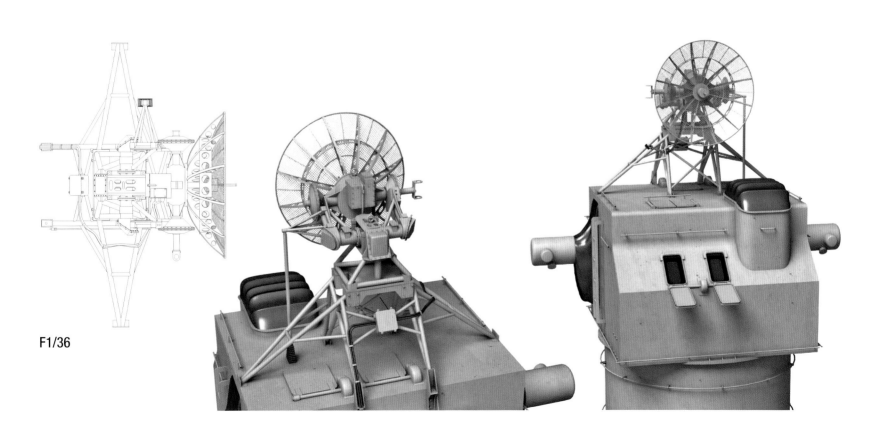

F1/36

MK51 DIRECTOR, 1943–1955 (1/25 SCALE)

F1/37 RIGHT PROFILE

F1/38 LEFT PROFILE

F1/39 FRONT VIEW

F1/40 BACK VIEW

F1/41 PLAN

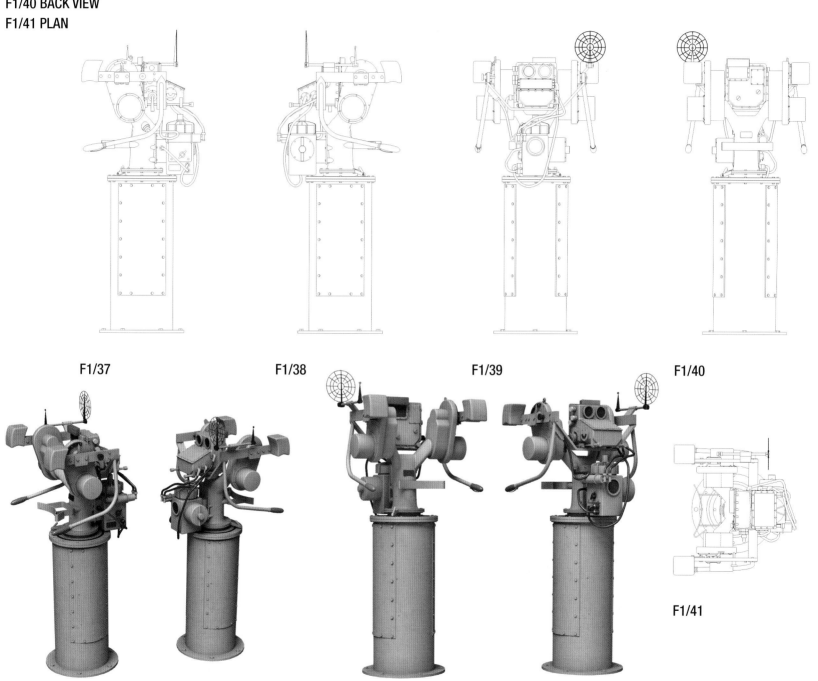

F1/37

F1/38

F1/39

F1/40

F1/41

MK57 DIRECTOR WITH A MK34 RADAR ANTENNA, 1945–1955
(1/25 SCALE)
F1/42 RIGHT PROFILE
F1/43 LEFT PROFILE
F1/44 FRONT VIEW
F1/45 BACK VIEW
F1/46 PLAN

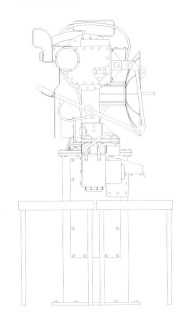
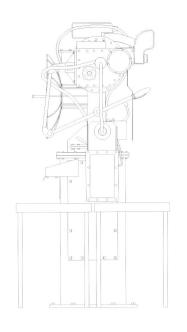
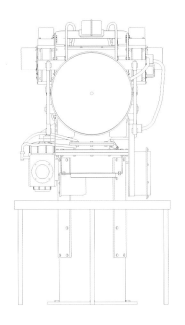
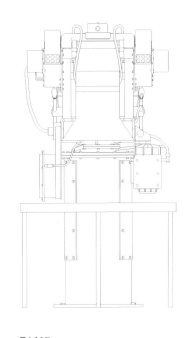

F1/42

F1/43

F1/44

F1/45

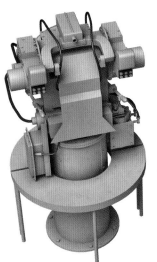
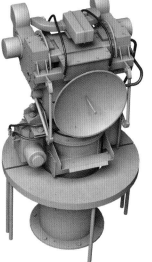

F1/46

MK63 DIRECTOR, 1951–1958 (1/25 SCALE)

F1/47 RIGHT PROFILE

F1/48 FRONT VIEW

F1/49 PLAN

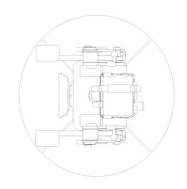

F1/49

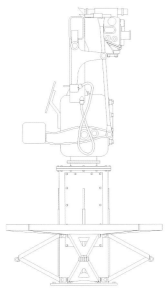

F1/47

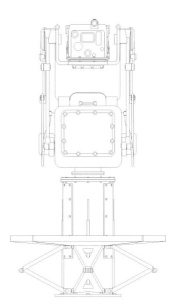

F1/48

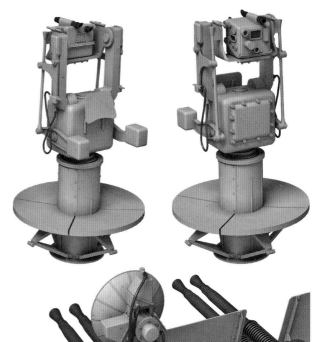

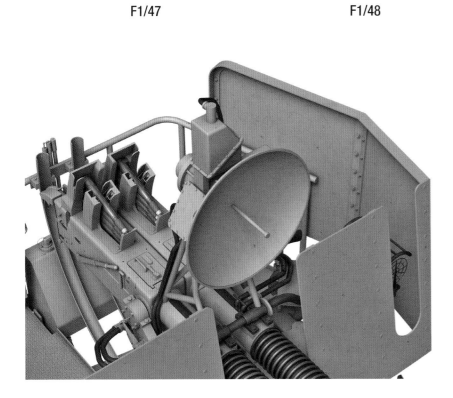

MK34 RADAR ANTENNA FOR THE MK63 DIRECTOR FITTED ON TOP
OF THE LEFT PAIR OF BOFORS GUNS, 1955–1958 (1/25 SCALE)

F1/50 RIGHT PROFILE

F1/51 BACK VIEW

F1/52 PLAN

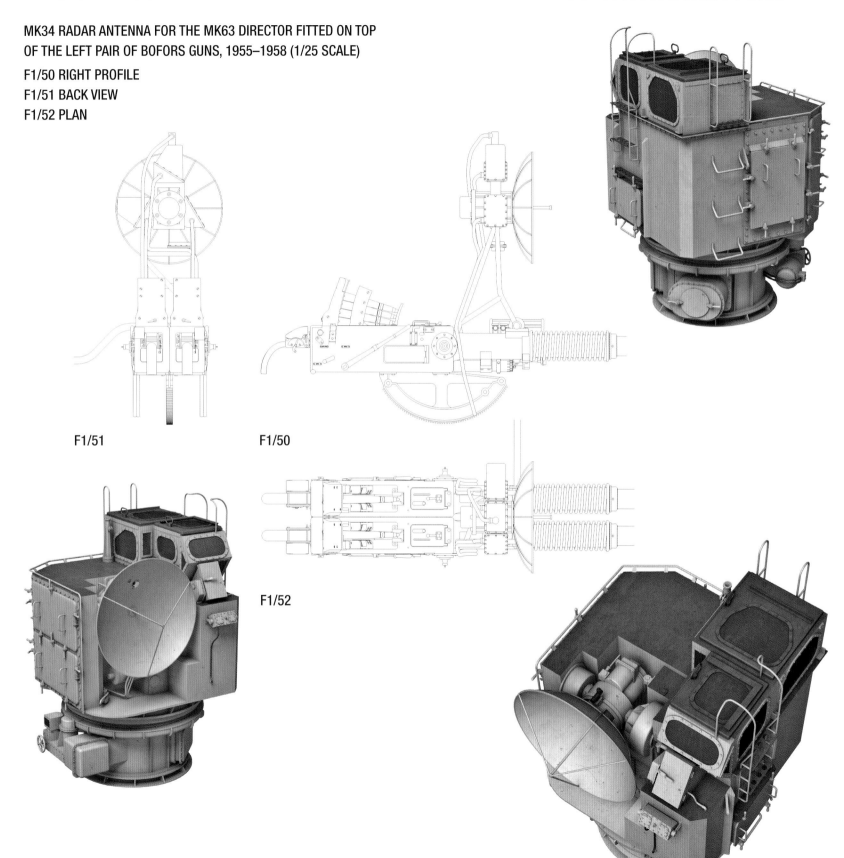

F1/51

F1/50

F1/52

MK56 DIRECTOR WITH A MK35 RADAR ANTENNA,
1955–1958 (1/37.5 SCALE)

F1/53 RIGHT PROFILE
F1/54 LEFT PROFILE
F1/55 FRONT VIEW
F1/56 BACK VIEW
F1/57 PLAN

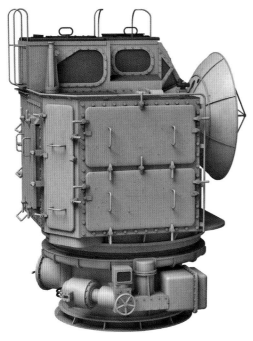

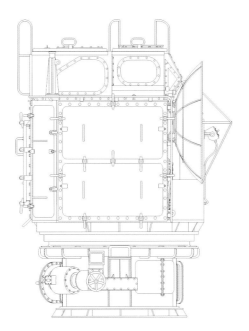

F1/53

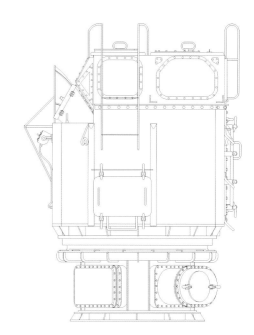

F1/54

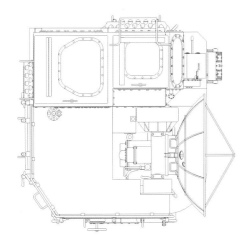

F1/57

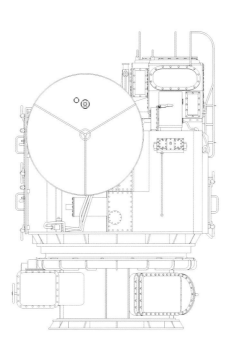

F1/55

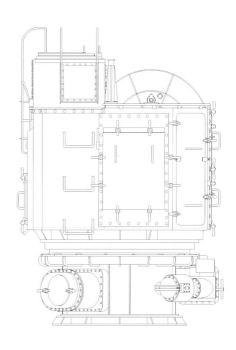

F1/56

SK AIR SEARCH RADAR ANTENNA, 1943–1946 (1/75 SCALE)

F2/1 PROFILE
F2/2 FRONT VIEW
F2/3 BACK VIEW
F2/4 PLAN

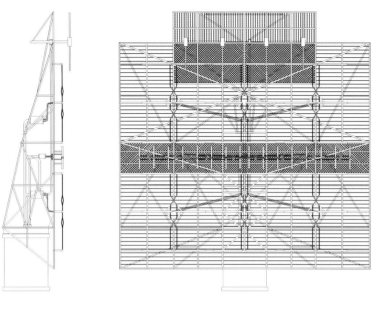

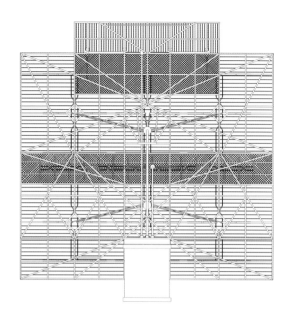

F2/1                    F2/2                                        F2/3

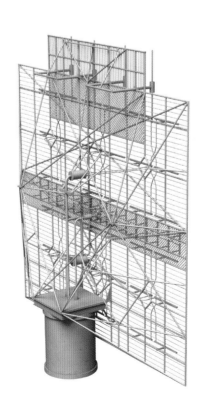

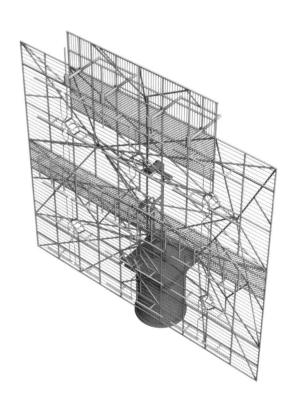

F2/4

SK-2 AIR SEARCH RADAR ANTENNA, 1946–1951 (1/75 SCALE)

F2/5 PROFILE
F2/6 FRONT VIEW
F2/7 BACK VIEW
F2/8 PLAN

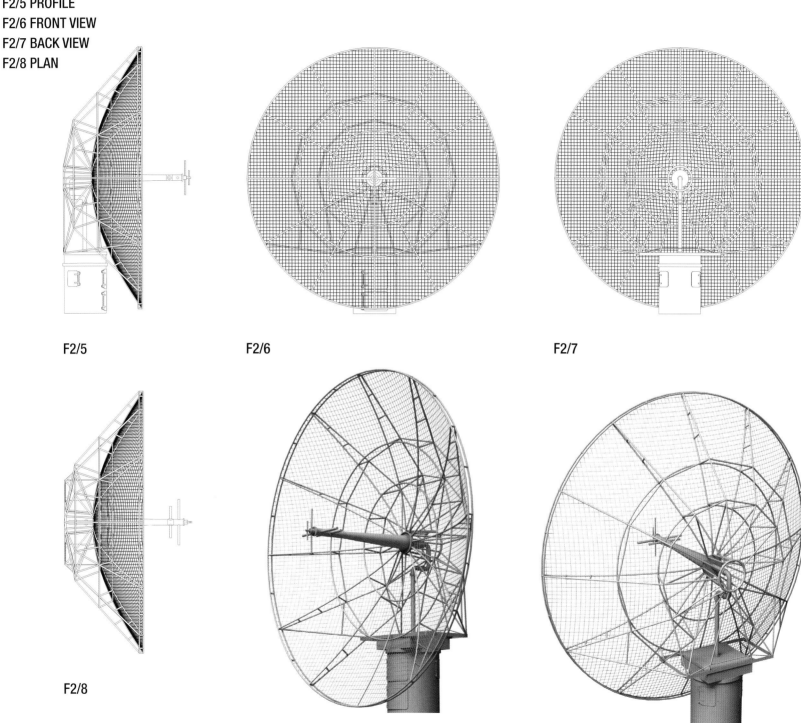

F2/5

F2/6

F2/7

F2/8

SR AIR SEARCH RADAR ANTENNA, 1945–1948 (1/50 SCALE)

F2/9 PROFILE
F2/10 FRONT VIEW
F2/11 BACK VIEW
F2/12 PLAN

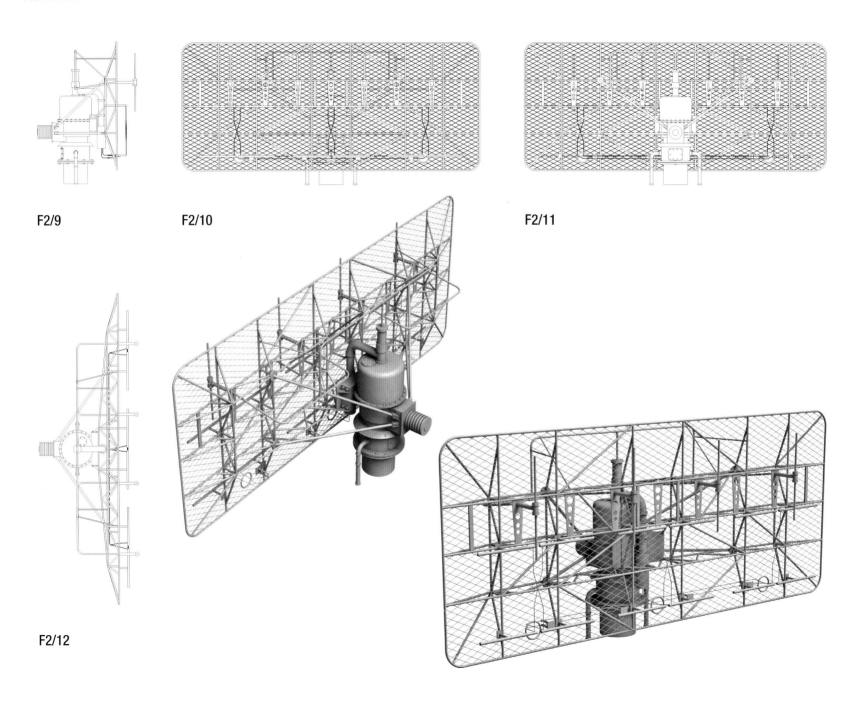

F2/9       F2/10                                      F2/11

F2/12

SP AIR SEARCH RADAR ANTENNA, 1948–1955 (1/50 SCALE)

F2/13 PROFILE
F2/14 FRONT VIEW
F2/15 BACK VIEW
F2/16 PLAN

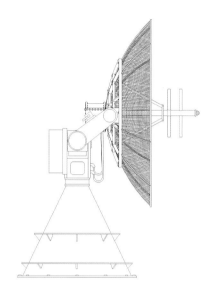

F2/13

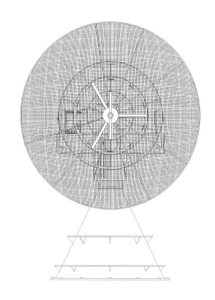

F2/14

F2/15

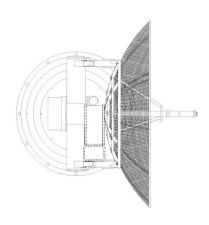

F2/16

SPS-6 AIR AND SEA SURFACE SEARCH RADAR ANTENNA, 1951–1955
(1/50 SCALE)

F2/17 PROFILE
F2/18 FRONT VIEW
F2/19 BACK VIEW
F2/20 PLAN

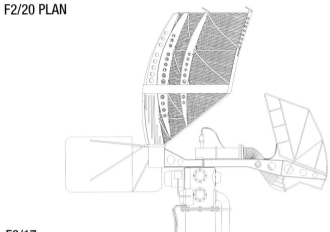

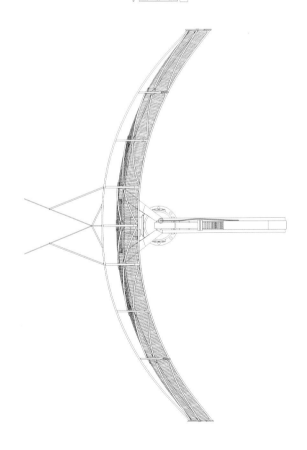

F2/17

F2/20

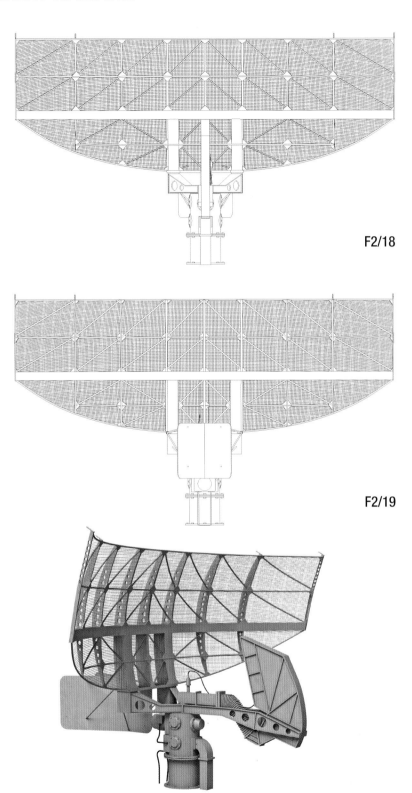

F2/18

F2/19

SPS-12 AIR AND SEA SURFACE SEARCH RADAR ANTENNA, 1955–1958
(1/50 SCALE)

F2/21 PROFILE
F2/22 FRONT VIEW
F2/23 BACK VIEW
F2/24 PLAN

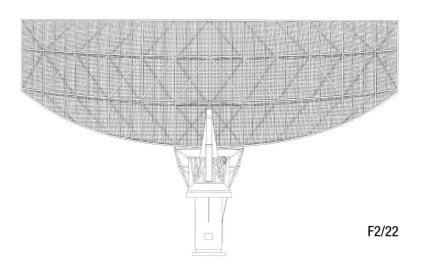

F2/22

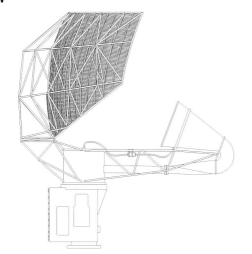

F2/21

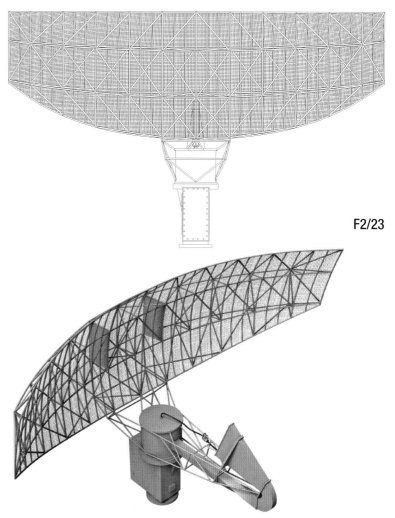

F2/23

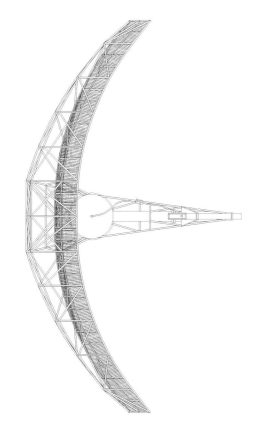

F2/24

SPS-8 HEIGHT METER RADAR ANTENNA, 1955–1958 (1/75 SCALE)

F2/25 RIGHT PROFILE

F2/26 LEFT PROFILE

F2/27 FRONT VIEW

F2/28 BACK VIEW

F2/29 PLAN

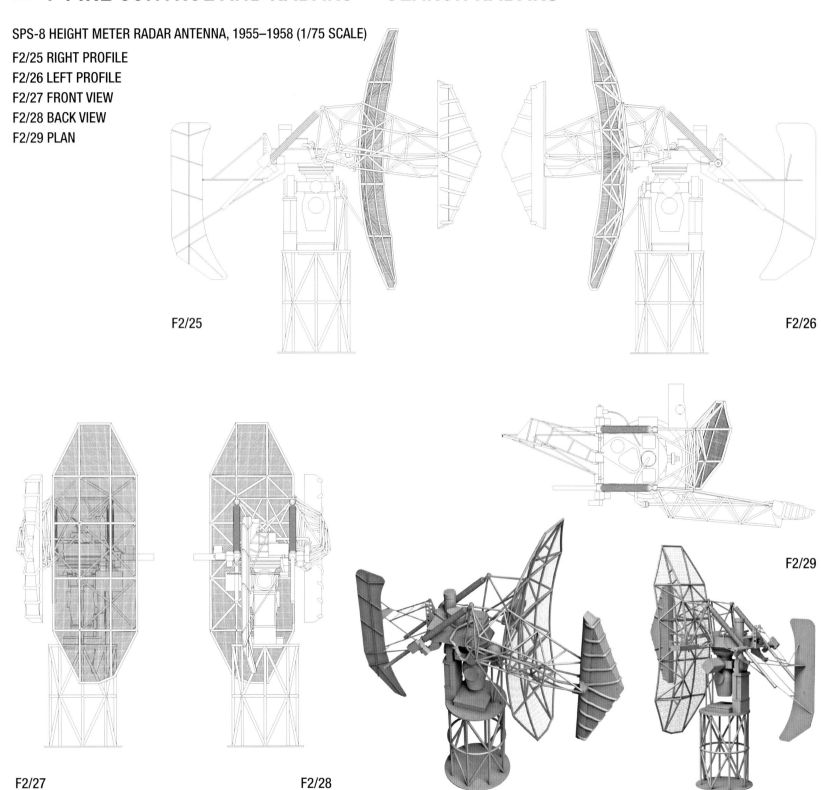

F2/25

F2/26

F2/27

F2/28

F2/29

SPS-49 AIR SEARCH RADAR ANTENNA, 1984–1990 (1/75 SCALE)

F2/30 RIGHT PROFILE
F2/31 LEFT PROFILE
F2/32 FRONT VIEW
F2/33 BACK VIEW
F2/34 PLAN

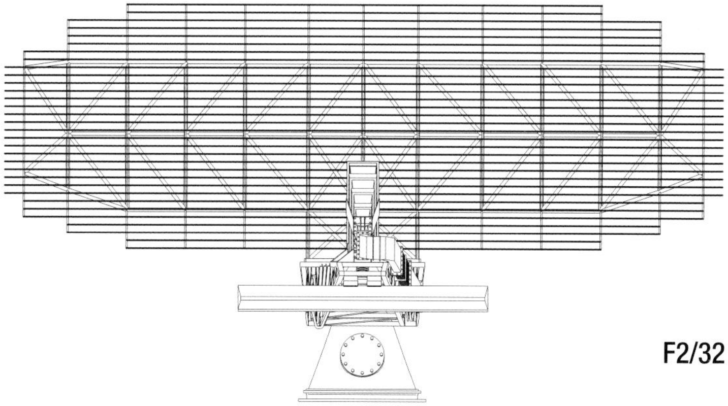

F2/32

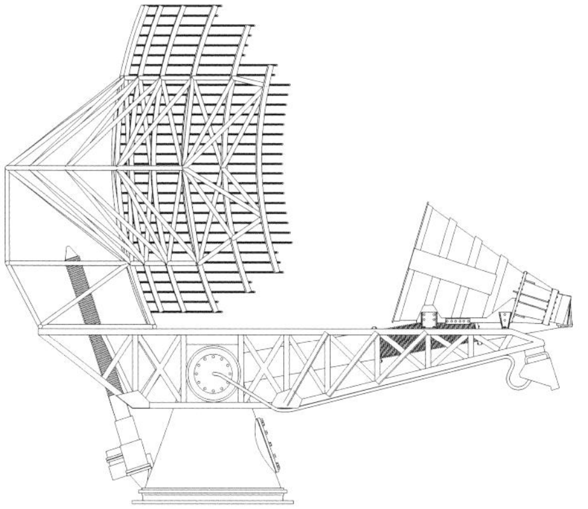

F2/30

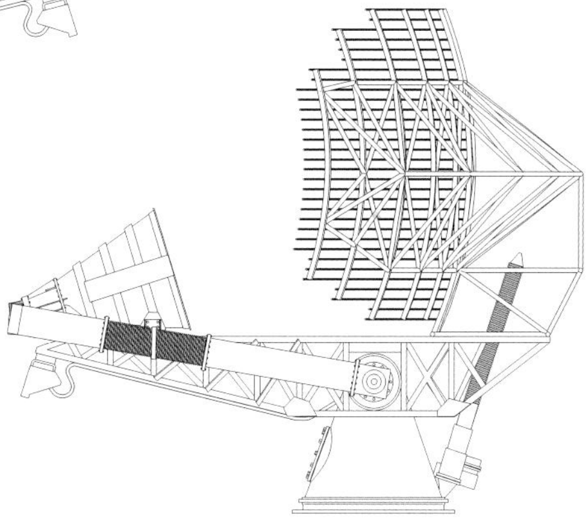

F2/33

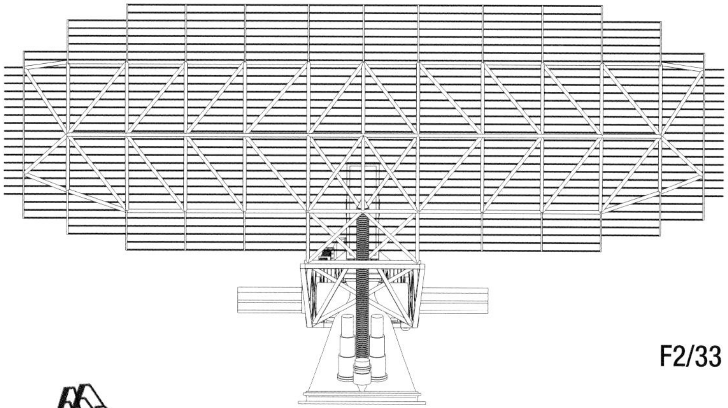

F2/31

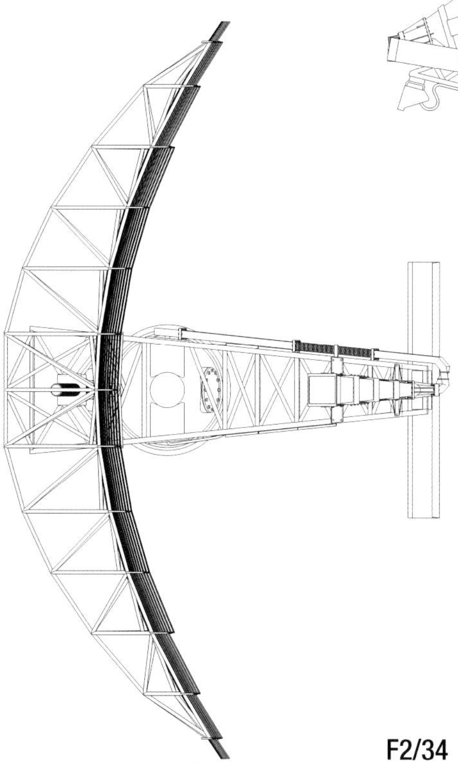

F2/34

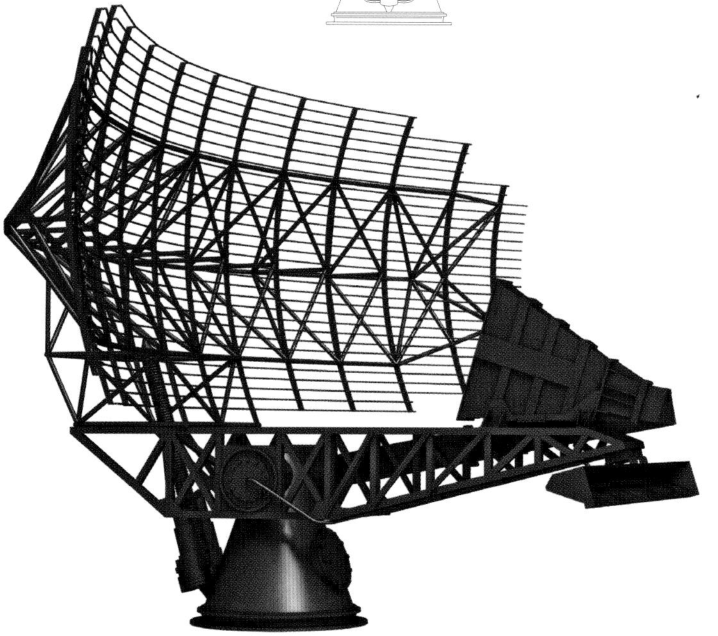

SG SEA SURFACE SEARCH RADAR ANTENNA,
1943–1948 (1/37.5 SCALE)

F2/35 PROFILE
F2/36 FRONT VIEW
F2/37 BACK VIEW
F2/38 PLAN

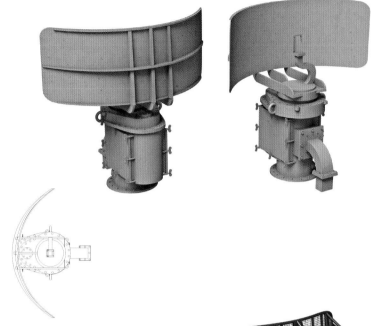

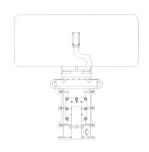

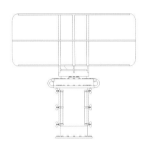

F2/35

F2/36

F2/37

F2/38

SG-1B SEA SURFACE SEARCH RADAR ANTENNA,
1948–1955 (1/37.5 SCALE)

F2/39 PROFILE
F2/40 FRONT VIEW
F2/41 PLAN

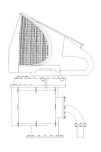

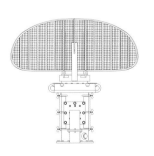

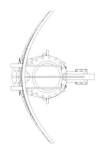

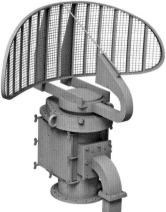

F2/39

F2/40

F2/41

SG-6 AIR AND SEA SURFACE SEARCH RADAR ANTENNA,
1948–1958 (1/50 SCALE)

F2/42 PROFILE
F2/43 FRONT VIEW
F2/44 BACK VIEW
F2/45 PLAN

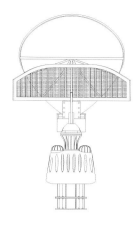
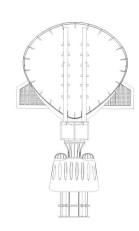

F2/42    F2/43    F2/44

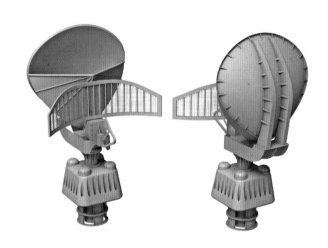

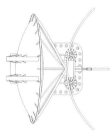

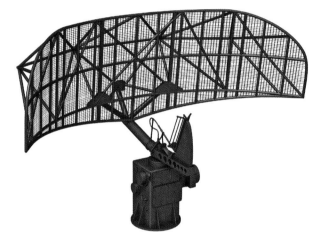

F2/45

SPS-10/SPS-67 SEA SURFACE SEARCH RADAR ANTENNA,
1984–1990 (1/50 SCALE)

F2/46 RIGHT PROFILE
F2/47 LEFT PROFILE
F2/48 BACK VIEW
F2/49 PLAN

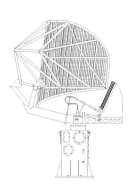
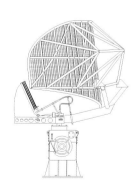
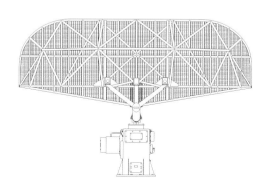
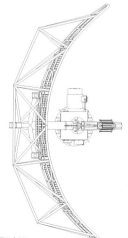

F2/46    F2/47    F2/48    F2/49

36IN. SEARCHLIGHT, 1943–1955 (1/25 SCALE)

F3/1 RIGHT PROFILE
F3/2 LEFT PROFILE
F3/3 FRONT VIEW
F3/4 BACK VIEW
F3/5 PLAN

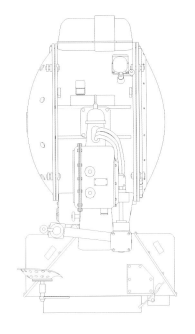

F3/1

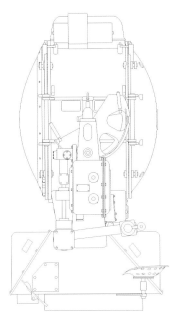

F3/2

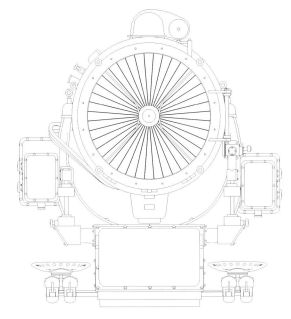

F3/3

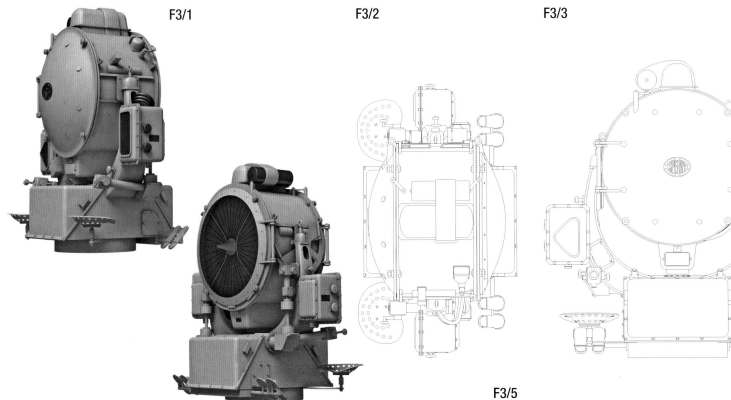

F3/5

F3/4

**24IN. SEARCHLIGHT, 1943–1958 (1/25 SCALE)**

F3/6 RIGHT PROFILE
F3/7 LEFT PROFILE
F3/8 FRONT VIEW
F3/9 BACK VIEW
F3/10 PLAN

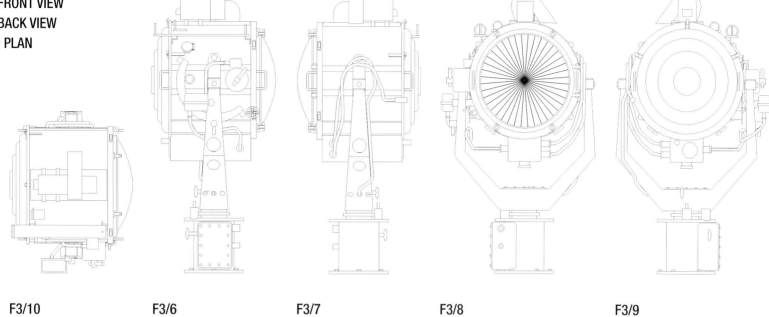

F3/10          F3/6          F3/7          F3/8          F3/9

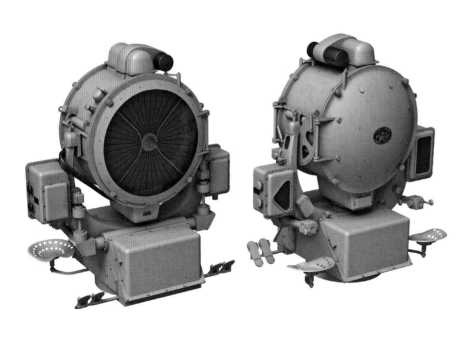

**12IN. SIGNAL LAMP, 1943–1990 (1/25 SCALE)**

F3/11 RIGHT PROFILE

F3/12 LEFT PROFILE

F3/13 FRONT VIEW

F3/14 PLAN

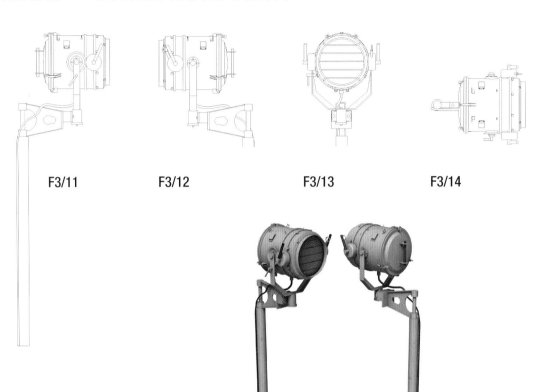

F3/11    F3/12    F3/13    F3/14

**TARGET DESGINATOR, 1943–1958 (1/25 SCALE)**

F3/15 RIGHT PROFILE

F3/16 LEFT PROFILE

F3/17 FRONT VIEW

F3/18 BACK VIEW

F3/19 PLAN

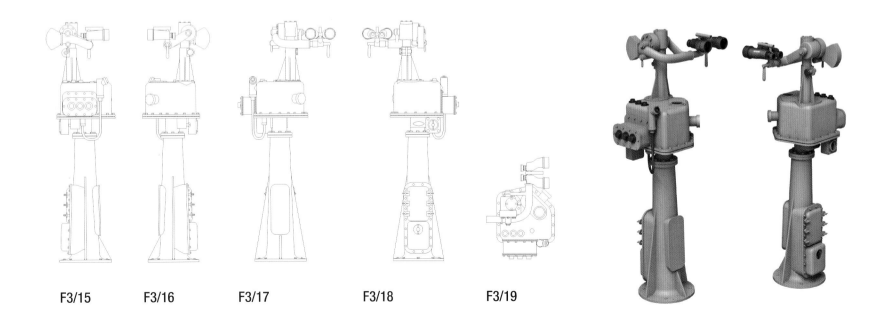

F3/15    F3/16    F3/17    F3/18    F3/19

## SKY LOOKOUT, 1943–1955 (1/25 SCALE)

F3/20 PROFILE
F3/21 FRONT VIEW
F3/22 PLAN

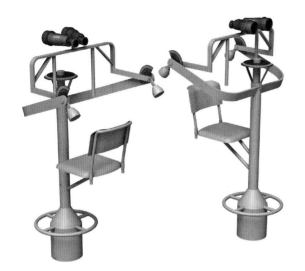

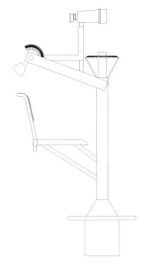

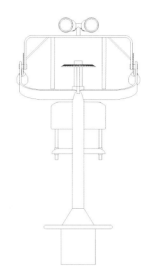

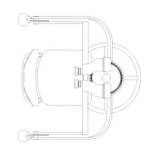

F3/22

F3/20

F3/21

## TDY RADAR JAMMER ANTENNA, 1944–1951 (1/50 SCALE)

F3/23 PROFILE, FRONT VIEW AND PLAN

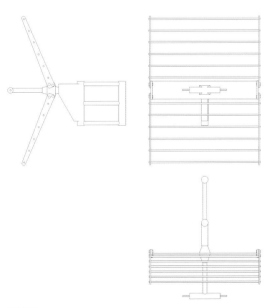

F3/23

TDY RADAR JAMMER ANTENNA, 1945–1955 (1/50 SCALE)

F3/24 PROFILE, FRONT VIEW AND PLAN

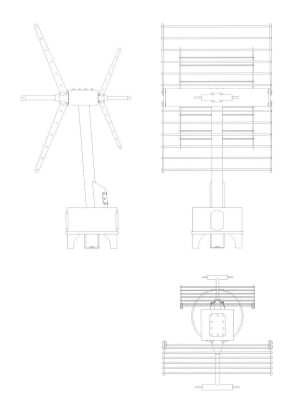

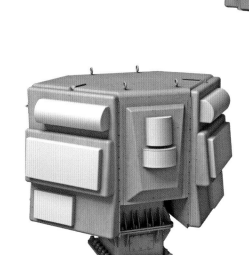

F3/24

SLQ-32 ELECTRONIC WARFARE ANTENNA, 1984–1990 (1/50 SCALE)

F3/25 PROFILE
F3/26 FRONT VIEW
F3/27 PLAN

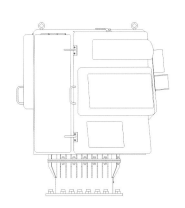

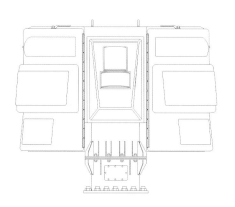

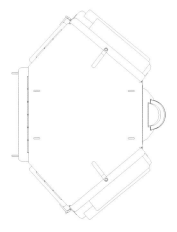

F3/25

F3/26

F3/27

OE-8 SATELLITE COMMUNICATION ANTENNA, 1984–1990
(1/37.5 SCALE)
F3/28 PROFILE
F3/29 FRONT VIEW
F3/30 BACK VIEW

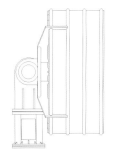

F3/28

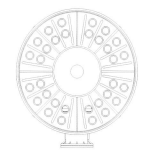

F3/29

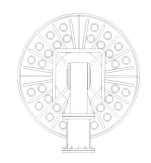

F3/30

NTDS (NAVAL TACTICAL DATA SYSTEM) ANTENNA, 1984–1990
(1/150 SCALE)
F3/31 PROFILE
F3/32 BACK VIEW
F3/33 PLAN

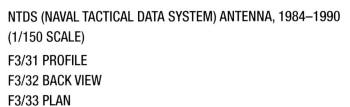

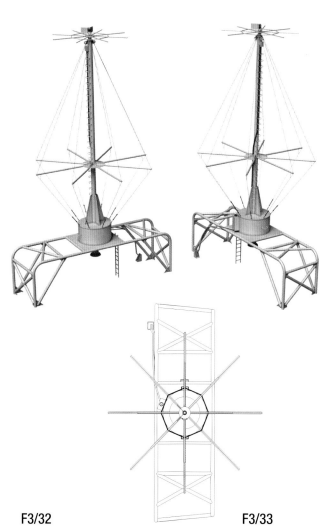

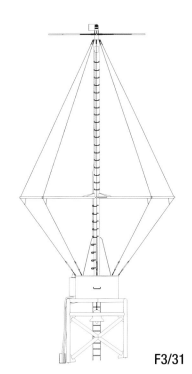

F3/31

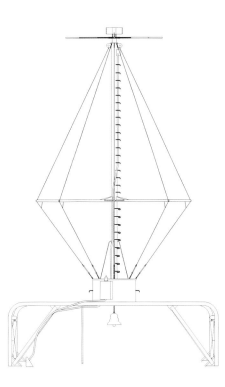

F3/32

F3/33

## HULL AND DECK FITTINGS, FRAMES 0–31 (1/200 SCALE)

### G1/1 RIGHT PROFILE, MID-1943–1949

### G1/2 PLAN, MID-1943–1949

### G1/1–2 HULL AND DECK FITTINGS, FRAMES 0–31

1 30,000lb anchor
2 Ship's hull number painted in white, 1943–1949
3 Draught marks
4 Eyeplate
5 Oerlikon gun tub (added in mid-1943)
6 Paravane chain (removed in 1946)
7 Jack staff
8 Single Oerlikon mount (replaced with twin mount in 1946; twin mount removed in 1949)
9 Single Oerlikon mount (removed in 1949)
10 Spare barrel tube
11 20mm magazine loading frame

12 20mm ammunition locker
13 20mm ammunition locker (added in mid-1943)
14 Roller
15 Paravane windlass
16 Non-skid chain plate
17 Anchor hawse pipe
18 Anchor chain
19 Chain stopper
20 Padeye
21 Fire plug
22 Anchor chain swivel
23 Deck hatch
24 Davit socket
25 Twin bitt

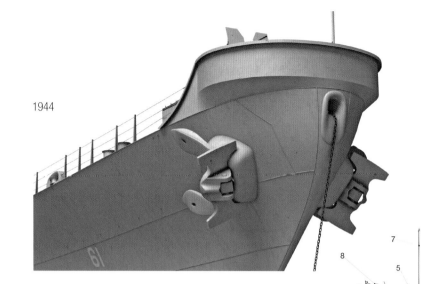

1944

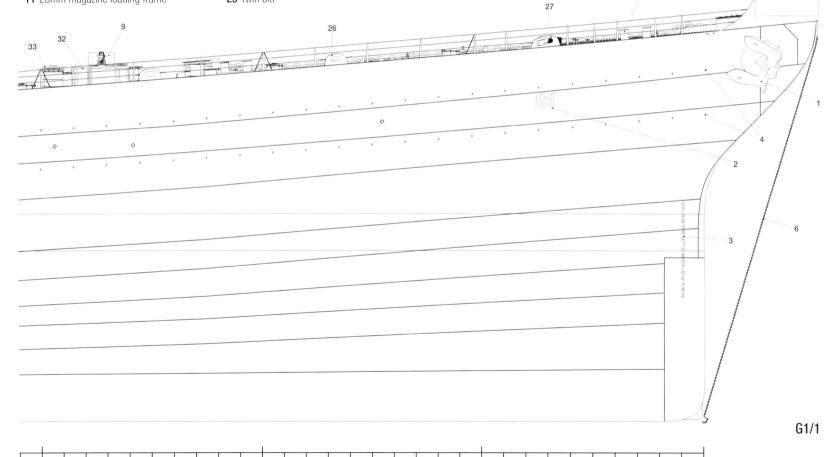

G1/1

26 Closed chock
27 Roller chock
28 Capstan
29 Wildcat
30 Capstan and wildcat controls
31 Phone box
32 Oerlikon shield (removed in 1951)
33 Bucket vent
34 Deck drain

1944

G1/3

G1/3 FRONT VIEW, 1943–1949

G1/4 RIGHT PROFILE (FRAGMENT), EARLY 1943
G1/5 PLAN (FRAGMENT), EARLY 1943

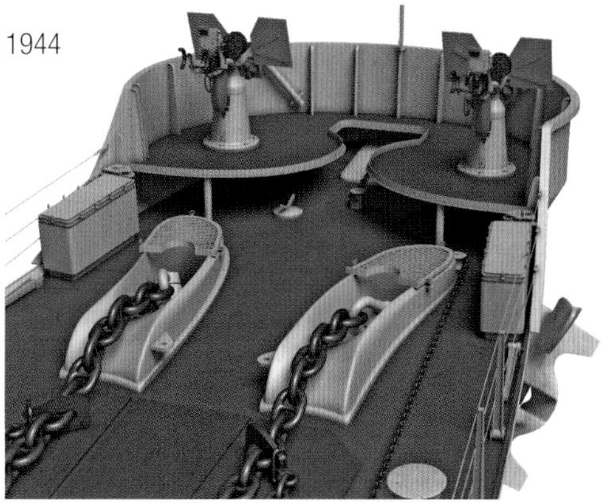

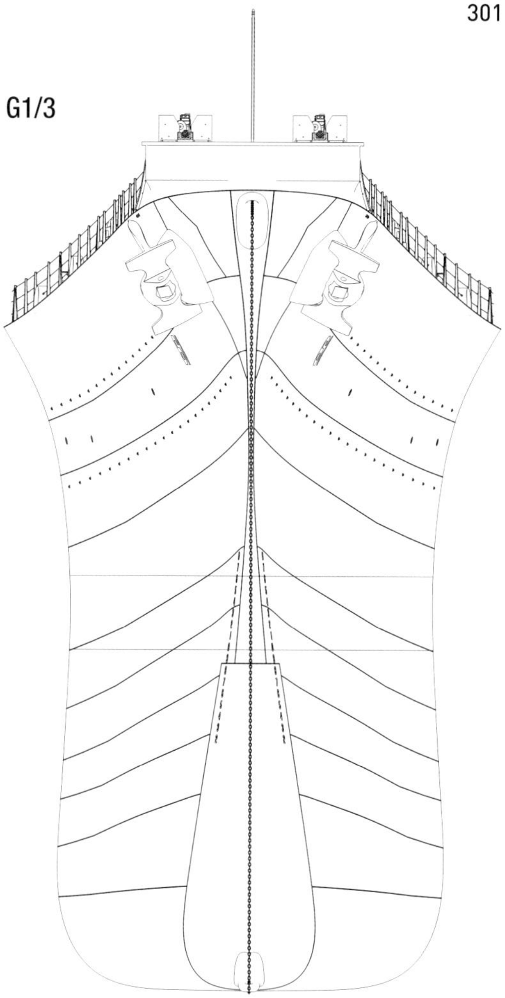

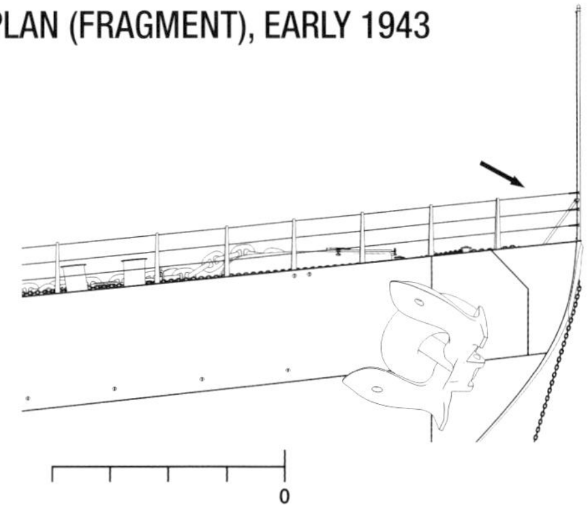

G1/4

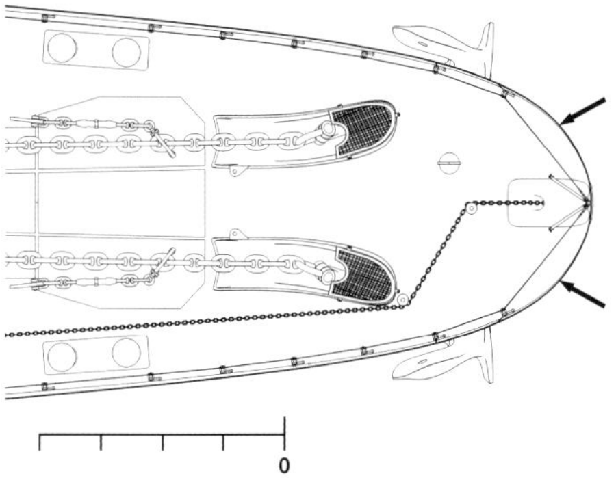

G1/5

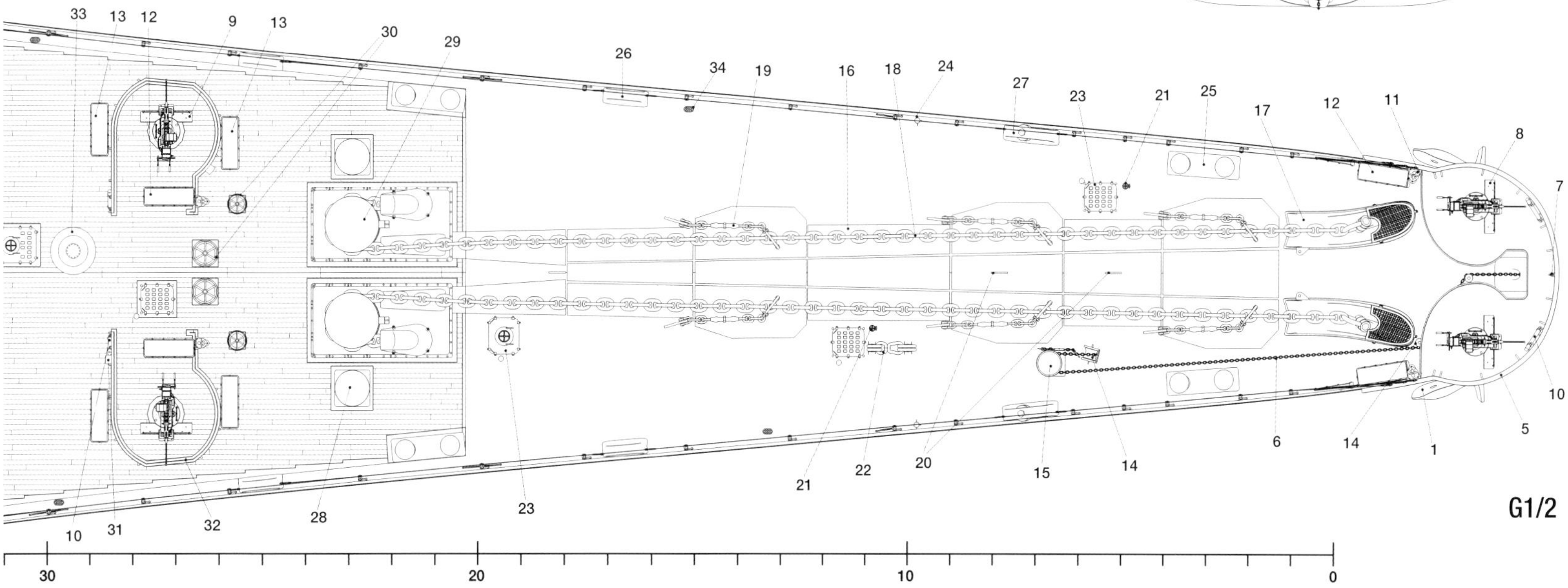

G1/2

**HULL AND DECK FITTINGS, FRAMES 0–31 (1/200 SCALE)**

**G1/6 RIGHT PROFILE (FRAGMENT), 1984**

**G1/7 PLAN, 1984**

**G1/6-7 HULL AND DECK FITTINGS, FRAMES 0–31**
  1 Ship's hull number painted in white with black shadows, 1951–1990
  2 Third row of eyeplates (fitted in 1955)
  3 Pipes added to drainage holes along the hull (from 1951)
  4 New shape of bow tub platform (from 1951)
  5 Wind baffle (added in 1951)
  6 NTDS antenna (added in 1984)
  7 Goose vent (added in 1984)
  8 New form of bucket vent (modified in 1955)

1984

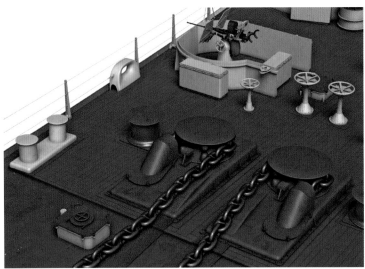

1944

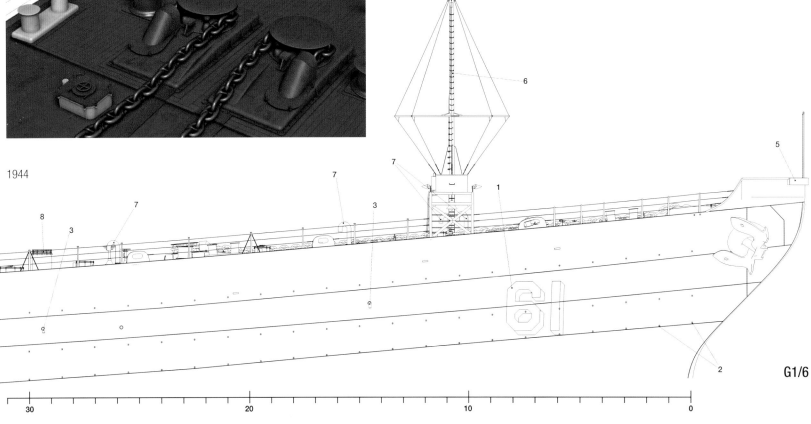

G1/6

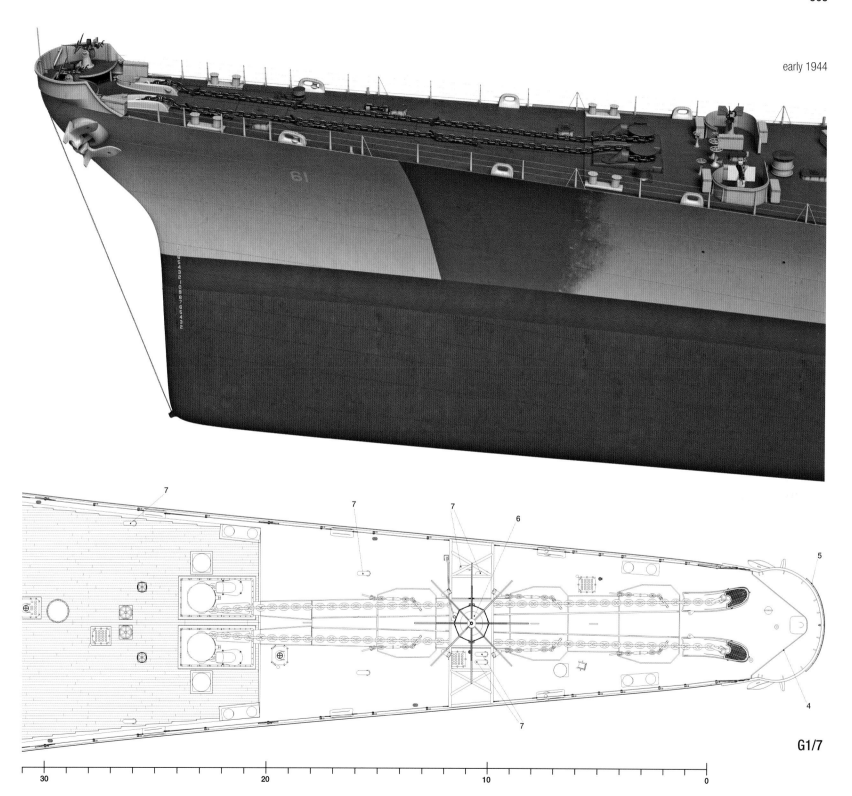

early 1944

G1/7

30 20 10 0

**30,000LB ANCHOR AND CHAIN (1/75 SCALE)**

G1/8 PROFILE

G1/9 FRONT VIEW

G1/10 BOTTOM VIEW

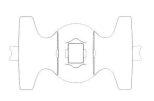

G1/10

**ANCHOR CHAIN STOPPER (1/75 SCALE)**

G1/11 PROFILE

G1/12 PLAN

G1/11

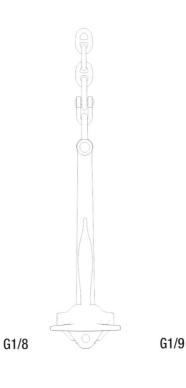

G1/8

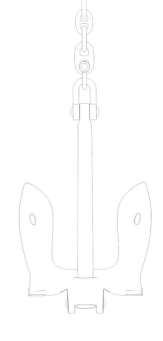

G1/9

G1/12

**ANCHOR HAWSE PIPE (1/75 SCALE)**

G1/13 PROFILE

G1/14 PLAN

G1/13

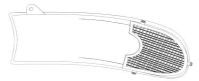

G1/14

1944

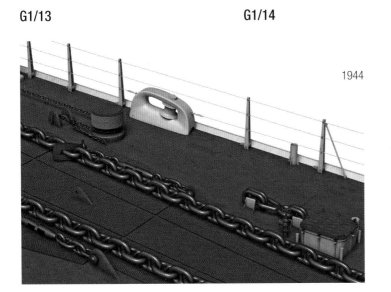

CHOCKS AND BITTS (1/50 SCALE)

G1/15 CLOSED CHOCK

G1/16 ROLLER CHOCK

G1/17 TWIN BITT

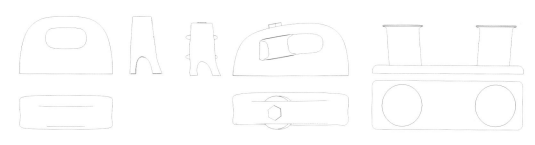

G1/15

G1/16

G1/17

PARAVANE WINDLASS AND ROLLER (1/50 SCALE)

G1/18 PROFILE AND PLAN

G1/19

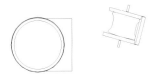

CAPSTAN (1/50 SCALE)

G1/19 PROFILE AND PLAN

G1/18

G1/20

WILDCAT (1/50 SCALE)

G1/20 PROFILE

G1/21 FRONT VIEW

G1/22 PLAN

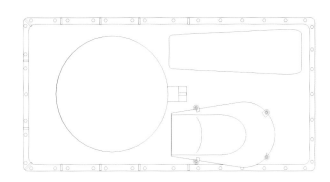

G1/21

G1/22

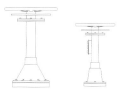

CAPSTAN AND WILDCAT CONTROLS  (1/50 SCALE)

G1/23 PROFILE AND PLAN

G1/23

FIREFIGHTING GEAR (1/25 SCALE)

G1/24 FIRE PLUG
G1/25 FIRE HOSE RACK
G1/26 FIRE HOSE REEL

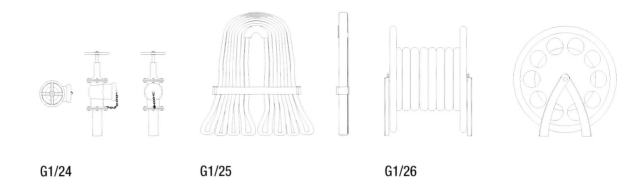

G1/24            G1/25            G1/26

FIRE PLUGS ADDED IN 1984 (1/50 SCALE)

G1/27 TRIPLE FIRE PLUG
G1/28 QUADRUPLE FIRE PLUG

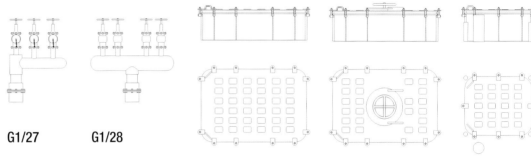

TYPICAL DECK HATCHES (1/50 SCALE)

G1/29 PROFILE AND PLAN

G1/27       G1/28

G1/29

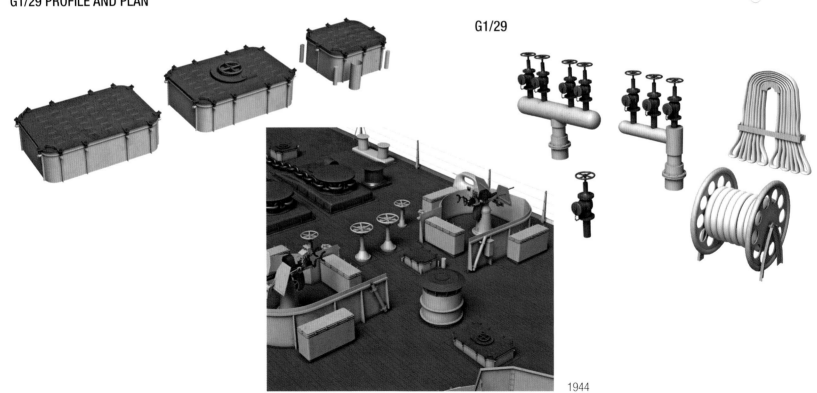

1944

# TYPICAL DECK VENTS (1/50 SCALE)

G1/30 BUCKET VENT, 1943–1955
G1/31 BUCKET VENT AFTER MODIFICATION, 1955–1990
G1/32 MUSHROOM VENT

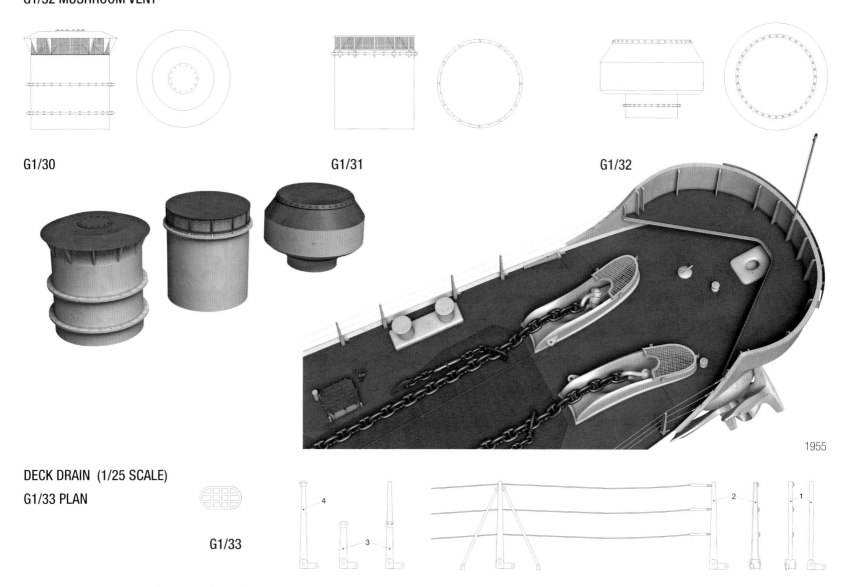

G1/30

G1/31

G1/32

1955

# DECK DRAIN  (1/25 SCALE)

G1/33 PLAN

G1/33

1

2

3

4

# GUARD RAILS  AND VARIOUS STANCHIONS  (1/50 SCALE)

G1/34

## G1/34 PROFILE AND FRONT VIEW

**1** Simple stanchion
**2** H stanchion
**3** H stanchion near the catapults
**4** H stanchion with an awning stanchion bracket (after 1951)

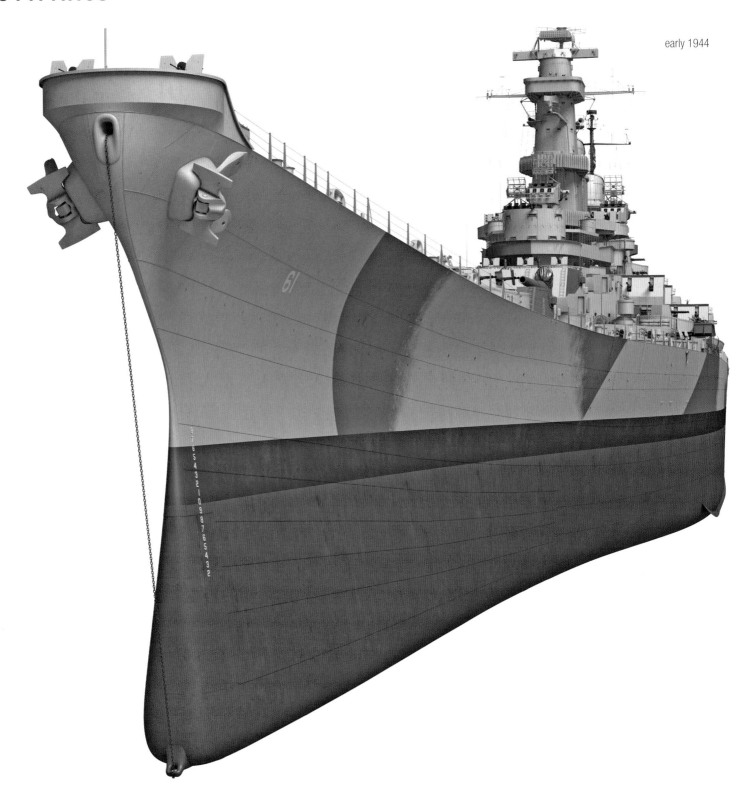

early 1944

early 1944

early 1944

**HULL AND DECK FITTINGS, FRAMES 31–64 (1/200 SCALE)**

**G2/1 RIGHT PROFILE, MID-1943–1949**

**G2/2 PLAN, MID-1943–1949**

**G2/1–2 HULL AND DECK FITTINGS, FRAMES 31–64**
1 Closed chock
2 Roller chock
3 Twin bitt
4 Bucket vent
5 Mushroom vent
6 Deck hatch
7 Stowed helmets
8 Bofors mount shield with ammunition stowed on its inner side (fitted in mid-1943, removed in 1955)
9 Quad Bofors mount (fitted in mid-1943, removed in 1946, fitted again in 1951 and permanently removed in 1955)
10 Hinged door in Bofors shield
11 Mk51 director (fitted in mid-1943, removed in 1946, fitted again in 1951 and permanently removed in 1955)
12 Mk51 director shield on pedestal (fitted in mid-1943, removed in 1955)
13 Stowed paravane (removed in 1955)
14 20mm ammunition locker (fitted in mid-1943, removed in 1946)
15 Tool box
16 Loudspeaker
17 Vertical ladder
18 Paravane boom attachment points
19 Flush watertight hatch
20 Deck drain
21 Fire hose
22 Stowed chain jacks
23 Stowed paravane boom (removed in 1955)
24 Breakwater
25 Davit socket
26 Fire plug
27 Fire hose reel
28 Barbette no.1

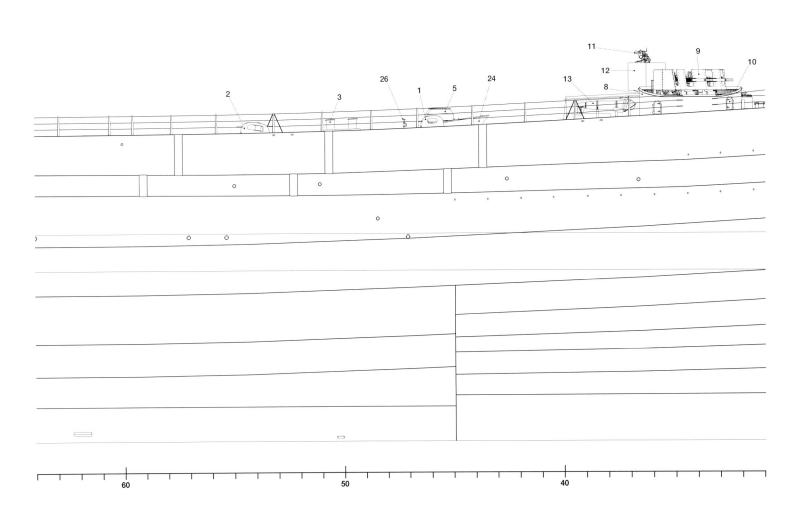

G2/1

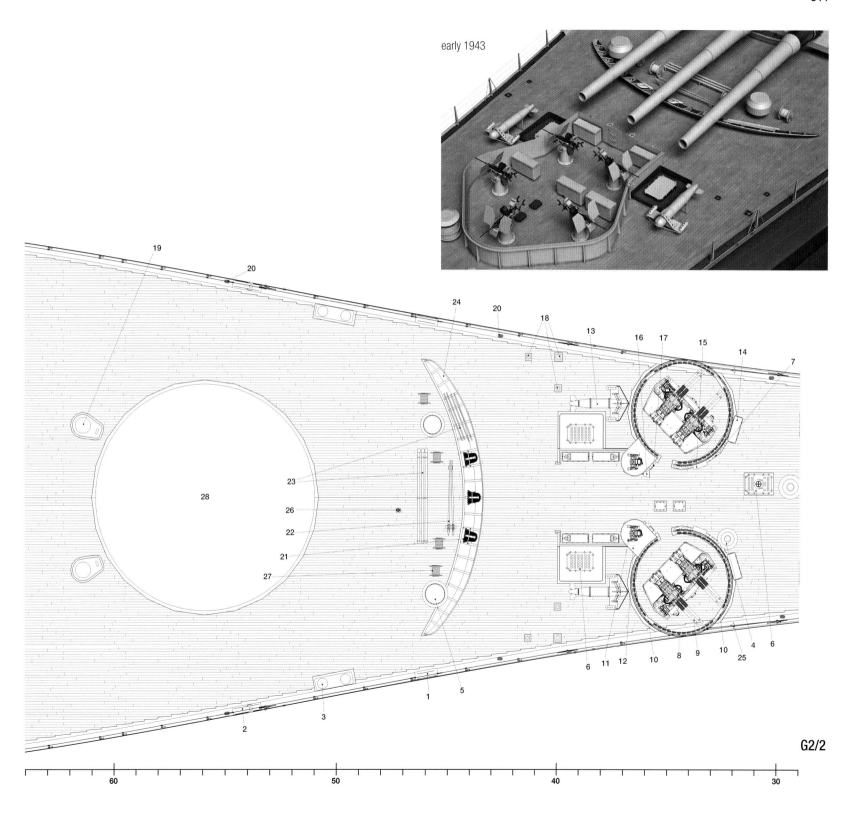

early 1943

G2/2

60    50    40    30

**G FITTINGS**

HULL AND DECK FITTINGS, FRAMES 31–64 (1/200 SCALE)

G2/3 BOFORS TUBS AND MK51 DIRECTOR SHIELDS – VIEW FROM
FRAME 37 TOWARDS THE BOW, MID-1943–1949

G2/4 RIGHT PROFILE (FRAGMENT), EARLY 1943

G2/5 PLAN (FRAGMENT), EARLY 1943
  **1** Oerlikon gun tub (removed in mid-1943)
  **2** Single Oerlikon mount (removed or relocated in mid-1943)
  **3** 20mm ammunition locker (removed or relocated in mid-1943)

G2/6 RIGHT PROFILE (FRAGMENT), 1951–1955
  **1** Boat boom
  **2** Pipes added to drainage holes along the hull

G2/7 RIGHT PROFILE (FRAGMENT), 1955–1990

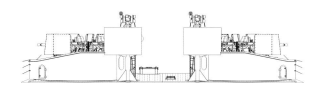

G2/3

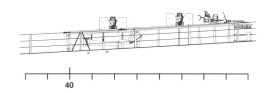

G2/4

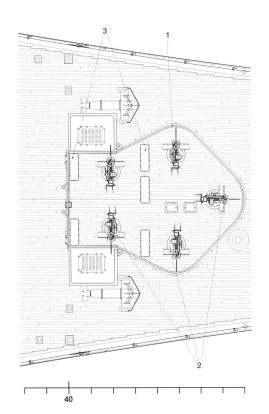

G2/5

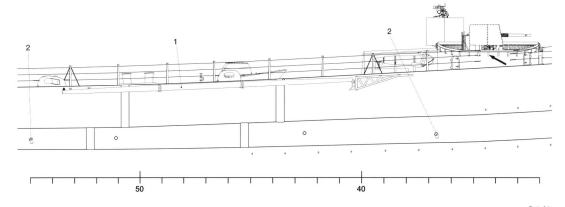

G2/6

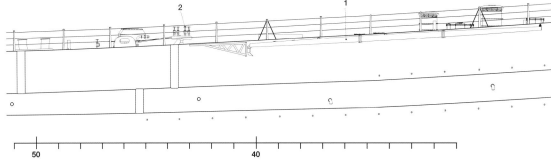

G2/7

G2/8 PLAN (FRAGMENT), 1955–1990

G2/7–8 HULL AND DECK FITTINGS,
FRAMES 31–64 (1955–1990)
1 Relocated boat boom (1955–1958)
2 Quadruple fire plug (added in 1984)

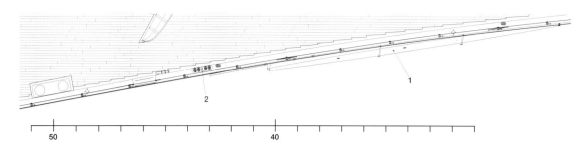

G2/8

PARAVANE (1/50 SCALE)

G2/9 PROFILE
G2/10 FRONT VIEW
G2/11 PLAN

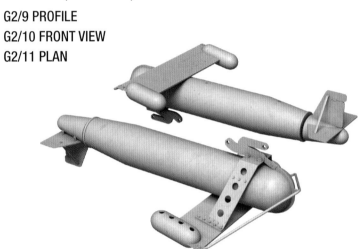

G2/9

G2/10

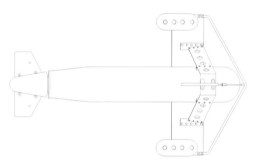

G2/11

BREAKWATER (1/100 SCALE)

G2/12 VIEW FROM THE CENTRE LINE
OUTBOARDS
G2/13 BACK VIEW, STARBOARD SIDE FRAGMENT
G2/14 PLAN, STARBOARD SIDE FRAGMENT

G2/13

G2/12

G2/14

## HULL AND DECK FITTINGS, FRAMES 64–94 (1/200 SCALE)

### G3/1 RIGHT PROFILE

### G3/2 PLAN

### G3/1–2 HULL AND DECK FITTINGS, FRAMES 64–94

1 Bilge keel
2 Accommodation ladder davit
3 Bracket for accommodation ladder upper platform wishbone
4 Davit socket
5 Single Oerlikon mount (removed in 1946)
6 Oerlikon shield (removed in 1951)
7 20mm ammunition box (removed in 1946)
8 Fuel and diesel fill
9 Bucket vent (modified in 1955)
10 Flush watertight hatch
11 Barbette no.2
12 Franklin lifebuoy (removed in mid-1943)
13 Pipes added to drainage holes along the hull (from 1951)

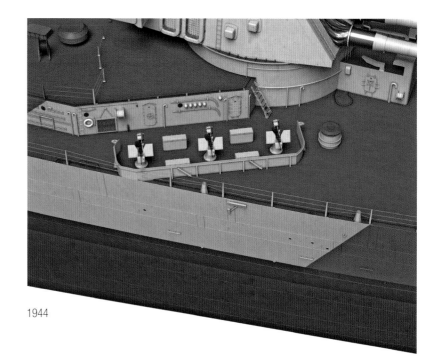

1944

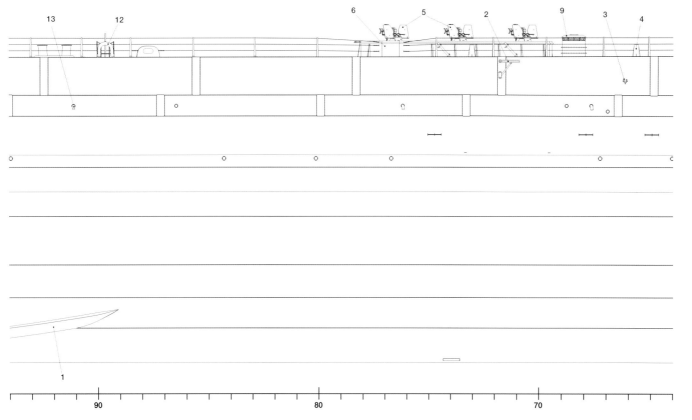

G3/1

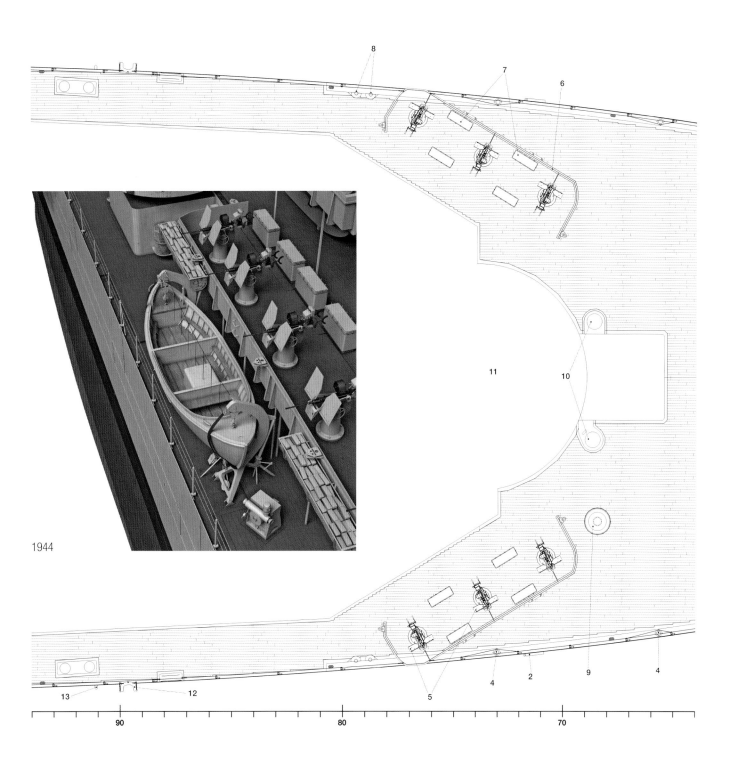

1944

G3/2

HULL AND DECK FITTINGS, FRAMES 94–123 (1/200 SCALE)

G4/1 RIGHT PROFILE, 1943–1949

G4/2 PLAN (STARBOARD SIDE FRAGMENT), 1943–1949

### G4/1–2 HULL AND DECK FITTINGS, FRAMES 94–123
1 Bilge keel
2 Crescent boat davit
3 Boat davit winch
4 26ft motor whaleboat Mk2

### G4/3 PLAN (STARBOARD SIDE FRAGMENT), 1951–1958
1 Modified wooden deck border
2 Boat davit heightened and moved inboards
3 Boat davit winch moved inboards
4 Pipes added to drainage holes along the hull

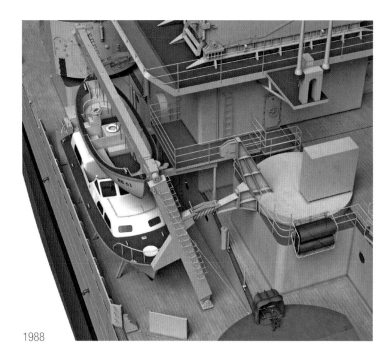

1988

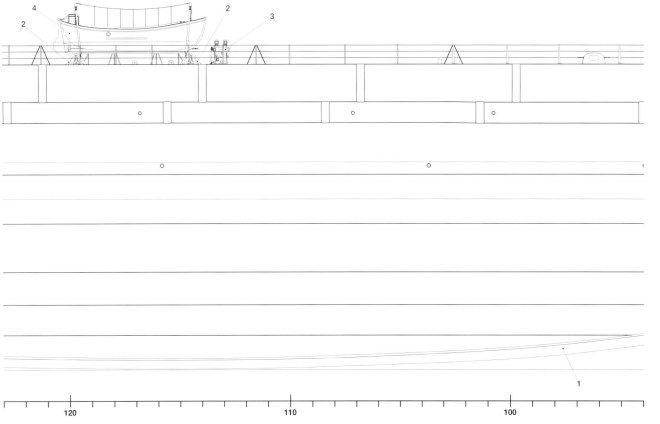

G4/1

120        110        100

G4/4 RIGHT PROFILE (FRAGMENT), 1984–1990

G4/5 PLAN (STARBOARD AND PORT SIDE FRAGMENTS), 1984–1990

G4/4–5 HULL AND DECK FITTINGS, FRAMES 94–123
  **1** Bulwark
  **2** Boat davit
  **3** Cleat
  **4** Boat davit winch
  **5** 33ft personnel boat cradle
  **6** 40ft utility boat cradle

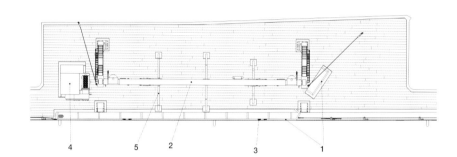

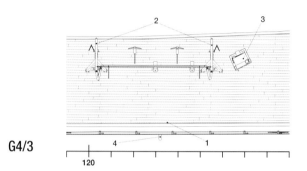

G4/3

G4/5

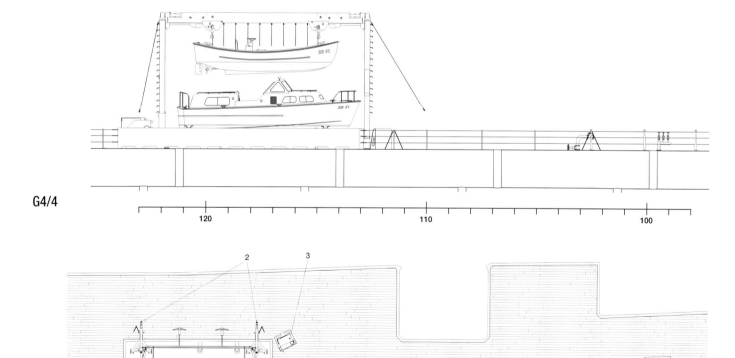

G4/4

G4/2

HULL AND DECK FITTINGS, FRAMES 123–152 (1/200 SCALE)

G5/1 RIGHT PROFILE, MID-1943–1958

G5/2 PLAN (STARBOARD SIDE FRAGMENT), MID-1943–1955

## G5/1–2 HULL AND DECK FITTINGS, FRAMES 123–152

**1** Bucket vent
**2** Quad Bofors mount (fitted in mid-1943, removed in 1946, fitted again in 1951 and permanently removed in 1955)
**3** Bofors mount shield with ammunition stowed on its inner side (fitted in mid-1943, removed in 1955)
**4** Davit socket
**5** Portable bolted plate (removed around 1946)
**6** Pipes added to drainage holes along the hull (from 1951)

## G5/3 RIGHT PROFILE (FRAGMENT), EARLY 1943

G5/4 PLAN (STARBOARD SIDE FRAGMENT), EARLY 1943

**1** Oerlikon gun tub (removed in mid-1943)
**2** Single Oerlikon mount (removed or relocated in mid-1943)
**3** 20mm ammunition locker (removed or relocated in mid-1943)
**4** Floater net basket (removed in mid-1943)

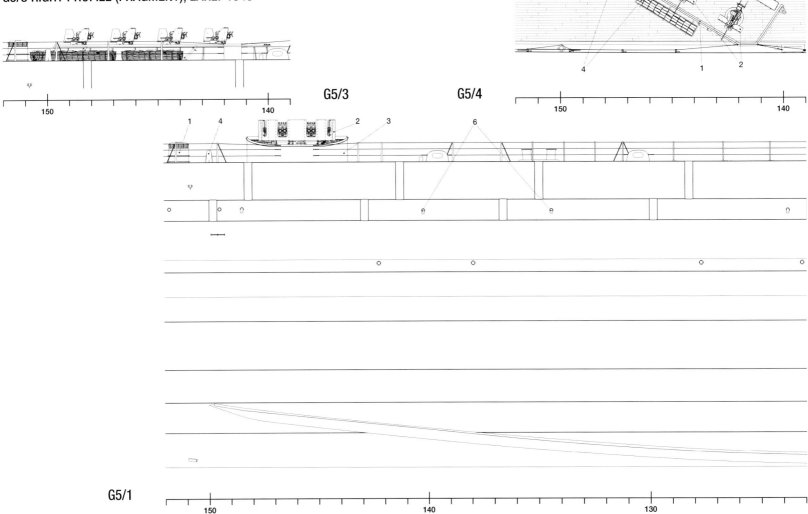

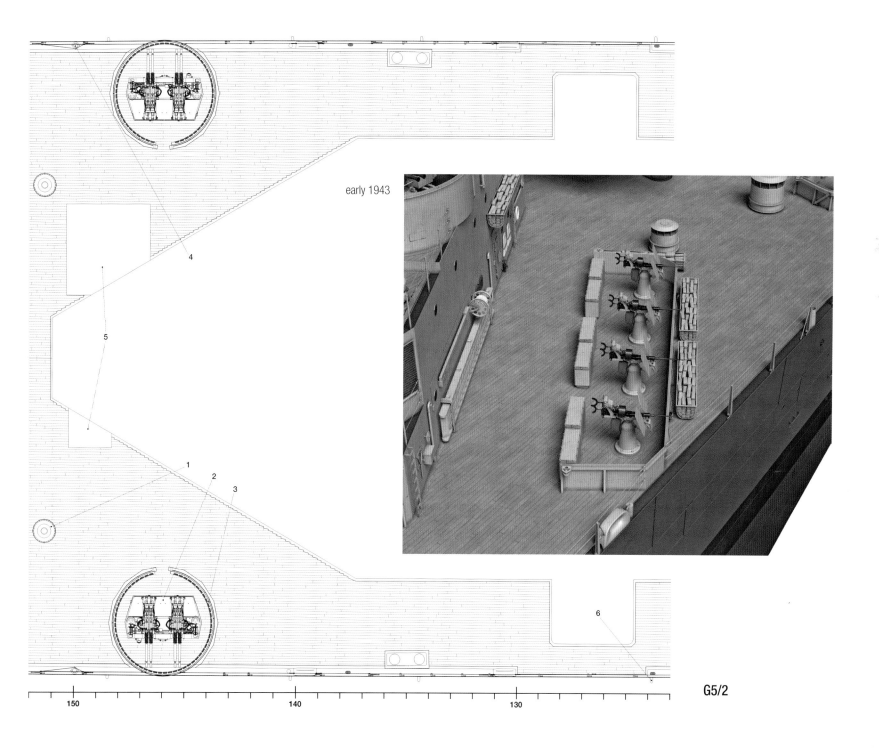

early 1943

4

5

1

2

3

6

G5/2

150          140          130

HULL AND DECK FITTINGS, FRAMES 152–182 (1/200 SCALE)

G6/1 RIGHT PROFILE, 1943–1949

G6/2 PLAN, 1943–1949

### G6/1–2 HULL AND DECK FITTINGS, FRAMES 152–182
  **1** Long pipes added to drainage holes along the hull (1945–1949)
  **2** Franklin lifebuoy (removed in mid-1943)
  **3** Accommodation ladder davit
  **4** Floater net basket (removed in 1951)
  **5** Barbette no.3
  **6** Bucket vent
  **7** Flush watertight hatch
  **8** Deck hatch
  **9** Fire station
  **10** Fire hose reel
  **11** 20mm ammunition box (removed in 1946)
  **12** 20mm ammunition box (removed in 1949)
  **13** Single Oerlikon mount (removed in 1946)
  **14** Single Oerlikon mount (replaced with twin mount in 1946;
      twin mount removed in 1949)
  **15** Oerlikon mount shield (removed in 1951)
  **16** Deck winch
  **17** Wire cable reel

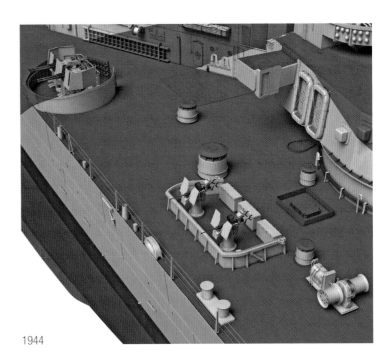

1944

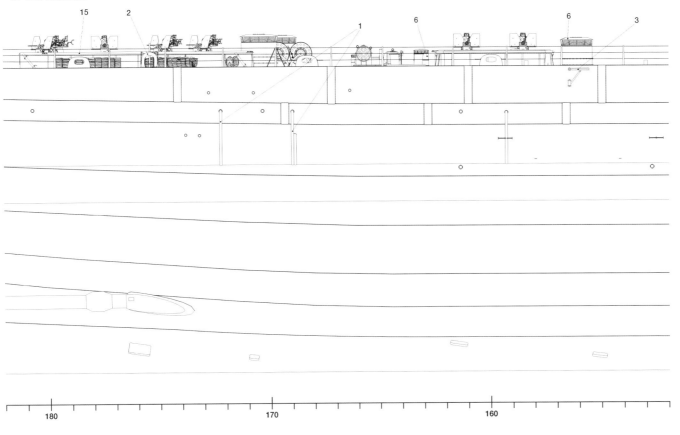

G6/1

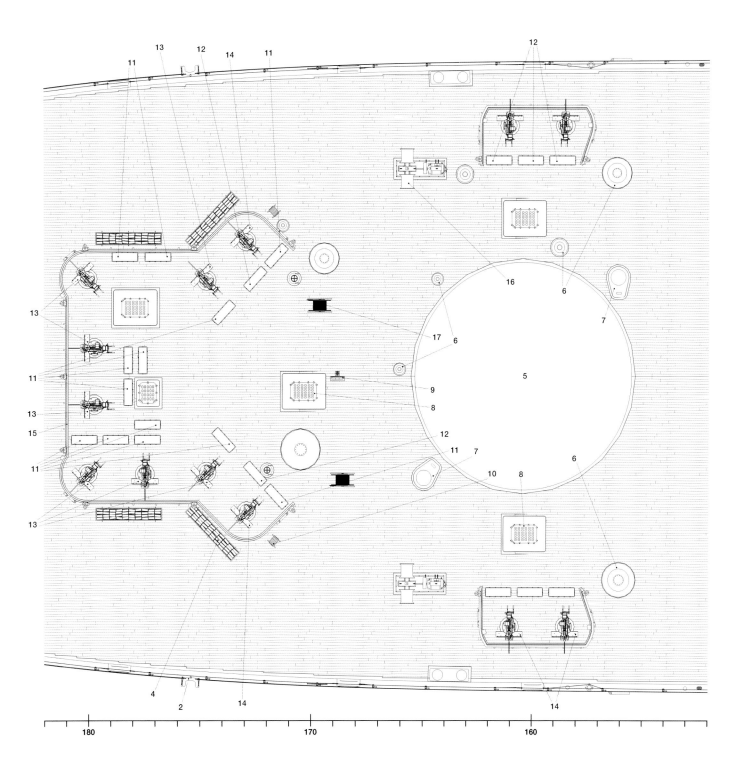

G6/2

180    170    160

HULL AND DECK FITTINGS, FRAMES 152–182 (1/200 SCALE)

G6/3 RIGHT PROFILE (FRAGMENT), 1951–1958

G6/4 PLAN (STARBOARD SIDE FRAGMENT), 1951–1958

**G6/3–4 HULL AND DECK FITTINGS, FRAMES 152–182**
1 Helicopter service area (added in 1951)
2 Deck winch relocated inboards and towards the stern (from 1955)
3 Pipes added to drainage holes along the hull (from 1951)
4 Empty deck after the removal of Oerlikon tub used for boat stowage (see drawings I1/32–I1/34)
5 Vertical ladder

G6/5 RIGHT PROFILE (FRAGMENT), 1984–1990

G6/6 PLAN (FRAGMENT), 1984–1990

**G6/5–6 HULL AND DECK FITTINGS, FRAMES 152–182**
1 Boat boom
2 Triple fire plug
3 Loudspeaker
4 Helicopter service area
5 Light array
6 Trussed whip antenna
7 Vertical ladder
8 Raised helicopter deck
9 Deck drain

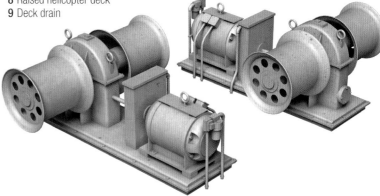

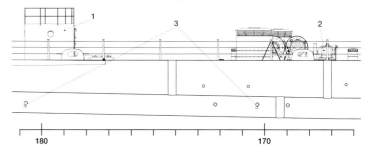

G6/3

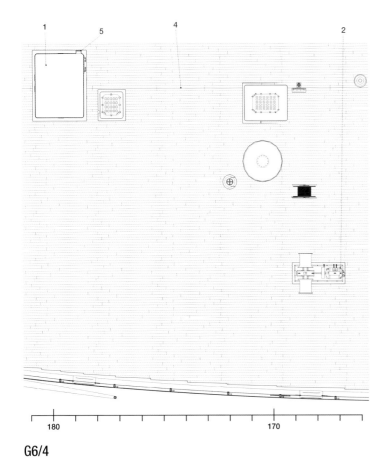

G6/4

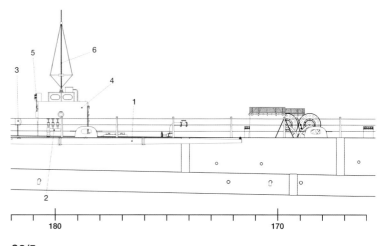

G6/5

HELICOPTER SERVICE AREA,
1984–1990

G6/7 LEFT PROFILE
G6/8 FRONT VIEW
G6/9 BACK VIEW

G6/6

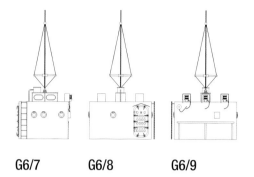

G6/7    G6/8    G6/9

DECK WINCH (1/50 SCALE)

G6/10 PROFILE
G6/11 BACK VIEW
G6/12 PLAN

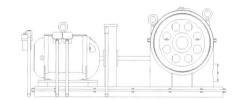

G6/10

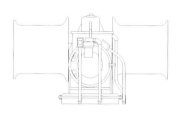

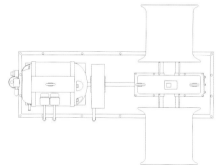

G6/11

G6/12

WIRE CABLE REEL (1/50 SCALE)

G6/13 PROFILE
G6/14 PLAN

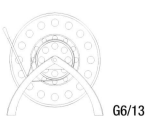

G6/13    G6/14

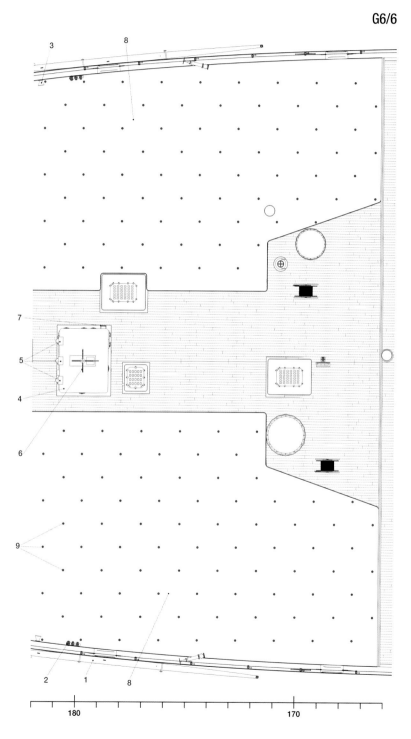

HULL AND DECK FITTINGS, FRAMES 182–215 (1/200 SCALE)

G7/1 RIGHT PROFILE, 1943–1949

G7/2 PLAN, 1943–1949

1944

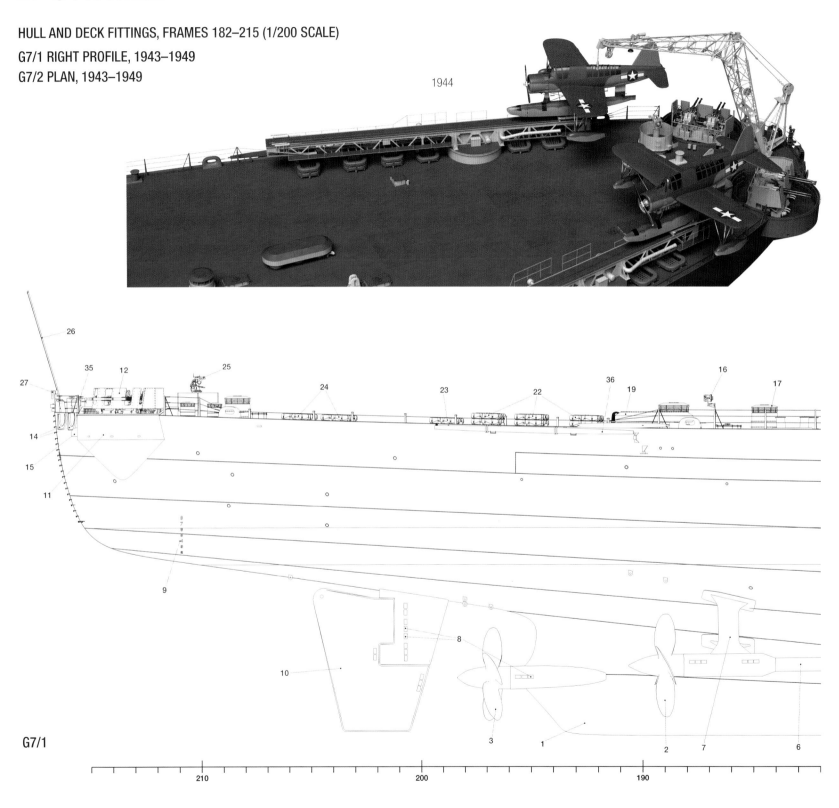

G7/1

210                    200                    190

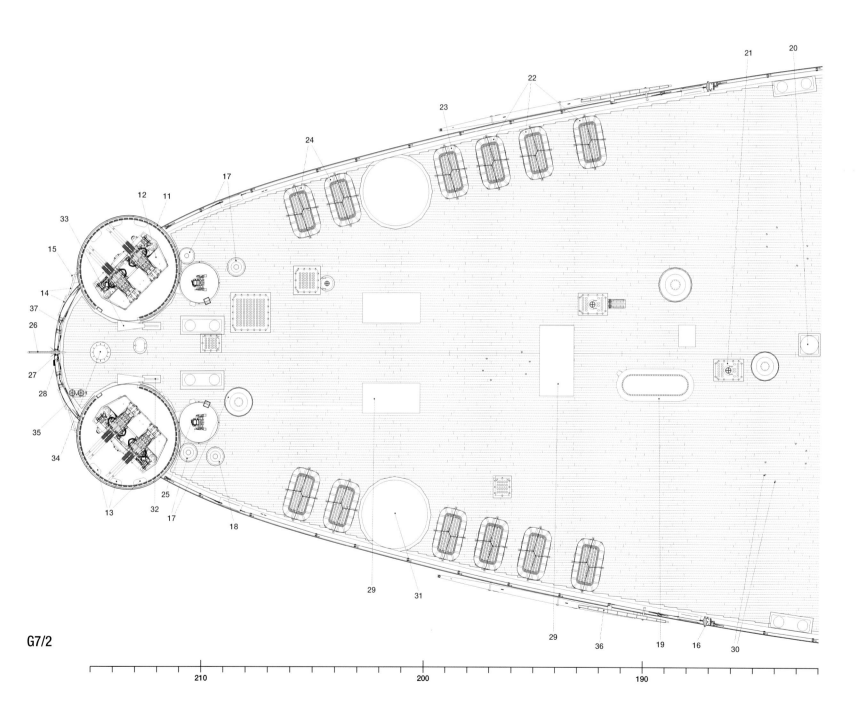

G7/2

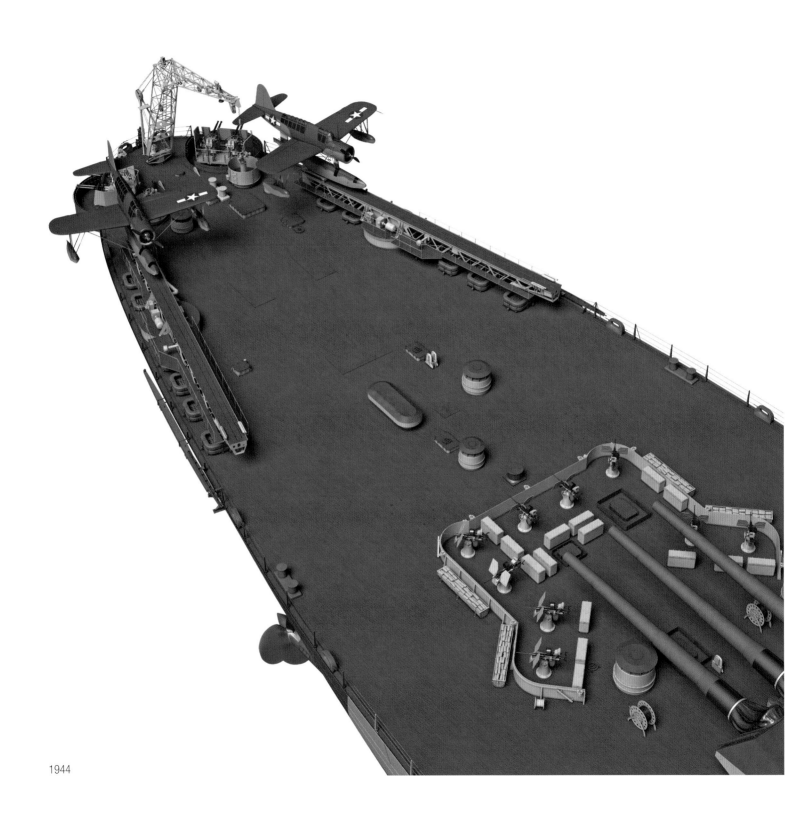

1944

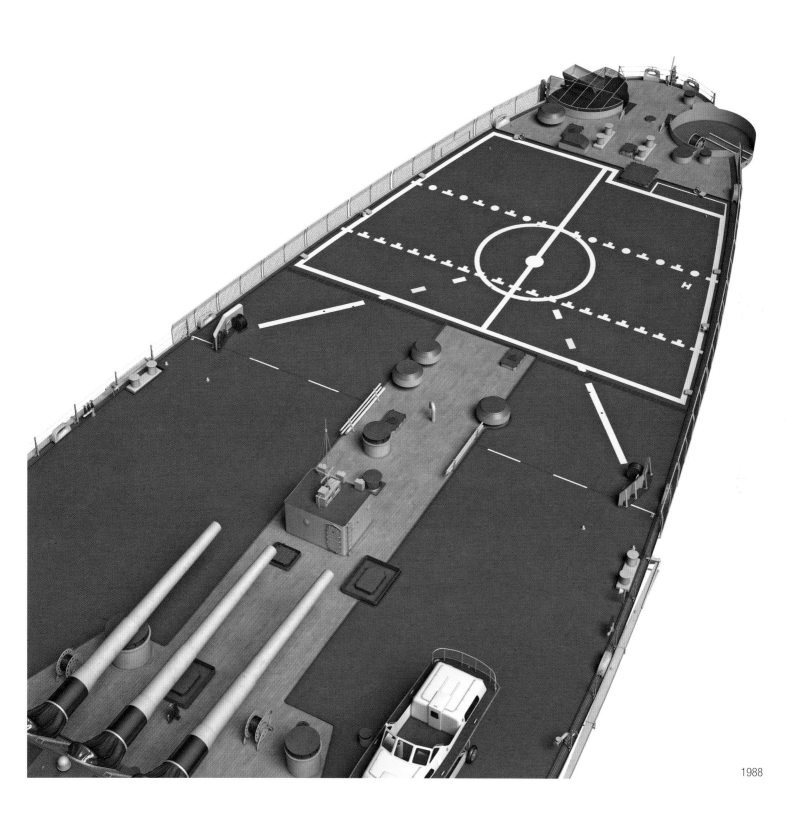

## HULL AND DECK FITTINGS, FRAMES 182–215 (1/200 SCALE)

### G7/3 BACK VIEW, 1943–1949

### G7/1–3 HULL AND DECK FITTINGS, FRAMES 182–215

**1** Skeg
**2** Starboard side outer propeller (four-bladed, right-handed – clockwise rotating)
**3** Starboard side inner propeller (five-bladed, right-handed – clockwise rotating)
**4** Port side outer propeller (four-bladed, left-handed – anticlockwise rotating)
**5** Port side inner propeller (five-bladed, left-handed – anticlockwise rotating)
**6** Outer propeller shaft
**7** Outer propeller shaft strut
**8** Zinc strips
**9** Draught marks
**10** Rudder
**11** Stern Bofors tub
**12** Quadruple Bofors mount
**13** Empty shell scuttle
**14** Hinged aircraft recovery sled cradle (fitted in mid-1943, removed in 1946)
**15** Freeing port (fitted in mid-1943)
**16** 12in. signal lamp (removed in mid-1943)
**17** Bucket vent
**18** Bucket vent (fitted in 1945)
**19** Triple mushroom vent (replaced with bucket vents in 1945)
**20** Mooring capstan
**21** Deck hatch
**22** 2 stowed life rafts (removed in 1948)

**23** 1 stowed life raft (2 rafts from 1945, both removed in 1948)
**24** 1 stowed life raft (removed in 1945)
**25** Mk51 director (removed in 1949)
**26** Ensign staff (fitted in 1946)
**27** Stern lights
**28** Davit socket
**29** Portable bolted plate (removed around 1946)
**30** Aircraft padeyes
**31** Catapult base (both catapults removed in 1948)
**32** Towing padeye
**33** Non-skid plate
**34** Aircraft crane base (crane removed in 1955)
**35** Aircraft crane controls (removed in 1955)
**36** Stowed boat boom (replaced with another type in 1951)
**37** Stern chock
**38** Welded ship's name

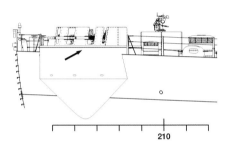

G7/4

210

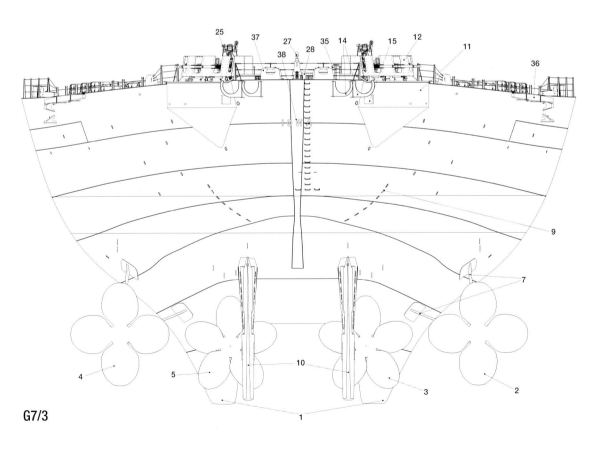

G7/3

# G7/4 RIGHT PROFILE (FRAGMENT), EARLY 1943

# G7/5 RIGHT PROFILE (FRAGMENTS), 1951–1958
# G7/6 PLAN (FRAGMENTS), 1951–1958

## G7/5–6 HULL AND DECK FITTINGS, FRAMES 182–215
**1** Pipes added to drainage holes along the hull (from 1951)
**2** Ship's hull number painted in white with black shadows, 1951–1990
**3** Life rafts (1951–1958)
**4** Enlarged boat boom (fitted in 1952)
**5** Bofors mount equipped with a Mk34 radar antenna (1951–1958)
**6** Mk63 director in a heightened tub (1951–1958)
**7** Bucket vents replacing a triple mushroom vent (from 1945)

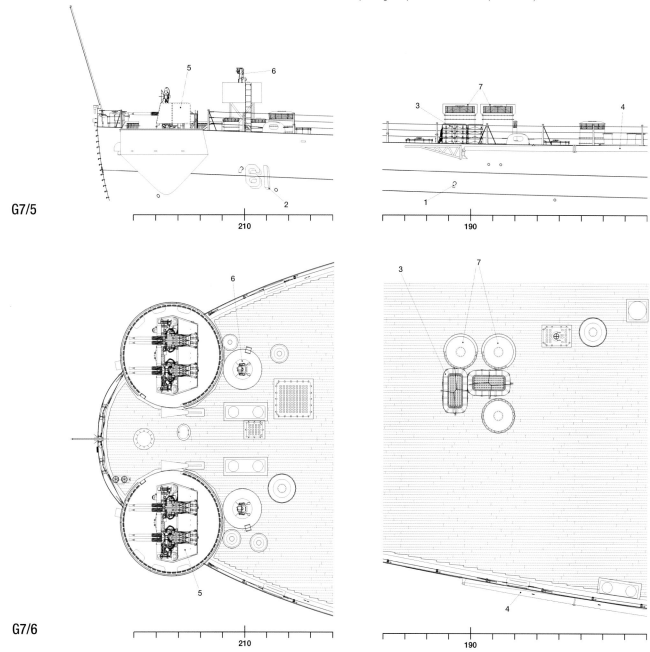

G7/5

210

190

G7/6

210

190

HULL AND DECK FITTINGS, FRAMES 182–215 (1/200 SCALE)

G7/7 RIGHT PROFILE (FRAGMENT), 1984–1986

G7/8 PLAN, 1984–1986


G7/9 RIGHT PROFILE (FRAGMENT), 1986–1990

G7/10 PLAN (FRAGMENT), 1986–1990

G7/11 BACK VIEW (FRAGMENT), 1986–1990


G7/7–11 HULL AND DECK FITTINGS, FRAMES 182–215

1 Drain
2 Hinged safety net
3 Boat boom
4 Light array
5 Opening for SLQ-25 Nixie decoy launcher
6 Raised helicopter deck
7 Deck drain
8 Fueling station
9 Fire station
10 Vertical shield
11 Loudspeaker
12 Cleat fitted on closed chock
13 Stern tub with an opening (cut in 1986)
14 Aviation gasoline trolley (from 1986)
15 Slipway for quick disposal of trolley in case of danger (fitted in 1986)


G7/12 STERN LIGHTS (1/50 SCALE)

1 Stern light
2 Wake light

G7/10

G7/11

G7/7

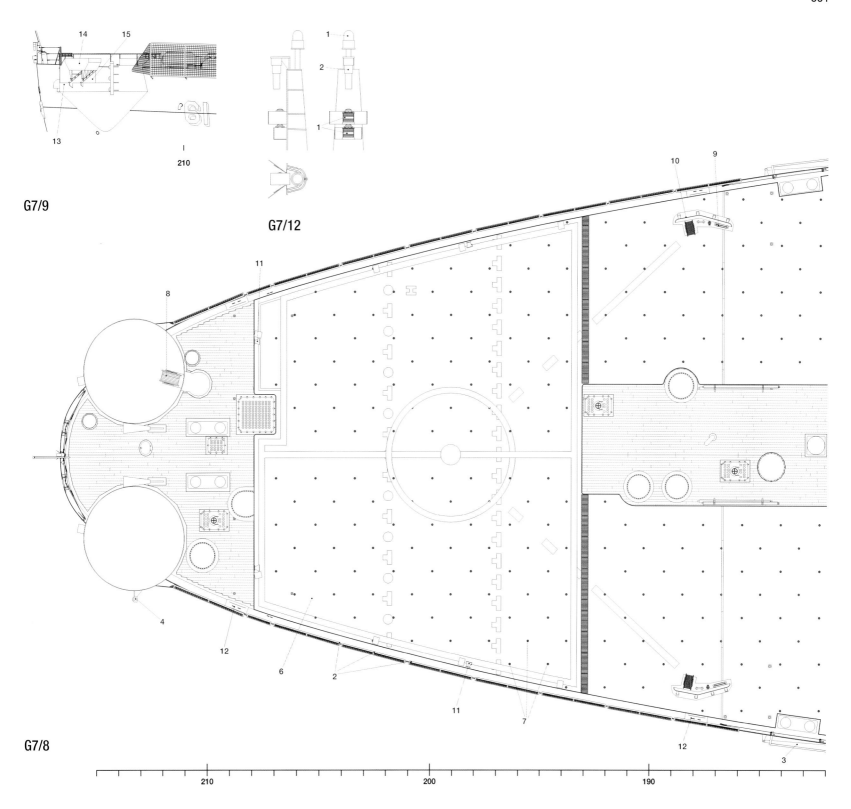

G7/9

G7/12

G7/8

210               200               190

early 1944

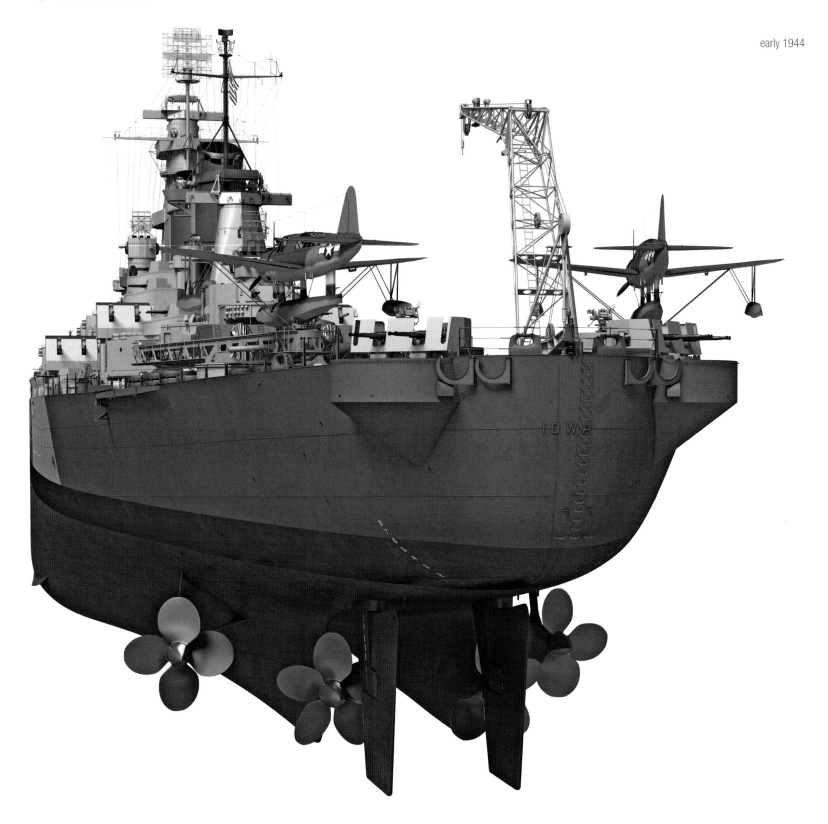

1952

1988

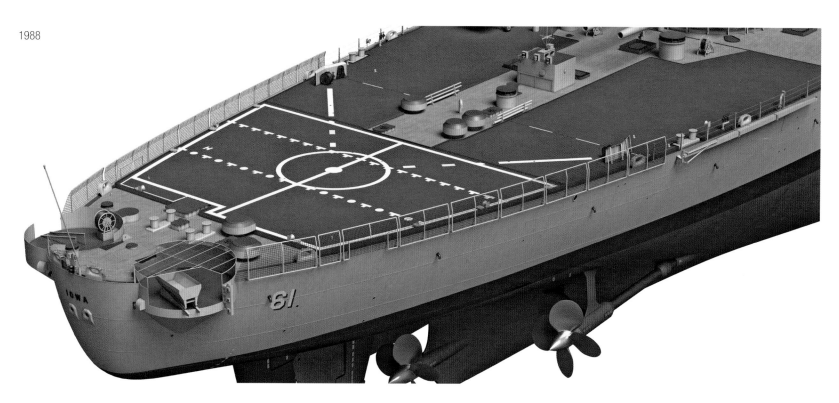

SUPERSTRUCTURE FITTINGS

G8/1 TYPICAL DOORS AND SCUTTLES (1/50 SCALE)

G8/2 TYPICAL PORTHOLES AND PEEP HOLES (1/50 SCALE)

G8/3 TYPICAL LADDERS (1/50 SCALE)

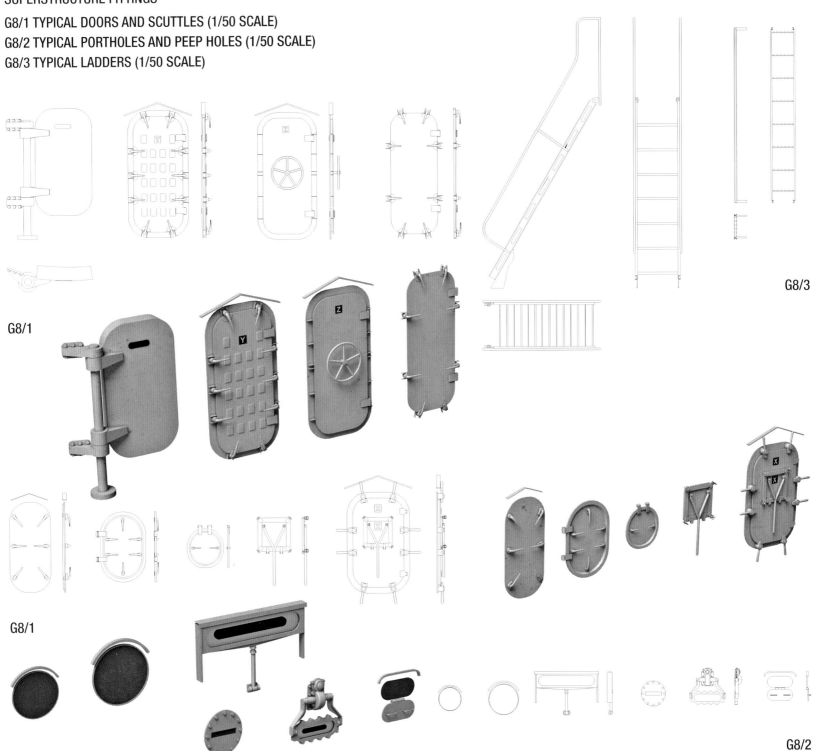

G8/1

G8/1

G8/2

G8/3

G8/4 COMPASS (1/50 SCALE)
G8/5 PELORUS (1/50 SCALE)
G8/6 STOKES STRETCHER (1/50 SCALE)
G8/7 POSITION LIGHTS (1/50 SCALE)
G8/8 LIFE RING (1/50 SCALE)
G8/9 WIND INDICATOR (1/50 SCALE)
G8/10 FLAG BAG (1/100 SCALE)
G8/11 LOOKOUT BINOCULARS,1984–1990 (1/50 SCALE)

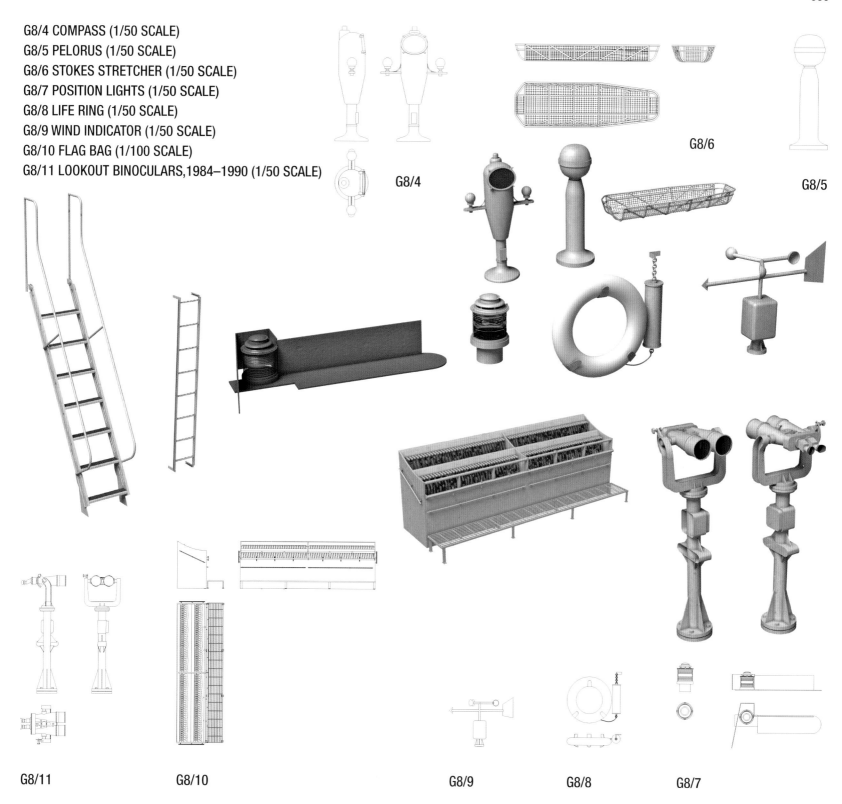

G8/4

G8/6

G8/5

G8/11       G8/10                    G8/9         G8/8        G8/7

VOUGHT OS2U KINGFISHER FLOATPLANE, 1943–1944 (1/100 SCALE)

H1/1 PROFILE
H1/2 FRONT VIEW
H/3 BACK VIEW

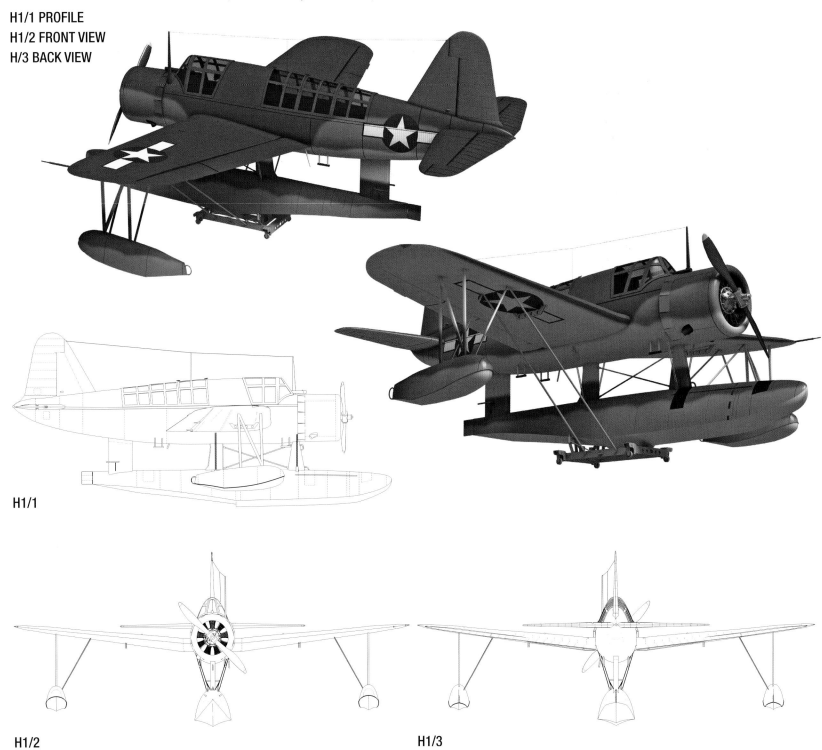

H1/1

H1/2

H1/3

H1/4 PLAN
H1/5 BOTTOM VIEW

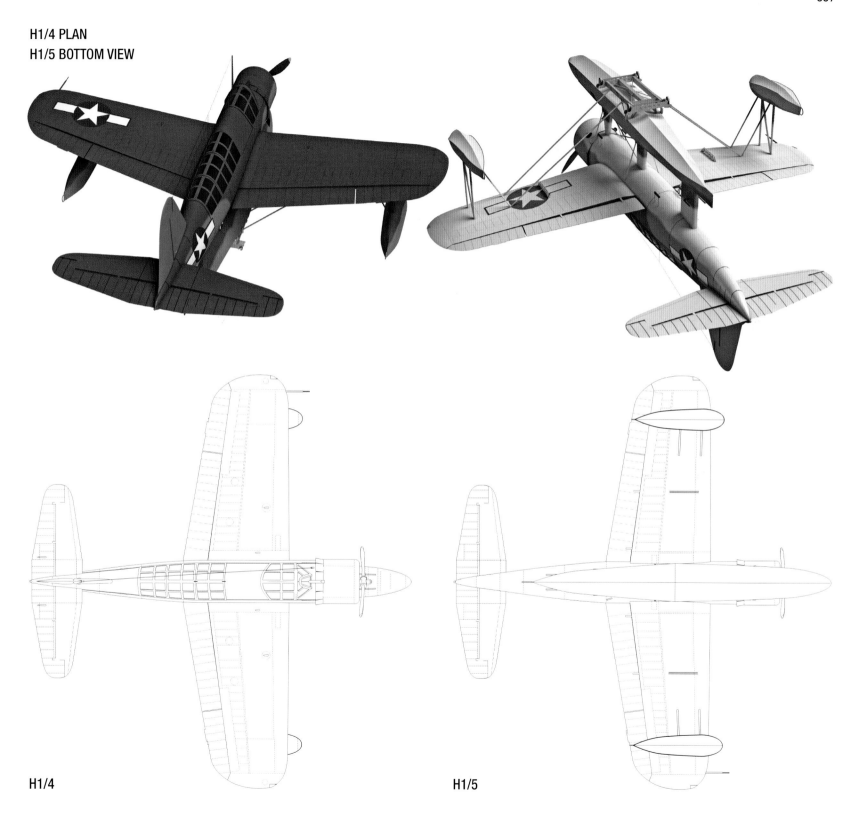

H1/4                    H1/5

CURTISS SC-1 SEAHAWK FLOATPLANE, 1945–1947 (1/100 SCALE)

H1/6 PROFILE

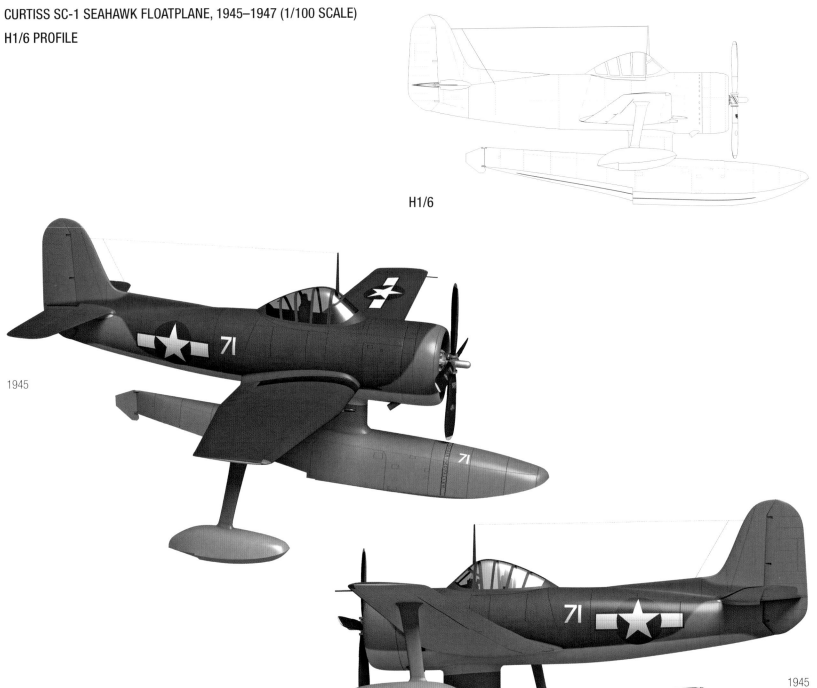

H1/6

1945

1945

H1/7 FRONT VIEW
H/8 BACK VIEW

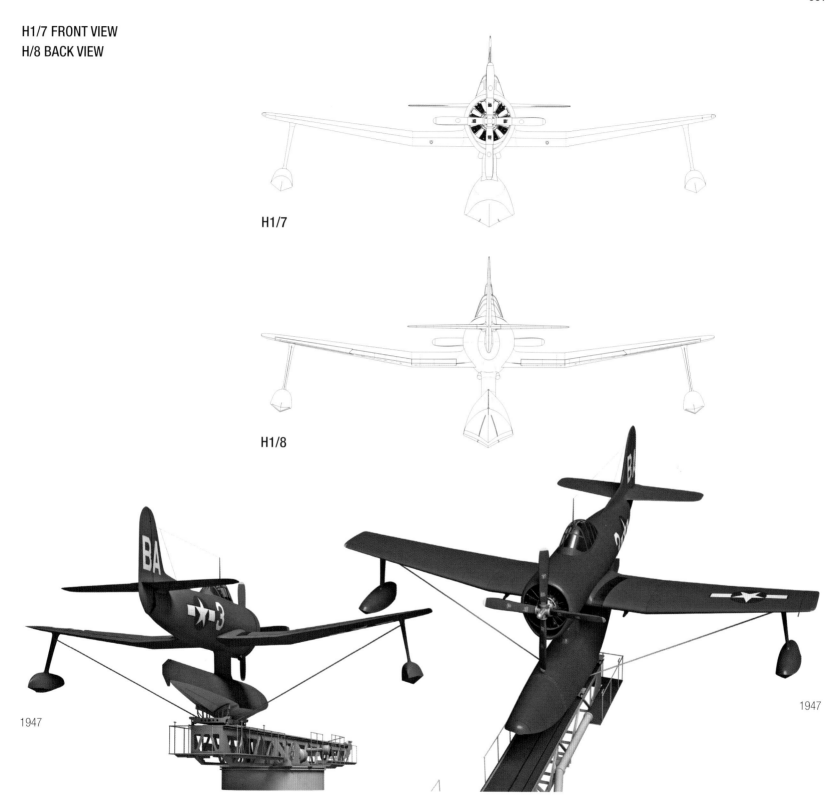

H1/7

H1/8

1947

1947

CURTISS SC-1 SEAHAWK FLOATPLANE, 1945–1947 (1/100 SCALE)

**H1/9 PLAN**
**H1/10 BOTTOM VIEW**

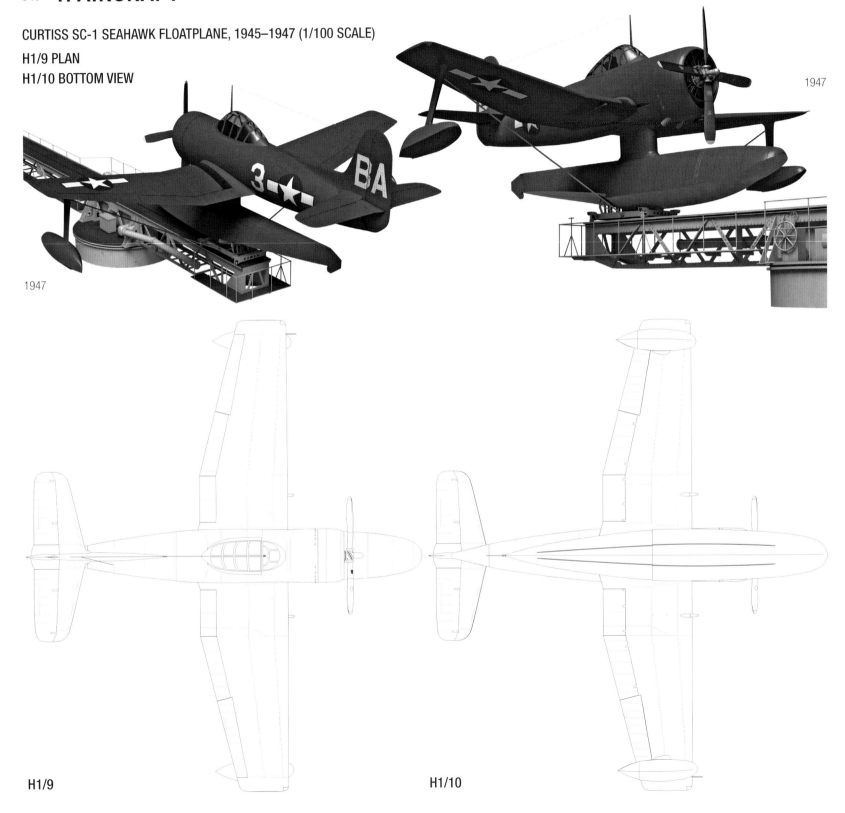

1947

1947

H1/9

H1/10

AIRCRAFT CRADLE (1/50 SCALE)

H1/11 PROFILE

H1/12 BACK VIEW

H1/13 PLAN

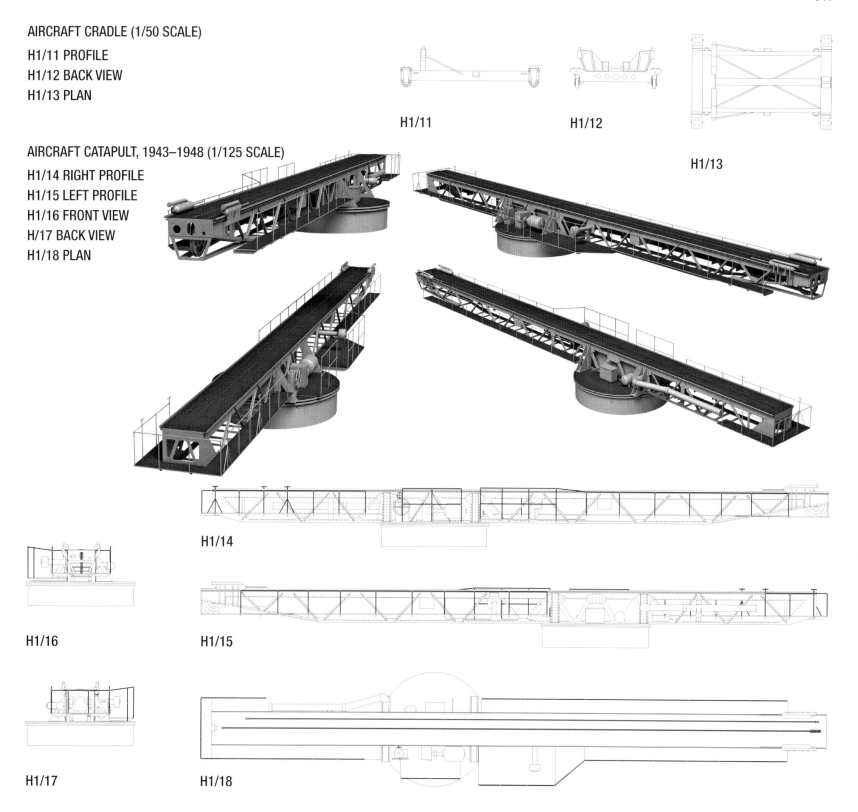

H1/11

H1/12

H1/13

AIRCRAFT CATAPULT, 1943–1948 (1/125 SCALE)

H1/14 RIGHT PROFILE

H1/15 LEFT PROFILE

H1/16 FRONT VIEW

H/17 BACK VIEW

H1/18 PLAN

H1/14

H1/16

H1/15

H1/17

H1/18

50FT MOTOR LAUNCH, 1955–1958 (1/75 SCALE)
I1/1 PROFILE
I1/2 PLAN
I1/3 FRONT VIEW
I1/4 BACK VIEW

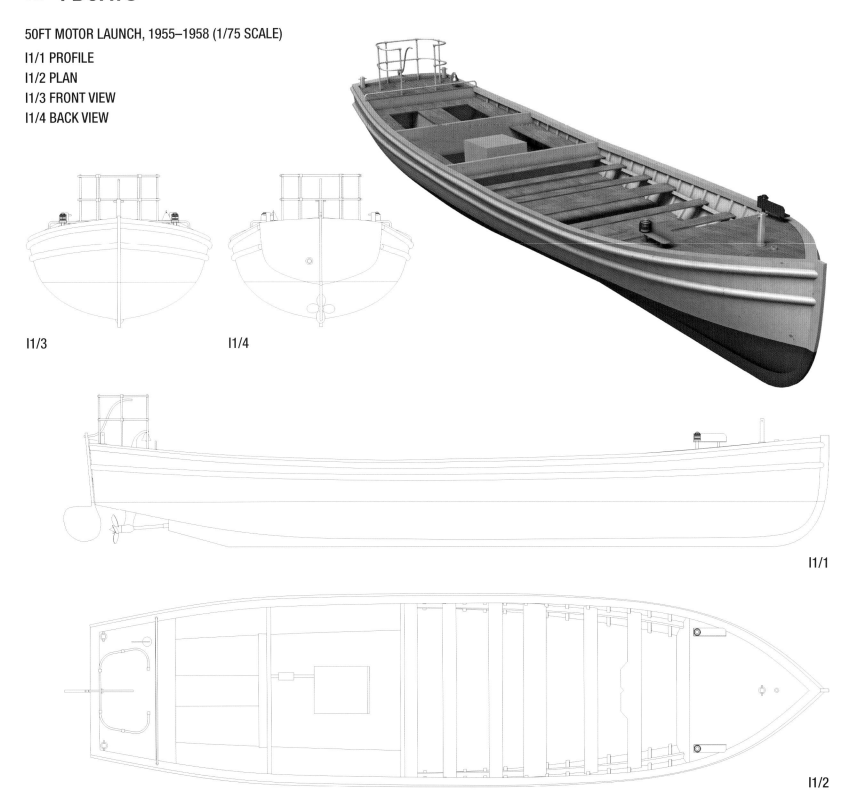

I1/3

I1/4

I1/1

I1/2

40FT MOTOR LAUNCH, 1955–1958 (1/75 SCALE)

I1/5 PROFILE

I1/6 PLAN

I1/7 FRONT VIEW

I1/8 BACK VIEW

I1/7

I1/8

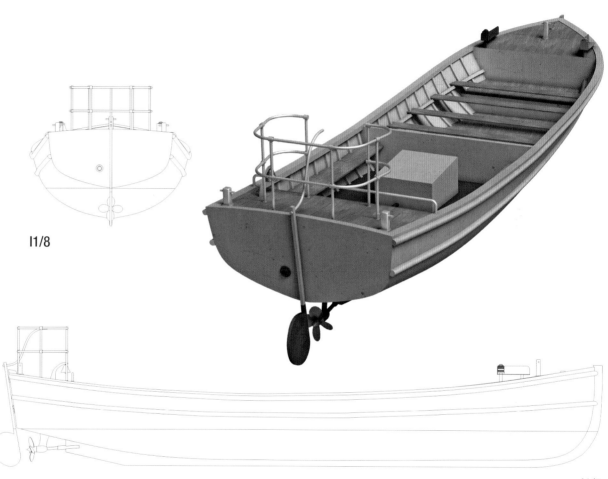

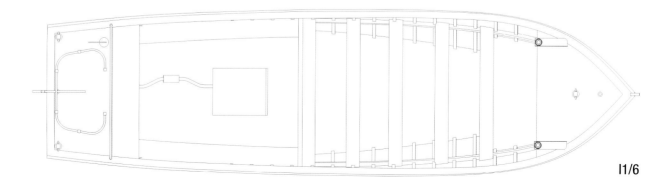

I1/5

I1/6

**30FT MOTOR LAUNCH, 1952–1955 (1/75 SCALE)**

I1/9 PROFILE
I1/10 PLAN
I1/11 FRONT VIEW
I1/12 BACK VIEW

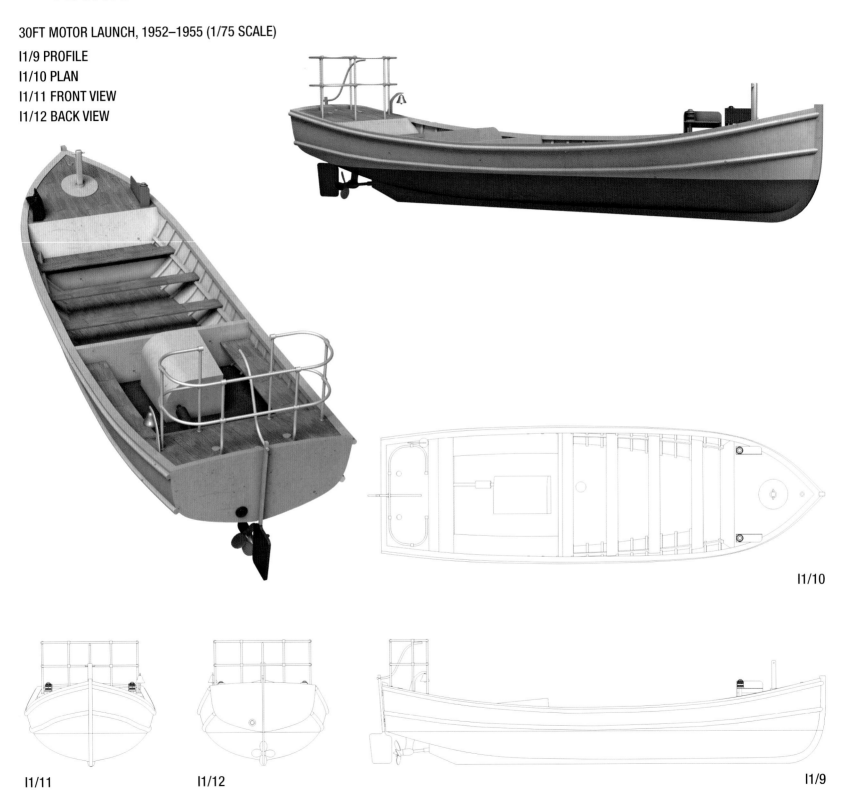

I1/10

I1/11

I1/12

I1/9

35FT MOTOR BOAT, 1955–1958 (1/75 SCALE)

I1/13 PROFILE
I1/14 PLAN
I1/15 FRONT VIEW
I1/16 BACK VIEW

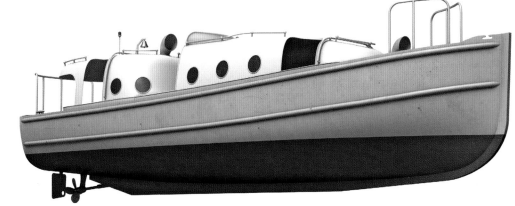

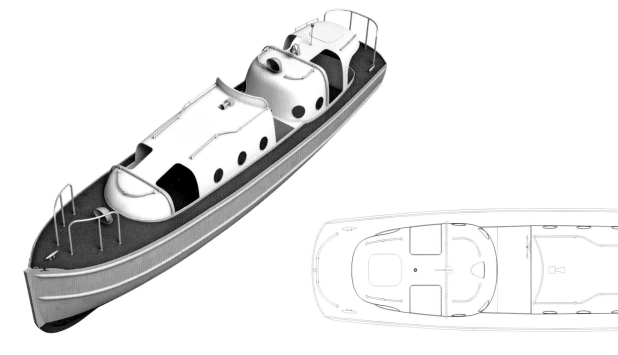

I1/14

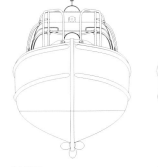

I1/15

I1/16

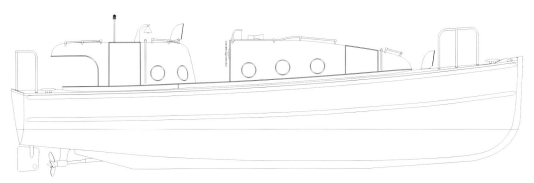

I1/13

28FT PERSONNEL BOAT, 1952–1958 (1/75 SCALE)

I1/17 PROFILE

I1/18 PLAN

I1/19 FRONT VIEW

I1/20 BACK VIEW

I1/18

I1/19

I1/20

I1/17

26FT MOTOR WHALEBOAT MK2, 1943–1958 (1/75 SCALE)

I1/21 PROFILE
I1/22 PLAN
I1/23 FRONT VIEW
I1/24 BACK VIEW

I1/23

I1/24

I1/21

I1/22

25 MAN BALSA LIFE RAFT, 1943–1958 (1/50 SCALE)

I1/25 PROFILE
I1/26 PLAN

I1/25

I1/26

FLOATER NET BASKETS,
1943–1958 (1/50 SCALE)

I1/27 TYPE 1 – PROFILE
I1/28 TYPE 1 – PLAN
I1/29 TYPE 1 – FRONT VIEW
I1/30 TYPE 2 – FRONT VIEW
I1/31 TYPE 3 – FRONT VIEW

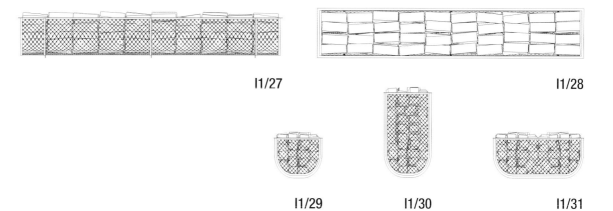

I1/27

I1/28

I1/29

I1/30

I1/31

**I1/32 BOAT ARRANGEMENTS, 1944 – PLAN (1/1500 SCALE)**

1 26ft motor whaleboat Mk2

**I1/33 BOAT ARRANGEMENTS, 1952 – PLAN (1/1500 SCALE)**

1 26ft motor whaleboat Mk2
2 30ft motor launch
3 28ft personnel boat

**I1/34 BOAT ARRANGEMENTS, 1955 – PLAN (1/1500 SCALE)**

1 26ft motor whaleboat Mk2
2 28ft personnel boat
3 35ft motor boat
4 40ft motor launch
5 50ft motor launch

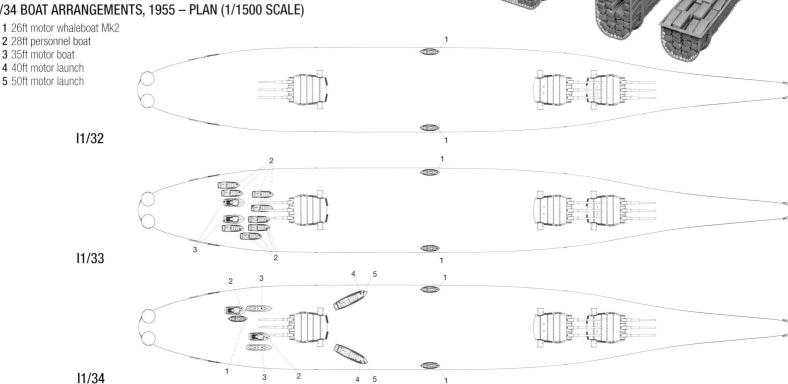

I1/32

I1/33

I1/34

40FT UTILITY BOAT, 1984–1990 (1/75 SCALE)

I1/35 PROFILE
I1/36 PLAN
I1/37 FRONT VIEW
I1/38 BACK VIEW

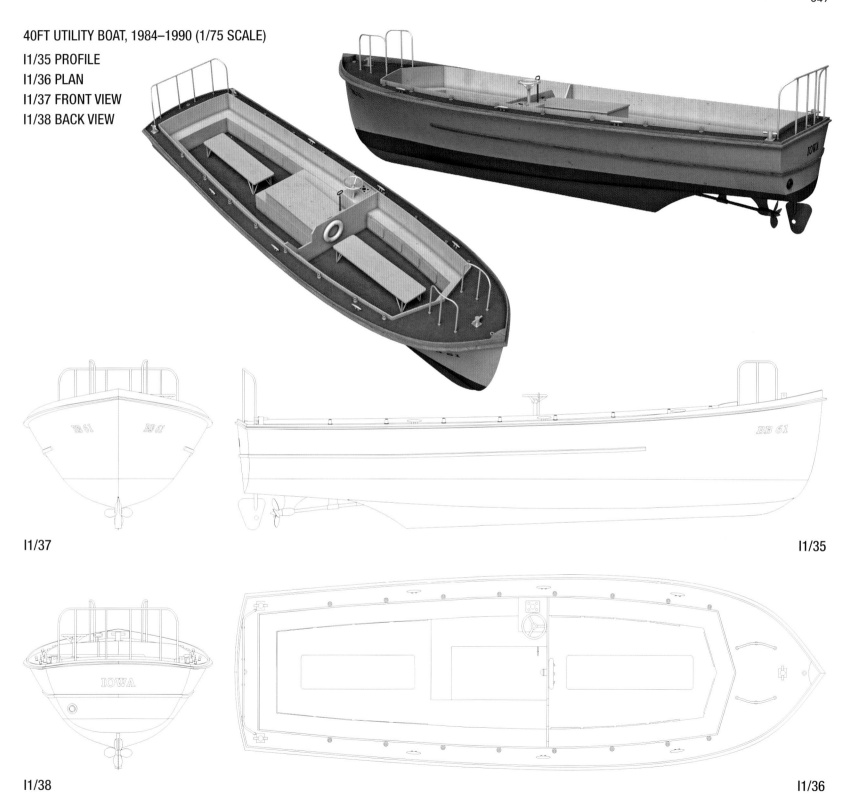

I1/37

I1/35

I1/38

I1/36

40FT UTILITY BOAT, 1984–1990 (1/75 SCALE)

I1/39 PROFILE
I1/40 PLAN
I1/41 FRONT VIEW
I1/42 BACK VIEW

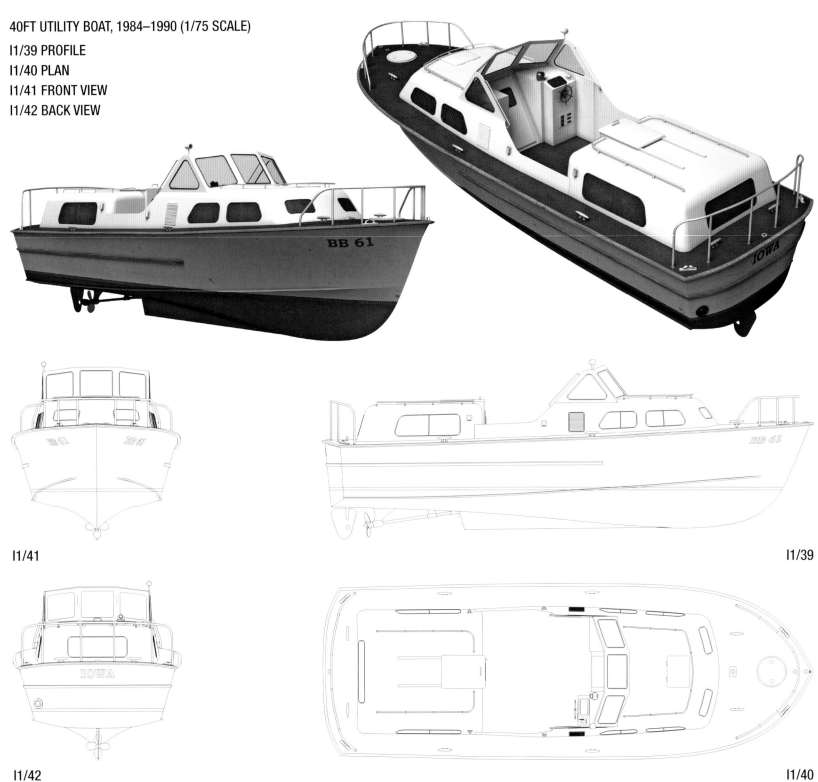

I1/41

I1/39

I1/42

I1/40

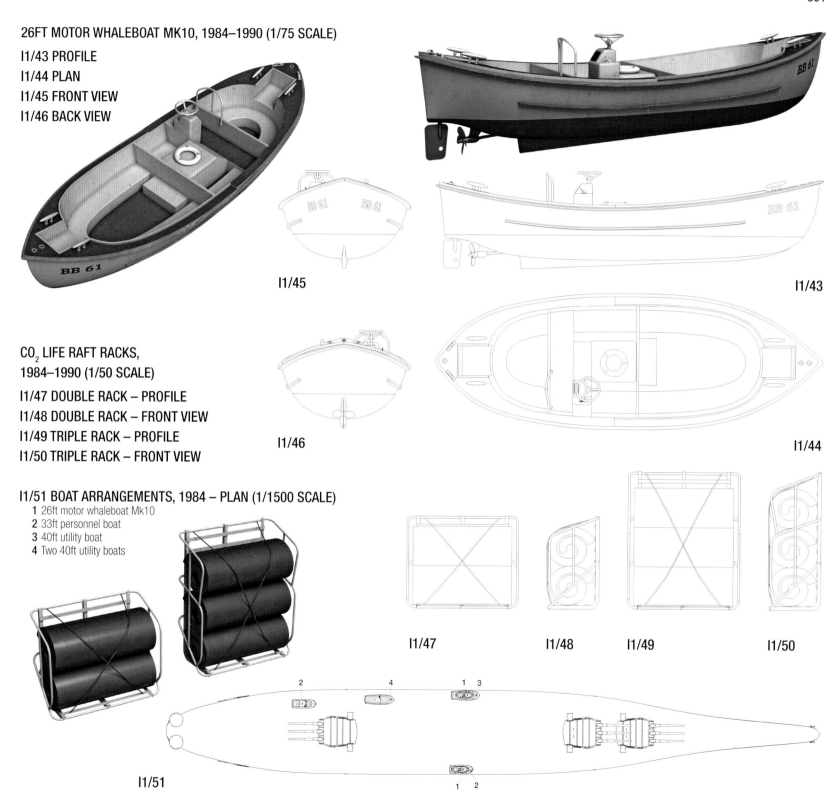

## 26FT MOTOR WHALEBOAT MK10, 1984–1990 (1/75 SCALE)

I1/43 PROFILE
I1/44 PLAN
I1/45 FRONT VIEW
I1/46 BACK VIEW

I1/45

I1/43

## CO$_2$ LIFE RAFT RACKS, 1984–1990 (1/50 SCALE)

I1/47 DOUBLE RACK – PROFILE
I1/48 DOUBLE RACK – FRONT VIEW
I1/49 TRIPLE RACK – PROFILE
I1/50 TRIPLE RACK – FRONT VIEW

I1/46

I1/44

## I1/51 BOAT ARRANGEMENTS, 1984 – PLAN (1/1500 SCALE)

1 26ft motor whaleboat Mk10
2 33ft personnel boat
3 40ft utility boat
4 Two 40ft utility boats

I1/47

I1/48

I1/49

I1/50

I1/51

# BIBLIOGRAPHY

Caresse, Philippe, *Le cuirassés de la classe Iowa. Tome I: genèse & technique*, Lela Presse, Le Vigen (2015), 978-2-914017-90-9

Dulin, Robert O., Garzke, William H., *Battleships. United States Battleships in World War II,* Naval Institute Press, Annapolis, Maryland (1976), 0-87021-099-8

Palasek, Jarosław, *Pancerniki typu Iowa. część I*, Okręty Wojenne, Tarnowskie Góry (2016), 978-83-61069-39-3

Palasek, Jarosław, *Pancerniki typu Iowa. część II*, Okręty Wojenne, Tarnowskie Góry (2017), 978-83-61069-40-9

Sumrall, Robert F., *Iowa Class Battleships: Their Design, Weapons and Equipment*, Naval Institute Press, Annapolis, Maryland (1989), 978-0870212987

Sumrall, Robert F., *USS Iowa (BB 61)*, The Floating Drydock (1986), 0-933126-77-8

Walkowiak, Thomas F., *USS Missouri BB63. 2 September 1945. Plan Book* (2006), 0-94405-07-9

Wiper, Steve, Warship Pictorial 34. *USN Battleships in color*, Classic Warships Publishing, Tucson, Arizona (2010), 978-0-9823583-5-1

## WEBSITES

https://www.history.navy.mil – Naval History and Heritage Command

https://maritime.org – San Francisco Maritime National Park Association

http://www.navsource.org – Naval History, Photographic history of the U.S. Navy

http://www.navweaps.com – Naval Weapons, Naval Technology and Naval Reunions

http://www.researcheratlarge.com – Researcher @ Large